A Clinical Introduction to Freud

A Norton Professsional Book

A Clinical Introduction to Freud

Techniques for Everyday Practice

Bruce Fink

W.W. Norton & Company
Independent Publishers Since 1923

New York • London

Note to Readers: Standards of clinical practice and protocol change over time, and no technique or recommendation is guaranteed to be safe or effective in all circumstances. This volume is intended as a general information resource for professionals practicing in the field of psychotherapy and mental health; it is not a substitute for appropriate training, peer review, and/or clinical supervision. Neither the publisher nor the author(s) can guarantee the complete accuracy, efficacy, or appropriateness of any particular recommendation in every respect.

For information about permission to reproduce selections from this book, write to Permissions, W. W. Norton & Company, Inc., 500 Fifth Avenue, New York, NY 10110

For information about special discounts for bulk purchases, please contact W. W. Norton Special Sales at specialsales@wwnorton.com or 800-233-4830

Manufacturing by Maple Press
Production manager: Christine Critelli

Library of Congress Cataloging-in-Publication Data

Names: Fink, Bruce, 1956- author.
Title: A clinical introduction to Freud : techniques for everyday practice / Bruce Fink.
Description: First edition. | New York, NY : W. W. Norton & Company, Inc., [2017] | "A Norton professional book." | Includes bibliographical references and index.
Identifiers: LCCN 2016029074 | ISBN 9780393711967 (hardcover)
Subjects: | MESH: Psychoanalytic Theory
Classification: LCC BF173.F85 | NLM WM 460.2 | DDC 150.19/52—dc23 LC record available at https://lccn.loc.gov/2016029074

W. W. Norton & Company, Inc.
500 Fifth Avenue, New York, N.Y. 10110
www.wwnorton.com

W. W. Norton & Company Ltd.
15 Carlisle Street, London W1D 3BS

1 2 3 4 5 6 7 8 9 0

To my friends who provided such helpful comments on and criticism of this manuscript as it gradually became a book, including Yael Baldwin, Kristen Hennessy, Derek Hook, Mike Miller, Stephanie Swales, and Adam Szmerling. Their contribution was considerable, as were the suggestions of Deborah Malmud at Norton.

Contents

metonymy of desire p 149
self disclosure, transference p 182
                                          p 184

language + jouissance p220
" the symptoms constitute the
   patient's sexual activity" p275

Because of the novelty of my therapeutic method, I see only the severest cases, which have already been under treatment [by other practitioners] for years without any success.

—Freud, SE VII, p. 21 n

Words were originally magic, and even today words retain much of their ancient magical power. By words, one person can make another blissfully happy or drive him to despair.

—Freud, SE XV, p. 17

Introduction

The division of the psychical realm into what is conscious and what
is unconscious is the fundamental premise of psychoanalysis.
                                        —Freud, SE XIX, p. 13

WHAT IS PSYCHOANALYTIC practice other than the invention and use
of a whole series of techniques designed to access and impact
the unconscious? Freud claimed that "the theory of repression is the
cornerstone on which the structure of psychoanalysis is built,"[1] and in
this book I shall examine Freud's work with a view to explaining and
exemplifying the myriad techniques he devised with which to get at the
unconscious and thereby undo many of the ill effects of repression.

My impression, based on some three decades of psychoanalytic teaching, practice, and supervision, is that the most basic methods Freud
developed for accessing the unconscious are no longer taught to the
vast majority of students of psychology and psychoanalysis. The latter are, instead, instructed only in roundabout ways of broaching the
repressed—ways that stem from what appears to be an almost century-
long fascination (on the part of post-Freudians) not with the repressed
itself but with the *obstacles* to reaching it, obstacles that Freud encountered early on in his work as he encouraged his patients to remember
the events that led to the onset of their symptoms.

One such obstacle includes everything that falls under the heading
of "resistance"—including such minor forms of resistance as embarrassment, moral compunction, and a sense that certain things simply are not
talked about, being socially "inappropriate," as well as more insidious
and tenacious forms—and analysts' preoccupation with resistance gave
rise to a whole trend within psychoanalysis known as "the analysis of
resistances."[2] Another obstacle, referred to by Freud as "defense" (which
includes a long list of self-defensive maneuvers like denial, displacement, isolation of affect, compromise formation, omission, conversion,
turning against the self, reaction formation, suppression of affect, projec-

tion, and undoing), spurred the development of a type of work known as *the analysis of defense*.[3] A third phenomenon, which Freud dubbed "transference" and also characterized as an "obstacle,"[4] has led to the now decades-long attempt on the part of many contemporary schools of psychoanalysis to work with and analyze this further obstacle, as though it were the key to all things analytic.[5]

All three of these endeavors have a fatal flaw, I would argue, which is to mistake the obstacle for the goal. An obstacle is something we attempt to get around, not focus on for its own sake. It is not by trying to understand every facet of resistance, defense, or transference that we are better able to have an impact on the unconscious—indeed, it might be truer to say that by focusing so exclusively on resistance, defense, and transference, the unconscious is forgotten.[6] We lose sight of the goal we are supposedly seeking—that of determining what thoughts and wishes have become unconscious owing to the action of repression—as we attend so assiduously to the obstacles that arise during our search. Investigating and interpreting the obstacles to our pursuit of a goal is not the same as pursuing the goal itself, even if it may occasionally be necessary.[7]

Jacques Lacan—a French psychoanalyst (1901–1981) who is arguably the 20th-century analyst who took Freud's work the most seriously and attempted to extend and at times rectify it, which is why I will refer to his views on numerous occasions throughout this book—said something about the May 1968 protesters in France, protesters who seemed determined to directly face off with heavily armed police, that might well apply to psychoanalysis as a whole: "To run straight at the obstacles placed before you is to behave just like a bull. The point is to find a different path than the one where the obstacles lie—or, in any case, not to be especially interested in obstacles."[8]

Lacan views transference as arising primarily at moments of stagnation or breakdown in the dialectical movement of psychoanalysis, not as a quintessentially useful part of the therapeutic work (see Fink, 2007, Chapter 7). Even if transferential reactions ineluctably arise at certain points in every analysis, in the best of cases the analyst manages to proceed in such a way that such reactions are few and far between. And the analyst strives to foster an atmosphere in which the least possible quantity of remembering of the past goes on via transferential "acting out" (a term often confused in our times with "acting up," which simply means "behaving badly," whereas in psychoanalytic theory *acting out* implies behaviorally performing something that one is unable to remember or feels unable to say to one's analyst), while the greatest possible quantity of remembering occurs without any such roundabout circuit being required. Lacan suggests that when transference shows its face in an analysis, it is not the Holy Grail that tells us we are on the right track; rather, "Transference is the means by which communication of the unconscious is interrupted, the means by which the unconscious closes up again. Far from being indicative of the signing over of powers to the unconscious, transference is, on the contrary, the shutting down of the unconscious" (Seminar II, p. 130).

In this book, I shall focus primarily on the techniques Freud developed for going *directly* toward the unconscious, illustrating how we can use them and perhaps even improve on them today. (Readers interested in knowing how I would respond to certain people who have critiqued Freud's technique and biases, whether recently or not so recently, are referred to Appendix I.) I will not explore Freud's personal life here, for a wide variety of reasons, not the least of which is that I find psychobiography incredibly reductionistic, but also because I find Freud the man far less interesting or compelling than Freud the theorist of psychoanalytic practice.[9] Did Freud realize that emotions begin to fester when they are not expressed because of the story his father told him of one day being forced off the pavement for being a Jew and not having retaliated? This is, in my view, the sort of pointless speculation psychobiographers engage in.[10] Freud undoubtedly gleaned a great deal from his own life experience, but also from all that he read and all that he heard from his patients. How could anyone ever know exactly what inspired a specific insight? Perhaps Freud himself would have been unable to tell us in many instances.

Nor shall I elaborate here on the particulars of Freud's intellectual development from the 1880s to the 1930s[11] or say much about the historical shift over the course of a few centuries from mesmerism to hypnosis to catharsis and on to free association.[12] As indicated above, my focus here is primarily on the clinically useful techniques Freud developed for getting at the unconscious; thus, I do not go into the intricacies of certain of Freud's abstract concepts (such as the pleasure principle, the death drive, the Oedipus complex, penis envy, and so on), forays into social and religious commentary (I say nothing here about *Totem and Taboo*, *Civilization and Its Discontents*, *The Future of an Illusion*, or *Moses and Monotheism*), or attempt to sift out which ideas he may have borrowed from this or that other theorist. Unlike Jean-Michel Quinodoz, in his *Reading Freud: A Chronological Exploration of Freud's Writings* (2005), I shall not examine everything Freud ever wrote, much less attempt to exhaustively explain everything in any of the texts by Freud that I do discuss. And unlike Jonathan Lear, in *Freud* (2015), I do not stress the aspects of Freud's work that might appeal to a philosopher who believes in the power of self-awareness.[13] My concern is to highlight what in Freud's work seems to me to be of most direct relevance to clinicians who wish to bring out what an analysand (a term I prefer to *patient*, as *analysand* implies that it is the person who goes into analysis who does the lion's share of the analyzing) is unaware of in order to impact his or her unconscious.

There are perhaps as many different readings of Freud's work as there are readers of it, and there are often wide divergences between the Freuds that various readers see. For Bruno Bettelheim (1982), Freud is a humanist who talks extensively about man's "soul." For Frank Sulloway (1979), Freud is a scientist and a "biologist of the mind." For some, Freud can be viewed as a phenomenologist, whereas for Lacan—at least at a certain point in his work—Freud is rather more of a structuralist. For Barbara Low, Freud's "attitude to his material . . . might almost be called *joyous*," his exposition expressing "profound emotion and the greatest freedom to use that emotion."[14] For others still, Freud was little more than a misogynist. And for Herman Hesse, Thomas Mann, and Albert Einstein, Freud was above all a great stylist, a man of letters, and a master of the German language (he won, for example, the Goethe prize for literature in 1930).

For my purposes here, Freud will be viewed primarily as a clinician who developed a whole series of theories and practices in order to grapple with problems he successively encountered while treating patients over the course of some five decades. As we shall see (especially in Chapters 4 and 5), Freud—as a clinician who, like most innovators, learned largely by trial and error—made his fair share of mistakes with patients and, like everyone else, had his own personal flaws, rarely if ever living up to his own compelling *theory of practice*. I shall argue, nevertheless, that the rigorous theory of practice he bequeathed us goes well beyond his own foibles and failings as an individual and has a great deal to teach us even today.

Although I initially began to read Freud's work on my own, the take on Freud's work that I present here is heavily colored by Lacan's many yearlong seminars, from about 1952 until the late 1970s, which arguably provided closer readings of Freud's work than any other course or text ever had. I studied these extensively during my analytic training in Paris in the 1980s and have been learning from them (and translating a few of them into English) ever since, finding them quite inexhaustibly fascinating.

To those potential readers who might be inclined to dismiss Freud's work out of hand—having heard that it is hopelessly out of date, his theories disproven by one and all, or that his theories were the product of a "perverted sex maniac"—but who are being asked, if not required, to read this book for a course, let me point out that for every expert in a scientific field who has supposedly debunked Freud's theories, there is another who endorses them and believes he or she has found evidence for them (see, for example, Adams, Wright, & Lohr, 1996; Baumeister, Bratslavsky, Muraven, & Tice, 1998; Muraven & Baumeister, 2000; Newman, Duff, & Baumeister, 1997; Rosner, 2000; Solms & Turnbull, 2002; Solms & Panksepp, 2012; Solms, 2015). We hear less about the latter, for whereas Freud bashing still makes for "good copy" (Crews, 1993; Webster, 1995), findings that corroborate psychoanalysis are no longer considered newsworthy. In every scientific field, researchers often disagree as to the validity of theories for decades, if not centuries (consider those proposed by Galileo and Darwin, and theories like those of the ether and string theory)—this is a regular feature of scientific debate. I would ask you to try to momentarily set aside the views of the competing experts and judge for yourselves as to the clinical usefulness or uselessness of the theories and practices I will present here—the proof, after all, of a theory designed to guide psychotherapeutic practice is in the pudding: Does it help you help your patients or not? (I do not see how the clinical validity of a theory could be seen to depend on the character of its inventor, as if we could all agree, in any case, whether someone was a "good person" or not. When we learn about new theories in the sciences that seem to explain many things we find in nature, or when we are moved by poems, songs, or novels, do we rush to discover if their creators were good, honest, upright people before deciding whether their scientific, literary, or musical productions were valuable?)

To those readers who prefer other psychological approaches to the psychoanalytic one, I would simply ask that you entertain the possibility that you might find a couple of useful techniques here that may come in handy one day when a client spontaneously tells you a dream or a sexual fantasy, for example. You may find within these pages a few instruments to put in your therapy toolbox (I mean that figuratively, not in the sense of an actual physical toolbox containing slips of paper on which specific interventions or interpretations are written, as seems to be used by some in the therapy world these days), whose value you will be able to test for yourself someday during a session. I would hope that those readers who have *theoretical* objections to Freud's work—whether they do not accept the notion that there is anything truly unconscious in human beings or thoroughly dislike dialectical thinking of any kind—would at least grant Freud the same respect they might give to any other well-known thinker, whether it be Plato, Aristotle, Kant, Marx, Heidegger, or Wittgenstein.

I would ask them to at least briefly give Freud the benefit of the doubt, studying his work seriously for at least a few days to see what kind of evidence he musters for his claims, before consigning to the garbage heap the 24 volumes of his opus. Those who publicly criticize and reject an author's views are usually more convincing when they actually know something about that author's work. The most virulent and unconditional critics of Freud's work (and of Plato's, Marx's, and Wittgenstein's) are often those who know very little about it, and that gives a distinct air of intellectual dishonesty to their criticism. They often do not even realize that Freud explicitly indicates that not all dreams are sexual and that not all dreams necessarily contain wishes left over from childhood.[15] It is always better to know at least a little bit about a theory before attempting to refute it.

Certain readers who have just begun to see patients—whether they are training to be clinical psychologists, social workers, counselors, or psychiatrists—may come to psychotherapeutic practice preferring to be guided by their own life experience and intuition, rather than by any theory that might, they feel, skew or otherwise distort their perception of their patients' troubles. What I would point out to such readers is that what they think of as their own "non-theoretically warped" intuition and pre-existing views have most likely been shaped by everything they have heard and read growing up, much of which is informed by a mishmash of psychological theories, whether espoused by novelists, poets, filmmakers, songwriters, talk-show hosts, or their parents and friends. "Intuition" is nothing but a sense one has or a guess one makes that is based on unarticulated, unexamined notions that one has assimilated in the course of one's lifetime;[16] and commonly heard phrases about life and people in our culture bring a whole, albeit unacknowledged, metapsychology with them, some of which comes from Freud, some from a raft of other sources.

Consider, for example, the oft-repeated line "He keeps it all bottled up inside." The "wisdom" built into the idiomatic expression "bottled up" might well be likened to Freud's "energetics"—that is, his notion of the "damming up of libido" (SE XVI, p. 408)—as could its corollary that during a good talk or cry, we must "let it all out." As simple an expression as "I've got her under my skin" implies several quite theoretical notions: (a) that we can be "infected" by another person in such a way that it is both pleasurable and painful, if not downright unbearable, to be with her (it's rather like scratching an itch from a mosquito bite or poison ivy: The more we give into the temptation to scratch, the better it feels momentarily, but the worse the itch becomes); and (b) that, as opposed to Descartes' well-known *partes extra partes*—no two objects can occupy the same space at the same time (a philosophical view called into question by quantum physics)—in the human realm, we can and do take at least something about another person into ourselves, it coming to dwell inside us. Just as there is no such thing as value-free language, there is no such thing as completely atheoretical intuition about life and relationships.

The attempt to avoid having any sort of theoretical notions "contaminate" one's thinking and the spontaneity of one's understanding of patients is thus doomed to failure from the outset! Better to take cognizance of and examine the theories that inescapably inform one's way of seeing the world than to allow them to inform it willy-nilly—in other words, in an inescapably haphazard and probably convenient way (dependent, perhaps, on whatever one is inclined to think or do at any particular moment in time). It is probably safe to say that it is precisely when we believe we are most free of any "corrupting" theoretical influence (Bloom, 1973) that we are most under its sway.

Theoretical language does not take us any further away from so-called reality (or, as some might think of it, from the phenomena, or from the thing itself) than everyday speech does, insofar as what we call "reality" is itself rife with metaphors that have accumulated over the centuries and is thus theory-laden. Both everyday language and explicitly theoretical language provide ways of seeing and are simultaneously blindfolds: They blind us to certain things even as they allow us to see others. To rely only on everyday language is simply to resort to unanalyzed, unarticulated theory, which usually turns out to be bad theory, in the sense that it is rife with prejudices and stereotypes. One is *always already* functioning within a theory or relying on a grab bag of assorted (and potentially mismatched) theoretical notions. So-called ordinary language has its own genius but also its own demons.

When faced with a new theory, useful questions to ask are, "Does it allow me to see anything that I had not seen before that might be of use in my clinical work? Does this theory allow me to uncover blindnesses in my initial way of thinking about things or in other theories that I may have already assimilated?" I can only hope that my readers will consider that psychoanalytic theory may allow them to see and hear certain things they have never seen or heard before.

In Chapters 1 and 2, I discuss the most basic foundations of Freud's work by exploring how he was led to formulate the existence of the unconscious—which, for practitioners, is arguably his most important theoretical contribution—and I include examples from the very first patients he (and his friend Josef Breuer) worked with. In Chapter 3, I explain how Freud came to interpret dreams in the way that he did and how to interpret your own patients' dreams. I also briefly review there how to work with slips of the tongue, bungled actions, and other such slipups or "mistakes" that people make quite regularly.

In Chapters 4 and 5, I comment on the two most widespread diagnostic structures that Freud talks about: obsession and hysteria (which, for better or for worse, and somewhat misleadingly, today often go by the names of obsessive-compulsive disorder, or OCD, and conversion disorder, respectively). For each structure, I take up the major case study that Freud devoted to it—for obsession, the case of the Rat Man, for hysteria, the case of Dora—and highlight the technique he used at the time and where it fell short of his later recommendations regarding technique. I also indicate in what ways obsession and hysteria manifest themselves differently to clinicians today and suggest how psychoanalytic techniques can be used to treat them successfully (I will argue that obsession and hysteria are still alive and well, so to speak, despite concerted efforts on the part of the authors of the *Diagnostic and Statistical Manual of Mental Disorders* [*DSM*] to fragment and/or bury them; see, especially, Appendix V). I do not say much in this book about Freud's work with psychotics, since time has, I believe, shown that he often failed to recognize incipient psychosis (as in the case of the Wolf Man; SE XVII), was unable to adequately theorize the causes of psychosis, and did not adapt his approach to psychoanalytic practice to have much success with psychotics. The theorization of the origins of psychosis and the modification of psychotherapeutic technique to achieve success with psychotics was, in my estimation, accomplished by later analysts, above all by Lacan.

In Chapter 6, I summarize Freud's many and varied accounts of how and why symptoms form, illustrating the forces involved in symptom formation using examples discussed earlier in the book as well as cases of my own. In Chapter 7, I discuss a number of developments in psychoanalysis and psychiatry since Freud's time and raise the question whether it should be thought that we have improved upon psychoanalysis in the interim, gone beyond Freud altogether, or reverted to pre-Freudian positions.

Along the way, I attempt to introduce the reader to and exemplify a multitude of psychoanalytic concepts, including repression, isolation, undoing, transference, countertransference, acting out, resistance, trauma, latent content, manifest content, condensation, displacement, wish-fulfillment, id, ego, superego, obsession, hysteria, phobia, negation, denial, fantasy, anxiety, affect, ambivalence, jouissance, free association, somatization, parapraxes, overdetermination, repetition, and many others as well. The reader will, I hope, come away from this volume having a fairly good working knowledge of both the basic theory and practice of Freudian psychoanalysis with neurotics.

The attentive reader will note that, in citing material from the 24 volumes of *The Standard Edition of the Complete Psychological Works of Sigmund Freud*, I have often taken liberties with the translation, updating the grammar and style, for example. I have done so not because I believe I am a better translator from the German than James Strachey—indeed, I am no translator from the German at all[17]—but because I strive throughout to make Freud as accessible as possible to the contemporary reader. Each of Freud's texts is cited here simply as SE, followed by the volume and, when relevant, page numbers (e.g., SE VII, p. 34); the *Standard Edition* is, for the most part, laid out in chronological order, meaning that the higher the volume number, the later the date of composition. The same is true of the multivolume *Seminar of Jacques Lacan*, which is cited here as Seminar, followed by the volume and relevant page numbers (e.g., Seminar VII, p. 34); page numbers for those volumes that have not yet appeared in English correspond to the French editions published by Seuil in Paris; for those seminars that have not yet been published in French, I give the date of the class from which I am citing. The major collection of Lacan's papers included in *Écrits: The First Complete Edition in English* (1966/2006a) is simply referred to here as *Écrits*. Citations from all other authors follow typical APA format: author's last name, year of publication cited, and page number(s).

Much of the material in this book was initially developed in undergraduate and graduate courses on Freud that I taught at Duquesne University over the course of some 20 years; nevertheless, everything here has been significantly revised and updated, I having once again found in working on this project that writing seriously tests my grasp of texts and theories in ways that oral teaching often does not. It should be noted that the vast majority of what I discuss here concerns neurotic, not psychotic patients (on work with the latter, see Fink, 2007, Chapter 10).

Certain readers may be interested in consulting further texts in which I have discussed Freud's ideas in detail. They might consider looking at two papers I devoted to his work on fantasy in his article "A Child Is Being Beaten" in *Against Understanding* (Fink, 2014b), and several chapters in which I discuss his work on love, desire, and narcissism in *Lacan on Love* (Fink, 2016). They might also find of value my discussion of how to work with dreams, daydreams, and fantasies in *Fundamentals of Psychoanalytic Technique* (Fink, 2007).

Recommended Reading

Chapter 1: Tracing a Symptom Back to Its Origin

Studies on Hysteria (SE II). Although the entire book is well worth reading, Part I, the "Preliminary Communication" by Breuer and Freud, and Chapter 1 of Part II, the case history of Anna O by Breuer (about 43 pages of text in all), are most relevant to my discussion here. Freud's other cases in Part II are well worth the time, as is Part IV, especially his discussion of transference at the end. Penguin recently published a new translation of the book by Nicola Luckhurst (S. Freud & J. Breuer, 2004), which reads very well, but for whose accuracy I cannot vouch.

Chapter 2: The Unconscious Is the Exact Opposite of the Conscious

"Negation" (SE XIX, pp. 235–239).

Chapter 3: Dreams: The Royal Road to the Unconscious

The Interpretation of Dreams (SE IV & V). Although the entire book is well worth one's while—Chapter 1, for example, includes important historical material—the clinician can glean the major points by reading the following sections, which taken together shorten the book from over 600 pages to about 260:

Chapters II, III, and IV	pages 96–162
Chapter V	pages 163–164 (Introduction)
Section B	pages 189–204 and 218–219
Section D	pages 241–267 (Oedipus)
Chapter VI	
Sections A–B	pages 277–309
Section C	pages 310–330 and 337–338
Section D	pages 339–342
Section H	pages 460–487
Section I	pages 488–493, 498–501, and 506–508
Chapter VII	
Section A–B	pages 509–535
Section C	pages 564–568
Sections E–F	pages 592–621

Extras:

Later comments on dreams:

"The handling of dream-interpretation in psychoanalysis" (SE XII, pp. 91–96).
"Remarks on the theory and practice of dream-interpretation" (SE XIX, pp. 109–121).
"Some additional notes on dream-interpretation as a whole" (SE XIX, pp. 127–134).

On slips and bungled actions:

Introductory Lectures on Psychoanalysis, Lectures 1–4 (SE XV).
The Psychopathology of Everyday Life (SE VI).

Chapter 4: Obsession and the Case of the Rat Man (Ernst Langer)

"Notes upon a case of obsessional neurosis" (SE X, pp. 155–318). The new translation by Louise Adey Huish (S. Freud, 2002) strikes me as quite readable, but I cannot judge its accuracy.

Chapter 5: Hysteria and the Case of Dora (Ida Bauer)

"Fragment of an analysis of a case of hysteria" (SE VII, pp. 1–122). The new translation by Anthea Bell (S. Freud, 2013) strikes me as fine, but not much more readable than Strachey's; I cannot vouch for its accuracy. *Papers on Technique*, especially:

"Recommendations to physicians practicing psychoanalysis" (SE XII, pp. 111–120).
"On beginning the treatment" (SE XII, pp. 123–143).
"Remembering, repeating, and working-through" (SE XII, pp. 147–156).
"Observations on transference-love" (SE XII, pp. 159–171).

Chapter 6: Symptom Formation

Introductory Lectures on Psychoanalysis, Lectures 17, 18, 19 (pp. 294–302 only), 23, and 28 (SE XV & XVI).

All in all, the recommended reading comes to about 700 pages (without the extras listed for Chapter 3), an amount easily included in a semester-long course on psychoanalysis.

A Clinical
Introduction
to Freud

CHAPTER 1

Tracing a Symptom Back to Its Origin

ONE OF THE SIMPLEST techniques Freud bequeathed to us seems now to be rarely taught or employed by the vast majority of practitioners: to explore in detail with the analysand all the circumstances surrounding the very first appearance of a symptom. Having spoken at length with his friend Josef Breuer about the latter's work with Anna O, and having experimented himself with hypnotizing patients and asking them to recount all the particulars of the moment at which a specific symptom first arose, Freud already in the mid-1890s claimed to have had a good deal of success in alleviating people's suffering by tracing their symptoms (like making funny clicking or clacking noises with their tongues at odd moments) back to their origin—that is, back to what he calls their "precipitating cause" (SE II, p. 3).

In his *Studies on Hysteria* (SE II), coauthored with Josef Breuer, the technique is simplicity itself. Freud does not see any need yet here to *interpret* the predicaments in which patients found themselves that led to symptom formation. It seems sufficient to get patients to *recount* everything that was going on at the time their symptoms first arose.

There is one additional condition: Patients must not simply tell the facts in a deadpan, matter-of-fact style, but must, in the consulting room, mentally project themselves back in time and get worked up, shocked, frightened, or upset, just as they had been at that earlier time (SE II, p. 6). An impassive account of the bare facts leads nowhere, whereas speech laden with affect (i.e., emotion) brings resolution—indeed, Freud mentions many instances in which emotionally charged speech about the circumstances surrounding the first appearance of a symptom led to the permanent disappearance of the symptom from a patient's life.

Magic? Hardly. Freud and Breuer call it "catharsis" here, referring *catharsis*

back to Aristotle's view, expressed in his *Poetics*, that the viewing public enjoys a good tragedy because it experiences, during the performance, many of the same emotions as the characters onstage; this releases a kind of affective energy that, as Freud might have said, had previously been strangulated or suppressed. Today, many of us are more familiar with catharsis through the vicarious aggression we feel while watching a football or hockey game, as we imagine being one of the players ourselves; the exhilaration we experience in watching a heart-pounding adventure movie; or the release we derive from viewing a tragic romance or "having a good cry" during a tearjerker. We can get so caught up in these broadcasts, movies, and stories because we ourselves feel some of the same aggressiveness, longing for passion and adventure, or heartbreak, but have not found an occasion upon which to express it or have not allowed ourselves to express it even when the opportunity presented itself.[1]

Freud observed that when patients under hypnosis spoke about all of the circumstances surrounding the first appearance of their symptoms, while re-experiencing the emotions they had felt at the time but had never before expressed or vented, curative effects ensued: Their symptoms at least temporarily disappeared. (Sometimes patients had to speak about not just the initial appearance of their symptoms, but the whole series of such appearances.) This led Freud to formulate a first hypothesis: A symptom forms when someone has an intense reaction to a situation and yet feels obliged (or forces him- or herself) to stifle that reaction, to express nothing at the time, and indeed to try thereafter to forget the experience altogether. This leads to two consequences:

- The intense emotional reaction becomes bottled up, and needs to be "uncorked" with the therapist's help; and
- the memory of the situation disappears, as it were, no longer being part of the store of memories available to that person's consciousness.

The second consequence implies that the event itself is forgotten. During ordinary waking life, the person remembers nothing of it. Freud found that it was only when he hypnotized the person that he was able to get him or her to remember the event and put into words every detail of it and all of the reactions he or she had to it.

This led him to propose a very simple model:

M1 | M2—M3—M4

FIGURE 1.1. The Isolation of One Memory from All Others

The memory of one event, abbreviated here as M1, becomes cut off from our memory of all kinds of other events (abbreviated here as M2, M3, and M4). In most cases, our memory of one event has links to memories of other events in our lives (the links are represented in Figure 1.1 as long dashes), whether because they occurred in the same place or time, or because they involved some of the same actors. Not so with M1: Our memory of this event has no connection whatsoever with any of our other memories and cannot be evoked or brought to mind by our thinking about things that occurred in the same place, at much the same time, or with the same friends, neighbors, or family members. It has become completely isolated.

Repression

This is Freud's first model of *Verdrängung*,[2] known in English as "repression": M1 is forced out of the fabric of all of a person's memories that are accessible to consciousness. The memory of this event has not been altogether eradicated, but it has gone "elsewhere"—it has become "unconscious" (for the first uses of the term, see SE II, p. 45). As Freud puts it much later, it has become "internal foreign territory," insofar as it remains within the person but becomes foreign-seeming to consciousness (SE XX, p. 57).

By way of example, Freud discusses what happens when someone insults us publicly (SE II, pp. 8–9). Some of us may immediately retort and give back as good as we got; others may hit or slap the person who insulted us; and still others may say nothing but ruminate for some time thereafter about the horrible slight, wondering whether we deserved it or not, thinking about our good points, and likely concluding—ruefully, angrily, or tearfully—that the other person was in the wrong. In all of these instances, the event leads to a certain amount of physical activity in the present (e.g., slapping) or mental activity shortly thereafter, leading to an immediate or gradual diminishing of the sense of outrage or humiliation that got us worked up (this implies a draining away or "discharging" of the "excitation"). We do not forget the event and, in the cases in which we react to it immediately, it may have few if any enduring effects. Should we ruminate, the emotion sooner or later becomes spent (in most cases), as we contextualize the humiliating event in relation to other more positive events in our lives, situating it as but a minor misfortune in an otherwise relatively fortunate existence. Freud (p. 9) refers here to "the disappearance of the accompanying affect through the process of association"—the linking up of one of our memories with many others.

There are, however, certain people who are positively *mortified* by such public insults. They are so taken aback when the insult comes that they are incapable of responding in the moment, and so shocked or hurt that they refuse to even think about what was said. Better to pretend it never happened, they seem to believe.[3] Why, we might wonder, would somebody be so shocked or hurt by a mere insult, no matter how coarse, degrading, or vociferous? People are obviously all the more mortified if the insult somehow hinted at, if not downright pinpointed something they knew to be true and that they wished to keep concealed. Had there been no truth to it whatsoever, it probably would have had little enduring impact. As the French say, *Il n'y a que la vérité qui blesse*—which one might render literally as "Only the truth smarts" or figuratively as "Nothing hurts quite like the truth."[4] Freud himself says something similar on at least two occasions: "As we all know, it is only reproaches which have something in them that 'stick'; it is only they that upset us" (SE V, pp. 482–483), and "A reproach that misses the mark gives no lasting offence" (SE VII, p. 46). But a reproach, insult, accusation, or affront that *hits* the mark (or comes close to hitting it) can be traumatizing; in other words, it can lead one to strive to forget it had ever been made.

An analysand of mine cheated on his wife for many years with a number of different women, and, as so often happens, would occasionally accuse *his wife* of sleeping around. When, one day, she finally accused him of being unfaithful to her, he became so infuriated he was beside himself, having believed he had been so careful to hide his affairs that no one could ever have suspected him of infidelity. He remained distraught and incensed for weeks thereafter, even as he tried to forget the whole incident and get his wife to forget it as well.

Yet *try as we might to forget the truth, the truth does not forget us.* No matter how hard we try to forget an event, to isolate it, to cut it off from everything else in our lives, it lives on and looks, as it were, for outlets, moments at which to reveal itself.[5] It continues to eat away at us, festering, as it were, or growing and metastasizing like a cancer (choose your favorite metaphor), requiring us to expend ever-greater amounts of energy to keep it under wraps. In short, it becomes "pathogenic"—that is, it generates something pathological. As Freud puts it, "The repressed idea takes its revenge by becoming pathogenic" (SE II, p. 116); that is, it takes revenge against us for having repressed it.

Like a population that is brutally oppressed by a tyrant, the greater the suppression, the more explosive the population's reaction is likely to be when it finally comes. My outbursts that are at least in part motivated by repression are the ones most likely to be viewed as "irrational" by my entourage, given how incommensurate they appear to be with my present circumstances—when, for example, I have repressed years of angry thoughts about a family member and some small incident finally triggers a volcanic eruption in me, everything coming spewing out. The more I have suppressed my own wish to retaliate against, criticize, or punish that person—that is, the more I have given up on my own desire to do something, swept aside or renounced my own will—the worse I feel, the guiltier I feel,[6] the greater the buildup of angry emotion in me (SE II, p. 8), and the more extreme my eventual explosion is likely to be. "In cases such as this, the affect is justified in its *quality* but not in its *quantity*. . . . The excess arises from sources of affect that had previously remained unconscious and suppressed" (SE V, p. 479).

Public insults may seem to be rather rare and minor events to many of us today, hardly capable of inciting the kind of emotional reaction that could give rise to repression. Times were obviously different when Freud wrote this, people keeping a far closer rein on their public persona and reputation, whereas today we have become accustomed to people being called crooks, liars, whores, or gigolos with nary a lawsuit in the offing. Freud, however, furnishes myriad examples of other emotionally charged situations that lead to repression, which we shall examine further on in this chapter.

The Ubiquity of Isolation Strategies

No one wants to get to know his unconscious and the most conve-nient plan is to deny its existence altogether.
—Freud, SE VIII, p. 162

If this isolation-based model of repression seems somehow obvious to us, it is because we are familiar with it from many other realms. Elemen-tary military strategy involves isolating one's enemy, cutting off all his lines of communication so he cannot call for possible reinforcements, preventing all attempts at retreat, and blocking all his supply chains of munitions, food, and water (when done to a city, this is known as *laying siege*). The criminal justice system isolates a prisoner not only behind bars, but also behind barbed-wire fences manned with gun-toting sentries. The medical corps attempts to quarantine a patient who has a contagious disease for which there is no known cure, cutting the patient off from all physical contact with others as far as possible (being unable, however, to protect its own medical personnel from the possibility of infection). Economic sanctions against a country often include boycotting its products or exports and blockading its ports and other trading platforms. Religions resort at times to isolating techniques such as anathematizing, excommunicating, and shunning when it comes to people, and blacklisting or burning when it comes to books. And ethnology teaches us that in cultures where certain foods are considered to be clean and others unclean, rituals are developed by which to keep them completely separate (just as all contact by men with menstruating women was sometimes restricted in the distant past, as they were considered to be unclean during their menses; in certain religions, such contact is still prohibited today).[7]

Isolation is employed as a strategy in many human realms, and thus we should not be that surprised to find that it is employed in the mental realm as well.

Being of Two Minds

We must always be prepared to drop our conceptual framework if we feel we are in a position to replace it with something that more closely approximates to the unknown reality.

—Freud, SE V, p. 610

A further hypothesis that Freud makes in 1895 is that although a memory of an event may be cut off from association with other memories that *are* available to us, it is not cut off from association with other memories that are *not* available to us. In other words, he hypothesizes that connections become established between one isolated memory and another isolated memory, such that they begin to form what he, following Charcot, calls a *condition seconde*—a "second consciousness," so to speak, a sort of split-off, disassociated, second self (which we tend to think of as a "non-self," as something that is radically "not me"). As more and more memories are shoved aside,

> groups of ideas . . . become cut off from associative connection with other ideas, but can become associated among themselves, thereby forming the more or less highly organized rudiment of a second consciousness [*condition seconde*]. (SE II, p. 15)[8]

The resulting web or chain of isolated memories becomes the foundation for what Freud calls the unconscious. And since so much of what we remember is recorded in words and verbal expressions (that is, signifiers)—it often being when someone uses a specific word or idiomatic expression that a particular memory is triggered in us—we can easily see why Lacan began referring to the unconscious as a "signifying chain"—that is, as a web or chain of signifiers.

$$M1-M2-M3 \quad | \quad M4-M5-M6$$

FIGURE 1.2. The Formation of a Web or Chain of Isolated Memories

Note that the "highly organized" chain on the left consists of thoughts, memories, and wishes that we considered so disturbing and distasteful that we put them out of mind. And all of them are related to hurtful things that others have said or done to us, or to feelings or desires that we have refused to accept in ourselves. In fact, the chain on the left consists essentially of all the "bad" things about ourselves that we would rather not know about, whereas the chain on the right consists of the things about us and our lives that we are at least willing (if not happy) to know about. Dreaming, intense daydreaming, and violent intrusive thoughts generally stem from the left-hand chain. And as we shall see when we take up the case of Anna O a bit further on, the chain on the left becomes associated with what we might call the "bad me," the chain on the right becoming associated with what we might call the "good me." The thicker (or more solid) the barrier between the two, the more likely it is that trouble will ensue.

The Radical Inaccessibility of Repressed Thoughts and Wishes

> *The unconscious is* inadmissible to consciousness.
> —Freud, SE V, p. 615 (emphasis in the original)

To highlight the degree to which isolated/repressed memories are inaccessible to ordinary waking thought, let me momentarily liken them to something that occasionally occurs in the realm of computing. As inexact as this analogy may be in many ways, it may help certain readers grasp what Freud means by isolation or dissociation.

What is at present in a computer's random-access memory (RAM)—that is, simplistically stated, what one sees displayed currently on the screen—can be likened to what we as human beings are *conscious* of at this very moment; let us call it M4. We are presently thinking or talking about M4, and it is obviously accessible to us. We are not currently thinking or talking about M5 or M6, but we might easily begin thinking or talking about them insofar as they are connected in our minds to M4. Rather than being conscious, M5 and M6 are—to get ahead of ourselves by employing Freud's vocabulary as developed in *The Interpretation of Dreams* (SE IV and V)—"preconscious." In the world of computing, we could associate M5 and M6 with other files that can be opened and read just by clicking on them. They are not currently in the computer's RAM, but the merest double click suffices to place them there.[9]

Anyone who has owned a computer for some time is aware that there are, however, files stored on its hard drive that either cannot be opened or cannot be effectively read, even though they are still obviously present (like unconscious material, computer files we try to erase rarely are truly deleted). In recent years, it has become possible to lock files, such that they can only be opened by their creator (assuming he or she remembers the proper passwords!), or encrypt files, so that they can only be read by those who have the key. But more insidious for most of us is what results from the successive versions of word processing software like Microsoft Word that can no longer open older Word files that were created while running earlier operating systems. A maddening message Mac users often receive is that one of their older files "uses a file type that is blocked from opening in this version." In years past, Apple computers would all too often surprise the unwary with the following message: "That file cannot be opened. The application that created it is not available."

The memories, thoughts, and wishes that have become unconscious are like such files: We might say that the application that created them is no longer available. Better still, we might say that the application that can locate, open, and read them has yet to be created. Psychoanalytic practice involves inventing a whole series of applications that *can* locate, open, and read the contents of the unconscious ("the ideational contents"; SE II, p. 15), which are products of a *unidirectional* application known as repression. Repression is designed to make things disappear, not to undo its own effects by making them reappear.[10]

Psychoanalysts must engage in a process we might roughly liken to "reverse engineering": taking a product apart to see how it was put together in the first place such that it works as it currently works. Analysts do not do so in order to learn how to bring about repression themselves,[11] but in order to reverse the effects of the application known as repression.

Freud at first believed he had found the necessary reverse application when he discovered hypnosis (through the work of Liébeault and Bernheim in Nancy, France, and Charcot in Paris). A subject in a deep hypnotic or somnambulistic state could remember, it seemed, virtually everything he was asked to recall by the hypnotist, things that he seemed absolutely unable to remember when asked by the same person while not under hypnosis.

Yet Freud soon discovered that hypnosis was not the skeleton key to all locks: Even in cases in which he was able to bring about deep hypnosis, which he admits to having found impossible in numerous instances,[12] the patient did not always immediately recover the information requested, time and encouragement by the hypnotist being necessary.[13] The "file" still could not be opened, something more being required to get around or overcome what appeared to be considerable resistance. And given the number of cases in which no good, reliable hypnotic state could be achieved, Freud soon developed other "reverse applications," including a combination of what he called "concentration" (with eyes closed, lying on a couch), suggestion, and pressure (of his hands on a patient's head), and then relaxation and free association (SE II, pp. 109–110 and 268).[14] The less often specific memories and wishes would come out just by Freud asking his patients to tell him about themselves, the more he turned to working with dreams, fantasies, daydreams, intrusive thoughts, slips of the tongue, and bungled actions of all kinds—in short, things that are generally overlooked if not deliberately ignored in most people's everyday lives—as indirect ways of gaining access to the "files" that seemed to be under lock and key.

To take this approximate computing analogy a step further, I would venture to liken the contents of the unconscious to a computer virus, which—like a "foreign body" (SE II, p. 290) or cancer in a living organism that eats away at healthy tissue—covertly works away at the data stored on your hard drive, progressively corrupting one bit of data after another, one file after another. Human memories ordinarily have almost automatic connections with other memories, based simply on where and when the events they memorialize took place and the actors involved, which are usually places and people well known to us. Thus if we are to cut off or isolate one memory from the rest of our memories—if we are to successfully "forget" them—we must also forget those other memories that cannot help but bring the one we wish to forget to mind. In other words, the memory we push out of mind begins infecting other closely related memories, drawing them out of mind as well.[15]

Let us imagine that a traumatic event in my life occurred in a shower in a relative's house. To effectively forget that event—that is, to ensure that I never consciously think about it again—I must also forget everything else that happened in that bathroom and perhaps even in that portion of the house. If other things that happened the same day were also memorable, I may find that I need to withdraw my memories of those, too, from consciousness, as well as a whole series of memories concerning the other person or persons involved in the traumatic incident. The greater the trauma, the greater the number of thoughts that could lead me there by a chain of associations (or stream of consciousness) and that will thus have to be disposed of. In this way, a considerable fabric of memories ends up being withdrawn from consciousness (i.e., they are no longer part of the web of memories stored in my "preconscious," the accessible portion of the hard drive; the hard drive is now, as it were, "partitioned").[16] Like a computer virus, the repressed memory goes on working behind the scenes, often creating larger and larger blanks in one's "data banks," so to speak.

An everyday and usually temporary example of this occurs when we cannot remember someone's name, and suddenly we cannot remember a number of other names that just a moment before were on the tip of our tongues, we being sure we could remember them. The inaccessibility of these names may not last long, but a link has formed between the one name we suddenly cannot find and the others, blocking any of them from coming to consciousness. Here the amnesia is generally only momentary, but in other cases it can be far more enduring, the person being "genuinely unable to recollect it" (SE II, p. 3). As Lacan says, "It is this very inaccessibility that we must always posit as the foundation of the unconscious" (Seminar VIII, p. 182).

The Unconscious Is Not a Kind of "Latency"

> The most complicated achievements of thought are possible without the assistance of consciousness.
>   —Freud, SE V, p. 593 (emphasis in the original)

It is often by studying the most extreme cases that we begin to grasp the functioning of far less extreme cases as well, if not of virtually everyone (this is true in medicine as well, where disease processes are often clearer in the worst cases than in more benign cases). Thus it was that by working with quite severe cases, Freud was able to draw a radical conclusion: Thinking (i.e., the establishment of associative links between different memories or ideas) goes on at two different levels: at a level that *is* accessible to awareness and at a level that is *not* accessible to awareness. The kind of thinking that goes on in the latter is quite automatic, requiring no conscious intentionality on our part; and its very existence implies something that Freud first formulated in *The Interpre-*

tation of Dreams: We are not masters in our own homes—that is, in our own heads (see also SE XVI, p. 285, and SE XVII, p. 143). Insofar as we think of ourselves as aware of all of our own thoughts and intentions, we are quite thoroughly mistaken. This "splitting of consciousness" (a splitting into a first and a "second consciousness"; SE I, p. 12) goes on in virtually all of us.[17]

Many a psychiatrist and philosopher has objected to this initially startling theory. Psychiatrists in the 19th and early 20th century often argued that hysterical patients were faking, and simply did not want to remember what they said they could not remember (they also taxed hysterics with faking in virtually every other realm as well, especially as regarded illness, considering them to be malingerers). Philosophers asserted that such people were acting in "bad faith," that they were unwilling to try hard because they willfully did not wish to face their own past or present. Such unwillingness or "bad faith" often intervenes when patients are telling therapists about their past, and Freud himself gives us examples in which he asked a patient who was *not* hypnotized what might be the reason for something (a symptom, for example), and the patient *immediately* claimed to be able to think of nothing. But after Freud had applied pressure to the patient's head a few times, assuring the patient that the answer would come to him, the patient finally admitted that something had come to mind, adding, "I could have told you that the first time" and explaining that he had found it too "trivial" or "stupid" to mention when first asked the question. As Freud later taught us, it is precisely when the patient says that something is stupid or trivial that we must give it our utmost attention!

As analysts, we must often use our own guesswork to prompt an analysand to reveal an association to an element in a dream (that is, something that comes to mind in connection with an element of the dream, whether that element be a word, an image, or an action) that had already come to the analysand's mind but that he or she was loath to admit to.[18] These could be considered to be instances of embarrassment, shyness, shame, or even bad faith (should we wish to adopt Sartre's pejorative term, which I should not), but they are far different in feel and presentation to both the analyst and the analysand from the first articulation of something that has been forgotten and remained inaccessible for decades.

Many analysands at some point have an experience in which something comes to light, after a long period of analytic work, which they have the dim sense that they had always known but never expressed or owned up to. (Freud writes that patients would sometimes comment, "As a matter of fact, I've always known that, I've just never thought of it"; SE

XII, p. 148.) This might correspond to what phenomenologists refer to as *latency*, but once again it is experientially (dare I say "phenomenologically"?) very different from the sometimes shocking and upsetting revelation of what was truly unconscious, and which often initially gives rise to confusion and discombobulation on the analysand's part, and then to a long and sometimes unsettling period of productive associational work. So-called latency is a far cry from repression. What is unconscious is not that which one is dimly aware of: It is, rather, something that is usually quite surprising, if not downright alarming, especially early on in one's analysis;[19] it is something that one does not easily take in stride, but regarding which one must do a good deal of associational work in order to connect the repressed up with one's other impressions and thoughts (that is, to connect the repressed M1 with M4, M5, and M6).[20]

Freud's view is that all significant events are registered or inscribed *somewhere* in the mind[21] and our task is to figure out how to render them accessible—that is, we must invent techniques that make it possible to access the ideas, wishes, and memories that have been locked up, encrypted, blacked out, or corrupted. Free association is the major technique we use to access them and, as we shall see in Chapter 3, it requires time and ingenuity on our part to help analysands learn how and becoming willing to free-associate.

Traceable Symptoms: Trying Too Hard, for Example

What sorts of symptoms were Breuer and Freud able to alleviate when they *were* able to gain access to those memories via hypnosis and trace symptoms back to their origins? Here is an example from the case of Frau Emmy von N., who is the subject of the second long case history related in *Studies on Hysteria*.

For many years, Emmy von N. involuntarily made a kind of clicking or clacking sound with her tongue whenever she was "excited." Under hypnosis, this was traced back to a moment at which she had been caring for her young daughter, who had long been unable to fall asleep owing to a serious illness. When her daughter finally did fall asleep, the mother "concentrated her whole willpower on keeping still so as not to awaken her." Freud then adds that, "precisely on account of her intention [not to awaken her daughter] she made a 'clacking' noise with her tongue" (SE II, p. 5). When she recounted all the particulars of this first instance of clacking to Freud while hypnotized (along with a later instance), her somewhat minor symptom, which we might refer to today as a "nervous tic," disappeared for quite some time.[22]

Freud refers to the clacking noise she made on that occasion as "an instance of 'hysterical counter-will'" (SE II, p. 5) and as "the putting into effect of antithetic ideas" (p. 92), without really explaining what he means by these expressions. Today we would be inclined to hypothesize that the mother was aggravated and exasperated with this daughter whom she felt to be uncooperative, and wished, at least at some level—in other words, at least some part of her wished—to punish the girl by waking her up again by making noise. Emmy von N. knew full well that to do so would be self-defeating, as it would lead Emmy von N. herself to further prolong her exhausting vigil by her daughter's bedside, yet something in her wanted to do so anyway. That is, we would hypothesize that Emmy von N. was conflicted or of two minds: relieved her daughter had finally settled down and yet angry and/or frustrated at having been made to wear herself out at her bedside and wishing to lash out at her.

Why would someone have to concentrate her willpower so diligently on not making any noise unless she herself was somehow tempted to make noise? Had no such intention to punish her daughter inhabited Emmy von N., there would have been no need for her to monitor herself or concentrate so hard on *not* making noise. This is a crucial yet all too often overlooked facet of every instance of intense intentionality (or "trying so hard"): One has to focus one's attention so acutely on doing one thing precisely because something in one wants to do the opposite! If I have to be extra, extra careful not to miss an appointment, it is obviously because something in me does not want to go to it. Trying too hard is symptomatic of a mind divided.

Later in his case study, Freud confirms what we were able to hypothesize about Emmy von N. even before reading the bulk of the case history, for he tells us that "she had hated her child for three years" (SE II, p. 63), having had a whole series of "grievances against this child [who] had been very odd for a long time; she had screamed all the time and did not sleep, and she had developed a paralysis of the left leg which there had seemed very little hope of curing" (p. 60). At least one of the reasons why Emmy had hated this daughter for so long was that her beloved husband died suddenly right before her eyes while she was in bed, still weak from having given birth to this daughter. Although even the doctors were unable to revive her husband, Emmy somehow believed that "she might have been able to nurse her husband back to health if she had not been in bed on account of the child" (p. 63). Thus her fury at her daughter dated back almost to the very day of her birth.

She later told Freud that, although she had never been fond of the child, "no one could have guessed it from my behavior, for I did everything that was necessary" (SE II, p. 64); this suggests that she obliged herself to act a part that she did not feel, and no doubt resented the child still more because she forced herself to appear to be a good mother in the eyes of the world. This led her to doubly hate her daughter.

Thanks to Freud, it is elementary psychoanalytic thinking in our times to realize that people overemphasize or over-accentuate one thing because they mean the contrary (they say, "Oh, your talk was *so* interesting" when they found it boring, or "We would never even dream of hurting you" when they have not just been dreaming about hurting you but even been planning how to do so), and that they are often led to focus a huge amount of their attention ("concentrate their willpower") on doing *x* precisely because they wish to do the opposite of *x*!

One of my analysands experienced terrible anxiety whenever he had to write a paper for a particular course; it turned out that he thought the course ridiculous and the professor a fool, and was tempted to say so whenever he began writing. The paper required so much concentration and effort on his part precisely because he was working so hard not to say what he wanted to say in it, and was constantly apprehensive that he had in fact let some of his true feelings about the course and the professor leak out in his writing. The more he wanted to criticize this professor and his course, the more uneasy he grew.

The fact that Emmy von N. continued clacking her tongue for some 15 years after her daughter's illness whenever she was "excited" suggests that part of the excitement she experienced on the subsequent occasions when she clacked derived precisely from the fact of being of two minds about something: both wanting to do something and not wanting to do it.

It appears, in any case, that Freud had no need to interpret this to his patient as I have just interpreted it here in order for the tic to disappear for quite some time: He believed that it sufficed to help the patient "ventilate" the emotions she had felt at the time for the pent-up excitation to disappear (SE XI, p. 8); other terms for such "ventilating" that he uses are putting into words, giving verbal utterance to (SE II, pp. 29, 30, 101), talking out, talking off (p. 70 n), talking away (p. 35), abreacting, and narrating (pp. 32, 34). It was undoubtedly true that inciting her to ventilate helped her, for her tic disappeared for a time, but it came back again later; and mere ventilation certainly did not do anything to forestall the creation of new symptoms in future situations in which she found herself of two minds (pp. 261, 264).

For a case in which we see many such situations where the patient is of two minds, let us turn to the one that can be rightly said to be at the origin of all talk therapy: that of Bertha Pappenheim (1859–1936), the patient who has come down in history to us under the pseudonym Anna

O. She was treated for a year and a half in 1881–1882 by Joseph Breuer, an older medical colleague of Freud's, and it was at Freud's insistence that about a decade later Breuer wrote up and published the case, Freud having convinced him of the importance of the method alighted upon in the course of the treatment.

The Very First Case: Anna O

For those of us who are used to reading contemporary case studies, Breuer's account of Anna O's history often seems confusing and surprising. He tells us his 22-year-old patient's story twice over: first from an "external" or "objective" medical perspective—including what a physician of the time would have noticed as to the unfolding of the illness, starting from the moment he was first called in to see her—and then from a chronological therapeutic perspective, indicating how her therapy proceeded as it traced things back to their "first causes." More astonishing to us still is the virtually complete absence of interpretation by Breuer of what might have been going on in the girl's mind.

Anna O suffered from such a wide range of symptoms over the course of her two-year illness that I would be hard-pressed to enumerate them all here briefly. Let us instead read Freud's (1910) succinct account of them:

> She suffered from a rigid paralysis, accompanied by loss of sensation, of both her right arm and leg; and the same trouble from time to time affected her left arm and leg. Her eye movements were disturbed and her power of vision was subject to numerous restrictions. She had difficulties over the posture of her head; she had a severe nervous cough. She had an aversion to taking nourishment, and on one occasion she was for several weeks unable to drink in spite of a tormenting thirst. Her powers of speech were reduced, even to the point of being unable to speak or understand her mother tongue. Finally, she was subject to conditions of "absence," confusion, delirium, and alteration of her whole personality. (SE XI, p. 10)

This list of symptoms—to which we should add at least headaches, complaints that the walls of her room were closing in on her, inability to speak at all for a couple of weeks, and then for some time only in a confusing mixture of English, Italian, and French, even though she could still understand German (SE II, p. 25)—is quite astounding by modern standards, and it is not surprising that Breuer refers to her as having a "psychosis," even though her case is proffered up as (and obviously is) one of hysteria. (*Psychosis* in his terminology seems to refer to a temporary condition rather than to an enduring clinical structure.)

The first symptom that Breuer was able to help her with—using a technique that she herself spontaneously invented, which involved speaking of every occasion on which the symptom had appeared and going back in time from its most recent occurrence to its first occurrence, without skipping any, and thereby following the thread back step by step—involved her inability to drink water, no matter how thirsty she might be (SE II, pp. 34–35). It turned out that the symptom arose owing to what seems like a fairly trivial event: She saw the dog of her English "lady companion" drink water out of a glass in that lady's bedroom. We are told precious little else about this event, other than that Anna O "did not care for" this lady companion, and that she did not say anything on this occasion to her about it as she wanted to be "polite" (p. 34). All we are told is that she suppressed any and all expression of astonishment and disgust, and that once she expressed these emotional reactions to Breuer some six weeks later, while under hypnosis, "the disturbance vanished, never to return" (p. 35).[23]

It goes without saying that not every situation in which we suppress an expression of surprise and/or disgust gives rise to a symptom, for we often think over the situation in our minds afterward (laughing to ourselves, condemning the actors involved in our minds, or mustering comforting thoughts of our own superiority, for example) or eagerly tell someone else about the situation, thereby draining away whatever "excitation" may have arisen at the time. The fact that Anna O seems to have done no such thing, and instead *isolated* her memory of the event from all of her other memories, suggests several, if not many, possibilities: that she had heard something rather awful about diseases that could be communicated by dogs; that she truly hated this English lady companion, but had been told she must tolerate and perhaps even make a show of liking her by someone in the family (that someone probably being her mother, but it might have been her father); that she secretly wished this lady companion might contract an illness from such indiscriminate contact with her dog; that she associated this lady with her own mother, against whom she presumably had a number of grudges, as we shall see further on, if not outright death wishes; and/or that every time she tried to drink water from a glass thereafter she was reminded of her thoughts about communicable diseases or of her hateful wishes toward this lady and/or her mother. There may well have been other components of the situation as well, but we can only guess at them since we are given so little information.

What seems clear is that some nasty thoughts or wishes must have been aroused in her by the sight of this lady's dog drinking from her glass—thoughts or wishes that she felt to be so reprehensible that she tried to put them out of mind once and for all. In order to do so, she needed forever thereafter to avoid coming into contact with water glasses, for they might, by association, remind her of those "inexcusable" thoughts and wishes. To put it in the kind of contemporary terms we hear around us every day, she was not "in touch with her anger" at her friend and/or mother—indeed, she wanted to know nothing whatsoever about it!

Neither Breuer (in 1895) nor Freud (in 1910) comments on the considerable psychological forces that must have been at work in her at the time in order to produce such a life-impeding symptom. And insofar as those forces were never truly elucidated, even as their momentary affective charges were released through the "chimney sweeping" (as Anna O herself called it) she and Breuer engaged in, those same forces could and did go on to create new symptoms on many other occasions. It is not a wild extrapolation, I think, to form a picture of her late 19th-century household as one in which filial piety and duty played a preponderant role, and in which few personal reflections or feelings were ever aired, encouraged, or tolerated.

When such reflections and feelings are stifled or choked back, they tend to fester and bother their suppressors, making the latter "suffer mainly from reminiscences" (SE II, p. 7)—that is, from remembering and ruminating about painful situations from the past regarding which they have regrets. *Why do people who stifle themselves have such regrets? Because they did not say or do what they wanted to say or do in those distressing situations.* Many of us have, at one time or another, stifled ourselves, but we are conscious of our regrets and ruminations, which stem from having given up on our own desire to express something or take some action. We often replay in our minds what we did and did not say or do, thinking of what we with hindsight feel we should have or could have said or done that we would now feel better about. Freud's hypothesis here is that for some people, these regrets and ruminations—that is, this reminiscing, but not in a positive sense, about a particular event and how they did or did not react at the time—go on not in consciousness but, rather, outside of the realm of consciousness, "working" them, so to speak, eating away at them, and even unexpectedly emerging in dreams, daydreams, and other so-called altered states.

When Freud claims that "hysterics suffer mainly from reminiscences" (SE II, p. 7), he does not mean that they are nostalgically reminiscing about the past, thinking about how wonderful it was; he means that they are wracked with regrets and guilt about having given up on their own desire to say or do something. And when Lacan says that we feel guilty when we give up on our own desire, he is merely summarizing what Freud has already laid out for us here.[24] Lacan points out that the term Freud usually uses in this context is *Versagung,* which means several things, including privation (being deprived of something), denial, refusal, and disallowance (not being allowed to have or do something); Lacan interprets *Versagung* as meaning renunciation, perhaps basing this on the various uses of the verb *versagen* (implying, in certain instances, to fail, bungle, break down, or botch), not frustration, as it is usually rendered in English (the German term for frustration is *Frustration*). "Renunciation" implies that one wanted to do something and gave up on it, often as if one were giving in to someone else's wishes (as in self-denial, as if giving in to someone who said something like, "Bite your tongue, girl!"). In other words, it suggests a situation in which one allows someone else's will to prevail over one's own (or allows what one *imagines* someone else's will to be to prevail over one's own) and regrets it forever thereafter. In short, for such people, and Anna O seems to have been one of them, *renunciation is often a recipe for disaster.*[25]

For the Love Of . . .

In the beginning of analytic practice was love.
—Lacan, Seminar VIII, p. 4

The physician makes use of some of the components of love.
—Freud, SE XIV, p. 312

According to Breuer's account, Anna O fell ill as she attempted to perfectly care for her father during his terminal illness, and Breuer seems to have taken this at face value (this is perhaps what he felt any daughter was expected to do at the time, and he never mentioned any possible grievance she might have had against or ambivalence she might have felt toward her father). But reading between the lines—and without going too far out on a limb, I believe—we might wonder why virtually the entire task of caring for her father fell to her instead of to her mother, or to other possible siblings (we hear only once about a younger brother [SE II, p. 36], despite the fact that families tended to be quite large at the time) or relatives. She had a more trying shift than her mother, insofar as she watched over her father all night long, and her mother even left home for several days during the father's illness, leaving still more of the responsibility for his care to Anna. Breuer confined himself to telling us that Anna was "passionately fond" of her father (p. 22), and that she led a very isolated life at home, but we might wonder to what degree she was stuck on her father or felt that she had—whether in his mind, her mind, her mother's mind, or all three—in some sense taken over the role of wife from her mother.

Bolstering the notion that she was seriously attached to her father is the fact that every one of the major symptoms Breuer detailed first arose in the presence of or in relation to her father (SE II, p. 36):

- not hearing when other people would come in the room where she was;
- not understanding when other people were talking to each other;
- not hearing when she was directly addressed;
- and deafness brought on by a wide variety of circumstances.

The girl had strong feelings about her father, some of which were no doubt extremely positive and others of which may well have been negative (though the latter were never mentioned by Breuer). Some of the latter perhaps originated with her feeling obliged to care for him so unstintingly.

If indeed she was seriously attached to her father, we could quite easily conclude that it was her treatment with Breuer that led her to displace or transfer her great affection for her father onto someone else for the very first time (onto her doctor, she seeming to have had few if any suitors, much less lovers, prior to Breuer's appearance on the scene). For Breuer provides us with a similar, albeit scattered, list regarding not symptom formation but rather *forms of alleviation that could only occur in his presence*:

- He was the only person she always recognized when he came in the room (p. 26);
- at times when she refused nourishment altogether, she nevertheless allowed Breuer to feed her (p. 26);[26]
- he was the only one who could overcome her "obstinacy" (p. 30);
- her reaction to the sleeping medication she was often given (chloral) was euphoric when he was present but highly disagreeable when he was not (p. 30);
- she would always request that he shut her eyes in the evening and tell her that she would not be able to open them until he himself opened them the following morning (p. 38).

Breuer never commented on the degree to which Anna would do things for him that she would not do for anyone else and trusted him as she trusted no one else; nor did he seem to realize that to ask him to shut her eyes in the evening and open them again in the morning was to make it seem as though they had spent the whole night together! Indeed, he did not appear to take much notice of the degree to which Anna had transferred her love from her father onto him and in fact got better for him—that is, out of love for him.[27] Hers might truly be understood as what Freud later called a "cure by love" (SE IX, p. 90; SE XIV, p. 101; see also SE XVI, p. 441)—insofar as the forces at war within herself were obviously not "worked through" by the end of the treatment—but such a cure could last only as long as the doctor-patient relationship did.

Yet Breuer only came to realize the degree to which Anna had grown to love him after he had called off the treatment. He did so at least in part after having finally realized that his wife had grown bored and quite depressed hearing him talk endlessly about this beautiful young patient whom he saw morning and night, often spending several hours a day with her in all, and perhaps finally realizing that he himself had become enamored of Anna. As we learn—not in *Studies on Hysteria*, but in Ernest Jones' account of what Freud told Jones about what Breuer had admitted to him (assuming this account is trustworthy)—the very day Breuer told Anna and her family that he felt she was sufficiently improved to end the treatment, he was urgently called back in the evening to find Anna going through what is known as an "hysterical pregnancy" (or pseudocyesis), claiming, "Now Dr. B.'s child is coming!"[28]

This was hardly the only incident that showed how clueless Breuer was about the powerful feelings Anna had for him. For at one point well on in the treatment (10 days after her father's death), once she had grown to trust Breuer implicitly, he brought in a medical colleague whom he apparently wished to consult with regarding the peculiarities of her case. In what Breuer calls a "negative hallucination" (SE II, p. 27), Anna failed to see this unwanted intruder, obviously not wanting him to be there or to observe her as though she were an animal in a zoo, and thus blocking him out. This seems to have so infuriated the consultant that he blew smoke in her face to force her to perceive him—which she then did, leading her to attempt to run out of the room but instead fall unconscious to the floor.

This incident led to a marked worsening of her condition (SE II, pp. 27, 29), and Breuer had quite a tough time regaining her trust. She had no doubt felt she was cooperating with him and telling him all of the most intimate details of her existence because of the very close relationship between them, and he had suddenly tried to bring in a third party acting the part of an objective, outside observer. What a betrayal she must have felt it to be!

A psychotherapeutic technique that relies solely on getting a patient to detach from a parental figure by attaching to the therapist is obviously a risky one; and it is one in which, even if the therapist were available to serve as a long-term lover for the patient, conflicts related to the earlier love object would likely be repeated in relation to the later one, ultimately solving nothing (SE II, p. 304). The same old problems would arise in relation to the new love object, even he were more acceptable in societal terms—for example, a doctor somewhat older than herself instead of her father. (According to Freud's later conceptions of the role played by transference in psychoanalytic practice, as we shall see, patients' conflicts with their parents are in effect displaced onto the analyst, but there they are interpreted and worked through, not simply repeated.)

Such a transfer of love from father to physician may perhaps have been at the crux of Breuer's work with Anna O, but <u>a number of factors suggest that Anna was not necessarily quite so stuck on her father as we might think, and that she in fact felt she had been thrust into the role of wife, whereas she would rather have been pursuing a life of her own.</u>

Consider, for example, what is discovered to be at the origin of her nervous cough (*tussis nervosa*): It first arose one night while she was caring for her father—as did most of her other symptoms (SE II, pp. 36–37)—and heard the kind of music people would dance to at the time coming from a neighbor's house. Breuer tells us that "she was very fond of dancing" and that upon hearing the music she "felt a sudden wish to be there," dancing with other young people, rather than taking care of her sick father at home. Such a wish conflicted, however, with her strong sense of duty (Breuer refers to her "self-reproaches"; p. 40), and she obviously thought herself wicked to be entertaining such selfish thoughts of personal pleasure while her father was lying on his deathbed.

Since whenever she would suppress something in herself (whether a rejoinder she thought of making to something disobliging someone said to her, or a wish she wanted to express), it would lead to "a spasm of the glottis," Breuer makes the following hypothesis: "The motor impulses that she felt [in her throat when a "twinge of conscience" (SE II, p. 43) would lead her to choke back her wish to express a desire to go dancing] transformed the spasms [of the glottis] into a *tussis nervosa*" (p. 44). If this were all there were to it, we would have to wonder why the spasms of the glottis did not lead to something more like hiccups, a choking sensation, or even vomiting. It strikes me that the specific symptom that arose on this occasion, <u>coughing, was pretty transparently designed to *cover over the sound of the music that was giving rise to the conflict in herself.*</u> This is corroborated by the fact that the cough would appear thereafter whenever she heard "any markedly rhythmical music" (p. 40) and was reminded of the very same conflict between filial duty and personal pleasure.

Note the way in which the resulting symptom—the nervous cough—tried to solve a certain kind of problem: If she allowed herself to hear the music, she would want to leave her father's side and go off dancing; this desire she considered to be reprehensible, given her father's condition, and she would then reproach herself harshly for having such a desire. Better not to hear the music in the first place! As soon as the first notes began to force their way into perception, she unwittingly masked them with her coughing. Thus it was as if she had not heard them at all ("out of hearing, out of mind," we might say).

$$\text{Cough}$$
$$\downarrow$$
$$\text{Wish} \Rightarrow \Sigma \Leftarrow \text{Self-reproach for having the wish}$$
$$\uparrow$$
$$\text{Covers music (that is its purpose)}$$

Her wish plus her self-reproach for having the wish led to suppression of the wish and the creation of a compromise formation: a symptom (the nervous coughing). The coughing "spoke of" or came to signify—but only to one in the know, as is true of any symptom, whether it affects the body or just the mind—the simultaneous existence of a wish and a reproach leading to the suppression of that wish.

It is the fairly transparent conflict in Anna's mind between filial duty and a wish to be out dancing with young people in her neighborhood that leads us to call into question the notion that Anna was totally stuck on her father. And we can see that this conflict gave rise in her to an "inability to act" in the world and an "inhibition of the will" (Freud calls these "abulias"),[29] finding a sort of resolution solely by the creation of a somatic symptom. Freud refers to this as "conversion": the conversion of a psychical conflict into a chronic bodily symptom (SE II, pp. 86, 147, 203–208; see also SE III, p. 49).[30]

Precipitating Causes

Breuer indicates that "Each of [Anna's] hysterical symptoms arose during an affect" (SE II, p. 39)—*affect* and *excitement* being code words in his account for an internal conflict—and shows how so many of her symptoms appeared precisely when she was trying to suppress something

(p. 40). The *cause* of the symptom seemed here to be not the event itself—for example, hearing dance music while attending to her father in his sickbed—but the attempt at self-suppression, at suppressing one of the conflicting forces to such a degree that all memory of it was isolated from the rest of her memories. Breuer and Freud were naturally struck by the tenacity of the symptoms that result from such attempts (which often take but a few seconds), commenting on "the disproportion between the many years' duration of an hysterical symptom and the single occurrence that provoked it" (p. 4).

For the most part, events are not in and of themselves traumatic—it is how we react to them that makes them traumatic or not. Experienced, war-hardened soldiers react very differently to extreme battle situations than do new recruits; whereas the latter may be traumatized by the first shedding of blood in their platoon, and repeatedly play over the horror in their minds day and night, more experienced soldiers may simply talk about it with each other and move on. Even one and the same person may react very differently to similar situations at different times and under different circumstances. A moderately serious car crash will always be a moderately serious car crash, but we are likely to be more traumatized by it if we ourselves are at fault, as opposed to the other party or so-called black ice or what is known by insurers as an "act of God" (such as a tornado). If we ourselves were at fault and ended up harming people other than ourselves, we are more likely to try to completely forget the incident or replay the crash over and over in our minds to figure out what we might have done differently.[31]

Many factors go into the constitution of a symptom-inducing trauma, and what is traumatic for one person will not necessarily be traumatic for another. The "precipitating cause" (SE II, p. 3) of a symptom is thus not the event itself per se but the attempt to isolate or forget it. Hence the importance of mentally bringing the patient back to the moment at which the attempt to isolate or forget the event occurred, in order to flesh out all the forces acting upon the subject at that exact moment in time.

Breuer and Freud speak here in fairly standard cause-and-effect scientific language, and they conclude that if the cause had not been present (i.e., if the attempt at forgetting or isolation had not occurred), there would have been no such effect—that is, no symptom formation. And vice versa: In cases in which there is no such effect (for example, in people who do not have such symptoms), there was no such cause.

They also hypothesize, for the psychological realm, the same sort of principle of *inertia* we are familiar with from physics: If we apply a force to something in a vacuum and thereby set it in motion, that motion will continue unchanged—that is, in the same direction and at the same speed—until some opposing force stops it. In the real world, which is not characterized by a complete vacuum, what stops most bodies is friction (from air, water, or more solid substances) or opposing forces such as gravity. Freud and Breuer can be understood to be saying here that a "traumatic cause"—a cause that has a traumatic effect on someone—continues to have that effect (in other words, continues to produce the same symptom) *forever* unless a stop is put to it by some countervailing force, which in most cases is some form of talk therapy. As they put it in SE II,

> We may reverse the dictum *"cessante causa cessat effectus"* ["when the cause ceases the effect ceases"] and conclude from these observations that the determining process continues to operate in some way or other for years—not indirectly, through a chain of intermediate causal links, but as a directly releasing cause, just as a psychologically painful event that is remembered in waking consciousness may still lead one to cry long after the event. (p. 7)

Symptoms, therefore, do not "work themselves out" or "gradually fade" over time: They persist endlessly unless resolved by some form of therapy. The usual "wearing-away process" to which nontraumatic memories are subject does not occur in these cases (p. 8; see also SE V, p. 578); "The repressed is unaltered by the passage of time" (SE XXII, p. 74).

This is borne out by the kinds of symptoms that we see all around us in everyday life. The number of people who have a fear of flying or of taking elevators is quite considerable, and when we encounter adults who have such fears, we note that these fears tend to persist for the rest of the adults' lives unless they go into treatment. These fears may not be terribly visible to casual outside observers because such adults tend to organize their lives in such a way as to avoid flying or taking elevators whenever possible (and avoidance is one of the defining features of neurosis), but their fears tend not to wane, remaining just as paralyzing at age 80 as they were at age 20 (leading these adults at times to have a few good, stiff drinks or take antianxiety medication before boarding a plane, or simply to avoid planes altogether).

This contradicts contemporary psychological "wisdom," which maintains that patients' current symptoms are usually due to current problems and that there is no need to explore the past to resolve them, short-term, "problem-oriented," "solution-focused" therapy (like cognitive-behavioral therapy) being sufficient. And, running counter to a good deal of "folk wisdom," Freud seems to suggest that there are few self-reparative tendencies in the human psyche (unlike in the human body, where even crippling physical traumas can be overcome to at least some degree after a number of years); this makes it such that people are unlikely to "grow out of" such fears over time.

The Unconscious Does Not a "Depth Psychology" Make

What were four or five years in comparison with a whole lifetime, especially considering that the patient's existence had been so very much eased during the treatment?

—Freud, SE V, p. 437

There is no need to postulate some *depth* into which unwanted memories are shoved, as it were: There is no need to think of that which is isolated or cut off as sinking or being pushed down into some deep, dark place. It suffices to imagine a barrier between different sets of perceptions and memories, the ones on the left being associated, for example, with the naughty or evil Anna—after all, she herself described her absentmindedness or daydreaming as her "bad self" (SE II, p. 46)—the ones on the right being associated with her good self (p. 24).[32]

$$M1-M2-M3 \quad | \quad M4-M5-M6$$

Should it seem to the reader to be outmoded to talk about split consciousness,[33] one side of the split being associated with the "bad self" and the other with the "good self," it suffices to listen to children who often speak of themselves in these very same terms—good Jim and bad Jim, for example—and who, in more extreme cases in which we see incipient forms of multiple personality (or so-called dissociative identity disorder), even give slightly different names to their bad selves: good Jim and bad Tim.

Note that the good and the bad selves are precise opposites of each other, and that Anna O considered herself to be a good girl when devotedly caring for her father and a bad girl when failing to do so because she wanted to do something else with her life. Lacan talks about conscious and unconscious as though they were located on a Möbius strip (Seminars XIV and XV), one being locally the flip side of the other, thus illustrating how intimately connected they are: What is considered to be good is precisely what is not bad, and vice versa.

Parents, caretakers, and educators obviously all contribute to this good/bad split, although some clearly reject or chastise the supposedly

good = not bad

bad = not good

bad aspects of the child far more than others do. There are, after all, households in which one is not simply punished for expressing anger at a parent but is even expressly forbidden to *be* angry at a parent (it is said to be irrational, immoral, unfair, unjustified, illegitimate, or even evil and inspired by the devil). So, too, are there children who so desperately want to please a parent that they themselves go beyond the "call of duty" and repress in themselves any sort of disobliging thought or feeling about that parent.

This is not to say that we would be better off were no split of any kind to ever form, were nothing to *ever* be split off or isolated from consciousness (or from potential consciousness, in the form of the preconscious), for that theoretically leads to psychosis, something we will not delve into in this book. And one might plausibly argue that the split in each of us who is not psychotic gives rise to a primary symptom or set of symptoms (see Chapter 6). Yet these symptoms are often ones with which we can live without them driving us crazy or making us miserable (until such time, that is, as they perhaps do begin driving us crazy or making us miserable, at which point we, in the best of cases, seek out a qualified analyst). But there are some people in whom the split is so all-encompassing and rigid that myriad symptoms form, and they quickly become crippled by them.

Such is the case of those who, like Anna O, find themselves in predicaments where powerful internal psychic forces are pushing in different directions simultaneously:

$$\text{Force 1} \Rightarrow \text{Symptom} \Leftarrow \text{Force 2}$$
Libido   Prohibitions (Superego)
$$\text{"Bad self"} \Rightarrow \text{Symptom} \Leftarrow \text{"Good self"}$$
Id   Ego

Cast in the terms that Freud presents much later (SE XVI, p. 360), we have on the left the impersonal force of the "it" (rendered in English translations of Freud's work as the "id," which includes the drives that we feel we have no control over, as when we say, for example, "I don't know what came over me" or "I couldn't help myself"); and we have on the right the force of the "me" (rendered in English translations of Freud's work as the "ego," which includes those aspects of myself that I am happy with or at least willing to accept as part of me, aspects that often coincide with broader social, cultural, and religious notions regarding what constitutes a good person). Cast in still other Freudian terms, we could characterize the conflict here as that between the libido on the left and the forces of prohibition (or superego) on the right.

Let us note that James Strachey, Freud's official translator, often seems to have sought to make Freud's very simple and intuitively understandable language sound more scientific in English by choosing words of Latin origin. For example, Freud's German term *Ich*—which has been translated into English as "ego"—simply means "I" or "me"; you would use it, for example, when you ring someone's doorbell and he or she asks, "Who is it?" at which point you might simply respond, "It's me." Freud's German term *Es*—which has been translated into English as "id"—simply means "it," as in the expressions "It is raining," "It is snowing," or "It happened." And Freud's German term *Über-Ich*—which has been translated into English with the term "superego"—literally means "over me," in the sense of something that stands over me and that disciplines and orders—like a superior, a parent, or a boss.[34]

Returning to our conflict model, we can imagine a situation in which Forces 1 and 2 somehow cancel each other out, the subject being left with little or no energy to do anything at all, all of her energy being tied up in this titanic struggle—and such is sometimes the predicament of those who complain of depression.[35] Their total lack of energy might be thought of as a symptom by some, but it is not a fully constituted symptom in the way a tic, nervous cough, squint, or paralysis of a limb is, for these latter are compromise formations that create something new, something that somehow manages to extract the subject from the predicament in which she finds herself.

Recall, for example, that it was by attempting to take such perfect care of her father that Anna O became exhausted to the point that she had to take to her bed for about four months. If the main conflict in her can be understood as one between her filial duty and her desire to have a life of her own, she found a way to renege on her filial duty by falling ill. Her "state of weakness, anemia, and distaste for food became so bad that, to her great dismay, she was no longer allowed to continue nursing the patient" (SE II, p. 23). We might understand this result to have been a "secondary gain" from her illness, as Freud was to formulate such things later (and this concept is still widely used today), or perhaps to have even been its "primary aim," albeit unconscious. For, as we saw in the case of Anna's nervous cough, in many instances what is effectively achieved by a symptom (drowning out the sound of music) is the very purpose of the symptom. Anna's breakdown presumably forced Anna's mother to take over the lion's share of nursing during the final four months of her husband's life.

Granted, retiring to a sickbed did not offer Anna much of a life of her own—except indirectly insofar as a handsome young doctor by the name of Josef Breuer was brought in to treat her, with whom she quite clearly fell in love—but it did, arguably, help solve at least part of the problem. (We will discuss the way in which symptoms form as solutions to problems in greater detail in Chapter 4).

Forcing Yourself to Do What You Don't Want To

Before we leave Anna O to turn to the many things Freud learned from work with his own patients, let us briefly discuss the very beginning of her illness, at least as defined by the first visible symptom that appeared when she was 21.[36] Given the way her treatment unfolded, by following the thread from the most recent manifestations of her symptoms to the earliest ones, it is no doubt significant that *she only recalled the incident that first precipitated her illness on the very last day of the treatment* (SE II, p. 40).[37] What she remembered that last day was as follows: She had been sitting by her father's bedside, anxiously awaiting the arrival of her father's doctor; her mother had gone away, and her father was in very bad condition, running a high fever. Her right arm, draped over the back of her chair, had fallen asleep and she had a dream, fantasy, or intense daydream of some kind in which a snake was slithering toward her father to bite him (p. 38). She tried to fend off the snake, but her arm refused to move. She then looked at her hand and her fingers looked like snakes with "death's heads" (i.e., skulls) in the place of her fingernails. The snake finally vanished and she tried to pray, but no words came to mind. The only words that finally occurred to her were some nursery rhymes in English, and she eventually "found herself able to think and pray in that language" (p. 39).

Anna was obviously quite frightened by this dream or intense daydream, but no symptom formed just then. The next day, however, she saw a branch that reminded her of the snake and her arm suddenly became stiff—that is, rigidly extended (SE II, p. 39). After that, anything that reminded her of snakes made her arm stiff.

Breuer provides no interpretation of the dream as we might now, and as Freud certainly would have done only a few short years later. He merely mentions that there were snakes in the field behind the house and that she had been frightened by one, no doubt. She had never said as much herself, making this a total supposition on his part.

What might we say about the dream today, after having studied Freud's plentiful work on dreams? The first question we must always ask is *Why have such a dream in the first place?* In other words, why imagine that her father is about to be bitten by a snake and that she is unable to help him? (Those who might be immediately tempted to see in the snake a phallic symbol have probably been influenced by a rather stereotyped version of Freud, the kind found on the back jacket of mass-market paperback editions of *The Interpretation of Dreams* where we are encouraged to revert to pre-Freudian way of interpreting dreams, using universal symbols, rather than interpreting them contextually and using the analysand's associations whenever possible.) We are aware that her father was quite ill—and thus already in mortal danger—and that she probably felt somewhat powerless to help him, but why dream such a thing? Freud teaches us that a dream is not simply a reproduction, replaying, or re-presentation of reality, but rather that we dream, day-dream, or fantasize about something that at least some part of us wants to have happen.

It is hardly rocket science to surmise that if a poisonous snake were to bite her father, who was already quite ill, he would die in fairly short order. One of the results of his death would be that Anna would no longer have to watch over him all night long. Her overriding sensation might be one of grief but, as anyone who has ever taken care of a loved one for months at a time during a terminal illness will tell you, it would be accompanied by a sense of relief (cf. SE V, p. 430). Her father would finally be out of his misery and Anna could move on with her life.

Considering the dream in this light allows us to hypothesize that when she looked at her hand and fingers and saw skulls instead of fingernails, she was condemning herself as a murderer for having wished her father dead, feeling that by her own hand she had allowed him to be in such mortal danger. Note that Anna, like most of us, had two hands, and if one was paralyzed (having apparently fallen asleep in reality), she still had another with which she could have protected her father; and yet she did not in the dream, suggesting that she did not want to protect him from this threat. The partially paralyzed arm was thus used in the dream as a pretext or excuse for not going to her father's rescue and perhaps being bitten herself—she was not willing to sacrifice herself for him, so that he might live a short time longer. Recall that she had, on one occasion, imagined seeing "her father with a death's head" in the place of her own image in a mirror, perhaps having the sense that he and his illness might soon be the death of her (SE II, p. 37).

We are told that when the snake vanished, she tried to pray but no words came to mind. We are not told what she might have been trying to pray for—was it for the snake to return and bite her father? Or was it to thank God that her father had been spared? Assuming it was the latter, we have to note that she is unable for quite some time to find any words of thanks, as if she did not wish to thank God for having spared him. The only words that eventually came to mind were some nursery rhymes in English; again, we don't know their content, but such nursery rhymes are often a far cry from words with which to pray or thank God—consider, for example, "Jack fell down and broke his crown and Jill came tumbling after"![38] And it was after such nursery rhymes came to mind that she was finally able to think and pray in English (again, we do not know what she prayed for), which may have something to do with why she later spoke only English for quite some time during her illness.

Anna had turned herself into a true human wreck nursing her father, and few of us would, I imagine, condemn her for having wanted his terminal illness to end sooner rather than later. But she condemned herself for wanting this, and engaged in a behavior that we see in a great many cases: The less she wanted to be attentive to him—finding herself daydreaming off in "la la land," thinking about dancing with young men and failing to hear her father request something—the more she tried to force herself to be attentive and concentrate all of her will on doing the opposite of what at least a part of her wanted to do (for she considered her own fun-seeking wishes to be frivolous). I have had many an analysand who no longer wanted to stay with his partner and who tried to force himself to be good to her and do what she wanted; the less he wanted to be with her, the harder he strove, and the less successful he was in his striving, as the part of him that did not want to be with her would always manage to show through.

This was precisely what happened to Anna: The harder she tried to listen so that she would hear her father's requests, the deafer she became! The more vigilant she tried to be at her father's bedside, the more absent she would become and the less she would notice that he actually needed or wanted something from her. It is precisely because she was sick of caring for him that she felt that her care could never be good enough.

It was the repeated attempt to put her "frivolous" desires entirely out of mind that constituted the precipitating cause of so many of her symptoms.

Altered States

Speaking of Anna O's intense daydreaming, note that Breuer and Freud mention a second way in which isolation-based repression can come about: When someone is in what in the 1960s and 1970s would have been referred to as "an altered state of consciousness" (SE II, p. 214). They refer to such altered states here as "hypnoid states," because they resemble the state of someone who is hypnotized (they also use the French term *absences*, absences), even though they are "fallen into" spontaneously, without the help or intervention of a hypnotist.

Many of us, today, are not terribly familiar with such states—which, like many of the earlier manifestations of hysteria, including psychosomatic contractures, paralyses, inability to speak, deafness, blindness, and so on, have given way to other manifestations—and the closest some of us come to such states are moments of intense daydreaming. Such daydreaming, which seems to be overlooked by the vast majority of practitioners today but is already mentioned by Freud and Breuer in 1895 (SE II, p. 13), can become so all-engrossing at times that we temporarily forget everything going on around us and can only be jolted out of it by a teacher angrily or sarcastically calling us to account in front of a roomful of jeering classmates. To describe it, we resort to euphemisms like being "out of it," "spaced out," "zoned out," "in la la land," "gone," in "a twilight state" (SE II, p. 4), "in a trance," or, as the French say, "on the moon" (*dans la lune*); contemporary psychologists and psychiatrists often refer to it as *dissociation.*

For some people, the fantasies that occur to them during such moments seem so vivid that they can no longer determine whether they actually occurred or not. This is familiar to almost all of us after having had an especially vivid dream that takes place in a familiar context: We cannot recall whether we in fact slept through an important appointment or not, or slept with someone we really should not have. How relieved we sometimes are after opening our eyes, seeing that we are still in bed, and realizing that it must have been but a dream!

Such altered states of consciousness are often so far removed and cut off from our more ordinary states of consciousness that many of us find it terribly difficult to remember what was going on while we were dreaming or daydreaming; and our memories of the fantasized events that occur during such states remain isolated and "dissociated" (SE II, p. 12) from our memories of what occurs during waking life, dreaming life and waking life staying separated by a wide divide. It often takes a great deal of practice to stop ourselves from ignoring or even actively overlooking (SE II, p. 68) what we were imagining during such dream states; such practice is encouraged by at least those psychoanalysts who continue to strive to work in a recognizably Freudian vein.[39]

A male patient of mine told me that he was so dissociated on his wedding day that he remembered virtually nothing of the marriage ceremony and had no recollection of having said "I do." He could easily deduce what he had probably done that day, but for a long time could recall nothing of it. (In an amusing episode of *I Dream of Jeannie*, Jeannie is so caught up in her own fantasies of what the perfect wedding should be like that she literally disappears every time she attempts to walk down the aisle with her husband-to-be.)

Yet even analysands who become adept at remembering their dreams are often still incapable of recalling all kinds of intrusive thoughts (Freud called them "involuntary ideas," SE V, p. 523) that flash through their minds while they are staring off into space, sitting idly on the subway, or even just walking down the street. Such intrusive thoughts are often considered by those who have them, when they do actually remember them, to be unforgivably nasty, cruel, and violent. Consider, for example, the thought that flashed through Elisabeth von R.'s mind at her sister's deathbed and that was instantaneously pushed away: "Now he [her sister's husband, whom she found charming] is free again and I can be his wife" (SE II, p. 156). The very fact of recalling such thoughts is already a first step toward drawing them into relation to other thoughts and memories, taking them out of their isolation and dissociation and connecting them up with the rest of our lives (see Figure 1.3). Which is not to say that we are then immediately willing to accept them as being part of ourselves! But admitting that they are there and that we are the ones who have such thoughts (i.e., that they are not implanted in us by some external alien source) is an important first step.

$$M1--|--M2-M3-M4$$

FIGURE 1.3.   Drawing a Memory out of Its Isolation from Other Memories

Indeed, what we might loosely call "denial" takes at least two distinct forms:

1. First we deny that any such event (e.g., a violent fantasy) ever occurred.
2. Once we feel forced to admit that it did occur, we deny that it has anything to do with us and loudly proclaim that wishing for such reprehensible things is the furthest thing from our minds; that is, when something's existence can no longer be disputed, its having any possible connection with ourselves is disputed.

In recent years, I have heard students in psychology classes claim that such intrusive thoughts and fantasies undoubtedly result from "random firings" of neurons in the brain. They often assert the same of slips of the tongue, slips of the pen, slips of the keyboard—in short, all of what Freud called "bungled actions" or "parapraxes."[40] Far better, they seem to feel, to believe "random" things go on in their minds than to accept that such thoughts and fantasies might have something to do with them and in fact be telling! Many people who decide to go see a therapist begin from this same position of denial and only give up its two sub-positions (existence and connection) with great difficulty and in the face of over-whelming evidence to the contrary.

Another "altered state of consciousness" (that is not drug induced) many of us may be familiar with arises at the moment of an accident of some kind, whether we inadvertently give ourselves a bloody gash, get into a bicycle or car crash, or are unfortunate enough to be involved in a plane or train crash. In such situations, we often experience time as slowing down, events unfolding in an uncanny sort of slow motion, and we do not appear to really register what is going on. We seem to be dazed, and it often requires considerable effort for us to remember after the fact exactly what transpired and in what order. What we were feeling at the time often seems altogether unknowable, as though we were in it up to our ears, so to speak, being too close to it to be able to put a label of any kind on it.[41]

What makes public insults traumatic for some (as we saw earlier in this chapter) and car crashes traumatic for others (even when those involved are not or are only very slightly injured physically) is the fact that they isolate the memory of the experience, either because they actively put the memory out of mind or because they are, in a manner of speaking, "out of their minds" when the experience occurs.

Deferred Action

Putting memories out of mind leads to symptom formation, and Freud attempted to figure out how and why people put memories out of mind. Anna O's nervous cough was traced back to the conflict she felt between filial duty and personal pleasure, provoked by the music coming from a neighboring house while she was sitting by her father's sickbed, leading her to suppress any expression of a wish to go dancing. Here a single "precipitating cause" of her symptom was located, and this constituted a classic form of scientific explanation.

This is not, however, the model of causal explanation that Freud is perhaps best known for, it not being the best model for explaining the genesis or origin of a great many symptoms. In his (1895) unpublished "Project for a Scientific Psychology," Freud discusses an 8-year-old girl, whom he refers to pseudonymously as Emma, who went into a shop to buy some candy and whose genitals were grabbed at through her cloth-ing by the shopkeeper there (SE I, pp. 353–354). No symptom of any kind formed after this event (which she repeated, going back into the shop a second time, only to have the grabbing behavior repeated), but around the age of 12, shortly after reaching puberty, Emma went into a different kind of shop to buy something and saw two shop assistants (one of whom she was attracted to) laughing together about her clothing, it seemed; she rushed out in some kind of a fright and thereafter suffered from a compulsion not to go into shops alone.

The shop assistants' laughter reminded Emma unconsciously of the grin with which the shopkeeper in the first incident had accompanied his grabbing, establishing a link between the two events, and <u>allowing her to reread the first event in light of her *recently acquired knowledge of sexuality*.</u> (Freud also hypothesizes that her attraction to one of the shop assistants at age 12 may have been accompanied by a sexual "release," i.e., some libido or lust, which then turned into anxiety.) In other words, similar features of the earlier and later incidents (shops, laughter, and clothing) allowed for a retroactive comprehension of the earlier events as having been imbued with sexual meaning, something she had presumably been unaware of at 8 years of age. In the interim, she had acquired knowledge of sex and had undergone the hormonal changes associated with puberty. It was thus only in conjunction with the later event that the earlier events gave rise to a symptom.

The later event (call it E2) thus turned the earlier events (call them E1) into something they were not at the outset. In Figure 1.4, we have a simple timeline:

Ogden
The present of
the moment of
the past

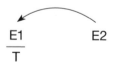

FIGURE 1.4.

In Figure 1.5, the later event gives the earlier event new meaning: a sexual meaning, which, in this late 19th-century Victorian context, was a traumatic meaning (T).

E1   E2
—
T

FIGURE 1.5.

E1 did not serve as the precipitating cause of Emma's symptom (i.e., being unable to go into shops alone) all by itself, but only when taken in conjunction with E2. Freud was led to this notion because it was not always possible to isolate one single precipitating event, but sometimes two or more connected events could be isolated.

He referred to this as *Nachträglichkeit,* which we might translate as "deferred action," "retroaction," or "ex post facto action." In such cases E1 apparently has no effect until much later—that is, until E2 has occurred. Had E2 never occurred, no symptom might ever have formed. But we might also think of <u>E1 as a problem waiting to happen,</u> insofar as Emma was going to hit puberty within a few years, and some situation that reminded her of E1 was bound to occur sooner or later.

Lacan (*Écrits*, pp. 681–684) generalizes this model, by replacing events 1 and 2 by signifiers 1 and 2, <u>since events are often remembered by us largely in words or signifiers, and traumatic meaning T with *s* for the signified.</u>[42]

$$\frac{S1}{s} \qquad S2$$

<u>It may be that this kind of retroactive causation is found only in fields where language and meaning predominate,</u> as in psychoanalysis, corresponding, as it does, to the way in which meaning is created through human speech and writing.[43]

Freud and Breuer also talk about the summation of traumatic events (SE II, p. 6), whereby many events function together by summation or addition to create an effect; this latter form of causation can be found in other fields. For example: Smog is a product of several elements in the atmosphere that are added together. However, in Emma's case, something other than mere summation was at work: <u>The causality was ex post facto, because the second event could occur four years after the first, as long as there was a mental link (e.g., shops, laughter, and/or clothing)</u> between the two events. Once the two events and the links between them were brought to light, Emma's symptom presumably disappeared.

What Can Be Alleviated Today by Tracing Things Back

The connections [or links] are unconscious.
—Freud, SE XVI, p. 278

Can we still alleviate symptoms by tracing them back to their origins, even today? In certain cases, yes—especially when they are what I would call microsymptoms, like moments of guilt or anxiety, or somatic complaints that have only recently appeared in someone's life. And sometimes even when analysands have been suffering from them for a long time.

I was able to help eliminate an adult analysand's longstanding sensation of being physically cold—which was resistant to exposure to the Southern California sun, taking hot baths, and continually imbibing steaming hot food and liquids—by tracing it back to the day she, as a child, having overheard something that sounded like fighting going on in her parents' bedroom, peeked in through their door, while standing on the freezing cold tile floor in the hallway, and saw her "father on top of [her] mother, his penis erect." Not all of the details came out at once and, as I was practicing the talking cure and not hypnosis, the memory of the scene did not come out by my asking directly about the origins of her sensation of being cold but rather in a more roundabout manner. Nevertheless, this and other psychosomatic symptoms, complained of by a modern-day hysteric, were resolved by tracing them back to their source;[44] this does not always mean back to the first time the symptom itself occurs, for this girl's coldness upon peeking into her parents' bedroom was not psychosomatic—rather, it was the real effect of the coldness of the tile floor (see Fink, 1997, Chapter 8). The psychosomatic coldness began some three decades later.[45]

In another case, anxiety that had lasted for about a week was overcome when my analysand traced it back to its not-nearly-so-distant origin. He had been asked by his much-hated boss to help convince younger physicians on his unit that they should be happier with their work schedules; having been excluded from a leadership role on his unit for some years, he was happy to finally be asked to do something and yet unhappy to be asked to convince people of something he did not himself believe. His anxiety got worse and worse the longer he delayed talking with the younger physicians; although he did not want to do it, he was worried that the moment in which he could play a leadership role would slip away and that he would never be asked again if he did not cooperate now. Recognizing that he did not want to engage in this form of leadership—and that he had felt this very strongly from the very moment at which it was proposed by his boss, but had put it out of his mind (he had, in other words, isolated it)—he decided that he would not do what his boss had asked, and the anxiety tied to this particular conundrum subsided.

I would argue that even if many symptoms are not definitively dissipated by discussing their origins, *few if any symptoms are ever eliminated without a thoroughgoing discussion of their origins.* Now, a major obstacle to getting at the origin of a symptom is that therapists often content themselves with the first sketchy version of a story that the patient tells them, forgetting that stories are virtually always much more complicated and detailed than they are upon first telling. Freud often indicates that he had to "insist a second time" to get a patient to complete a story

(SE II, p. 98); that he started "from the assumption that [his hypnotized] patients knew everything that was of any pathogenic significance and that it was only a question of obliging them to communicate it" (p. 110), something few clinicians do today, forgetting that patients need to be greatly *encouraged* (more than they need to be "obliged," as Freud puts it) to overcome their own resistance to delving into what they feel to be delicate or morally reprehensible topics; and, more importantly still, that he "accustomed [him]self to *regarding as incomplete any story that brought about no improvement*" in the patient's condition (p. 79, my emphasis)—a fabulous rule of thumb, in my view!

In my experience as a supervisor of other clinicians' work, I find that it is the therapists who complain that they cannot get anywhere with their patients' dreams, daydreams, or fantasies who assume that there is no more to such mental productions than their patients' initial accounts of them, whereas many facets of them are deliberately held back and others perhaps less deliberately censored during the telling, patients often commenting that some detail seemed "too irrelevant," "too banal," or "too obviously Freudian" to be worth relating. Other details or associations to such mental productions are often left out of patients' accounts because they are loath to admit to them, responding, once we have managed to guess what they had omitted, "It's true, I thought of that, but I hoped that wouldn't be it" (i.e., wouldn't be the most germane association or memory).

One of my analysands told me a dream in which he had to slog through mud up to his knees on the way to see me. I asked, "What about mud?" a question that was met with silence on his part. "Nothing came to mind?" I asked. "No," he replied. "It was brown?" I inquired to try to incite him to say *something* about it—indeed, anything. At that point he burst out laughing and admitted that "shit" had come to mind along with the thought that he felt like he had to slog through knee-high shit to get to his session with me. This had struck him as impertinent and he had been loath to relate it until I prodded him.

If we do not encourage our analysands to tell us important stories from the past and current (or even former) dreams and fantasies in what I sometimes refer to as "four-part harmony," meaning in the fullest detail possible and including all of their voices (in other words, all of their conflicting thoughts and emotions at the time), there is no way we will get to the bottom of them. This requires that we feel quite sure that our technique is valuable (as Freud put it, the laborious work of reconstruction of events in a patient's past "required that I have complete confidence in my technique"; p. 114 n), and my sense is that one only acquires such confidence from having experienced the value of fully exploring past events and dreams in one's own analysis. Today we are grappling with a vicious cycle in which fewer and fewer trainees are encouraged to explore such memories in four-part harmony in their training analyses, and hence they develop little confidence in the value of doing so in their later work with their own analysands.[46]

Even when we do manage to isolate the origin of a longstanding symptom an analysand has been plagued by, it rarely disappears altogether. Why not? Because over the course of time it has acquired multiple meanings and supports from myriad other events in the analysand's life. The initial event's connections with later and still earlier events must still be traced out and explored exhaustively. This cannot always or perhaps even often be done deliberately, for an analysand usually remembers certain of the events connected with the symptom only at distant intervals—in connection, for example, with a dream in one instance, and in connection with a name that floats into consciousness in another instance. In such cases, it is only once all the relevant connections have been explored that a symptom gives way.

Freud (SE II) discusses the case of Miss Lucy R. in which, although certain improvements occurred as the patient told him of her symptoms and the occasions upon which they arose,

> the key to the whole situation lay only in the last symptom to be reached by the analysis.
>
> The therapeutic process in this case consisted in compelling the psychical group that had been split off [M1—M2—M3] to unite once more with ego-consciousness [M4—M5—M6]. Strangely enough, success did not run *pari passu* [keep pace] with the amount of work done. It was only when the last piece of work had been completed that recovery suddenly took place. (p. 124)

We might say that, even though M2 and M3 had been fully explored, it was not until M1 was found that the symptoms (depression, fatigue, and having the impression that she smelled burnt pudding and cigar smoke) all at once evaporated. I, like many other analysts, have had cases in which little improvement seems to have occurred despite years of intensive work, and then suddenly a great deal changed in a very short space of time. Such is often the nature of therapeutic work, whether one is employing hypnosis—as Freud did with Lucy R.—or not.

In theory, as soon as a memory that had been isolated is drawn into relation with memories that are accessible to the subject, that memory stops producing symptoms; in practice, the many links that memory has established with other isolated memories must also be elucidated for symptom formation to cease.

This is not to say that every isolated memory can become un-isolated, as it were, or completely withdrawn from the unconscious; for one would then have to hypothesize that the very barrier between conscious and unconscious could disappear in someone in whom it had formerly existed. But long experience on the part of analysts, many of us having spent numerous years in analysis ourselves, makes it clear that the unconscious itself is never completely evacuated of all isolated memories, never completely absorbed back into our accessible memory: There are always motives of which we are unaware that can lead even the most well-analyzed and experienced analysts to do things in our everyday lives—and even in our consulting rooms—for reasons that are opaque to us. In other words, the barrier between the two realms continues to exist even after a great deal of exploration.

What is promising, however, is that it generally becomes easier for those of us who have been through a long course of analysis to gain access to recent memories that have become isolated than it was before the analysis, and that work with supervisors or other colleagues often suffices to make us see what we had not been seeing without having to head back to the couch for another long stint of personal analysis. Those of us who have done extensive analytic work can often wake up from a dream and locate in fairly short order what the dream may have been about. But this does not mean we should underestimate the degree to which even we, no matter how experienced we are as analysts, can fool ourselves into thinking we know all about what goes on in our own minds!

CHAPTER 2

The Unconscious Is the Exact Opposite of the Conscious

How the Unconscious Manifests Itself in Speech and Symptoms

> *Opposite thoughts are always closely connected with each other and are often paired in such a way that the one thought is excessively, intensely conscious while its opposite is repressed and unconscious.*
>
> —Freud, SE VII, p. 55

A CCESS TO THE REPRESSED is rarely gained in one fell swoop. Intermediate steps along the way are usually required, as if the barrier between M1 and M2—M3—M4 had to be softened up or rendered permeable little by little. Although this perhaps makes the work harder and slower for the practitioner, it makes the result more palatable for the analysand; for to be confronted with the contents of the unconscious all at once is likely to either frighten the analysand or give rise to perplexity, if not outright rejection.

In the absence of hypnosis, how do we gradually pave the way to the repressed? In a multitude of manners, including in-depth discussion of dreams, daydreams, fantasies, slips, bungled actions, and so on. We will touch on all of these in the course of this study of Freud's work, but we will begin with what are perhaps even simpler ways of approaching the repressed, the first being through negation. Even though Freud only wrote up his five-page paper entitled "Negation" in 1924, long after the majority of his work on dreams and bungled actions, it outlines one of the most elementary techniques he ever developed. This is not to say that his discussion in that paper is elementary—indeed, it is so complex that numerous interpretations of it have been proposed (by Lacan and by the philosopher Jean Hyppolite, for example). But we will not go into the theoretical complexities it introduces here, confining our attention to its practical uses.

Removing the "Not" from Negative Assertions

Negation

The content of a repressed image or idea can make its way into consciousness, on condition that it be negated. Negation is a way of taking cognizance of what is repressed.

—Freud, SE XIX, p. 235

Imagine that we ask an analysand who is relatively new to psychoanalytic treatment to tell us about her mother and she responds, "Well, I can't say she was a terrible mom."

We might reply, "You can't? Yet 'terrible' seems to be the first word that popped into your mind about her."

The analysand is then likely to retort something along the following lines: "Yes, but she had her good sides, too, so I can't really say that."

"Yet you perhaps feel in some ways that 'she was a terrible mom'?" we might continue—assuming her tone of voice does not suggest total rejection of the idea—by quoting the exact second half of her first response about her mother (i.e., "Well, I can't say *'She was a terrible mom'*").

In this way—and the exact exchanges could, of course, be quite different than the specific ones I have provided here—we underscore the adjective ("terrible") that came to her mind in response to our request that she tell us about her mother, without lending much credence to how she qualified it. In other words, we don't take at face value the fact that she may have put a yes or a no, a plus or a minus, or a quantifier before it—that is, whether she said her mother was not terrible, always terrible, never terrible, occasionally terrible, terribly terrible, quite terrible, or only somewhat terrible. For Freud's important contribution in this context is to say that when we encourage analysands to free-associate—that is, to say the first thing that pops into their minds in response to a question we ask—things often occur to them that upon consideration, even just split-second consideration, they will probably want to negate. What popped into their minds is, we hypothesize, connected to the unconscious (by a longer or shorter series of links) and can only be brought forward by them in speech insofar as it is denied: "I *can't say* 'She was a terrible mom.'" As long as it is denied, it *can* be mentioned by them, for they do not see anything fishy in such denials; in other words, they do not believe that they are revealing anything in particular by making a negative claim like this.

Indeed, in the ordinary course of affairs, few people other than psychoanalysts seem to see anything suspect in such negative claims. At least, not until the stakes are high. When, for example, a high-ranking politician says, "I can't say that the war in the Middle East is going badly" or "I wouldn't say the economy is doing poorly," some in the audience usually begin to wonder why, if things are going so swimmingly, the politician didn't say something positive like, "I'm happy to announce that the economy is doing quite well," instead of something so negative. When a CEO says, "Our performance last quarter was not disastrous," certain investors probably begin to wonder why the head of a corporation would ever mention a word like "disastrous" if the company were doing well. Similarly, if you ask your spouse how work went today and she responds, "I never left my desk all day," you may well wonder why she said that, provided you had never implied that you suspected she was doing anything other than working at her desk all day long. Indeed, you may begin to wonder why, of all the things she could have told you about her day, she felt the need to tell you *that* when you were not accusing her of, say, goofing off on the job or having an affair with someone behind your back! When the stakes are high, people seem to instinctively become as suspicious as psychoanalysts.

Freud's genius was to wonder why, of all the things our analysand could possibly have said about her mother, she picked this particular adjective: "terrible." A mother can be warm, cold, loving, spiteful, funny, or morose; she can be evenhanded or unfair, play favorites or ignore her children; and she probably has myriad different characteristics at different times. So why single out this one particular word? Why this specific selection? *Freud's approach was to consider everything the analysand says to be of the utmost importance,* which is very different from the way the analysand herself usually regards what she says; for, when questioned about a particular term she used to describe someone, she is likely to immediately change the term, temper it, or even retract it. *Freud teaches us not to lend credence to retractions* (we should apply this to Chaucer's famous retraction, too!).[1] When the analysand says something, it has to be allowed to stand, even when the analysand rushes to qualify it or tone it down.

Negating is an attempt to go still further—it is an attempt to take something back even as it comes out of one's own mouth.[2] Freud's way of formulating what happens here is that <u>a particular thought about the mother can only roll off the analysand's tongue under erasure, as it</u> were—that is, with a big X written over it, crossing it out: ~~terrible~~. The thought that her mother was terrible can only come to mind insofar as it is disguised from the analysand's consciousness, only insofar as it is unrecognizable to her as revealing her true sentiments. (As we shall see momentarily, thoughts can be disguised in other ways as well, not just by negation.) She believes that with her negative assertion—"I can't say she was a terrible mom"—she is not saying something telling about her own feelings but, rather, that she is making a true claim—in other words, that she is stating the truth as she understands truth.

Attempting to get at the truth as she conceptualizes it, the analysand is often led to say something like, "I know that *I* think my mother was terrible, but she always claimed she was a great mother, and my sister and brother think she was great, too." Here the patient discounts her own feeling about her mother because she is not sure it is "objectively true"; perhaps, she thinks, it is "merely subjective," that it is her own misconception or misrepresentation of her mother. Freud talks about this concern in terms of one of the functions of what he calls "judgment"[3]: <u>We seek to determine whether an</u> idea <u>(Freud calls it a</u> *Vorstellung,* <u>which Strachey translates as "presentation" or "representation") that we find in our own minds corresponds to something "real," something outside of ourselves</u> (SE XIX, pp. 236–237).

The analysand here seems to believe that the question whether her mother was terrible or not is as simple as the question of whether or not unicorns exist: We have an idea and a picture of unicorns in our minds, but experience and research show that no one has ever seen a real, living, breathing unicorn (even if this does not yet constitute absolute proof that no one will ever encounter one). Hence it seems pretty transparently obvious that there are no unicorns, and that unicorns are "just in our heads."[4]

But determining whether something is real in the psychological realm poses a far thornier problem: If two of my siblings think my mother was a good parent, does that make it truer or realer than my own feeling about her? Couldn't they be mistaken? Maybe they just bought our mother's story about herself, when she claimed to be a fine mother? Or perhaps she was actually better to them than she was to me, having preferred them to me? (Or was it that there was something about me that made her mean to me—for example, something about the way I looked or acted that annoyed her?) Analysands are often concerned, above all at the outset of our work with them, with giving what they believe to be an "accurate portrayal" of their parents, siblings, spouses, and friends, one that is not influenced—or at least not "overly influenced"—by their own subjective experience of those people.

Yet our concern as analysts is not to weigh how many people think the patient's mother was a good parent and how many a bad parent and come up with some supposedly objective rating; our concern is to explore in every way possible the analysand's experience of her mother! To do so, we often have to work hard to stop the analysand from seeking some objective yardstick by which to measure reality and encourage her to focus instead on her own "psychical reality," as Freud calls it.[5] (This is where psychoanalysis and cognitive-behavioral therapy part ways, cognitive-behavioral therapists professing to be able to know reality directly and objectively and to be able to teach their patients to do the same.) So should our analysand lapse into silence, and we ask what was going through her mind, and she answers, "I was thinking about what we said about my mother, and on further reflection, I think she wasn't so bad after all"—another negation—we may want to insist that each of the things she thinks about her mother is important in its own right and that even though it isn't necessarily the only thing she thinks about her mother, it should not be dismissed out of hand.

Thoughts that are articulated in such a negative fashion ("I don't think *x*" or "I think she isn't *x*") don't necessarily lead us directly to the unconscious, but they are often incredibly useful in steering us in the right direction. And the more the analysand becomes attuned to hearing her own denials and negations and wondering what they hide, the more permeable the barrier between unconscious and conscious is likely to become.[6]

Disguising Unconscious Thoughts

I don't want to say it felt good . . .

—An analysand

Presenting a thought that occurs to you under erasure—that is, while negating it—is only one of many ways of disguising a thought. Let us now turn to a second way of doing so.

Imagine that an analysand you have been working with for some time has a dream with a woman in it and you ask him to tell you about this woman, who had, in the telling of the dream, remained unidentified. He responds (immediately or after a pause), "I'm sure you're thinking it's my cousin."[7] If everything in the analysis up until that time has revolved around the cousin, then his response is not especially telling; but if the cousin has been just one of several important actors in his life and but one of a plethora of people discussed in the analysis, the fact that his cousin came to mind is what should be underscored.

The fact that he situates the thought as *your* thought—that is, as having arisen in your mind, not his—is like the yes or no, plus or minus, or quantifier we saw earlier, which adds little if anything useful to the thought itself. What it tells us is either that his cousin could only come to mind (that is, to consciousness) inasmuch as he attributed the thought to you; or that his cousin came to mind and, because it was immediately disturbing, he attributed its coming to his mind to what he perhaps believes to be your suspicious or dirty-minded nature! In the former case, Freud's hypothesis would be that the thought of his cousin would ordinarily have been "censored"—that is, blocked from coming to mind by the barrier between the unconscious and the conscious—but that since it was attributed to you, it could come to mind. In the latter case, censorship comes into play after the fact (that is, after his cousin came to mind), leading what was perhaps more likely to have been a preconscious than an unconscious thought to be projected onto you.[8]

In both cases, thoughts that are deemed objectionable by the analysand—by his ego or superego, to use Freud's more technical terms—are able to come to mind (in the former case) and be spoken (in the latter case) on condition that they be repudiated: "Such a thing would have never occurred to me," the analysand seems to claim, "but it's just the sort of thing *you* would think of." (Freud indicates that his patients would sometimes say things like, "Something has occurred to me now, but you obviously put it into my head," or "I know what you expect me to answer. Of course you believe I've thought this or that"; SE II, p. 280).

Projection is an incredibly important way of disguising unconscious thoughts, and we see it in a multitude of accusations that people make toward those around them. The husband who most belligerently accuses his wife of cheating on him is (as we saw in Chapter 1) usually the one who has most persistently cheated on his wife, or at least fantasized about doing so; by reproaching her he hopes to stave off or allay his own self-reproaches. By thinking of and treating his wife like a "slut," he diverts attention away from his own slutty behavior, and tries to convince himself that he is morally superior to her—even though in his heart of hearts he probably believes he is vastly inferior to her. The employee who most strenuously accuses his employer of being unbearably authoritarian is often far more authoritarian himself, but refuses to own it.

As in the case of denials, *in the case of projections we analysts concern ourselves far less with the person to whom the thought is attributed than to the content of the thought itself.* The analysand's cousin came to mind (to someone's mind, in any case), so we encourage him to talk about that. Cheating came to mind, regardless of who the analysand says is doing the cheating, so we prompt him to discuss cheating.

Fishy Assertions

I can't believe I just said that!

—An analysand

People are often quite unaware of the degree to which they signal their own intentions without thinking they are doing so. When someone says to you, "I don't mean to be rude, but . . . ," you can be pretty sure that he or she is about to be rude to you. When someone says, "I don't mean to be critical, but . . . ," you can be pretty sure he or she is about to launch into more or less harsh criticism of you.[9]

The proverbial man in the street seems to believe that providing a disclaimer as to his intentions suffices to eliminate any appearance of rudeness or criticism from what he is about to say, whereas it simply announces that he himself is aware that what he wants to express is likely to be perceived as rude or critical. He would like to somehow attenuate or obviate that perception—cut it off at the pass, as it were—with his denial, and yet he himself brings it to the fore, alerting us to the fact that something important is about to be said even before he gets started. He does not realize that the more effort he puts into downplaying something, the more he brings it to our attention and makes our ears prick up.

It should be noted that such disclaimers are not always formulated in a strictly negative fashion. One of my analysands would occasionally tell me that she had had "an innocuous dream"[10] or "a silly little dream," her conscious intent being to downplay the dream's importance. But such attempts to minimize the significance of a dream are rarely, if ever, gratuitous: They usually signal the fact that the analysand has sensed that there is something troubling or disconcerting in the dream and wishes to divert our attention away from it or insinuate that we should not give it much thought. Even more common examples of this occur when analysands fall silent for a bit, and when we ask what was going through their minds, they respond, "Nothing"; if we persist in asking, perhaps by repeating the word *nothing* with a questioning intonation, they often reply, "No, nothing, just something stupid" or "just some random thought." (Freud indicates that his patients would often say, "Something has occurred to me now, but it has nothing to do with the subject"; SE II, p. 279). If we encourage them to articulate that "stupid" or "random" thought, as we should, we often find that it is in fact one of the most important things that they say in the course of the entire session! This is what led Lacan to say that it is with such "stupidities" that we do analysis" (Seminar XX, pp. 11–13). The first thing that pops into their minds—that is, a free association—often seems irrelevant, out of the blue, or incoherent, and although many analysands' first inclination is to discount it altogether as though it had never occurred to them at all, it is precisely what must be spoken in order for the analysis to go forward.[11]

Another of my analysands often began sessions, at one point in the treatment, with the statement, "I'm sorry I'm late." The uttering of such a statement in everyday life serves, when one's lateness is exceptional rather than the rule, to *excuse* one's lateness; it is speech that is designed to do something (it is, in other words, a "speech act"),[12] which in this case is to *apologize* for an unusual tardiness and *express an intention* to go back to being more on time in the future. The very repetition of this statement by my analysand, however, suggested an apology with absolutely no intended follow-through, for he was just as late for his subsequent sessions.

After a number of such latenesses accompanied by the same formulaic apology, "I'm sorry I'm late," I asked, "Are you?" The analysand was rather taken aback at this unusual response to such an ordinary speech act, so I continued, "Are you sure you are sorry about being late? If you were sorry about it, wouldn't you try to ensure you're not late so often?" This led to a long, fruitful discussion of what the analysand seemed to get out of believing that he was making me think about him in his absence, and out of keeping me waiting while he snuck in a sort of secret pleasure reading something or looking at something that he knew was likely to make him late for his session.[13]

Disclaimers that seem designed to dissimulate one's actual intentions may thus be formulated either positively ("I'm sorry . . .") or negatively ("I don't mean to be cruel . . ."), but the attentive interlocutor, instructed by psychoanalysis, will not take them at face value. For, indeed, each analysand has his or her own particular ways of couching things so as to downplay them, divert attention away from them, or hide them, and the analyst must become familiar with each person's rhetorical style in order to flush out and elucidate what it is designed to dissimulate.

Certain analysands have a habit of repeating claims that they make again and again—for example, one analysand repeated the assertion "Everything in my family was great" three times in a row in one of his first sessions with me—such that we begin to wonder who they are trying to convince: themselves or us? If they are so convinced of what they are stating, why would they feel the need to repeat it so often? To convince themselves by convincing us? Insistent repetition of positive assertions begins to smack of negation, and seems to be the habitual way in which certain analysands proffer denials (i.e., they do not really believe everything was so great, but wish it had been).

Every Fear (or Worry or Concern) Covers Over a Wish

Certain analysands regularly indicate that they are worried about someone when in fact they wish them harm. I would be hard-pressed to tally up the number of times I have heard analysands say they were "worried" or "afraid" their father (or someone else close to them) would have a heart attack when their father had no heart condition whatsoever, nor was there any history of heart disease in his family! In such cases—*not* in cases in which it is clear that their father is in poor health and under great stress—analysands' wishes that something bad would happen to their father or that he would simply disappear are disguised more or less automatically into worry, concern, anxiety, or fear. It is not the case that these analysands are conscious that they wish their fathers dead but, feeling it is unacceptable to express such wishes in public, deliberately opt to express them differently; rather, they are conscious only of the worry, stress, concern, or fear—in other words, they are just as duped by their own affective experience as it seems they would like everyone around them to be.

To put this as plainly as I can, such analysands have an unconscious wish for their fathers to die (or at least to be greatly harmed), and thus they either do not think about their fathers at all consciously, or if they do, they do it only in a distorted or disguised form (SE IV, pp. 259–261, 266–267). It is obviously not the father himself as a person or the word "father" that has been repressed, but a specific wish or thought they have regarding him. In Figure 2.1 (and elsewhere), I represent the fact that a wish is repressed by placing it under a bar or barrier, and represent the fact that something quite different comes to consciousness by placing what is conscious over the bar or barrier:

I worry my father might die

I wish my father dead

FIGURE 2.1.

This could be represented, alternatively, in the way in which we represented repression (as isolation) in Chapter 1:

I wish my father dead | I worry my father might die

We see here that a certain thought and affect related to my father can only come to mind (i.e., to awareness or consciousness) because both the thought and the affect have undergone a transformation: "Wish" has been replaced by "worry," and the anger that I feel toward him that makes me wish him dead has been transformed into anxiety or concern. The intensity of my affect remains the same—in other words, the quantity of feeling is the same on both sides of the barrier—but fear and anxiety seem to me to be far less objectionable feelings to have about my father than angry death wishes.

Such transformations of wishes into worries, concerns, anxiety, or fear are extremely common, so common indeed that *it is a useful rule of thumb in psychoanalysis to consider virtually every fear, worry, concern, or anxiety an analysand expresses as at least potentially covering over a wish*.[14] We will turn to Freud's discussions of this further on when we take up symptom formation, for Freud formulates a crucial hypothesis, which is that *every feeling that is deemed inappropriate or unconscionable by a person's moral scruples can be transformed into anxiety*. Indeed, anxiety is the universal currency of emotion (SE XVI, pp. 403–404), all emotions being able to be converted into anxiety when suppressed by one's self-critical faculties (the ego or superego). Anxiety must thus not be taken at face value, but as always potentially indicative of some other emotion that is being self-censored (see SE IV, pp. 266–267, and SE X, p. 162).

Freud goes so far, in the case of the Rat Man, as to formulate an almost universal rule that things are quite the opposite of what they seem: "The unconscious is the precise contrary [i.e., the exact opposite] of the conscious" (SE X, p. 180). This rule flies in the face of our habitual ways of seeing the world, and many practitioners initially have a hard time wrapping their heads around it (those familiar with the political uses of ideology may have a less difficult time with this, being aware that the official reasons given for governmental actions are very often the exact opposite of the unofficial, true reasons). We are so used to taking at face value what people tell us about their motives and intentions that the "logic of suspicion" (as I call it; see Fink, 2007, pp. 14–17) built into psychoanalysis—which requires us to consider the possibility that virtually everything people tell us is only a partial truth if not an outright lie—seems hard to digest.

"The unconscious is the exact opposite of the conscious" implies that virtually everything we believe about ourselves upon entering our own personal analysis must eventually be turned on its head. It also implies that, as analysts, we must not be duped by what our analysands initially tell us about themselves and their lives, but must always entertain the possibility that the truth (insofar as it can be said to be singular, which is in fact rarely the case) is often closer to the opposite of what they initially maintain. Those who prefer to believe that most people know themselves pretty well will find this exceedingly hard to swallow, but those who have been through a thoroughgoing analysis themselves are likely to realize that an important turning point is reached in one's own personal analysis when one comes to the realization, as one of my witty analysands once put it, that one is "full of shit."

Less crudely stated, we could say that both the analysand and the analyst would do well to take nothing for granted, and to seriously consider the possibility that virtually everything the analysand says at the outset of their work together might well be a cover for something else.

Dissimulated Aggression

Not every repressed wish will necessarily manifest itself in the form of fear, worry, concern, or anxiety. Some repressed wishes are considered by something within us to be so reprehensible that the topic or person they concern is better left unmentioned altogether, for fear that something of our true feelings or wishes might burst forth; these often end up giving rise to symptoms (whether tics, phobias, vomiting, fear of flying, repeated checking that doors are locked or gas turned off, or what have you). Still, many repressed wishes can be found out owing to such typical disguises (fear, worry, concern, or anxiety), once one has come to grasp that they are disguises.

Another very common way in which analysands dissimulate their intense anger at someone is by expressing a need to *protect* that person. If we take such expressions at face value, we often fail to discover that, in fact, the person they wish to protect is quite capable of taking care of him- or herself and is in no danger of any obvious kind. What, then, is to be made of their concern with protecting that person? What we usually discover is that they themselves wish that person harm and feel they pose a threat to that person; they thus feel a need to protect that person from themselves! They themselves are so busy wishing that person harm that they become anxious to protect him or her from themselves. Many is the analysand who refers to his or her mother as "my poor mother" or "that poor woman," or to his or her lover as "that poor guy" or "that poor girl," when the only reason to pity them would be that they are so hated and/or persecuted (at least in thought) by the analysand him- or herself!

The Heuristic Value of Hypotheticals

In his paper on "Negation" (SE XIX), Freud provides us with a method for getting analysands to unwittingly reveal certain of their unconscious thoughts and hidden intentions without our having to work hard to turn everything they tell us on its head and make what may seem to them to be improbable interpretations. Rather than attempting to directly soften or puncture the barrier between unconscious and conscious, this method executes an end run around the barrier (an end run as in American football, where one goes around the far edge of the opponent's defensive line rather than trying to find or force a way through it):

> There is a very convenient method by which we can sometimes obtain a piece of information we want about unconscious repressed material. "What," we ask, "would you consider the most unlikely imaginable thing in that situation? What do you think was furthest from your mind at that time?" If the patient falls into the trap and says what he thinks is most incredible, he almost always makes the right admission. (p. 235)

Freud leaves the "situation" abstract here, so let me provide an example. Imagine that an analysand tells you about a dream in which she is reading a letter. Upon awakening she could no longer recall who the letter was from or what it was about, even though these things seemed to be very clear while she was dreaming. Asking her if anything comes to mind about letters, whether she has received any recently or can think of any significant letters she has received in the past, leads to no associations. Freud's method or trick, as we might call it here, involves asking one of the following kinds of questions:

- "Since you cannot recall who it was from, who do you think it most certainly could not have been from?"
- "As you cannot remember what the letter was about, what do you think it could not possibly have been about?"
- "Who would be the last person to write to you?" or
- "What would be the last thing you would expect to hear about in a letter?"

Freud's notion here is that when we ask the patient what is the fur-thest thing from her mind or the most far-fetched, we free her up to tell us what is in fact the closest thing to her mind and the most probable. When we ask her what would be the last thing on her mind, by couch-ing it in this way, we make it easy for her to tell us the first thing on her mind. Whereas, in response to our initial question as to what occurs to her about letters, she may have consciously been running through the list of possible girlfriends or boyfriends who might have written to her, this hypothetical question may suddenly lead her to think of receiving a letter regarding the death of a parent or grandparent, regarding an inheritance, or regarding a fatal illness in her extended family. None of these had perhaps occurred to her upon waking or even as she attempted to associate to the dream at our prompting during the session; but the permission given to her to think of the most unlikely of letter writers and the most unlikely of topics may well free her up to take us in the most fruitful direction.

Why would such a gimmick work? Because it encourages her to say something without any "skin in the game"—that is, without anything apparently being at stake. Such techniques are designed to do an end run around the censorship, for how could what she says be considered morally reprehensible by her when she is simply saying what is furthest from her mind?

The fact that the furthest thing from my mind is actually the clos-est, and the last thing on my mind is actually the first, accords with the abovementioned claim by Freud that "the unconscious is the exact opposite of the conscious" (SE X, p. 180). And as Freud puts it later, the unconscious is like a "foreign language" (SE XIX, p. 112) that con-sciousness (or the ego) cannot understand, insofar as its contents, to the degree to which they manifest themselves in awareness, are distorted, disguised, and inverted: My (conscious) fears represent (unconscious) wishes, what I believe is the most implausible is the most plausible, the person I believe I am most anxious to protect is the one I most seek to harm, and so on. Through their personal analyses, analysts slowly learn how to read this "foreign language," how to "translate" the conscious dissimulation back into the unconscious thought or wish from which it stemmed, engaging in a kind of "untranslating" activity in order to undo the distorting "translation" that had been brought on by censorship.[15] And analysts in some sense teach each new analysand they work with to do so as well.

Excursion on Technique

When we analysts propose a hypothetical of the kind mentioned in the previous section, which aims to release the analysand from any responsibility for the thought that is "the furthest from her mind," we obviously must not then suddenly hold her responsible for the "stray thought" or "absurd idea" that occurred to her. We must not seize upon the idea for which we had implied she would not be held accountable, cry "Aha!" and immediately try to make her see the truth value of the far-fetched thought.

Instead, and this is especially true with those who have not already been in analysis with us for some time, we must broach the "absurd idea" discreetly, asking questions like:

- "What about that grandparent?" (the one whose death might have been announced in the letter in her dream), or "Tell me about that grandparent."
- "What about an inheritance?" (news of which might have been announced in the letter in her dream). "Is there any inheritance that you have heard about, might be expecting, or could be hoping for?"
- "What about pancreatic cancer?" (the fatal illness that might have been announced in the letter in her dream). "Is there something you have heard about it or someone you know who has had it?" (One of my analysands mentioned Apple Computer's Steve Jobs in this connection, which led to a long discussion of the illnesses of prominent people and how he, too, would like to be a prominent person.)

With questions of this kind, we do not automatically insinuate that the far-fetched thought that came to mind has an immediate connection with the analysand, but use it as a springboard to learn more about the analysand, her situation, her family, her experience with illnesses, and so on. By following these different threads, we may together find a connection between the furthest thing from her mind and her own life by a somewhat long series of associations and related links. When we are able to do so again and again with the analysand, she is likely to begin to realize herself that the strangest and seemingly least probable thoughts that occur to her actually do have a connection to her, and this generally serves to loosen up the barrier between the unconscious and conscious and facilitate our task as analysts in the course of the work we do together.

The Disconnection Between Thought and Affect

In the many different forms of obsessional neurosis, forgetting is mostly restricted to dissolving thought-connections, failing to draw the right conclusions, and isolating memories.

—Freud, SE XII, p. 149

I wasn't going to give my parents the satisfaction of watching me graduate. I had to shoot myself in the foot to spite them.

—An analysand

This is not to say that the analysand is likely, the moment we have found she has reasons to be angry with the relative whose death might have been announced in the letter received in the dream, to immediately feel the full extent of her fury at that particular relative and cry, "Yeah, I'd really like to kill him!" or "I wish he would waste away like Steve Jobs did!" Freud often found that it was far easier for analysands to *intellectually* accept that they had reasons to be angry at the people who seemed to suffer a thousand deaths in their dreams than it was for them to actually get angry at those people—that is, to really experience their fury at them. Indeed, he often found that despite having made some such very specific connection, his analysands would seemingly become angry at everyone except the relative in question, including Freud himself.

Insofar as we ourselves, as analysts, are the ones who bring the analysand to the point of realizing or remembering that she has reasons to be furious with her relative, fury is often directed toward us first, perhaps for having done so, but more likely by way of displacement of anger from the relative onto us. After all, if the analysand's death wish toward the relative was unconscious, she presumably felt that there were considerable obstacles in the way of her expressing anger at the relative, perhaps (a) because she felt she had a great deal to lose were she to do so—be it esteem, love, or a legacy—or (b) because that relative intimidates her and she would have to steel herself to angrily assert what she remains not entirely sure of when faced with that relative's mild-mannered appearance, denials, protestations, or explosive temper. How much easier to get angry at the analyst, who seems so unlikely to fly off the handle or punish any sort of outburst? How much easier to spew invectives at inconsiderate drivers on the highway on the way home from the session? Or at the cashier at the supermarket? Or at her boss, husband, neighbors, or children? Drivers, cashiers, relatives, and neighbors can generally do little to deflect or allay her anger, since they have no clue as to what is fueling it; but the analyst can forestall fury so great as to threaten the continuation of the treatment in many cases by gentle, sensitive questions and answers as opposed to brutal interpretations and defensive disclaimers (e.g., "I have never been horrible to you like your relative was," a useless disclaimer if ever there was one).

Although it seems safe enough to assume that, in the course of ordinary life experience, thought and affect initially go hand in hand—for example, that my uncharitable or negative thoughts about my uncle (let us call him Bob) are accompanied by feelings of revulsion toward him—Freud found that such thoughts and feelings often became detached from each other. Let us represent the initial situation in which thought and affect are connected as follows:

$$\text{Thought} \leftrightarrow \text{Affect}$$

Freud hypothesized that repression often acts or takes effect by breaking the link between thought and affect; let us depict the subsequent situation in which thought and affect are disconnected owing to repression as follows:

$$\text{Thought} \quad \| \quad \text{Affect}$$

Repression, understood in this way, may lead to a wide variety of consequences:

1. My negative thoughts about my uncle may be forgotten even though my aversion toward him remains; I loathe him but I don't really know why, having forgotten the events that led me to despise him (perhaps he once punished me harshly for breaking something I hadn't broken).

In this first instance, thoughts have undergone repression, while their corresponding affect persists in consciousness. We may represent this, simply enough, as follows, where what is under the bar (or fraction-like line) is unconscious and what is above it is conscious:

$$\frac{\text{Affect}}{\text{Thought}}$$

In this instance, my affect strikes me as incomprehensible, and I may well latch on to some minor or unrelated incident to explain it to myself and others. Indeed, I may begin to find odious his religious beliefs, political convictions, profession, or lifestyle, and vehemently criticize all and sundry that espouse or practice them. I alight upon all kinds of reasons to criticize such beliefs and practices, and perhaps even formulate an entire counter-ideology to my uncle's, but my original impetus for doing so remains opaque to me (i.e., my feelings about the early events that involved my uncle have shifted to or become displaced onto his belief system or lifestyle). We might depict the situation here as follows, with Thought₁ representing my negative thoughts about my uncle owing to one or more events in my past, and Thought₂ representing my negative thoughts about certain religious beliefs, political convictions, professions, or lifestyles that I initially heard him express but that I may no longer even consciously associate with him:

$$\frac{\text{Thought}_2 \leftrightarrow \text{Affect}}{\text{Thought}_1}$$

Another possible scenario that follows the same logic is one in which, rather than despising my Uncle Bob, I begin to despise my brother Bob (who, let us suppose, was named after Uncle Bob). The conflict in my mind that led me to forget what happened with my uncle does not exist in relation to my brother, and the affect that I formerly felt toward one Bob becomes attached to another Bob. We might refer to this, with Freud, as a "verbal bridge" or "switch word" (SE V, p. 341 n. 1),[16] or simply as a "false connection" (SE II, p. 67 n)—and transference of feeling from one's uncle to one's analyst would be another kind of false connection—or we might refer to it as a substitution of one Bob for another (or one signifier, S₂, for another signifier, S₁):

$$\frac{\text{Bob}_2 \leftrightarrow \text{Affect}}{\text{Bob}_1}$$

$$\frac{S_2 \leftrightarrow \text{Affect}}{S_1}$$

Note that both the quality and quantity of affect (in this case, extreme loathing) remain the same; it is merely the object of my loathing that has changed.

Recall, now, that *forgetting is not a necessary component of repression; repression can take effect by breaking the link between thought and*

✦ *affect without any events or thoughts becoming unconscious*. The following is therefore another possible consequence of repression:

> 2. I remember the events that occurred that led me to think Uncle
>   Bob atrocious, but I don't abhor him—I abhor his wife instead,
>   without being able to say why or providing only reasons that seem
>   incommensurate with my feeling of repulsion.

Here nothing has been forced below the bar (or fraction-like line), but
the repulsion I felt toward Uncle Bob has drifted, shifted, or been transferred to another person—not to another person who has the same name
as him, this time, but to someone whom I associate with him owing to
their so often being together. In other words, rather than there being
here a substitution of one person for another who are alike in some
respect (e.g., name and sex), we have here what we might call a slippage
or "metonymic" sliding from one person to another with whom the first
is closely associated in many of my thoughts and memories. We might
represent this in either of the two following ways:

$$\text{Person}_1 \rightarrow \text{Person}_2 \leftrightarrow \text{Affect}$$

or

$$\text{Person}_2 \leftrightarrow \text{Affect} \ \| \ \text{Person}_1$$

More schematically, these could be written as follows:

$$S_1 \rightarrow S_2 \leftrightarrow \text{Affect}$$

or

$$S_2 \leftrightarrow \text{Affect} \ \| \ S_1$$

If we wanted to depict *something* as having been forced below the bar,
we could situate the original link between thought (or person or signifier) and affect itself as having been forgotten:

$$\frac{S_2 \leftrightarrow \text{Affect} \ \| \ S_1}{\leftrightarrow}$$

We are all, I suspect, familiar with the tendency of pent-up anger to find an outlet of some kind, no matter how far it may be from the original source of the anger: A father who has been upbraided at work by his boss finds reasons to severely rebuke his son for some minor oversight at home, picks a fight with a neighbor, or ends up kicking the dog. As Freud reminds us in *The Interpretation of Dreams* (SE V, pp. 552–553), affect is ever on the lookout for a means of "discharge"—a way to express itself or come out. When one avenue is blocked, it will sooner or later find another.

A further way in which repression may occur is as follows:

3. I do not remember the events that occurred that led me to loathe my Uncle Bob, but I am always anxious around him, or I develop a fear of being alone in a room with any man around his age.

In this instance, thoughts have been forgotten, and so as to ensure that they will not be remembered, the affect that had originally been associated with them (loathing) transmogrifies into something less tangible or legible: anxiety.

$$\frac{\text{Affect}_1 \rightarrow \text{Affect}_2}{\text{Thought}}$$

Again, we could depict the connection between thought and affect as having been pushed below the bar as well:

$$\frac{\text{Affect}_1 \rightarrow \text{Affect}_2}{\text{Thought} \qquad \leftrightarrow}$$

We might hypothesize that such transformations of one affect into another (indicated by the unidirectional arrow) occur precisely when the thought is not altogether repressed and there seems to be a danger of my recalling what happened that made me loathe my uncle in the first place. On rare occasions, the transformation of affect goes so far that instead of abhorring him, I begin—strangely enough—to adore him; this is obviously the most perfect of disguises, which neither he nor I nor virtually anyone else can see through.

Repression may lead to yet another result:

4. I remember nothing, nor do I feel angry in general or hate anyone, but I develop a facial tic around the eyes or mouth, or move my head or arm in a curious way, whenever I am around a man who reminds me of Uncle Bob; or I feel sick to my stomach and vomit whenever I am around any man who reminds me of him.

Compromise formation

Note that many such odd bodily movements are at least in some small measure associated with what one might initially expect from someone who is about to explode at someone else, whether verbally or physically. A nervous twitching might develop in my jaw muscles related to a tension owing to my desire to yell or bite, which is simultaneously suppressed; or I might begin to stutter, trying to express my fury and yet squelching it before I can get the words out. The two warring factions within myself— the desire to attack and my self-condemnation of it—combine to create a "compromise formation" (SE V, pp. 517, 596–597, and 676; SE XV, p. 66) which few, if any, can decipher as indicative of my fury.

I might, on the other hand, begin moving one or both of my eyebrows, which to an outside observer appears to be a kind of blinking, but which might well represent the first movements of the narrowing and focusing of my gaze upon someone I would like to attack, something I simultaneously refuse to allow myself to do. Some of the facial tics we encounter resemble, if we look closely, the first movements of snarling as we sometimes see it in the animal kingdom; it is because these movements are simultaneously being counteracted by an opposing force—some sort of censorship, some sort of agency forbidding the subject from attacking—that they take on such an odd appearance (if you have ever seen a dog sneeze instead of biting you during a bit of rough and tumble play, you will know what I mean). Certain movements of the head as a whole may involve an initial, perhaps jerky, attack posture; others are more suggestive of a ducking or defensive posture; and still others of an aborted shaking of the head as if to say "No!" And a number of erratic or spasmodic movements of the hand or arm may similarly indicate a wish to strike out at someone or to protect oneself from an expected blow. It is the jerky and repetitive nature of these movements that so strongly indicate the presence of warring factions within the person with the tic.

This situation seems more difficult to depict using the above-developed visual schemas. Two different affects seem to be struggling for supremacy here: a wish to attack Uncle Bob and a will not to do so. The latter may be motivated in many different possible ways: I may wish to protect him from my own fury, perhaps at least in part because I also like him in some respects; I may wish not to show that I grant him any importance in my life (feeling he would love it if he knew I felt so strongly about him, even if those strong feelings were thoroughly negative); I may worry I will lose my parents' love if they catch me attacking my uncle or hear about it; I may believe that it is immoral to hit anyone and that I should be above all fits and displays of anger; and so on. Neither of my opposing affects seems to ever get the upper hand here, unlike the case of those people who seem to easily blow up at others, only to exhaust their anger fairly quickly and become more comfortable around those others shortly after the explosion; we think of the latter as volatile and perhaps unpredictable, but they are rarely subject to symptom formation of the kind we see in those who never allow themselves to blow up in the first place.

Those who are ever at war with themselves end up expending huge quantities of their energy fighting their own tendencies, and to outside observers often seem quite dead, as if devoid of emotion (contemporary clinicians often characterize them as having "flat affect," overlooking the considerable affective forces that are warring within them). The tension they build up within themselves can, however, be quite self-destructive, leading to high blood pressure, muscular and skeletal problems, and—what is perhaps most common—the grinding of teeth. (Indeed, dentists are often the first professionals contacted by those who are fighting themselves in this way.) Self-destruction is tantamount, after all, to a kind of compromise—a compromise between the opposing forces that (a) wish to destroy another and that (b) seek to thwart any such violent activity. Instead of destroying others, I destroy myself; yet I do so in such a way that neither they nor I are any the wiser. Tics and daytime teeth grinding are thus true compromise formations (nighttime teeth grinding is more likely a direct expression of anger); the same is true of nausea and vomiting, which ostensibly harm no one but myself.

It would appear that my reasons here for hating Uncle Bob may or may not have become unconscious, but that what is at stake is a conflict between two affects, one of which Freud will later associate with the id (e.g., the one that wishes to attack) and the other with the superego (the one that prohibits any such attack). It is the incomprehensible nature of the symptom (abbreviated here as the Greek letter sigma, Σ), which is produced by these opposing forces, that keeps my reasons for hating Uncle Bob out of mind, there being no obvious link between those reasons and the symptom—that is, between thought and Σ.

$$\text{Affect}_1 \rightarrow \quad \Sigma \quad \leftarrow \text{Affect}_2$$
$$\overline{\phantom{\text{Affect}_1 \rightarrow \quad \Sigma \quad \leftarrow}}$$
$$\text{Thought}$$

There are, undoubtedly, other possible ways in which thought and affect diverge, each going its own way—thought either becoming isolated or persisting in consciousness, and affect either being displaced onto someone else or transforming into anxiety, fear, nausea, or a nervous tic. But let us turn now to some more general considerations on affect.

Affect May Drift but Is Not Repressed

Repression [can] make use of another mechanism. The trauma, instead of being forgotten, is deprived of its affective charge, such that what remains conscious is merely its ideational content, which is completely colorless and is judged unimportant.

—Freud, SE X, p. 196

Few practitioners today seem to recall that, according to Freud, there is no such thing as an unconscious affect. Thoughts may undergo repression, but feelings do not. Feelings undergo displacement, supression, and other kinds of transformations, but they never become unconscious.[17] As he says, "Strictly speaking . . . there are no unconscious affects" (SE XIV, p. 178); and, again, "We cannot assert the existence of unconscious affects in the same sense as of unconscious ideas" (SE XVI, p. 409). In other words, even though one may occasionally encounter in Freud's work a reference to a repressed feeling or an unconscious emotion, Freud makes it clear that these are somewhat sloppy or approximate ways of speaking that end up being misleading. When we formulate things as clearly as we can, "there are no unconscious affects."[18]

Whereas thoughts may well become repressed, what does Freud teach us about affects? He says, "The immediate vicissitude of [an] affect [tied to an idea that undergoes repression] is to be transformed into anxiety" (SE XVI, p. 409). In other words, when we encounter anxiety we often find that some thought (a wishful thought) has been repressed and the affect associated with it, regardless of its original tenor, has been set adrift, so to speak; it no longer seems to be connected in the analysand's mind to any event, circumstance, or thought and transforms into anxiety, anxiety being "the universally current coinage for which *any* affective impulse is or can be exchanged if the ideational content attached to it is subjected to repression" (pp. 403–404).

And in *The Interpretation of Dreams*, Freud provides a useful corrective to the absurdly widespread use of the notion of "inappropriate affect" when he says that the

> affects [of neurotics] are always appropriate, at least in their *quality*, though we must allow for their intensity being increased owing to displacement. . . . Psychoanalysis can put patients on the right track by recognizing the affect as being . . . justified and by seeking out the idea that belongs to it but has been repressed and replaced by a substitute. (SE V, p. 461)

Such statements, which span almost two decades of Freud's work,[19] make it clear that in his view affects may drift, become attached to other objects (making "false connections" with them), or transform into anxiety or even into their opposites, but they are not repressed per se, in the sense of becoming unconscious. They are always visible somewhere in the person's life, assuming we know how to look. The same cannot be said of the thoughts to which they had been initially attached.

It has often been noted regarding obsessives that they recall many important memories from their past, and can tell you about them in great detail, but without the slightest bit of emotion being attached to them; and regarding hysterics that they, on the contrary, have forgotten many important memories from their past, but the feelings that were undoubtedly attached to them initially are still present in their lives or bodies, appearing in "crazy," incomprehensible ways insofar as they are detached from the thoughts and memories that initially gave rise to them. In the former we wonder where the emotion has gone—presumably into displaced objects of love or hatred, or into symptoms; in the latter we know that the memories have been repressed, and that the affects have been set free to drift.

Part of our goal as clinicians is thus to find ways in which to bring thought and affect back together, which is what has to happen for symptoms to get resolved. One might, without exaggeration, say that virtually all of psychoanalytic technique is designed to do just that. Getting analysands to talk in great detail about hurtful events in their lives is our best bet for bringing painful and/or distressing affects into contact with the events that first gave rise to them and with all their subsequent thoughts about them. And helping analysands free-associate about both past and present happenings, intrusive thoughts, perplexing reactions, dreams, slips, and fantasies is our ticket to bringing the "inexplicable" experiences in their lives into contact with the affects that went into their construction.

CHAPTER 3

Dreams

The Royal Road to the Unconscious

There is nothing imaginable that is too absurd, complicated, or abnormal for us to dream about it.
                                    —Cicero, *On Divination* II, lxxi, p. 146

Although over a century has elapsed since the first edition of Freud's magnum opus, *The Interpretation of Dreams* (SE IV and V), was published, dreams continue to be absolutely crucial to psychoanalytic work. Despite the fact that the vast majority of present-day psychoanalytic practitioners probably do not do even *half* of what Freud recommended we do when interpreting dreams—the lion's share of them almost certainly never having read more than a few chapters of the book—people who have been through analysis often say that the most important thing in their analysis was their dreams and the discussions they had with their analysts about them.

In the 2000s, a Lacanian psychoanalytic institute in Paris published the results of a long-term study of analysts-in-training who had completed their academic program and personal/training analyses[1] and had requested to undergo the institutional procedure adopted by certain Lacanian institutes known as the Pass (a procedure that qualifies them to become members of their schools or members with a special status). Virtually all of these candidates stressed the importance to them of their dreams and their work on them to the progress and completion of their analyses. This was, to many analysts at the time, quite an astonishing finding, perhaps all the more so in that Lacanians have no fixed method of interpreting dreams (even if they tend to be quite conversant in Freud's work), and there is thus probably as much variation among the different Lacanian practitioners when it comes to dreams as there is in virtually every other school of psychoanalysis.

Let us thus take it to be established by patients themselves that dreams are incredibly important to psychoanalytic work, and let us consider one of the probable reasons why this is so, even before we enter into Freud's specific theory and practice of dream interpretation.

What We Learn from Dreams: Almost Everything

⭐ A dream is a (disguised) fulfillment of a (suppressed or repressed) wish.
—Freud, SE IV, p. 160 (emphasis in the original)

✳ *Within an analysis far more of the repressed is brought to light in connection with dreams than by any other method.*
—Freud, SE XIX, p. 117

One of the very first things Freud tells us in *The Interpretation of Dreams* announces what is probably still the most important aspect of dreams today: It seems that "dreams have at their command memories that are inaccessible in waking life" (SE IV, p. 12). In other words, myriad things that are "beyond the reach of our waking memory" (p. 11) are presented and represented in dreams. In our times, work with dreams has largely taken the place of hypnosis, for it provides us with much of the same material that could formerly only be accessed by patients in the hypnotic state.

Psychoanalysts of many different persuasions can thus agree on at least one thing: We learn an awful lot about analysands' backgrounds and childhood experiences by getting them to relate their dreams to us and associate to them. Memories that come up in connection with dreams shed light on a great deal that would otherwise be inexplicable to us in our analysands' waking thoughts, feelings, and symptoms.

This does not mean that earlier events and experiences are reproduced in dreams exactly as they occurred at the time. Indeed, they are rarely re-depicted so faithfully and are often merely alluded to, one small element from a childhood event appearing in a dream. As Freud puts it, "A dream very seldom reproduces recollections in such a way that they constitute, without abbreviation or modification, the whole of [a dream's] manifest content" (SE IV, p. 198), scenes from the past often being merely evoked or considerably transformed in the scenario of the dream. He goes on to say that, "as a rule, [a] childhood scene is only represented in the dream's manifest content by an allusion" (p. 199).[2]

Nevertheless, it is in thinking about the dream and talking with one's analyst about it that one is reminded of something from the past that one perhaps had not thought about for many years—if indeed one had ever thought about it since it first occurred—and certainly would not have mentioned when initially invited to tell the story of one's life. This is obviously true in the case of things we have done that we feel to be shameful, but it is true of many other things as well. Indeed, so many things that it would never occur to us to tell our analysts about ourselves during the initial days or weeks of analysis are alluded to by dreams and brought into the conversation with our analysts as we discuss those dreams that one might venture to say that our initial account of our upbringing to our analysts was a mere bare-bones skeleton that needed to be fleshed out, when it was not in fact largely a fabrication designed to help us forget (or at least dissimulate) what had indeed happened. For we have a tendency to "paper over" unseemly or disagreeable experiences from the past and to rewrite our own history to cast ourselves in a more favorable light. The story about ourselves that we have become accustomed to telling others—and perhaps even to believe ourselves—is by no means adequate in analysis, and is at least part of the reason why our present predicament seems to be so opaque to us. This story has become an official history, from which myriad crucial facts have been expunged.

Talking about dreams therefore helps fill out, correct, and at times even overturn this official history. This is absolutely crucial to situating our symptoms in their more complete context—in other words, in the context of the whole of our experience, not just a small part of it. Even if the "whole picture" is an ideal that is never attainable, one merely approaching it asymptotically over the course of time, there is no way to grasp the origin and development of our symptoms without a serious enlargement and revision of the official history. And as we saw in Chapter 1, tracing symptoms back to their origin is a very important first step toward alleviating them.

Backdrop to Freud's Study of Dreams

> The interpretation of dreams is the royal road to a knowledge of unconscious mental activities.
> —Freud, SE V, p. 608 (emphasis in the original)

Freud's earliest patients would, while under hypnosis or in a relaxed state, sometimes spontaneously tell him about dreams they had had, and Freud was thus led to try to grasp the connection between their dreams and the symptoms of which they complained. He made a fairly exhaustive study of the literature on dreams that was available at his time, running the gamut from the use of dreams for purposes of prophecy in biblical times and in ancient Greece and Rome to the 19th-century medical discourse about dreams as caused merely by physiological stimuli that went unnoticed during one's busy daytime activities but were noticed by the otherwise unoccupied mind during sleep. Virtually all the same theories about dreaming that we hear around us even today were current in Freud's time, including that dreams are nothing but nonsense, the mind's "higher faculties" being deactivated during the night; that dreams help discharge all the "junk" that accumulates in the mind during waking hours, especially details that one did not or was unable to pay much attention to in the course of the day; that dreams discharge tension or mental pressure that builds up during the day (SE IV, p. 80); that dreams are caused only by slight noises or other sensations that reach us during our sleeping hours, whether from the outside or the inside (e.g., sounds of passing vehicles, the ringing of chimes, digestive difficulties, being too hot or too cold, or needing to urinate); and that dreams foretell the future. Freud notes that theories propounded in the *early* 19th century paid far more tribute to the imaginative and creative power of dreams than those proffered in his own sad times (the second half of the 19th century), which were characterized by a kind of reductionistic scientific discourse that stigmatized dreams as stupid, useless, and intellectually bankrupt.

In his review of the extant literature on dreams, he found that those philosophers and psychologists who attentively recorded and studied their own dreams—as well as those of family, friends, and colleagues (who would relate their dreams to them in person or in letters, as was so common at that time)—generally considered dreams to be connected, whether directly or indirectly, to their actual lives. Some argued that dreams continue to work over the same material that had occupied their minds during the day; others that dreams provided a nice break from daytime problems; some that dreams focus on mundane details to which they had barely paid any attention while awake; others that dreams creatively present and re-present important issues and conflicts in one's life. Although each writer tended to argue that what he found in his own dreams (and in those of his small circle of friends and colleagues) held true for everyone, the reader may well come away instead with the impression that we are not all necessarily the same kinds of dreamers, or at least that each author focused on a different subset of his own dreams. Perhaps some of us are more imaginative dreamers than others, even if we are not necessarily that creative in everyday life;[3] some of us solve more of the problems we confront during the day while sleeping than others; and some of us have unremittingly boring dreams.

More important in the present context is the fact that these philosophers and psychologists often believed that the immoral and at times even criminal acts committed in their dreams were not wholly foreign to them, feeling that the thought of such acts had at least at one time or another flashed through their minds. In that sense, they were willing—unlike the "medical researchers" of Freud's own time—to accept some personal responsibility for what happened in their dreams, even if it did not reflect particularly well on their own moral character.

As Hildebrandt, whose contribution to the study of dreams Freud found to be "the most perfect in form and the richest in ideas" (SE IV, p. 67), put it, "It is impossible to think of any action in a dream for which the original motive has not in some way or other—whether as a wish, desire, or impulse—passed through one's waking mind" (cited by Freud, p. 69). Hildebrandt believed that "dreams give us an occasional glimpse into depths and recesses of our nature to which we usually have no access in the waking state" (cited by Freud, p. 70). Radestock, another author mentioned by Freud, held that "dreams often do no more than reveal to us what we would [rather] not admit to ourselves" (cited by Freud, p. 71). Erdmann commented that "dreams have never shown me what I ought to think of a man; but I have occasionally been astonished to learn from a dream what I do, in fact, think of a man and how I actually feel about him" (cited by Freud, p. 71). And the philosopher Fichte remarked that "the nature of our dreams gives a far more truthful reflection of our whole disposition than we are able to learn of it from self-observation in waking life" (cited by Freud, p. 71).

The French writer Maury went still further when he said that, when we are dreaming,

> it is our penchants that speak and make us act, without our conscience holding us back, even if it sometimes sends us warnings. I myself have certain flaws and lascivious impulses, which I struggle to counter in the waking state and generally manage not to give into. But in my dreams I always yield to them, or, to put it more felicitously, I act upon their impetus without any fear or remorse. . . . The scenes that unfold before me in my dreams are obviously suggested to me by the urges that I feel and that my will, being absent during sleep, does not seek to repress. (Cited by Freud, p. 73)

Both Hildebrandt and Maury thus argued, before Freud, that dreams give free reign to certain of our impulses—of which we may or may not be fully aware during everyday life, but which we generally suppress—while our moral conscience appears to be swept aside. Urges that are usually suppressed are enacted in dreams, while our moral sense is at least partially put to sleep (SE IV, pp. 72–73).

Thus the idea that dreams are intimately related to the rest of our lives and perhaps even show us things about ourselves that, in waking life, we would rather not know, is hardly a Freudian invention (as Lynkeus put it, "It is always the same man, whether he is awake or dreaming"; cited by Freud, p. 309 n. 2). Although in our own times, scientists are again hard at work seeking some purely physiological explanation for dreams (see, for example, Jouvet, 1993/1999, and Hobson, 2015), seeming anxious to either invalidate all of Freud's work or place what little can supposedly be salvaged of it on a strictly biological footing, it would not be going too far, I think, to say that "those who are engaged in what is described as 'research' into dreams" (SE IV, p. 93) have returned to what are essentially *pre-Freudian positions*, and provide us with yet another "shining example of the repugnance to learning anything new which is characteristic of [many] scientists" (p. 93). For while they willingly endorse the idea that there is "a causal connection between the somatic and the mental" spheres—that is, between body and mind—the connection only seems to go in one direction for them: In other words, they believe that even if at the present, given the current state of medical science, they cannot find the physiological cause of the lion's share of mental activities, they are sure that "deeper research will one day trace the path further and discover an organic basis for [every] mental event" (pp. 41–42). The authors of the *DSM-5*, too, believe that, *someday*, "incontrovertible etiological or pathophysiological mechanisms [will be] identified to fully validate specific disorders or disorder spectra" (American Psychiatric Association [APA], p. 20).

Freud, although he occasionally paid lip service to this same hubristic belief in the eventual omnipotence of science, nevertheless retorted, "The fact that, for the time being, we cannot see beyond the mental [to its grounding in the physiological], is no reason to deny the existence of the mental realm" (SE IV, p. 42). Yet a great deal of contemporary research continues to view the mental sphere as a mere epiphenomenon of the biological sphere; and a mere epiphenomenon has no ability to give rise to changes in the body, much less to meaningful mental phenomena worthy of interpretation in their own right (research on mindfulness perhaps constitutes an exception to this). In 1900, Freud already emphasized the importance of viewing the products of the mind as significant in and of themselves; in other words, he asked us to entertain the idea that *mental phenomena like thoughts or wishes could be the cause of a symptom,* whether that symptom affected the mental realm alone, the somatic realm alone, or both the mind and the body. Yet most "scientific" researchers today (especially in medicine and psychiatry), even though they may acknowledge that mental/psychological stress at work or at home can lead someone to have physiological problems, seem to continue to believe that fantasies, daydreams, and dreams are merely epiphenomenal, and that talking about such will-o'-the-wisps can have no curative effect on anyone. The only curative effects they seem to acknowledge are those that come from directly biological interventions: surgery, medications, and the like. Transformative ideas and feelings that can grow out of the discussion of fantasies and dreams—related to human meaning-making and the impact of speech—are simply not on their radar.

What Is a Dream?

A hungry person dreams of eating but wakes up still hungry. A thirsty person dreams of drinking but is still faint from thirst when morning comes.

—Isaiah 29:8

It is the very narrative of a dream—the verbal material—that serves as a basis for interpretation.

—Lacan, 1976, p. 13

A dream is quite obviously a sensory experience—it is primarily visual for most of us, but it can also include auditory, tactile, gustatory, and olfactory sensations—and often an emotional experience as well. And yet as soon as we attempt to recollect a dream, we begin to translate, in a manner of speaking, that sensory and affective experience into words; in this sense, we begin to tell ourselves a story about the dream, a story about what occurred in the dream. Some of us then remember far better the story as we have told it to ourselves than we do the images and feelings that constituted the initial experience, and in the morning may remember little else but that story. Those who write down their dreams in the middle of the night are probably familiar with the experience of remembering nothing whatsoever of the initial dream experience, having but their own nocturnal scribbling to remind them that they had had a dream and of what occurred during it. Analysands who record their dreams orally upon waking at night (on their phones or other recording devices) often tell me how shocked they are to hear their own voices recounting something of which they have retained no memory whatsoever.

When we *can* remember a dream, we may feel that our own verbal description of it is inadequate, believing that we have not found adequate words to render the sensations, images, or feelings that were so vivid at the time and that have perhaps even stayed with us in part. But this does not alter the fact that insofar as we talk about our dream with another human being, the only thing to which that other human being has access is our words about it. Our interlocutor can never experience the dream as we did, can never see the same images or have the exact same sensations (unless we are consummate filmmakers and manage to reproduce at least the visual and auditory sensations of the dream, even if we are not yet able to reproduce most olfactory and tactile sensations through film), much less feel the exact same emotions as we did. Our interlocutor has only our words at his or her disposal.

Put differently, *a dream, insofar as we work with it and attempt to interpret it in analysis, is a series of words—it is, in short, a text.* The analyst works with the text that is provided by the analysand, and that text (the "text of the dream" or dream text, as Freud calls it; SE XXII, pp. 9 and 13) is often added to as the analysand begins to associate to the dream. It may also be amended—and Freud cautions us to take seriously both the original and the "corrected" versions, not just the latter—and it may even be criticized as inadequate by the analysand who feels that it does not do justice to the dream, certain portions of the dream seeming to be missing altogether, others not entirely rendered by the words the analysand has come up with for it, there being doubt as to whether one scene came before another or as to whether a certain fabric was green or blue, and so on.

Regardless of its possible imperfections, this text is the main material with which the analyst and the analysand work. The dream itself is either gone or still partially, if not vividly, present to the analysand's mind; but in any case, it cannot be directly "transferred" (as if in some sort of mind-to-mind "video streaming" or "Vulcan mind meld" à la Mr. Spock of *Star Trek* fame) to the analyst. And even if it could be directly "transferred," the analyst would not necessarily experience the video "streamed" by the analysand exactly as the analysand experienced it— after all, each of us is affected differently by one and the same movie or video! If the analysand is an artist and paints pictures that seem to render portions of the dream, the analyst must nevertheless ask the artist to talk about those paintings, for even if a picture is worth a thousand words, it is hardly self-explanatory. Everyone sees different things in pictures, and they are fruitful ground for projection (hence the usefulness of pictures in projective tests); but what the analyst is primarily interested in are the *analysand's* interpretations of the pictures, not the analyst's own projections based on his or her own personality and life experience. Hence, *as far as psychoanalytic practice is concerned, a dream is the oral text or speech* (which can potentially be transcribed more or less accurately) *produced about the dream by the analysand.*[4]

This text is not, of course, a dead text: It does not involve a dead language but a living language that is spoken by at least two people, the analysand and the analyst. And it is spoken by a living, breathing human being who is affected by speaking this text aloud—who may become excited, sad, annoyed, bored, or angry while telling it during a session, or who may pause and/or make a slip of the tongue while recounting it or associating to it. The act of *enunciating* this text to the analyst thus adds another layer to the words themselves: Emotion appears to be attached to the recounting of certain portions of the dream, and stumblings and mumblings may appear as other portions of the dream are related. None of this need be taken at face value, yet it adds to the information available to the analyst.

Something that we can conclude from the above is that a dream, as it plays a role in analysis, is already a sort of translation: It is the rendering or translation of a primarily visual and affective experience into words. And spoken words are what we predominately work with in psychoanalysis.

It might be thought that our goal is then to work from the analysand's speech back to his or her initial experience of the dream; we might picture this as in the following figure (in which the arrow indicates the translation process):

Recounting a dream: Visual/affective experience $\longrightarrow$ Text/speech

Analyzing a dream: Text/speech $\longrightarrow$ Visual/affective experience

Were we able to "undo" the translation or reverse the translation process, this would presumably allow other people to experience the dream just as the dreamer had—that is, to have the same dream. Yet, as we saw regarding films, we do not all experience a film in the same way, even if we watch it side by side in the same movie theater, for we each situate ourselves differently with respect to the various characters and predicaments in the film depending on our own backgrounds, identifications, desires, fantasies, and so on. And *even if we were able to experience someone else's dream as he or she had experienced it, we would be no closer to being able to interpret it*—indeed, we would probably be just as confused about its meaning as the dreamer is! It is not by putting ourselves in the exact same place as the dreamer and feeling what he or she felt in the dream that we find the key to interpreting it.

Freud's fundamental thesis here is that what we need, in order to interpret a dream, is not an as-accurate-as-possible picture or replica of the initial visual/affective experience had by the dreamer; rather, we need to get at *the initial unconscious thoughts and wishes that went into the construction of the dream* as a visual/affective experience. In other words, what is more important to us than the dream as remembered is what caused the dream to come into being in the first place. Freud's hypothesis can be illustrated in the following manner (where the arrow again indicates a translation process):

latent content   manifest content
Initial thoughts/wishes ——→ Visual/affective experience

The visual/affective experience is usually confusing and opaque, when it is not altogether nonsensical by everyday standards; but there are, in Freud's view, thoughts and wishes that gave rise to the visual/affective experience that are not nearly so confusing or opaque. He calls the visual/affective experience the *manifest content* of the dream—it is what we may be able to remember upon awakening (and we might include in the manifest content the subsequent transformation of it into a written text or speech). And he dubs the initial thoughts and wishes that led to the construction of the dream the *latent content.*

Before turning to the nature of this latent content, let us note that Freud hypothesizes the existence of a twofold transformation process: (a) Thoughts are transformed into images (we witness "the turning of abstract thought into pictures," SE V, p. 341), and (b) latent content is turned into manifest content. The two happen simultaneously and are obviously overlapping processes, but they can, I believe, be at least theoretically distinguished, the former corresponding quite closely to what occurs in the visual and plastic arts,[6] the second to what is involved in certain forms of literature (perhaps, above all, allegorical literature, which Freud often refers to in *The Interpretation of Dreams*, and which we will turn to further on). The term by which he designates this twofold transformation is *Übertragung,* which in German means both "translation" and "transference," and is the same term that Freud uses for transference in the psychoanalytic sense of the transferring or displacing of a suspicion or misgiving an analysand has about his or her parent or spouse, for example, onto the analyst (*transference* in the psychoanalytic sense has numerous meanings, some more of which we will turn to in Chapter 5). At the very beginning of what is perhaps the most important chapter in *The Interpretation of Dreams*, Chapter 6, Freud (SE IV) writes as follows:

> The [latent] dream-thoughts and the [manifest] dream-content are presented to us like two versions of the same subject matter in two different languages. Or, more strictly speaking, the dream-content seems like a transcript [or translation: *Übertragung*] of the dream-thoughts into another mode of expression, whose characters and syntactic laws it is our business to discover by comparing the original and the translation. (p. 277)

Something in the dreamer is therefore a translator or transcriber of sorts, and the analysand and analyst must work together to decipher the "foreign language" (the visual manifest content) into which the dream thoughts have been translated. Although they both presumably know the "source language" from which the translation has been made (i.e., they are familiar with the language in which the latent dream thoughts and wishes are expressed), they do not know the "target language" into which it has been rendered.

Dreams Are Microsymptoms

No one should expect the interpretation of a dream to fall into his lap like manna from heaven.
—Freud, SE V, p. 522

The hypothesis, on Freud's part, of the existence of a transformation process (from the latent to the manifest content of a dream) is no more than an extension of what he learned by attempting to unravel hysterical symptoms. Consider, for example, Anna O's inability for six weeks to drink water (discussed in Chapter 1). Although Anna was often incredibly thirsty and dehydrated, whenever she would try to raise a water glass to her lips, she would push it away in disgust. This made no more sense to her than to anyone else, considering the intense heat of the summer and her need for liquids, not to mention the usually inoffensive or benign nature of water glasses and water itself (SE II, pp. 34–35). What Breuer and Anna O found by tracing the symptom back to its first occurrence was that a glass of water had taken on a significance for her that it had never had before (and has probably had for very few people in the course of history, for that matter): Her lady companion's dog had drunk out of such a glass in that lady's room, and such glasses and water itself had become connected in Anna's mind to physical intimacy between dog and mistress, illnesses carried by dogs, ill wishes toward her lady companion and/or mother, or something along those lines. For Anna to take a drink of water was to be reminded of her ill wishes toward her lady companion and/or mother, wishes which she considered to be reprehensible.

There is but one short step from this to concluding that, after seeing the dog drink from the glass, Anna O's every urge to drink water became equated with the thought, "I wish my lady companion (or mother) harm"; and that pushing the water glass away was tantamount to the thought, "It is unconscionable for me to wish my lady companion (or mother) harm." Otherwise stated, a symptomatic act (or symptomatic inability to act—in this case, to drink water) is a *translation into another register, medium, or "mode of expression"* (SE IV, p. 277; my emphasis) of a wish and simultaneously of the obstruction or suppression of that wish owing to one's self-criticism for having such a wish.[7] We saw much the same thing when we discussed certain facial tics as the transfer or translation into the physical realm of anger (accompanied by a wish to strike out at someone) and simultaneous self-stifling of that anger.

What allowed Freud to make headway in interpreting dreams was thus the fact that he formulated and then tested the hypothesis that one could *view dreams as like symptoms, as structured like symptoms, and indeed as minisymptoms themselves*. Just as individual symptoms each had a secret meaning—unknown both to those around the sufferer of the symptom and to the sufferer herself—dreams too each turned out to have a secret meaning that neither the dreamer nor those around the dreamer could easily guess. Just as Freud always found that there was more behind any individual symptom than met the eye, he postulated that there was more behind any specific dream than met the eye or ear: There were latent thoughts and wishes that had become transformed by the dreamwork into an illegible medium so as to be unrecognizable to waking consciousness.

It is worth pointing out, I think, that what counts as a symptom in psychoanalysis is something that a patient complains of—bemoaning that it is getting in the way of his or her life, if not outright ruining it—and professes not to be able to understand. Analysts do not take some sort of master-like stance and tell patients that this or that behavior that they are engaging in—whether drinking, taking drugs, binge eating, vomiting, or what have you—constitutes a symptom based on some supposedly "objective standard of normal behavior" against which to judge any individual's behavior; psychiatrists and psychologists often adopt such a stance, but psychoanalysts do not (or at least should not, as there is no basis for such a stance in psychoanalytic theory, even if certain individual analysts go astray here). In analysis, *a symptom is what the analysand considers to be problematic in his or her life,* not what the analyst considers to be symptomatic in the analysand's life.[8]

This is not a minor difference in perspective, for the only facets of patients' lives that are likely to be open to change are those that patients themselves identify as problematic, difficult to live with, and incomprehensible. It is their very incomprehensibility to patients that constitutes them as symptoms that are accessible to psychoanalytic treatment.

Similarly, a dream is just a dream to those who pay dreams no heed; to such people, there is nothing symptomatic about their dreams. But analysands who recount dreams (and sometimes we have to encourage them repeatedly to remember and recount them), characterizing them with adjectives like "bizarre," "perplexing," or "impenetrable," are telling us that they are symptoms for them—mini- or microsymptoms, perhaps, but the more they trouble and perplex our analysands, the more we are justified in treating them as full-blown (albeit short-lived) symptoms. Their seeming impenetrability is what justifies us in assuming the existence of a layer of meaning behind them. For example, the inexplicable attraction or repulsion we feel in them toward someone who in everyday life seems indifferent to us requires us to assume either that we are completely mistaken as to our true feelings about that person or that he or she is standing in for someone else in the context of the dream.

Just as those who suffer from spider phobias often cannot say what it is about spiders that terrifies them, and we find something else—indeed, usually *someone* else (a parent or close relative)—behind the spider once the phobia has been analyzed, so too the Bob who stars in my dream, who is a vague acquaintance of mine from my workplace, may be standing in for someone else: that despised Uncle Bob mentioned in Chapter 2, for instance. The tension and anxiety certain people feel around spiders has little, if anything, to do with spiders themselves and plenty to do with the parent or close relative that spiders have, unbeknownst to them, come to stand for in their psyches. This is what led Freud to claim, similarly, that "the affect felt in a dream stems from its latent and not its manifest content" (SE IV, p. 248); this is why we get nowhere when we attempt to find a connection between the repulsion we feel in a dream and the person who, in the manifest content, repulses us, that person often being someone to whom, in waking life, we feel either indifferent or even drawn.

The Nature of the Latent Content

*There are appetites of a terrible, savage, and lawless kind in every-
one—even in those of us who seem to be entirely moderate. This
surely becomes clear in sleep.*

—Plato, *Republic*, 572a

A dream's latent content generally includes thoughts and wishes that
some part of the dreamer would find too racy, dicey, or immoral to represent directly in a dream. This leads them to be represented indirectly,
in a disguised manner. It is not just our supposedly "realistic" or easily
realizable wishes that seek satisfaction; even our secret and/or "unrealis-
tic" wishes aim at being enacted in dreams in a way that we rarely allow
them to be enacted in everyday, waking life. Yet, if the secret wish that
is realized in a dream were transparently obvious to the part of us that is
"aware" of what is going on in the course of the dream (and this would
seem to be the part of us that is able to consciously remember the dream
when we awaken), we might well become so disconcerted or startled as
to simply wake up.

Freud postulates that secret wishes are fulfilled or come true in
dreams, but they do so only in a disguised manner. Why? To allow us to
go on sleeping. Were we to become even dimly aware of the unsavory
nature of the wishes being fulfilled in our dreams, we would likely wake
up owing to shock or horror in the middle of virtually every dream,[9] and
this would have two interrelated self-defeating effects:

1. It would destroy our health in short order. It is well-known that
   those who are deprived of the sleep cycles that involve dreaming
   (coinciding for the most part with what is referred to in contemporary psychological literature as REM or rapid-eye-movement sleep)
   quickly become irritable, increasingly paranoid, and eventually
   begin to hallucinate.[10] As Freud put it, "All dreams are, in a sense,
   dreams of convenience: they serve the purpose of prolonging sleep
   instead of waking up. *Dreams are the GUARDIANS of sleep and not its
   disturbers*" (SE IV, p. 233), and they resort to disguising their true
   nature so as not to shock us into repeated untimely awakenings.
   The disguises are there to allow us to go on sleeping; when the
   disguises are, as they occasionally are, insufficient—that is, overly
   transparent—we wake up.

2. It would interrupt the fulfillment of the wish in the course of the dream, leaving us far less satisfied and refreshed than we would be if we were able to continue dreaming until the "logical" end of the dream. Most of my readers will probably have had the experience of having been woken up by something or someone in the middle of what they felt to be "a good dream," and of trying to go back to sleep immediately in order to be able to finish the dream. When we are awoken before the end of our dreams, we do not enjoy the satisfaction dreams are designed to provide!

Now, no one need take at face value Freud's claim that the latent content of a dream includes unsavory material; it suffices to free-associate to all of the elements of virtually any of one's own dreams (or to get one's patients to free-associate to all of the elements in their dreams) in order to become convinced that material that is generally left out of one's waking thoughts about oneself shows up in what Freud refers to as the dream's "background thoughts"—in other words, the thoughts that form the backdrop to the dream. One need not be convinced that such thoughts and wishes are repressed, per se, to nevertheless realize that a dream's background thoughts often include the kind of things we would not really want other people to know about us, that we would consider "inappropriate" to bring up in most company, and that we ourselves might not even want to know about.

Freud did not, I would argue, presume that there must be nasty latent thoughts and wishes that go into the construction of all dreams because he had previously concluded that every human being is chock-full of nasty thoughts and wishes. Rather, it was owing to his extensive work with his own dreams as well as with his patients' dreams, based on eliciting their associations to them, that he came to believe there was a considerable hiatus between manifest content and latent content. Anyone can perform the same experiment today, and decide whether or not to come to the same conclusions as Freud did. There is no need to take it as a matter of faith. Indeed, I suspect that most practitioners who give dreams the time of day, so to speak, asking their patients to recount them and associate to them at length, fairly quickly come to many of the same conclusions as Freud did; and that most analysands who learn to remember their dreams and recount them and associate to them extensively in their own analyses soon realize how much more they learn about their own motives, fantasies, and urges from dreams than from virtually anything else.

Freud's hypothesis is that the latent content gives rise to the manifest content through a complicated translation process, the one obvious

[handwritten margin note: Thoughts + wishes → images]

facet of which we have touched on thus far is that thoughts and wishes become translated into images (we shall examine other facets shortly). This translation of ideas into images occurs in rebuses as well, which are games that have been played since at least Roman times, the Romans having been fond of deciphering rebuses during meals. Freud (SE IV, p. 277) proposes that we view a dream as like a rebus: Just as when faced with a rebus like

◊ O

we must work backward from the images to a phrase or sentence (here the usual solution is "diamond ring"), when faced with a dream we must work backward from the manifest content (images) to the latent content (thoughts and wishes). A simple rebus that might appear in a dream is B10 (appearing on a door or license plate, for example), which, when spoken aloud, might be pronounced "bee-ten"—that is, "beaten"—and evoke a violent scene the dreamer once witnessed or experienced. Another is the image of several feet protruding from under something; when asked how many feet there were, the dreamer who replies six may be struck by the notion of death implied by the phrase "six feet under."

Whereas the work that is performed by the dream (known as the *dreamwork*) turns the latent thoughts and wishes into a visual experience, the work that is performed in analysis translates backward from the (text devised to describe the) visual experience to the latent thoughts and wishes. Psychoanalysis thereby performs the exact opposite operation as the dreamwork, "undoing" what the dreamwork has done. What the dreamwork does, psychoanalysis undoes; what the dreamwork veils, psychoanalysis unveils (see Figure 3.1).

[handwritten margin note: undoing]

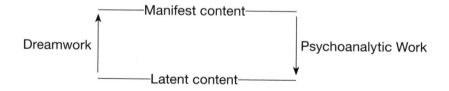

FIGURE 3.1. Psychoanalysis' "Reverse Engineering"

We have here once again a form of reverse engineering,[11] and indeed Freud's entire study of the translation process by which the latent content produces the manifest content of dreams can be understood as a way of figuring out how to take apart this product of the mind to see how it was put together in the first place. His goal, however, is not to be able to then make new dreams himself, but simply to learn how to discern the initial components when faced with the final product.

How to Approach a Dream

What we must take as the object of our attention is not the dream as a whole but the separate portions of its content.
—Freud, SE IV, p. 103

How does Freud approach the text of a dream? In other words, what parts of a dream does he highlight, and how does he even determine what constitutes a "part" of a dream? He furnishes a number of different ways of approaching dreams in order to elicit their backdrop and latent content, one of which involves simply asking the dreamer what occurred during the day prior to the dream. Another way is "to start from phrases that are spoken" in a dream (SE IV, p. 182) to see if the phrases actually come from some other context in either recent experience or from further back in the dreamer's past; for he argues that "whatever stands out markedly as speech in a dream can be traced back to something that has really been said or heard by the dreamer" (SE V, p. 420; other methods he recommends or himself uses will be discussed further on). Such spoken material is often a direct quote of something that was once said to the dreamer, is thrust into a completely foreign context in the fabric of the dream, "and is sometimes no more than an allusion to the occasion on which the remark in question was made" (SE IV, p. 304).

But let us consider a dream in which there are no spoken phrases by examining how Freud (SE IV) handles his own short "dream of the botanical monograph":

> I had written a monograph on a certain plant. The book lay before me and I was at the moment turning over a folded colored plate [a glossy reproduction of a picture]. Bound up in each copy of the book was a dried specimen of the plant, as though it had been taken from a herbarium. (p. 169)

To begin with, Freud tells us what appear to have been *the very first things that popped into his mind* about the dream (a sometimes excellent approach to interpretation): that he had seen a book on a particular kind of flower, cyclamens, in a bookshop window the previous morning; that cyclamens are his wife's favorite flowers; that he felt he had not been bringing his wife cyclamens often enough; and that a woman he had treated some years before, who had run into his wife two days earlier, was disconsolate when her husband once forgot to bring her flowers on her birthday, feeling it signaled that she was no longer as important to him as she had formerly been.

This is already a pretty good start, especially when taken in conjunction with Freud's comment that he had recently mentioned this latter anecdote to a circle of his friends to illustrate the unconscious intentions that may be implicit in the act of "forgetting" (even if popular wisdom would have it that forgetting is by its very nature unintentional).[12] We can probably conclude somewhat safely that—although Freud does not delve into this here (he tells us in several places in *The Interpretation of Dreams* that so as not to reveal too much about himself and his family, he has not included all of his associations in the book)[13]—the dream reminded him of *his* specific reasons for forgetting to bring his own wife flowers more often!

What Freud proceeds to do next is essentially to *cut the dream text up into small portions*—including such fragments as "monograph on a plant," "dried specimen of the plant," "herbarium," "lying before me," "folded colored plate," and so on (SE IV, pp. 169–173, 282–284)—and then associate to each of these fragments as fully as he can (even if he does at one point say, "For reasons with which we are not concerned, I shall not pursue the interpretation of this dream any further," presumably in order not to reveal any more embarrassing things about himself than he had already done by then; p. 173). How does he decide what is an important fragment to associate to? He provides a few indications, but they do not go very far in my view.[14] Whereas a butcher generally decides where to place his knife based on the natural joints in the animal carcass he is carving up (my apologies to vegetarian readers), how is an analyst to know how to divide up the text? What constitutes a significant portion of the dream to which to associate?

Clinicians who are new to psychoanalytic work are, in my experience, especially troubled by the apparent lack of guidelines here. One way of dealing with this is simply to ask about absolutely everything in the dream word by word, but imagine the result of asking someone what comes to mind in relation to the phrase *at the moment* or even just the word *the*! Anyone can locate the principal nouns in a dream—for example, *monograph, plant, book, plate, specimen,* and *herbarium*—and a few of the potentially important adjectives, like *folded, colored,* and *dried*. But who is to say that the verbs (e.g., *written* and *bound up*) and indicators of placement (*before me*) won't lead to useful associations? The fact is that *there is no hard-and-fast rule as to what constitutes an important portion of a dream,* and a given dreamer may associate to virtually anything in a dream, including the very style of the speech with which he or she recounts the dream to you. Many is the dreamer who has told me, "As I was describing it to you just now, I was struck by the way I did so, for it reminded me of when I . . ." or "It reminded me of the way so-and-so described such-and-such recently."

If there is a rule of thumb of any kind to be applied in breaking down a dream into portions (and then asking the dreamer to associate to each of those portions), it is as follows: *The portions we isolate should be words that potentially have more than one meaning* and that when taken out of the context in which they appear in the dream may well make the dreamer think of other contexts. Were we to isolate the word *plant* and repeat it back to Freud, assuming he was a contemporary of ours, a native English speaker, and had had the dream in English, he might think of certain kinds of plants, eggplant, the act of planting, implants of various kinds, a factory, or even a mole (aka "a plant") in an organization placed there, as it were, by a law enforcement agency. The word *plant* in English has a great many different meanings, and our hypothesis is that *although one potential visual representation of the word plant appears in the dream, another potential meaning of the word may be more important in the dream thoughts.*

This falls under the heading of what Freud, in Chapter 6 of *The Interpretation of Dreams*, calls "considerations of representability." Although perhaps sounding mysterious, it is as simple as the following: Let us say that my dream thoughts concern a wish that people around me at work would believe that I am a "plant," in the sense that I have been placed in the organization by a rival corporation or by some other nation's secret service (this would, perhaps, make me feel more important than I currently feel). How can the notion of "plant" in this specific sense be represented pictorially? Only with great difficulty, I think, which means that if the notion is going to appear in the dream, it will have to be in some displaced manner—for example, if I have seen a movie in which a particular actor plays the part of a mole in an organization, that actor may appear in my dream—or via a play on words, that is, through the depiction of a factory, garden plant, or implant of some kind. Many abstract notions, like "justice" (or someone getting what he deserves), are difficult to portray directly in dreams, and may be suggested by such things as the classic image of scales—"the scales of justice"—or even the appearance in a restaurant of a menu that includes only desserts, which is then described by the dreamer as containing "just desserts." A dream image of a cat being released from a sack of some kind may be described by the dreamer as someone "letting the cat out of the bag."

Naturally, it is not individual nouns alone that are polyvalent or

multivalent—that is, that have more than one meaning—and can usefully be highlighted. If the expression "I didn't buy it" appears in a
dream in the context of a shopping spree, "You didn't buy it" might
be repeated back to the dreamer afterward, the idea being that there
might well be something that the dreamer did not "buy"—in the sense of
"didn't believe"—in some recent or earlier experience evoked by the
dream. Plenty of idiomatic expressions in English (and probably in most
other languages as well) allow for more than one meaning, at least literal
and figurative (e.g., "give it to him," "take it back," "take that," "get her
back," etc.). And often even expressions that are usually unambiguous
can become quite ambiguous in context; for example, the simple statement "I closed it" might refer equally well to a deal the dreamer was
describing or to a door she had just mentioned. Often it is enough to
query, "You closed it?" for the dreamer to realize the ambiguity of what
she just said.

To state in more Lacanian terms the rule of thumb about how to
divide up dreams into portions to which to associate, we might say that
we try to break the dream text down into *signifiers*, and signifiers are
not necessarily just individual words but often groups of words with
one or more specific meanings (i.e., *signifieds*). "Diamond ring" is a single signifier, even if each of the words it contains is also a signifier in
its own right. "To beat around the bush" is, similarly, a single signifier;
it is a fixed or invariable expression, which generally cannot be in any
way altered (even if the British are more likely to say "to beat *about* the
bush"), that has a specific meaning.[15] Despite the number of words they
contain, expressions like "Throw in the towel," "Have someone wrapped
around one's little finger," "The grass is always greener . . . ," "That's
the way the cookie crumbles," "When in Rome . . . ," and "How do you
like them apples?" constitute single signifiers insofar as their meaning is
often not transparently obvious based on the words they contain; their
meaning derives from their usage in larger contexts, and they are the
kinds of expressions that often take children and non-native speakers
some time to grasp.

The analyst's goal, therefore, is to isolate ambiguous and/or polyvalent signifiers in a dream, and *repeat them back to the dreamer out of
context*—for example, after the dream has already been recounted and
the dreamer has begun to try to free-associate to it—to see if they bring
any other signifieds to mind. Clinicians who focus exclusively on trying
to "understand" what the analysand is saying—that is, on what they
believe to be his or her intended meaning—may have difficulty taking
a step back from that project and listening for possible ambiguities and

double meanings in what the analysand says. Hearing what people say at two different levels—at the level of what we believe to be the intended meaning and at the level of what people actually say, no matter how confused or equivocal—is a skill that may come easily to certain clinicians, but that others may have to work hard to acquire. They can work toward acquiring this twofold (or "multi-tasking") ability by listening distractedly to talk on the radio or television, focusing less on the "content" than on the form of expression, and listening especially for pauses, slips, slurs, and double entendres (whether intended or not). They can do the same in classes or seminars the content of which bores them, such attention to form often making them somewhat more interested in talks during which they might otherwise have fallen asleep.

Note that, in listening to news announcers, whether on the radio, television, or Internet, and practicing listening for slips, pauses, stumblings, and double entendres as opposed to content, it is perhaps best that they listen first to programs that they are not especially interested in, so that the content does not monopolize their attention. It is perhaps also best at first that they not look at the screen, in the case of television or Internet programs, since seeing the speaker is likely to interfere with their hearing (many analysts have remarked that they hear patients on the couch better than those sitting across from them, not because they are physically closer, but because the analysts are not distracted by their patients' looks, facial expressions, and so on). Once they are able to regularly hear the slips and slurs in speech about matters that are of not much interest to them, they can then turn to programs that are closer to their own hearts, practicing focusing on the sounds newscasters produce as much as possible while still taking in the meaning without dwelling upon it or trying to do anything in particular with it (for example, comparing it with things they heard before or fathoming its implications).

Once this skill is acquired, and clinicians have managed to easily hear both what appears to be the intended meaning (the signified) and the actual, and possibly divergent, form of expression (the signifier), things will never be the same: they will inevitably hear these two different levels in every aspect of their lives, whether in conversations with friends, family, and partners, or in listening to political speeches, lectures, and documentaries. Once turned on, this faculty is not easily turned off! It can be put to good purpose in interpreting dreams (taking certain signifiers out of context to see how they resonate for the analysand) and in psychoanalysis more generally.

I mentioned earlier that Freud proposes several different possible approaches to dreams, including asking the dreamer what had occurred the day or days before the dream and asking about any particular words or phrases enunciated by someone in the dream to attempt to see in what context they originated. A third way of approaching dreams he provides (SE V) concerns hesitations and vacillations in the dream text:

> In analyzing a dream I insist that the whole scale of estimates of certainty be abandoned and that the faintest possibility that something of this or that sort may have occurred in the dream be treated as a complete certainty. . . . Doubt produces an interrupting effect on an analysis that reveals it to be the offspring and instrument of psychical resistance. Psychoanalysis is right to be suspicious of it. One of its rules is that *whatever interrupts the progress of analytic work is a resistance.* (pp. 516–517)

The kind of doubt Freud is referring to here is not the product of some sort of conscious resistance that the analysand can simply turn off if requested to by the analyst. This resistance comes into being of its own accord, as it were, owing to the barrier between the unconscious and consciousness, and the analysand genuinely feels uncertain. How do we handle it?

If, for example, the dreamer cannot decide if a certain color—whether it is of paint, eyes, carpeting, or anything else in a dream—was green or blue, *we take the indecision itself to be particularly significant,* as if the dream thoughts behind that portion of the dream were so laden with unpalatable memories and/or meanings that, even in the remembering of the dream, some subterfuge had to be engaged in in order to throw the now-awake dreamer off the scent. We refuse to be distracted by the analysand's doubt as to whether it was green or blue and take both alternatives extremely seriously, asking for associations to both terms (SE IV, pp. 317–318).

An analysand of mine once recalled a very powerful scene from his past (a scene he professed not to have thought about in a very long time, perhaps not since it occurred some 25 years earlier) simply by associating to the color of an object that appeared in a dream he had had about selecting a notebook in a shop, the notebook being initially described by him as "blue or green." Even though the analysand felt he was correcting the former description ("blue") with the latter ("green"), I encouraged him to associate to both of them; he eventually concluded that the color of the object in the dream was the same as that of the "powder blue" carpet in his dining room growing up. At that point, he suddenly recalled that one day he had been lying on that carpet and had heard sounds coming from the next room; he had gotten up and looked through the louvered doors between the dining room and the family room, where he glimpsed his mother and brother having sex on the floor, their bodies being visually cut into odd horizontal slices by the louvers.

Having recollected this scene thanks to our associative work on the dream, the disturbing images he had been having around that time of partial bodies engaging in sexual acts tapered off. The scene alluded to by this dream element ("blue or green") could hardly have been guessed at from the manifest content of the dream (which initially seemed almost as boring as Freud's dream of the botanical monograph); nevertheless, this early childhood scene seems to have been one of the latent thoughts that went into the construction of the dream.[16] Had I taken the bait and allowed myself to be dissuaded from inquiring into the color owing to its supposed uncertainty, this memory might have taken much longer to come to light, and the distressing images that came with it might have persisted for quite some time.

Another analysand had a dream in which she was holding what she described as either a "file tub" (a sort of plastic tub or box in which to store papers and files) or a "tackle box" (for fishing equipment). Both descriptors led in fruitful directions: the "file tub" reminded her of the filing boxes in which she kept academic papers related to a research project of hers, a project she had grown quite sick of; the "tackle box" recalled the conflictual dynamics of fishing trips she had gone on with her father and brother as a child, her inability to keep lures, weights, and so on organized in her own tackle box, and her current difficulties staying organized in virtually all areas of her life.[17] Both of the alternative descriptions of what she was holding in the dream thus turned out to be important.

We can thus approach dreams in a number of different ways, and may well want to use several if not all of them in our everyday practice:

1) We can begin by asking the dreamer what is the first thing that occurs to him or her about the dream;
2) We can focus on words and/or phrases in the dream, as told to us by the analysand, that have two or more meanings (that are, in other words, ambiguous or polyvalent);
3) We can take idiomatic expressions (like "I didn't buy it") out of the dream context to see if they evoke anything in the dreamer's current life;
4) We can ask about what occurred in the dreamer's life the day or days before the dream was dreamt;

5) We can focus on hesitations and doubts—that is, on things the analysand professes to be unsure of in the dream (was the color green or blue?) or attempts to take back ("No, it wasn't green, it was blue");

6) We can focus on things that are left out of the first telling of the dream and only come to the analysand's mind later, while discussing the dream;

7) We can ask about the places where the scenes in the dream took place, inquiring whether they look familiar to the dreamer and, if so, whether he or she can recall anything that happened in those locales.

How to Get Someone to Associate to a Dream

We should disregard the apparent coherence between a dream's elements as an unessential illusion, and trace back the origin of each of its elements on its own account.

—Freud, SE V, p. 449

As odd as it may seem, what constitutes an "association" is not always crystal clear to analysands or even to analysts who are just beginning to practice. Nor does it always seem transparently obvious to analysts *how* to encourage analysands to free-associate.

How, for example, might we encourage a relatively inexperienced analysand to associate to the word *blue*? We might simply query, "Blue?" or "What about blue?" or even "What comes to mind about blue?" Faced with a shrug of the shoulders or the banal response, "The sky is blue," we might ask whether it seemed to be a particular shade of blue and, if so, can the dreamer describe it. The words with which he then describes it may lead off in a useful direction, but if he is unable to give any details about it, we might then ask whether he recalls ever having seen that particular shade of blue anywhere.

Should the attempt to encourage the dreamer to associate to the color blue go nowhere, there are other equally important avenues to explore, for the word *blue* may also imply melancholy, gloom, or mild depression—in other words, it is a signifier with several different signifieds, and may serve as what Freud calls a "switch-word" or "verbal bridge" from a visual image to an idea, or from one idea (usually a somewhat simple one) to another (SE V, p. 341 n. 1; SE VII, pp. 65 n, 82, and 90; SE X, p. 213). *Blue* may also designate a team (the blue team, for example, as opposed to the red team); it is part of expressions like "black and blue," "out of the blue," "the wild blue yonder," and "the deep blue sea"; it may make one think of "the blues," whether in reference to a musical tradition, a mood, or an army during a particular war (or even of bands like The Moody Blues or The Blues Brothers), or of bluebells (a type of flower), Blue Bonnet (a butter substitute, bluebonnet also being the state flower of Texas), baby blue (which may allude to the topic of having children), sky blue, "Little Boy Blue" (a nursery rhyme), blue balls (a painful male condition), or the homonym *blew*, as in "I blew it"—the list goes on and on. Depending on the analysand, any of these could prove to be extremely useful associations, reminding the analysand, for example, of events of the previous day, weeks, or years, previously unmentioned times in his life, or long-forgotten sexual experiences.

There is no way for the analyst to know in advance whether a particular way of associating to signifiers will be of use in someone's analysis; we can, however, gauge whether a particular way of associating turns out to be useful over the course of time in a specific analysand's work. One analysand may dwell on the letters contained within any particular signifier (*blue* making him think, for example, of *lube* and *lube job* in English or *bleu* and *cordon bleu* in French, *bleu* possibly linking up with the notion of rawness, as it is the term used to describe meat as raw in France, as opposed to medium or well done, and *Cordon Bleu* referring to the famous cooking school or the blue riband of the Order of the Holy Spirit, but *cordon* perhaps alluding to the umbilical cord), and this may lead to useful work; recall that Wolfgang Mozart signed his letters to his sister with a variety of anagrams of his own name, most often Gnagflow Trazom. (We ourselves may want to point to the literal connection between the prominent smile on someone's face in a dream and the fact that the dreamer's name happens to be Miles, of which *smile* is an anagram; see Freud's comments on "the analysis and synthesis of syllables," SE IV, p. 297 n). But another analysand may play around with the letters in a word and never alight upon anything that seems germane either to the dream or to his life experience. An old-fashioned poet (or a fan of Cockney rhyming slang) may usefully think, in connection with *blue*, of slough, brew, flu, stew, chew, hew, or loo, because that is how his mind works in general, whereas for most others such rhyming associations will lead nowhere. One analysand may be productively reminded of the stressful time when he wore blue in the Navy; another may recount a number of occasions on which he wore blue clothing to work in recent weeks, none of which seem to ever connect up with the dream itself.

Some analysands seem to take the invitation to free-associate as license to move further and further away from the dream in a kind of infinite "stream of consciousness." The analyst must thus not lose sight of the fact that the goal of association is to elucidate the backdrop of the dream, and must put a stop to seemingly fruitless trains of thought by calling the analysand back to some other portion of the dream to see if something more productive will arise from associating to other signifiers in it.

When faced with an immediate association on an analysand's part to a particular person in a dream whose looks were initially described as unclear, the analyst would often do well to probe further in order to discern whether in fact the figure in the dream was a collective or "composite figure" (Freud, SE IV, p. 293), which included characteristics of a number of different people (the analyst can do so by simply asking how the analysand would describe this person in the dream, and what features he or she shares with the person in real life who came to mind, and what, if any, features they do not share). The figures who appear in our dreams are often composites. When an analysand indicates that the person in the dream looked like her mother, but she actually had black eyes instead of her mother's blue eyes, and we inquire who she knows with black eyes, she often thinks of someone else.[18] This is a typical product of condensation, a prime example of which is found in Freud's own dream of Irma's injection (SE IV, pp. 106–118 and 292–293) where Irma condenses within herself a half-dozen women, including Freud's own daughter and wife! In many people's dreams, houses that they grew up in play an important role, and certain scenes in the dream often take place in parts of those houses, and yet the rooms simultaneously look somewhat different than they did in reality, alluding thereby to other houses or places as well. In such cases, two or more places or persons in the dreamer's life get conflated into one; each should be elucidated, and they may well turn out to share a characteristic that allowed them to be condensed in the first place. (Freud hypothesizes that two things that get condensed in a dream always have some feature in common.)

How are we to know whether we should be content with the first or second association to a person or place in a dream? We cannot be absolutely sure, and let us recall that, as Freud indicates, we can never "be sure that a dream has been completely interpreted" (SE IV, p. 279), there always being possible further associations that will occur to the analysand a day, a week, or even several years later.[19] Our rule of thumb should be to not necessarily encourage the analysand to move on to some other portion of the dream until we find something that seems to make some sense in terms of what we have thus far heard about her life and history ("It falls into place in the chain of the dreamer's thoughts and its interpretation is recognized by the subject herself"; SE V, p. 360 n), or until we alight upon something that seems to *overturn the sense* we had thus far made of her life and history, bringing with it a new perspective on things.

When the analysand immediately recognizes someone in her dream as a woman at work named Tess whom she barely knows anything about, and about whose looks, voice, position, or anything else she has little to say, it seems worthwhile to ask, "Do you know anyone else named Tess?" "Well, there is, of course, my Aunt Tess," might well be the response, and that Tess is likely to have been of far more importance in her life than the Tess at work. Here the censorship in the dream has used an easy ploy, replacing one Tess with another, in order to disguise the actual content of the dream—this is a perfect example of what Freud calls *displacement,* one Tess appearing in the stead of another. *Condensation* (as in Freud's dream of Irma's injection, where Irma stands in for many different women) and *displacement* are two of the major forms of disguise employed by the dreamwork/censorship to ensure that the unconscious dream thoughts (i.e., wishes) are not openly displayed to consciousness.[20]

Why Are the Wishes in Dreams So Often Counterintuitive?

A thought of something that is wished for is "objectified" in a dream: it is represented or, as it seems to us, experienced as a scene.
—Freud, SE V, p. 534

[margin note: dream → objectified wish]

Like symptoms, dreams are compromise formations: They are a compromise hammered out, in a manner of speaking, between (a) wishes that are unconscious and (b) the kind of semiwaking consciousness we have in the course of a dream (insofar as some part of us is aware of what is happening during the dream and can often remember what has happened after we wake up), which would be shocked by many of our unconscious wishes were they presented and fulfilled without any form of disguise. The second party to the compromise—the part of us that is attending to what is happening in the dream scenario and is imbued with some sense of right and wrong—is the reason for what Freud refers to as "the censorship" that disguises the unconscious wishes. The censorship acts in such a way that the unconscious wishes (which are imbued with no moral sense or conscience) become unrecognizable to the second party's semiwaking consciousness. The censorship thus constitutes an intermediary, go-between, or third party to dream construction.

Freud's model of the human mind is thus that it is not monolithic but rather multilayered, including conscious, preconscious, and unconscious (or conscious, censorship, and unconscious, since in his work on dreams he tends to equate the preconscious with the censor). To illustrate the structure of the psyche, Freud constructs an analogy between what goes on in the dreamer and what went on in the publishing world and postal system at his time. Postal censorship was such that a letter writer would write what he wanted to say, but then an official *censor* would go through what he had written and black out any parts of it that might be considered incendiary or unacceptable to the current regime in power, before it would be delivered to its addressee (SE IV, p. 142 n. 3). In order to avoid having his work censored outright, a letter writer or journalist would often be forced to disguise his ideas by speaking

> in allusions instead of direct references, or [concealing] his objectionable pronouncement beneath some apparently innocent disguise: for instance, he might describe a dispute between two Mandarins in the Middle Kingdom, when the people he really has in mind are officials in his own country. (p. 142)

Authors were thus driven to allusion, allegory, and displacement in order to get their message across to those who knew how to read it. This was as true in Freud's time as it was in Jonathan Swift's time (see his 1726 *Gulliver's Travels*) and as it is in certain countries (like China) even in the 21st century.

This state of affairs can be represented as follows, where we see the censor situated between the author and his or her public:

Public
———
Censor
———
Author

Insofar as the unconscious is the "author" of a dream, the preconscious plays the role of the filtering censor, which distorts the author's original message before allowing it to come to the dreamer's attention (the preconscious thus is not in and of itself a creative faculty, but rather a defensive one).

Public	Conscious
Censor	Preconscious
Author	Unconscious

Did Freud employ this analogy simply to illustrate his model of the mind, or did he in fact arrive at his theory of the different mental agencies (the

German, *Instanzen*, could also be rendered as mental "instances"; Freud also, and perhaps more felicitously, calls them "systems"; see, in particular, SE V, pp. 537 and 568, and in general the whole of Chapter 7) at least in part because of the kind of censorship that went on in his era?

We might ask a similar question about the physicists Ernest Rutherford and Niels Bohr: Did they arrive at the notion that an atom has a nucleus surrounded by electrons independently, or was it by analogy with the structure of the solar system (i.e., the nucleus is to the electrons in an atom as the sun is to the planets that revolve around it)?

$$\frac{\text{Nucleus}}{\text{Electrons}} \qquad \frac{\text{Sun}}{\text{Planets}}$$

Whatever the case may be, analogical thinking is common in many fields, and even if the Rutherford–Bohr model has been in many ways superseded, it certainly helped advance thinking in physics at the time. In Freud's case, postal and other forms of public censorship may have been decisive in shaping his thinking on the structure of the psyche, or may simply have supplied a useful analogy by which to illustrate his model of the mind when presenting it to his readers.

Referring back to the models we discussed in Chapter 1, we could designate the bar between two sets of memories (M1—M2—M3 and M4—M5—M6) as the censorship between unconscious wishes (on the left-hand side) and conscious dream experience (on the right-hand side), dream distortion, in the form of condensation and displacement, being what allows for the crossing of the bar:

unconscious wishes   conscious dream experience
$$\text{M1—M2—M3} \quad | \quad \text{M4—M5—M6}$$
censorship
condensation + displacement

And insofar as a dream, like a bungled action or symptom, is a compromise formation (SE V, pp. 517, 596–597, and 676; SE XV, p. 66), we could also represent a dream as a product of two warring forces or selves, censorship being necessary to reconcile the two parties (as a sort of convoluted peace treaty, we might say, wherein the right hand does not know what the left hand is doing):

(Unconscious wish) Force 1 $\Rightarrow$ Dream $\Leftarrow$ Force 2 (Moral conscience)

"Bad self" $\Rightarrow$ Dream $\Leftarrow$ "Good self"

What Freud adds to the political analogy of censorship is that each of us plays all three parts and therefore engages in self-censorship! Going against the grain of the dreamer's impression, which is that she (as semiwaking consciousness) is the simple spectator or witness of what goes on in her dreams, Freud asserts that we must realize that *we are, fundamentally, all of these different layers*—author, censor, and public; unconscious, preconscious, and conscious. We cannot shirk responsibility for unseemly wishes, and argue, "*I* would never even dream of such a thing!" because we have in fact just dreamt of such a thing and no one (presumably) put it in our heads for us.

To Freud's way of thinking, subjectivity includes all of these different layers. The subject is all of these things: (a) the urges, (b) the part of us that wants to know nothing about those urges, and (c) the part of us that would morally censure those urges severely if it were so unfortunate as to hear about them. Many analysands come to analysis with the sense that they have nothing to do with the form taken by their dreams, and that they are innocent bystanders to what happens in them, as it were, or victims of them when they are nightmares or "bad dreams." As one of my analysands put it, "A dream just happens to me—it's not something I have a part in." As another analysand put it, "I'm a victim of my dreams." And, indeed, our vernacular embodies this perspective insofar as we commonly say in English, "I had a dream," not "I made a dream," as they say in French.

This sense of being a simple witness to our dreams is responsible for the refusal, on many people's parts, to believe that their dreams (and even many of their nightmares) satisfy their wishes, because they do not identify with the wishes that appear to be satisfied in their dreams—as, for example, when a dream openly depicts the death of someone of whom they believe they are fond—feeling that they could never possibly wish for any such thing. Yet Freud shows, in many different texts, that we each *identify* with numerous persons from our pasts and persons around us in the present (SE IV, pp. 149–150 and 323; SE XIX, pp. 28–33), and take on their own urges and desires as if they were our own. Superficially speaking, we come to desire many of the same consumer commodities, trendy neighborhoods, "top" colleges, fine restaurants, and experiences that they tell us they desire; and we may even become attracted to people they are attracted to, even though there was nothing that initially drew us to them. This is so true that we may well say that *the wishes fulfilled in our dreams are, at times, not our own but are rather those of the people around us.*[21]

Lacan, following Freud's work on identification, states this still more plainly when he says that "man's desire is the Other's desire," by which he means, at least in part, that each of us ends up desiring many of the same things that those around us desire, and even ends up desiring those things in the same way as those other people desire them. It is as if we were—in some important way—those other people, as if we were the same as or identical to them. Insofar as the desires satisfied in our dreams seem not to be our own but rather those of people around us, we can conclude that we have assimilated their desires—that is, *those desires have become our own unbeknownst to us.*[22]

Now, this is as true of the desires fulfilled in our dreams as it is of the urges that are involved (and at times even at war with each other) in our symptoms: These desires and urges seem foreign to us, for we are not aware that we have identified with those whose desires and urges they originally were, and we may even be horrified at the idea that we could possibly have identified with such hated figures! This is so common that I would propose that we always keep in mind, as we attempt to interpret dreams and symptoms, the old Latin expressions—so useful to police inspectors and other crime solvers—*cui bono* and *cui prodest*. The latter is short for *cui prodest scelus is fecit* (he who benefits from the crime committed it), which is found in Seneca's classical play *Medea* (verses 499–501), and it implies that the guilty party is often the one who gains by the crime. *Cui bono* suggests that he who did the crime is he who profits from it.[23] The urges within us that seem so foreign to us and yet are played out and satisfied in certain dreams may have come to us from other people—others who, if we think about it, might well vicariously enjoy what goes on in our dreams (how dare they!).

Insofar as so many of our symptoms are ostensibly self-defeating or self-destructive—whether they involve continually arriving late for work, not paying attention to what we are doing and repeatedly hurting ourselves "accidentally" (this sometimes goes by the euphemistic name of "clumsiness"), reckless driving, drinking to excess, cutting ourselves deliberately, taking ever-higher doses of potentially lethal drugs, depriving ourselves of nourishment, destroying our own health through over-work, or any combination of the aforementioned activities—*we should always wonder who around us might be happy or might have been happy* (and I don't mean consciously or explicitly happy) *were we to self-destruct:* for example, lose our jobs, waste away to nothing, overdose, or contract a potentially fatal sexually transmitted or other illness.

A parent, sibling, or other family member has often communicated to us, whether directly or indirectly at one point or another in our lives (per-haps many years in the past), that they would prefer we not be around and that our presence bothers them, cramps their style, or positively drives them crazy. For many of us, one or more people in our past have given us the distinct impression, at one point or another, that they would prefer we not succeed in our endeavors (or at least that we not surpass them or leave them behind), that we be miserable, that we fail to thrive, and perhaps even that we disappear forever. (Given the frequency with which we ourselves wish, at one time or another, that others would fail or disappear, we should not be surprised that we ourselves have sensed the same thing from other people!) Hence when what we believe to be our greatest wishes are thwarted in a dream, we should always consider who around us seemed to want to stifle us and entertain the possibility that we have, for better or for worse, identified with their apparent desire to stifle us. Identifying who it was does not, naturally, fix the problem, but the problem most certainly cannot be fixed until we at least reckon with the fact that we are inhabited by what we believe to have been his or her desire, with the fact that this desire is inside us, part of us.

It quite often happens, curiously enough, that we identify with people's ill wishes or death wishes toward us and that we indeed enact them in our dreams and symptoms. We do the same with their at times adamant, passionate criticism of us and will to punish us for our short-comings and/or disobedience; we take that criticism and will to punish into ourselves in the form of the superego, which Freud views as getting its wishes fulfilled in what he calls masochistic "punishment dreams" (SE V, p. 476; see especially n. 2) and in certain symptoms as well. Freud comments that the wishes fulfilled in dreams

> must bring pleasure; but the question then arises, "To whom?" To the person who has the wish, of course. But, as we know, a dream-er's relation to his wishes is quite peculiar. He repudiates them and censors them—he has no liking for them, in short. So that their ful-fillment will give him no pleasure, but just the opposite; and expe-rience shows that this opposite appears in the form of anxiety. . . . Thus a dreamer, in his relation to his dream-wishes, can only be compared to an amalgamation of two separate people. . . . [And if] two people are not at one with each other, the fulfillment of the wish of one of them may bring nothing but unpleasure to the other. (pp. 581–582 n. 1)

Dreams that seem, on the face of them, to be self-destructive and symptoms that seem self-defeating may also be *designed to thwart the wishes of those around us.* Freud mentions a dream by one of his patients that seemed to thwart the wish of a friend of hers to be invited to the dreamer's house for a dinner party (this dream, told by "the butcher's wife," is quite complex and has led to considerable commentary; SE IV, pp. 146–151); her sense in the dream, and in telling Freud about it, was that her own desire (to throw a dinner party) was thwarted, and yet we might say that in it she thwarted her friend's desire as though it were her own or that she thwarted her own desire as though it were her friend's.[24]

An analysand of mine would manage to get so worked up about doing well at his job that he would sleep little and end up performing somewhat poorly; not surprisingly, he felt he was knocking himself out trying to succeed in a field he did not enjoy because his relatives wanted him to, they believing he was especially well equipped for such work and predestined to do it. They had, moreover, used their influence to help him get ahead in this field in a way he felt he did not deserve, and his symptom (tremendous anxiety over tiny work-related details that stopped him from sleeping) seemed designed to prove them wrong, thwart their wishes, and to reassert control over his own destiny, even if that meant failing at his current job. His behavior was symptomatic, insofar as it bothered him and he could not fathom why he was engaging in it; yet it seemed designed above all to foil the designs of those who had pushed him into his present career. We could say that it satisfied one of his wishes—his wish to thwart theirs—even as it simultaneously impeded others.

Analysands often find the wishes expressed in such symptoms and dreams counterintuitive, not even being dimly aware at the outset that they still harbor such resentment against those who pushed them in certain directions in life. They often consciously believe they owe their relatives a debt of gratitude, not hatred, and are astonished that they seem willing (in dreams and symptoms) to cut off their own noses to spite their relatives' faces, as it were.

An Unconscious Wish Is Formulated in a Complete Sentence (or, The Unconscious Is Structured Like a Language)

> *The construction of dreams is subject to the condition that it can only represent something which is the fulfillment of a wish and that it is only from wishes that dreams can derive their psychical motor force.*
> —Freud, SE V, p. 487

> *It is only too easy to forget that [the wish in] a dream is, as a rule, merely a thought like any other.*
> —Freud, SE XIX, p. 112

Spiteful and self-punishing dreams make for a ready-made introduction to the notion that an unconscious wish fulfilled in a dream can often be stated in the form of a complete sentence, like one of the following, which might apply to the dreamer him- or herself or to someone depicted or alluded to in the dream:

- "I wish he would fall flat on his face!" or "I hope he comes a cropper!"
- "Would that he fall in a manhole and disappear forever!" or "If only he would disappear!"
- "I hope he has a heart attack and dies!"
- "If only someone would attack him and he be fatally injured!"
- "If only a tidal wave would come ashore and wash her house away with her in it!"
- "If only a riptide would wash him out to sea!"
- "Would that she, in all her crazy sexual escapades, catch a sexually transmitted disease and die a horrible death!"
- "If only I could kill my father and my brother, I could have my mother and my sister to myself!" (This was the verbatim conclusion formulated by an analysand who dreamt that he killed first one soldier and then a second in one scene, and then in a subsequent scene found himself in the arms of a woman who resembled his mother in a specific way, he having recently had "a group hug" with her and a younger woman.)

These are all wishes from dreams analysands have told me—I could extend the list almost ad infinitum—and we see that these initially unconscious, repudiated wishes are articulated in everyday language just as our conscious thoughts and wishes are. They are formulated in language in the very same way that certain of our conscious wishes are (with such openings as "If only . . ." or "Would that . . ."), for example:

- "If only I could win the lottery!"
- "Would that my teacher not notice that I copied half my paper from a book and the other half from a website!"
- "If only he would finally notice me and ask me out!"
- "If only I could get into my top-choice college. . . ."
- "I hope that policeman didn't notice I didn't come to a full stop at that sign back there."

As we interpret dreams, we are looking for just such a formulation of one or more of the wishes that went into the construction of the dream, wishes that can be expressed in everyday language in the form of a more or less grammatically complete sentence (at times, the formulation can be as simple as "to be *x*"—whether *x* is "rich," "famous," "good-looking," "young again," "like so-and-so," "able to do things over again," or what have you—where it is implied that the analysand would really like that: "Oh, to be able to start over!"). This requires a kind of synthetic thinking on our part (after all the analytic thinking involved in breaking the dream down into small portions and associating to each of them) where we must now attempt to see the forest and not simply the ✶ individual trees. Lacan (Seminar VI, p. 71) commented, already in 1958, that analysts no longer knew how to decipher the wishes in dreams, and that this had led them to no longer be interested in dreams. Deciphering wishes is a creative process and can, indeed, be quite challenging at times! It is when we are unable to formulate anything in the dream in the form of a wish that we need to either encourage the analysand to continue to associate to the dream, work harder at reconstructing the wish in it, or let the dream go and hope that the next one will be more productive, transparent, or inspiring.[25]

It is the fact that in many instances we *can* arrive at a formulation of one or more of the wishes in a dream (and for that matter in daydreams, slips of the tongue, and other symptoms as well) that led Lacan to assert that "the unconscious is structured like a language" (see, for example, *Écrits*, p. 737),[26] for unconscious thoughts and wishes are made of the same stuff as our conscious thoughts and wishes—namely, language (including its signifiers and its grammar). And this is also what allowed Freud (SE V, p. 613) to make what was a startling claim at his time: Thinking can and does go on at a level outside of consciousness, and fully formed ideas and ✶ wishes come into being in us unbeknownst to us.

As shocking and dismaying as this was and still is to certain philosophers, it has been recognized since time immemorial in everyday speech; for in English, when faced with a conundrum, we might say, "Let me sleep on it," while in French one commonly says, *"La nuit porte conseil"*—literally, nighttime will bring good counsel, and more figuratively, the answer or solution will come to you while you sleep.

How *Not* to Approach a Dream

I should like to utter an express warning against overestimating the importance of symbols in dream-interpretation, against restricting the work of translating dreams merely to translating symbols, and against abandoning the technique of making use of the dreamer's associations.[27]

—Freud, SE V, pp. 359–360

Freud's method of interpreting dreams is not the old "symbolic method" whereby one takes the dream as a whole and makes a story out of it, above all regarding the future; this method is illustrated in the interpretation in the Old Testament of the pharaoh's dream of the seven fat cows and the seven skinny cows, which is taken to refer to the coming of seven years of plenty followed by seven years of famine. For most of us today, dreams do not predict the future except insofar as they perhaps make us aware of certain things that we want that we did not know we wanted, which we may then act on in the future.

Nor does Freud employ the old "decoding method," whereby the moon, for example, has the same meaning for every dreamer (regardless of age, culture, station in life, or anything else), serving as a kind of universal symbol. Anyone who had a copy of the official codebook could, in theory, for those who believed in this method, look up each of the symbols and construct a proper interpretation of a dream. The decoding method implied that if two different people had a dream including most of the same elements, it had much the same meaning for both of them. It also suggested that the interpretation arrived at by different interpreters should be identical, since they were all using the same codebook. The only question, then, concerned whether or not one had the proper codebook, and indeed whether any one codebook was better than any other.[28]

Freud broke utterly and completely with this tradition by maintaining that an image of the moon in someone's dream means whatever that person associates with it. And even if many people from the same culture may associate much the same thing with the moon, this is not necessarily the case, some being more inclined to think of blue moon (an astronomical event or the eponymous novel, song, or movie), others of Reverend Moon, and still others of Neil Armstrong, werewolves, vampires, zombies, menstruation, "Moon River," or mooning.

Yet, insofar as Freud recommends that we rely *not* on our own personal associations to elements in someone's dream but rather on the dreamer's own associations to them, different interpreters should still, at least in theory, come to more or less the same conclusions about the meaning of the dream. If the interpretation depended solely or primarily on the interpreter's associations, every interpreter would come up with something different. Working almost exclusively with the dreamer's own associations removes an element of *arbitrariness* from our interpretations of analysands' dreams (this is why we ask open-ended questions like, "What does 'moon' bring to mind?" or "What about 'moon'?" or "Why do you think the moon appeared in your dream?"). In practice, different analysts obviously devote more or less time to working with their analysands on any one particular dream, and to associating to any one specific signifier in the dream, and hence their interpretations may well differ because they end up eliciting different associational material. Nevertheless, they are all working at least primarily from the same dream text and from most of the same associations.[29] Reconstructing the wish or wishes in a dream is challenging, however, requiring a great deal of creative thinking on the analyst's part, and some analysts obviously have more facility with this than others. The best (and least arbitrary) way of working is no doubt, once numerous associations have been teased out, to begin by asking the analysand if he or she can now see any sort of wish in the dream.

Freud did himself a disservice, I would argue, when, under the influence of some of his colleagues,[30] he began to claim that we could interpret people's dreams on the basis of the general meaning of symbols in a culture. See, in this connection, *The Interpretation of Dreams*, Chapter VI, Section E, "Representation by Symbols in Dreams," virtually all of which was added after 1909, where Freud admits that "we shall feel tempted to draw up a new 'dream-book' on the decoding principle" (SE V, p. 351).[31] Much of the harshest criticism of psychoanalysis arose from the reductionistic tendency on analysts' part to dispense with patients' associations and interpret everything as some kind of universal symbol: "All elongated objects, such as sticks, tree-trunks, and umbrellas . . . may stand for the male organ, as well as all long sharp weapons, such as knives, daggers, and pikes" (p. 354). This inspired Melanie Safka's ironic line "A thing's a phallic symbol if it's longer than it's wide" in her 1970 antipsychoanalytic folk song "Glory Glory Psychotherapy."[32]

Freud also lapses at times, above all in this section of *The Interpretation of Dreams* that was added well after its first publication, into a type of interpreting that considers its job done as soon as a sexual interpretation of a dream-element is arrived at, or as soon as, in associating to some part of a dream, the analysand arrives at something connected to the analysand's father or mother—as if sex and mommy and daddy were the "ultimate meanings" of everything in dreams (though Freud does tell us about one dream in which, although "normally a dream deals with rebellion against someone else, behind whom the dreamer's father is concealed, the opposite was true here," SE V, p. 436). Yet the appearance of a bush in a dream need not always, nor perhaps even usually, allude to a woman's pubic hair; George or Jeb Bush may be lurking somewhere behind it, as may the Australian outback, the expressions "a bird in the hand is worth two in the bush" or "to beat around the bush," or even the partial homonyms *tush, mush, push*, or *Bolshevik*. Similarly, a so-called phallic symbol, like the Washington Monument in D.C., could lead to associations related to terrorism, rather than (or at least in addition) to sexual topics.[33]

Many of the dreams Freud interprets in *The Interpretation of Dreams* seem not to lead in either a sexual or Oedipal direction, at least as far as he takes them for us there (see, for example, SE IV, pp. 127–130, and SE V, p. 510), suggesting that the stereotype of the reductionistic analyst may come more from later practitioners than from Freud himself. Regarding the role of sexuality in dreams, Freud (SE V) writes as follows:

> The majority of the dreams of adults deal with sexual material [because] no other drive has been subjected since childhood to as much suppression as the sexual drive . . . ; from no other drive are so many and such powerful unconscious wishes left over, ready to produce dreams in a state of sleep. (p. 396)

And research on sleep over the last several decades might be understood to corroborate Freud's view here, inasmuch as it shows that during REM sleep, the sleep state most closely associated with dreaming, women generally experience clitoral arousal and men erections. Nevertheless, Freud adds that "we should also, of course, avoid the exaggeration of attributing exclusive importance to" sexual drives (SE V, p. 396). He observes, on the next page in a passage added in 1919 (mentioned here in an earlier footnote), that "the assertion that all dreams require a sexual interpretation, against which critics rage so incessantly, occurs nowhere in my *Interpretation of Dreams*" (p. 397; see also SE XXII, p. 8), where one instead finds many dreams whose interpretations have nothing to do with sexuality (see, for example, SE IV, pp. 127–130, and SE V, p. 510).

Similarly, although Freud maintains that "the deeper one carries the analysis of a dream, the more often one comes upon traces of experiences in childhood which have played a part among the sources of that dream's latent content" (SE IV, p. 198), the words "more often" imply "not always," and Freud discusses many dreams that are never traced back to childhood sources (see, for example, SE IV, pp. 248–250, and SE V, p. 510). Yet by the end of *The Interpretation of Dreams*, he waxes more categorical, proffering that every wish involves wishes dating back to childhood (SE V, pp. 553–554), despite what he himself has shown in the course of his book.

Freud's most overriding point—and the one I personally feel is of most enduring clinical relevance—is that the meaning of each dream-element is different for each individual, and that we cannot know what that meaning is in advance, before soliciting that individual's associations. Still, many of the people in a specific culture who speak the same language are likely to associate similar things with certain symbols. For example, a swastika is likely to have at least some of the same connotations for a large number of people in Europe. And each tongue has its own dream language, in the sense that if a piece of furniture known as a stool appears in the dream of a native English speaker, it is always possible that it may have at least two meanings (turd and barstool or step stool); and if a wooden stud appears, it may have as many as five other possible meanings. An English speaker who hears herself describe someone in her dream as having leaned over backward is likely to be reminded of the expression "to bend over backward for someone," an association that would not occur to a non-English-speaking French woman (for whom the more or less equivalent idiomatic expression meaning-wise would be *"se mettre en quatre"*: literally, to break oneself into four).

In the best of cases, the kinds of interpretations Freud proposed based on "symbols" were made only when the dreamer had no associations of her own to offer (SE V, p. 360 n. 1, and p. 372); and his interpretations were based primarily on Viennese idiomatic expressions or proverbs that were known to virtually everyone he worked with (much like the euphemism "deflowering" and the expression "filthy rich" are known to virtually all Americans of a certain age and educational background; see SE IV, p. 200). This led Freud to propose we "adopt a combined technique, which, on the one hand, rests on the dreamer's associations and, on the other, fills the gaps [in the dreamer's associations] with the interpreter's knowledge of symbols" (SE V, p. 353)—with the caveat, nevertheless, that dream-symbols "frequently have more than one or even several meanings, and, as with Chinese script, the correct interpretation can only be arrived at on each occasion from the context" (p. 353). We can also note that when Freud interprets dreams to which his patients seem to have had few if any associations, he generally bases his conjectures on extensive knowledge of the patients' backgrounds, upbringing, and current life situation, not on universal symbols.[34]

In one of my own cases, the dreamer was an avid reader of romance novels and dreamt of a cat that "arched its back." Although she initially had no associations to the dream, when I reiterated the words "arched its back" out of context—that is, not in connection with anything else in the dream—she immediately thought of orgasm (a woman arching her back is apparently a common image for a woman experiencing an orgasm in romance novels, making it part of what Freud calls "firmly established linguistic usage" [SE V, p. 342], at least in that specific context) and proceeded to tell me about her frustration with her sexual partner, other things in the dream then reminding her of that same frustrating partner.[35]

Overdetermination: A Simple Example

Productions of the dreamwork . . . are not made with the intention
of being understood.
                                        —Freud, SE V, p. 341 (emphasis in the original)

*Dreams, like all other psychopathological structures, regularly have
more than one meaning.*
                                        —Freud, SE IV, p. 149

One of my analysands told me the following very short dream: "My
cousin accidentally killed her husband." When I inquired if there were
not anything at all that she recalled in addition to that, she added, "She
killed him in the bathroom."

A first level of meaning arose from the simple fact that my analysand
did not like her cousin's husband and would have liked him out of the
way (thus, a conscious wish for his elimination). A second level of meaning arose from the fact—which became obvious as soon as I asked for
the names of the characters in the dream—that my analysand's first name
was the same as her cousin's. This analysand had, for some time prior
to the dream, complained bitterly about her own husband, which suggested that the dream simultaneously satisfied her wish to kill her own
husband (a rather less consciously acknowledged wish), the killer in the
dream condensing two figures—her cousin and herself—and the victim
condensing both the cousin's husband and the analysand's own husband.

A third level of meaning arose from the location of the murder. When
I asked about the bathroom, the analysand told me that it resembled the
bathroom in the house where she had lived in her prepubescent years.
Had anything memorable ever occurred there? I asked. The analysand
then recalled—for the first time in some 20 years—that her father had
slapped her mother in that bathroom. Why? She could not remember at
first, but then it came to her that it was because her oldest sister had
used their father's razor to shave her legs.

This led to a long discussion of the father's rages, of her own hatred of
her father, and of her mother's hatred of her father. "If only my mother
had killed my father (with the razor) in that bathroom," the dream
seemed to say, "my sister and I would have suffered so much less at his
hands and at the hands of men like him." Here we had stumbled upon a
still less conscious, possibly unconscious, wish.

All three wishes seemed to have found fulfillment in this very short,
highly condensed dream, where the killer stands for three different

women and the victim for three different men. The killer and the victim were thus "nodal points" (SE IV, pp. 317–318; see also SE II, p. 290) in the manifest content on which several different dream-thoughts in the latent content converged. Could we say that there was some ultimate meaning to the dream? Why would we when it seems that all three meanings are relevant and resonate with the analysand? This corroborates Freud's claim that dreams, like other symptoms, often have multiple meanings—in a word, they are "overdetermined" (SE V, p. 569).

Tools for Interpretation

There is no way of deciding at first glance whether any element that admits of a contrary is present in the dream-thoughts as a positive or as a negative.

—Freud, SE IV, p. 318

Freud provided numerous different tools by which to locate wishes in dreams, based on the fundamental principle that what accounts for the unrecognizability of the wishes fulfilled in them is that they are disguised. Not allowing ourselves to be fooled by the manifest content, we must work our way back to the latent content, and to do so we may have to take dream-elements differently than they initially present themselves: We may need to view them figuratively instead of literally, hypothesize that one element is standing in for its opposite (e.g., a crowd of people standing in for no one or just one crucial witness, or love standing in for hatred), associate to the words themselves (their form or possible anagrams) rather than to their usual meaning(s), and so on. As Freud puts it:

> A dream never tells us whether its elements are to be interpreted literally or figuratively, or whether they are to be connected with the material of the dream-thoughts directly or through the intermediary of some interpolated phraseology. In interpreting any dream-element it is in general unclear
>
> (a) whether it is to be taken in a positive or negative sense . . . ,
> (b) whether it is to be interpreted historically (as a recollection),
> (c) whether it is to be interpreted symbolically, or
> (d) whether its interpretation should depend on its wording. (SE V, p. 341)

We can view this as a list of heuristic devices by which to arrive at an interpretation (adding to it that what stands out most to the dreamer may well be a screen, proving to be less important in the interpretation of the dream than other elements or scenes; see SE IV, p. 305), but we might also wonder about the apparent lack of hard-and-fast rules about how to interpret individual dream-elements—that is, about how to use these tools and devices.

As a practitioner myself, I would argue that individual analysands tend to employ the same kind of disguises again and again in their dreams—something being turned into its opposite, for example—and that we come to learn whether it is condensation, displacement, reversal into its opposite, or anagrams that are most germane to interpreting a particular analysand's dreams (without forgetting that as such disguises are seen through again and again, the censorship may, over time, resort to new and different masks; this means that people's dreams do not necessarily become easier to decipher the longer they are in analysis). And let us note, first, that a similar set of interpretive tools is available to those who study literature, poetry, film, and other products of human creativity, going by names like metaphor, metonymy, analogy, allegory, symbolism, hyperbole, parable, periphrasis, hyperbaton, ellipsis, suspension, anticipation, retraction, negation, digression, irony, catachresis, litotes, antonomasia, and hypotyposis (see Lacan, *Écrits*, p. 433), without it being stipulated in advance which (if any) of these has been employed (wittingly or not) by the creative artist. The interpreter or literary, film, or art critic must try various approaches and see which yields fruit, which in this context means that it yields a provocative and perhaps even a compelling reading of the creative work.

In a less theoretical vein, we might consider how we try—in a rough and ready way—to see through the attempts made by those around us, whether friends, acquaintances, colleagues, or politicians, to disguise thoughts and wishes in everyday life. Certain friends of ours may tell us that we look tired or upset when it is they themselves who are tired and depressed, engaging in *projection*. (An analysand once opined that she was "worried this is just a fling for him"—her new partner—when she was actually preoccupied with the question of whether it was just a fling for her.) Other people tell us that everything is "just fine" when things are anything but fine (and the less fine they are, the more often and insistently they repeat that they're "just fine"), or that they are "so happy to see us" precisely when they are not, hiding the truth behind its opposite. Still others complain bitterly about politicians and government policies (about which there is assuredly plenty to complain) when what seems to be really irking them is their home life, engaging in some run-of-the-mill displacement.

Here are a couple of specific examples of acquaintances of mine. One is a musician who often complains bitterly that, because of her husband's preferences, she is stuck out in the countryside where *he* wants to live, whereas if she were in the kind of major metropolis where *she* says she would like to live, she could make it big in the world of music. Curiously enough, when she had the opportunity to spend part of every week in a major metropolis, she did not act on it. Speaking at another time, in a context unrelated to where people live, about a mutual friend, she proffered that only a small percentage of musicians actually make it to the big time, and that our friend is unsure he has the requisite talent. I began to wonder if in fact she was afraid that *she* might not make it as a musician even if she moved to the big city, and found it safer and more satisfying to be able to blame her lack of success on her husband than it would be to give it her all and potentially fall flat on her face. The world is, after all, full of people who blame their failure and dissatisfaction on someone other than themselves. And how else could we explain her failure to spend part of every week in a nearby city when the opportunity arose?

Another acquaintance complained bitterly to me about one of her daughters-in-law, the one who had married her favorite son. She maintained that no one liked this daughter-in-law—and, indeed, the list she gave me of those who disliked her was quite extensive, as if she needed to prove (and perhaps indeed overprove) that she was not the only one who felt that way about her. This acquaintance eventually came around to telling me that this daughter-in-law treats her own daughter very badly, a daughter who rather closely resembles my acquaintance. Might it not be that at least part of her dislike for her daughter-in-law derived from her identification with her daughter-in-law's daughter, who she felt was mistreated by her mother—just like my acquaintance felt she was mistreated by her own mother? We can perhaps see here a certain quantum of *projection* onto her daughter-in-law of her feelings toward her own mother.

An analysand I had been working with for some two years admitted, at one point, that he preferred to pity himself for having had a difficult childhood owing to his connection with a church (and he elected to spend the lion's share of his time petitioning that church as an adult), rather than put his precociously discovered artistic abilities to the test. He indicated, too, that he preferred to lament his uninspired marriage and less-than-perfect wife than find out whether he could actually make things work with the women in his life who truly inspired him. Here again, fears are covered over when blame for one's dissatisfaction in life is displaced onto others. Such distortions of the truth often fool friends and family, and sometimes even fool the tellers of such stories for a time, they coming to believe their own oft'-repeated versions of their personal history.

Governments and corporations regularly give altruistic and/or patriotic reasons for actions that are actually motivated by interests that are anything but praiseworthy, such reasons being designed to divert our attention from their real motives. A young child sometimes throws a fit when her mother leaves her at day care or school, but then settles down and begins to have fun as soon as her mother is gone; she feels that she has to put on a show for her mother, believing the mother wants her to feel bereaved when she leaves (perhaps to convince the mother of her importance in her child's life).[36] As we saw in Chapter 2, worry about someone often indicates the opposite of what it ostensibly manifests: It indicates aggressive impulses instead of loving ones (see SE IV, pp. 260 and 267). Similarly, in dreams, the *fear* of having left the house not completely or not at all dressed may well indicate its opposite: a *desire* to show one's body off to others, the kind of desire children often spontaneously satisfy by running around naked.

I hope these examples go some way toward showing that the kinds of disguises and distortions Freud recommends we be on the lookout for when we interpret dreams (and symptoms) are the very same disguises and distortions rampant in everyday life. On the stage of life, as on that "other stage" (the *andere Schauplatz*) of the dream world (see, for example, SE V, p. 536), things are often not what they seem, and people lie to others and to themselves all the time!

This still does not immediately tell us which form of disguise is being used in which specific case, and thus there is something a bit ad hoc about psychoanalytic method: Sometimes we need to look for a displacement (blaming one's spouse instead of oneself), sometimes a projection (seeing one's own mother in one's daughter-in-law), and sometimes we must notice that a show of despair at parting disguises joy (a smothered child being dropped off at school). Sometimes we have to turn an element around into its opposite to understand what it means; for example, my brother being extremely angry at me in a dream might be a disguise for my own explosive anger at him. But at other times, the very reversal in the dream of a real situation means "Would that it had been the other way around"—it implies, in other words, a wish that the opposite had been true. "If a dream obstinately declines to reveal its meaning, it is always worthwhile to see the effect of reversing some particular elements in its manifest content, after which the whole situation often becomes immediately clear" (SE IV, p. 327; see also p. 288). If, in a dream I have, I am furious at someone, and yet in everyday life I cannot think of any reason why I would be furious at him, we should perhaps consider that the fury in the dream is a cover for love and attraction (alternatively, it might reflect how I would respond to the rejection I expect from him if I show him love). Young boys often act aggressively toward the very girls they are interested in, and in work life we are sometimes the most concertedly polite to those we most thoroughly dislike. If we occasionally adopt such disguises in everyday life, why wouldn't we encounter them in dreams as well?

Dream interpretation is thus, obviously, not an abstract science in which we apply the exact same method in every instance. We cannot use the same tool in every case, but our goal is that by keeping enough of these heuristic devices in mind, we reach the point at which our interpretation of a dream:

- becomes internally coherent, at least to some degree (there might, nevertheless, be *a number of alternative or complementary meanings* that are coherent, as we saw in the dream of the cousin killing her husband in the bathroom);
- becomes convincing given the *context* in which the dream was dreamt in the analysand's life and everything that has been said up until that point in the analysis (SE V, p. 353);[37]
- fits in with at least some of the analysand's other thoughts and wishes, even if it includes new and surprising elements;
- fits in with some of our theoretical notions, such as the fact that shame, disgust, and fear indicate repressed desire, a fear covers over a wish, and so on (SE V, p. 341).

Freud thus proposes a kind of "hermeneutics": an approach to reading dreams that requires that a sort of "subjective certainty" be attained or acquired, which is contextual in nature ("The correct interpretation can only be arrived at on each occasion from the context," SE V, p. 353). When our associations to widely different dream-elements lead us to the same few people and overlapping topics, this suggests we are on the right track, the associations being mutually supporting.[38]

Still, I suspect that few analysts or analysands today are as concerned as Freud was in finding a virtually complete and thoroughly coherent interpretation of a dream (we will consider his concern with that when we turn to his work with Dora in Chapter 5). In the best of cases, we hope that the interpretations we arrive at *resonate* for the dreamers and help move their analyses forward, leading to the generation of new, useful material. An interpretation is only as good as the progress it leads to; and it proves to be completely useless if, no matter how complete and seemingly exhaustive, it brings no change or fresh food for thought in its wake. Hence *work with dreams must be subordinated to the progress of the analysis as a whole.*

Perhaps the very fact that we work with someone's dreams in a certain way in analysis affects the way they form after that, insofar as they participate in the dialogue with the analyst. As they are used in analysis, dreams become, after all, a message to the analyst, coming to address him or her, hiding and revealing simultaneously. Symbols and/or images return from dream to dream, forming links with earlier sessions, helping establish a common language between analysand and analyst. That language never, however, becomes transparent, and Freud himself indicated a limit to the legibility of dreams with his concept of "the dream's navel, the spot where it reaches down into the unknown" (SE V, p. 525), there being a thick tangle of associational threads at a certain point in the dream that defies our attempts to untangle it.

dream's navel

One of my analysands is quite preoccupied with physical places and spaces, and his dreams feature these prominently. As I often asked him, early on in the analysis, whether he recalled anything in particular having happened in the places the dream settings reminded him of (which, as indicated earlier, is a good question to ask about many, if not all, dreams), his dreams began to form, it seems to me, in such a way as to bring up different life experiences that something in him felt a need to discuss by alluding to the places where they occurred. As the analysis has evolved, his dreams about specific places almost always lead to the recounting of an incident that he had long since forgotten or never yet mentioned to me.

Does Absolutely Every Dream Fulfill a Wish?

The fact that dreams really have a secret meaning which represents the fulfillment of a wish must be proved anew in each particular case.
—Freud, SE IV, p. 146

As far as I can see at the present time, dreams that occur in traumatic neuroses are the only genuine exceptions, and punishment dreams are the only apparent exceptions, to the rule that dreams involve wish-fulfillment.
—Freud, SE XIX, p. 118

Few would, I suspect, disagree that *at least some of our dreams are wishful*—that is, fulfill one or more wishes—since virtually everyone has, as I mentioned earlier, been annoyed when awoken during "a good dream" and attempted to get back to sleep in order to be able to fin-ish the dream. And age-old and recent idiomatic expressions in English related to dreams (other languages have their own), like "It's a dream come true," "Never in my wildest dreams would I have imagined such a thing," and "Dream on!" imply that in dreams we imagine having things happen that we would find marvelous, even if unlikely. Freud mentions some similar idioms, as well as a couple of proverbs or dictums about animals: "What do geese dream of? Corn"; "What do pigs dream of? Acorns" (SE IV, pp. 132–133).

Yet Freud made the universal claim at several points in *The Inter-pretation of Dreams* that *every* dream fulfills a wish (see, for example, SE IV, p. 121). Faced with the objection that certain dreams seem not to fulfill wishes that are recognizable to the dreamer, Freud takes sev-eral tacks other than the one we saw above when he attributes their unrecognizability to dream distortion (including displacement, conden-sation, etc.). For example, he argues that the wishes satisfied in dreams are *unconscious* wishes, which are always at least initially rejected by the dreamer as not his own. And he explains instances in which the dreamer is filled with anxiety at the end of his dream as a last-ditch effort on the part of the censorship (whose usual role is to *"prevent the generation of anxiety or other forms of distressing affect,"* but which sometimes fails to adequately play its role; SE IV, p. 267), which has failed to sufficiently disguise the dream's contents up to that point. The censor brings in anxiety at the end as a kind of hand-waving designed to mask the fact that what has occurred in the course of the dream was in fact something that was wished for by some part of the dreamer;[39] upon waking, he is then fooled or reassured by the anxiety into thinking that he did not want what happened in the dream to happen (such dreams are usually referred to as *nightmares*). Furthermore, Freud argues that dreams in which the dreamer is made to suffer or is punished none-theless fulfill a wish: that of self-punishment. He refers to the latter as "punishment dreams."

It seems, in other words, that Freud is always able to pull a desire out of his hat, as it were: No matter how counterintuitive the desire fulfilled in the dream may seem, Freud always seems to find a way to explain it as a desire that truly belongs to some part of the dreamer (see, for example, SE V, p. 557). If it does not belong to the part of the dreamer that she recognizes as herself when awake (i.e., if it does not belong to her ego or fit in with her conception of herself, that is, if it is not "ego syntonic"), then it belongs to her unconscious; and if not to her unconscious, then perhaps to her superego (even though much of the latter may well be unconscious).[40]

Thus there seems to be something self-confirming about Freud's claim here, such that no matter what counterexample we come up with, he can always find a way to bring it back into the fold of his theory. This makes his theory unfalsifiable—in other words, it appears to be impossible to disprove. Karl Popper, the well-known philosopher of science, claimed that *"it must be possible for an empirical scientific system to be refuted by experience"* (1959, p. 41; emphasis in the original). We must, in his view, be able to at least imagine the existence of some possible fact or experiment that could disprove the theory or at least limit its field of application.

Whether we accept Popper's criterion of falsifiability or not (and there is debate among philosophers and scientists about its validity), we should note that Freud himself eventually qualified his own theory that every dream fulfills a wish. Twenty years after writing *The Interpretation of Dreams*, having worked with a number of soldiers who had been through the bombardments of World War I, he came to accept the notion that some people had dreams which repeatedly presented the same traumatic battle scene over and over again, and in which, try as he might, he was unable to locate any specific wish, conscious or unconscious. He came to the realization (and this is discussed at length in his 1920 text *Beyond the Pleasure Principle*) that there is something that goes horribly wrong and becomes fundamentally discombobulated and dysfunctional in the psyche when faced with certain forms of trauma: The psyche simply replicates the traumatic scene again and again in dreams, the dreamer repeatedly awakening in terror.

Just as Freud came to see that there is something fundamentally dysfunctional or excessive about repression—owing to its potentially infinite duration, which often seems so incommensurate with what occasioned it, and the unremitting character of its return in our lives in the form of symptoms ("the return of the repressed")—he concluded that trauma has a destabilizing effect. Whereas repression is initially designed to solve a certain kind of problem (namely, a conflict within a person who wants to do one thing and yet, for other reasons, feels obliged to do another, as we saw with Anna O), repression oftentimes becomes crippling, going too far, as it were, and creates myriad new problems: "Although it served a useful purpose to begin with, repression leads ultimately to a damaging loss of inhibition [of one's impulses] and mental control" (SE V, p. 617). Similarly, he notes that there is something about traumatic situations that contradicts the law he had laid out regarding the workings of the psyche in Chapter 7 of *The Interpretation of Dreams*, which is that the psyche always operates on the basis of a wish, the latter being understood as the accumulation of a quantum of tension that seeks discharge.[41] Repetition of a traumatic scene in a dream does not lead to the discharge of tension but rather to a repeated buildup of tension (note, too, that in such dreams scenes from reality are often reproduced *exactly* as they were remembered, not creatively reworked as they are in most dreams). This runs counter to the pleasure principle, which does not mean that it is part and parcel of the so-called reality principle. Rather, it seems to indicate some fundamental aberration, malfunction, or misfiring on the part of the psyche.[42]

Is there anything that corresponds to such an aberration in the animal kingdom? Do animals repetitively dream about traumatic situations they have experienced? It seems, as far as we know, that they do not (see Jouvet, 1960),[43] which implies that this is a distinctly human aberration. Is such an aberration rendered possible by the fact that we are speaking beings—in other words, that we are the only beings we thus far know of who are embedded in language? Some might try to explain this aberration on the basis of the size of the human brain or the existence of self-consciousness, but it is perhaps due more directly to the fact that we are linguistic beings, which is one of our fundamental differences from the rest of the animal kingdom.

Whatever the reason for such a fundamental malfunctioning may be, and this malfunctioning is at the root of what has come to be dubbed *post-traumatic stress disorder* (PTSD), Freud (SE XXII) finally came to accept that it constitutes a genuine exception to his universal claim that every dream fulfills a wish.

> With the traumatic neuroses things are different. In their case dreams regularly end in the generation of anxiety. We should not, I think, be afraid to admit that here the function of the dream has failed. I will not invoke the saying that the exception proves the rule: its wisdom seems to me most questionable. But no doubt the exception does not overturn the rule. . . . [We] can say still that a dream is an *attempt* at the fulfilment of a wish. . . . In certain circumstances a dream is only able to put its intention into effect very incompletely, or must abandon it entirely. (p. 29)

This at least opens the door to the possibility that *not every dream fulfills a wish* and that we should not relentlessly seek to reconstruct a wish behind every dream our analysands tell us. Rather, we should take it as a rule of thumb to look for conscious and unconscious wishes in every dream we are told, without taking it as gospel truth that we will necessarily find a wish if only we try long and hard enough. The fact that we do not succeed in finding one does not necessarily mean that there isn't one that was, in fact, at the origin of the dream; but, given our limited capabilities, we cannot expect to uncover *all* wishes, especially insofar as many of them are unexpected, well disguised, and only come out slowly over the course of the treatment.

We should not assume, however, that just because an analysand tells us she has the same disturbing dream over and over that her dream necessarily constitutes one of the exceptions to Freud's rule. First of all, in most cases when analysands claim to have the same dream over and over, there are actually numerous variations in the dreams, and those variations are usually quite significant.[44] (The same is often true of purportedly recurrent dreams from the analysand's childhood.) Secondly, a wish that is expressed again and again will often lead to a series of dreams that are like musical variations on a theme; and even if they are identical, this does not necessarily make them replicas of traumatic events—we still have to inquire about the affect that characterizes the dreams.[45] If it is total terror or horror, then yes, we are most likely dealing with exceptions to the rule.

[Handwritten margin note: Variations in recurrent dreams]

[Handwritten note: Affect of dream is connected to latent, not manifest, content]

Daydreams, Fantasies, Slips, and Bungled Actions (Parapraxes)

[Handwritten margin note: Thought + Wish]

> *All thought activity merely constitutes a roundabout path to wish-fulfillment. . . . Thought is, after all, nothing but a substitute for a hallucinatory wish [experience having taught us that thought is necessary if we are to fulfill that wish]; it is self-evident that dreams must be wish-fulfillments, since nothing but a wish can set our mental apparatus to work.*
>
> —Freud, SE V, p. 567

> *Truth will out.*[46]
>
> —Shakespeare, *The Merchant of Venice*, II:2, 645

> *[There are thoughts that are] cut off from consciousness and struggling to find expression. . . . Unconscious wishes are always on the alert, ready at any time to find their way to expression.*
>
> —Freud, SE V, pp. 546 and 553

Although Freud wrote quite extensively on daydreams, fantasies, slips of the tongue, and many forms of bungled actions (see his *Introductory Lectures*, Chapters 1–4, and *The Psychopathology of Everyday Life*), I will only comment on them very briefly here, as I have done so extensively elsewhere (see Fink, 2007, 2014a, 2014b). Like dreams, many daydreams, fantasies, and slips make some immediate sense (with many slips of the tongue, all we have to do is "take the speaker at his word" to grasp his not fully intended meaning; SE XV, p. 40), and, once associated to, make still more sense. Like dreams, they are "completely valid psychical acts" (SE IX, p. 73), not nonsensical neuronal misfirings, as some would have it. One of my analysands once consciously meant to say that he seemed to enjoy getting annoyed, but ended up saying, "I seem to annoy getting enjoyed." He realized that this was quite different from what he had intended to say, but was able, with very little prompting on my part, to talk about how annoying it was to him when people seemed to be getting some sort of enjoyment out of him. Another analysand came out with "at gun point" when she meant to say "at one point," and this brought out her sense of being "held up" and "forced" by various people in her life to do things she did not wish to do.

Freud explicitly indicates that daydreams and fantasies are similar in structure to dreams (SE V, pp. 491–493), and all of these phenomena can be understood as wish-based like dreams, even if the wishes satisfied by them are at times counterintuitive and initially unrecognizable or unacceptable to those who have them and/or to those who are affected by them.

> We may lay it down that a happy person never fantasizes, only an unsatisfied one. The motor forces of fantasies are unsatisfied wishes, and every single fantasy is the fulfillment of a wish, a correction of unsatisfying reality. (SE IX, p. 146)

Like dreams, daydreams and fantasies unfold in the present tense: we imagine our wishes being fulfilled in them here and now (SE V, p. 535). And like dreams, they have meaning, express intentions, and have purposes of their own, allowing the truth to speak. In bungled actions, in particular, "unconscious wishful impulses clearly try to get themselves acted on in daytime as well . . . ; they endeavor . . . to obtain control over the power of movement" (p. 567). Lacan even goes so far as to say that "bungled actions are the only actions that are always successful" (Seminar XVII, p. 58).[47]

Getting analysands to take seriously and associate to their slips and bungled actions—which might be thought of as speech acts and physical actions that *miss* their mark or target, leading to all kinds of *mis*-takes, including mishearings or misinterpretations of what people say, mislaying of objects, misreading and/or misremembering of instructions, misspelling or misprinting of words, misquoting other people, miscalculating simple sums, and so on—is much like encouraging them to recall and work with their dreams. It is not enough to mention once early on in the treatment that you want them to pay attention to their parapraxes for them to know what to do with them or how to think about them, and to go on working with them productively for the entirety of the treatment. Some analysands find slips and bungled actions—which are essentially mini-symptoms, that is, symptoms of small duration, involving at least two different intentions that collide and "interfere" with each other (SE XV, p. 42)—striking and meaningful from the outset.[48] Others must be gradually convinced that they can be valuable to the analysis, and analysts usually have the easiest time convincing them of this, not with garbled slips in which two or more words seems to have been smashed into each other (as in the slip I heard one day on the radio, where a female newscaster said "subpenises" instead of "subpoenas," and then burst out laughing), but with "the most usual, and at the same time the most striking kind of slips of the tongue: those in which one says the precise opposite of what one intended to say" (SE XV, p. 33). Analysts may also have a good deal of success early on with slips that say something that can be readily grasped, even if it is initially counterintuitive to the analysand, as when one of my analysands intended to tell me that he could not help feeling that "straight men want to kick [his] ass," but said "kiss" instead of "kick"; or when another analysand said that he wanted to continue on a path toward "instinctual renunciation," but instead came out with, "instinctual enunciation."

As in the case of dreams, analysts should encourage their analysands to interpret the slips themselves, first by immediately asking them what was going through their minds at the very moment they made the slip. Some analysands will be able to recall two different words (e.g., "left" and "right" coming out as "light," or "ask" and "answer" coming out as "ants") or trains of thought that collided and created a jumble of letters or sounds, in the case of a garbled word or words (for instance, a man's dual fascination with "omniscience" and "omnipotence" that came out more or less like "omnishitence," and the ideas of "include" and "enclose" coming out as "incluse"); some will comment that they had tried to suppress a certain word or thought that had come to mind earlier (SE XV, p. 66) and suspect that this is why it "spilled out" in the slip; and some will spontaneously laugh at the complete change in thought produced by what actually came out of their mouths, as opposed to what they had intended. The latter might at times altogether endorse Freud's claim that "anyone who has allowed the truth to slip out in an unguarded moment is in fact glad to be free of the pretense" (SE VIII, p. 106).

With certain analysands, the analyst will have to work very hard to get them to overcome their resistance to thinking about their own mental states and thought processes, and with each new slip may have to try to propose possible meanings of a slip (in the form of questions like, "Do you think some part of you might want *x*?" where *x* is what was actually said) based on the context in which it came out, the way it came out, and the analyst's provisional knowledge of the analysand's life. In the case of garbled words, in which an analysand professes to hear nothing, the analyst may need to propose possible words that may have been condensed into what was actually enunciated, hoping that the analysand will consider and perhaps even run with them, so to speak. I find that with most analysands, such encouragement eventually yields fruit, and they take up the project themselves. Some may, however, need to have it pointed out to them that if slips are random or just "sloppy ways of speaking," why aren't they made all the time or in every context? Why do they occur especially when they are talking about Mom and Dad, and not when they are discussing a distant relative or a rarely seen coworker? And if they are random, why did they say, "I could just kill him" instead of "I could just kiss him," when they could have said any number of other things instead?[49]

When faced with analysands, on the other hand, who make very few slips of the tongue—assuming the analyst has become adept at hearing them in virtually all circumstances—and who never seem to find anything of use in them, the analyst must seriously consider a diagnosis of psychosis, insofar as in psychosis there is no unconscious that is struggling for expression and that periodically breaks through in the form of parapraxes (on this complex theoretical point, see Fink, 2007, Chapter 10). But one must be careful not to jump to conclusions regarding a particular analysand's diagnosis when one is not yet terribly proficient at working with slips with the majority of one's other patients (Freud claimed, bizarrely enough, that "we often fail to hear our own slips, but never other people's" [SE XV, p. 68], but my experience supervising clinicians suggests just the opposite).[50] The fact that a patient regularly makes slips of the tongue and is eventually able to work with them productively (not simply agreeing to interpretations of them made by the analyst) is of capital importance in distinguishing neurosis from psychosis, and this is in my experience completely overlooked at this point in time by the vast majority of clinicians. We should keep in mind that on the very first page of the *Introductory Lectures on Psychoanalysis*, which constitutes a kind of summary of all of Freud's work up until 1915, Freud indicates that "psychoanalysis is a procedure for the treatment of neurotic patients" (SE X, p. 15)—psychoanalysis not having yet at that point in time been adapted in order to be able to work with psychotics—and that everything he discusses regarding parapraxes, dreams, and symptom formation in that book is based upon the dynamic conflict between the conscious and the unconscious as we find it in neurosis, and which we do *not* find in psychosis.[51]

Dreams and Memories

God speaks time and time again, but no one notices. In a dream,
in a vision in the night, when deep sleep falls on mankind as they
slumber in their beds, He may speak in their ears.

—Job 33:14–16

I mentioned earlier that according to Freud, dreams and fantasies do not necessarily reproduce memories from the past exactly as they occurred ("A dream is scarcely ever a simple memory"; SE IV, p. 245). This is of the utmost importance with regard to an early theory of Freud's, known as the "seduction theory," about which there has been much rather misinformed debate in recent decades (see, especially, Masson, 1984).

In the course of his initial work with hysterics and prior to working with dreams, Freud formulated the hypothesis that all neurosis resulted from sexual trauma—that is, some form of early sexual contact that was experienced by the child as traumatic. By the end of *Studies on Hysteria*, or thereabouts time-wise (1895), Freud had laid out two specific diagnoses: (a) obsession, which involves an early experience of pleasure that later leads to self-reproaches and guilt, and (b) hysteria, which involves an early experience of unpleasure due to the child's passivity or helplessness that leads to an overwhelming of the ego, discharge of excessive excitation, and disgust. The cause of both obsession and hysteria was, in Freud's view at that time, a specific event: "seduction" of the child by a parent, relative, neighbor, or caretaker—that is, early sexual contact of some kind between adult (or adolescent) and child, usually initiated by the older party (such contact is often referred to today, a bit too sweepingly, as *sexual abuse*), leading to guilt in obsessives and disgust in hysterics. Guilt arose supposedly because the obsessives were active in the process of the seduction, whereas hysterics were passive. (Later Freud modified this position somewhat: Such sexual experiences led, in his view, to aversion and guilt in obsessives and to disgust in hysterics; obsession and hysteria will be discussed at length in Chapters 4 and 5.)

In 1895, Freud tells us that he hoped to address the problems posed by such trauma directly by advancing at the level of theory. However, it was at the level of practice—in the analysis of dreams—that he made new headway. The practice of dream analysis led him to reject the seduction theory, because he found that dreams present multiple scenarios: In one dream the scenario plays itself out in one way, whereas the next dream presents things in another way and sometimes even in the opposite way (SE IV, p. 198). Freud thus came to believe that he could not take everything that happens in people's dreams (or daydreams) at face value—that is, as depicting historical events exactly as they unfolded in real life—dreams being as much based on people's fantasies about what happened, or what they would have liked to have happened, as on what actually did happen. This led him to conclude that *reality had to be bracketed,* in some sense, or held in abeyance, for we can't know for sure what happened on the basis of what transpires in our dreams. This concerns not just sexual material in dreams but all material: We cannot know whether any scene of any kind that is presented in a dream refers to something that actually happened in the dreamer's life or not.

Whereas formerly Freud had often attempted to corroborate what a patient reported in a dream by asking the patient's family and entourage whether or not certain events happened (and, if so, when), he came to realize that family members often did not know about any such events, thought they happened differently (each seeing events from his or her own perspective), or simply could not be trusted to tell him the truth about them (at times hoping to cover their own tracks, so as not to be blamed). Freud ultimately concluded that the whole question of *what really happened*—if, indeed, anything at all on the order of sexual contact occurred—was of less importance than the obvious effects of the real or fantasized event on the patient's life in the present.

The fact that dreams, daydreams, and fantasies do not necessarily reproduce memories from the past exactly as they occurred also takes on a great deal of importance with regard to many contemporary clinicians' immediate assumption that the slightest fantasy or dream a patient has about a sexual or violent encounter with a relative or neighbor automatically means such an encounter actually occurred in the patient's past. This has led to all kinds of problems around so-called recovered memories, which often appear not to have been "recovered" from the patient's memory at all but are rather *a creation of the therapist's own fantasies and/or projections* (an approach that a colleague of mine, Kristen Hennessy, terms *trauma hunting* on the clinician's part). Many patients have been led by such therapists to "confront" their relatives with "wrongdoing" from the past that, at least according to the relatives, never occurred; this has led to much unnecessary conflict within families (there are enough genuine reasons for conflict within families already, without adding spurious ones!) and many lawsuits against the therapists who encouraged it. (Note that some parents also countersued their own children simply in order to discredit them, whether the abuse had occurred or not.)

Our memories are sometimes very distinct, and sometimes not nearly so distinct; many readers have probably had the experience of having been somewhere, but their visual memory of it has been overridden and replaced by photographs or home videos they have seen of it; and they may have had the experience of having done or witnessed something, but their memory of it has been virtually erased and overwritten by a parent's account of the experience. Children and even many adults are quite suggestible, and can at times be convinced that something happened of which they have no real memory of their own!

Analysands often remember things in the course of an analysis that they had long since forgotten, and these memories often come to them in connection with something in a dream or fantasy, but not in the form of something that is *directly* represented in the dream or fantasy. The patient of mine whose sexual fantasies include the most physical domination and humiliation by others is precisely the one who seems to have been the least punished for anything in the course of his upbringing, even though he often felt he was doing things that were wrong and *believed that he ought to have been punished and harshly criticized for doing them.* Dreams and fantasies often stage what we wish would happen or wish had happened, not what actually happened.

As Freud put it in *The Interpretation of Dreams* (much of which was written in 1898), "Hysterical symptoms are not attached to actual memories, but to fantasies erected on the basis of memories" (SE V, p. 491); and "an analysis [of a dream] only gives us the *content* of a thought and leaves it to us to determine its reality. Real and imaginary events appear in dreams . . . as if they were of equal validity; and that is so not only in dreams but in the production of more important psychical structures" such as symptoms (SE IV, p. 288).[52]

This should not be thought to imply that, according to psychoanalysis, virtually no one is ever subjected to early sexual trauma: In many milieus and in many social classes, the sexual use and abuse of children all too obviously occurs and has multiple repercussions. Although psychoanalysis cautions us not to hastily jump to conclusions about what actually happened to a child based on that child's fantasy or dream productions (or play), it does not in any way presume that children's memories are *all* necessarily distorted by their own fantasies. A young child who, while engaged in play in the office of a therapist he trusts, has a large doll or figure inflict violence on a smaller one or portrays sexual acts between them and then comments that Daddy does this to him all the time at home, is worth taking seriously; below a certain age, few children are calculating in what they tell therapists during their play, even if they have already learned to hold back plenty of things at their parents' insistence while just "talking." Still, despite the demands of state agencies requiring that therapists report all instances of physical and sexual abuse, analysts must always continue to keep "reality" in brackets to some degree and be prepared to hear things from the child that contradict or render more complex the initial report. Strictly speaking, it is not the analyst's job to determine what really happened and what did not; that should be left to the patient.

CHAPTER 4

Obsession and the Case of the Rat Man (Ernst Langer)

[Without analysis,] the effect of a repression cannot be undone.
—Freud, SE VII, p. 241

FEW CASE STUDIES in the history of psychoanalysis have brought more people into treatment than that of the Rat Man. More people have seen features of their own thinking and behavior in Freud's write-up of Ernst Langer's[1] life and actions than in perhaps any other single case description, and have been struck by the nature and extent of their own pathology as they read about his.

Ernst Langer's life was characterized by *indecisiveness* and *uncertainty*: He could make up his mind about almost nothing, and especially could not decide whom to marry. Even regarding what might seem to be the most trifling things—for example, paying someone back who had laid out some money for him to receive a cash-on-delivery (COD) package at the post office—he would get into a quandary and would go back and forth again and again in his mind, and in his actions too, about how to return the money, going so far as to doubt at times to whom he actually owed it. Such indecisiveness, uncertainty, and *doubt* continue to be hallmarks of what is referred to as obsession (or *obsessive structure*, as I shall call it) in psychoanalysis even today, and of what in psychiatry currently goes by the moniker *obsessive-compulsive disorder* (OCD).[2]

Ernst (as I shall refer to him here) was plagued by worries about what might happen to people he ostensibly loved. He often imagined the most horrible things—accidents, illnesses, humiliations, and so on—happening to his fiancée, her grandmother, his young niece (Ella), and to his own father owing to the Ernst's actions or failure to act (e.g., negligence, oversight, or forgetting). These imaginings took the form of intrusive thoughts—that is, violent thoughts that raced through his mind at incredible speed (SE X, p. 167) and that confused and distressed him, seeming to him, as they did, to come out of nowhere,[3] and involving harm to people whom he believed to be his "loved ones" (see, for example, SE X, p. 226). He was full of rage at people which he could barely avow even to himself, felt himself to be morally and intellectually superior to virtually everyone (SE X, p. 177; S. Freud, 2000, p. 69), and yet secretly viewed himself as a failure, a fraud, a coward, and a base scoundrel (SE X, pp. 206 and 209). These latter features—rage, and a feeling of being superior coupled with concerns about being inferior (S. Freud, 2000, p. 141)—are shared by a large swath of the population in our times. Indeed, the belief that one is better than everyone else and the fear that one is actually quite worthless are perhaps the most widely expressed of all beliefs and fears in psychoanalytic consultations today.

Another feature of the Rat Man's case that resonates with many adults is the fact that he was already quite neurotic as a young child, being subject to certain superstitions (like our contemporary "Step on a crack, break your mother's back") and fears, and making repeated resolutions and vows to himself regarding what he felt to be his evil thoughts and wishes, both sexual and aggressive. He formed the conviction at one point that a girl he liked would pay more attention to him if a terrible misfortune befell him—for example, if his father died (SE X, p. 178).[4] Sexual impulses manifested themselves early in his childhood, as they do for many people; he even complained about his erections once to his mother (pp. 161–162),[5] even though he was dimly aware they were related to his wishes to see females naked. Freud's original notes inform us of many instances of spying on naked females (including his mother), touching housemaids, and even sexual exploration with his numerous siblings, especially one of his younger sisters, Olga (S. Freud, 2000, pp. 141, 151, 237–239).

All of Ernst's important relationships were characterized, starting very early on in his life, by intense ambivalence, including either conscious hatred alongside unrecognized love (and/or admiration) or conscious, intense love alongside unrecognized hatred (SE X, pp. 237–239). For we English speakers, *anger* is felicitously built right into his last name, Langer. Such ambivalence is characteristic of a broad cross section of the contemporary population, anger and hatred being especially frowned upon and suppressed today in countries like the United States far more so than certain facets of sexuality.

I will not give anything like a complete account or interpretation of the case of the Rat Man here (an obsessive task if ever there was one!), but will endeavor to highlight aspects of it that can teach us about psychoanalytic technique.

The "Precipitating Cause" of His Illness as an Adult

How bungling are our attempts to reproduce an analysis; how piti-
fully we tear to pieces the great works of art that Nature has created
in the mental sphere.
      —Freud, in a letter to Jung regarding the case of the Rat Man,
                                    cited in Jones, 1955, p. 264

When faced with a case history as floridly detailed and complex as that of the Rat Man,[6] it is of the utmost importance to be able to distinguish the forest from the trees—in this case, to distinguish (a) the general structure of obsession that afflicted the patient his entire life from (b) what Freud refers to as the "illness" that was consuming Ernst in the years prior to beginning analysis (which, to Freud's credit, he took the time to examine closely enough to find to be psychological in origin, even though many of his fellow nerve specialists would have immediately concluded it to be organic).[7] A general structure is something that can be chipped away at only a little bit at a time, lessening in severity over a period of years without ever entirely disappearing (more on this in the next chapter), whereas the particular illness that is running and ruining someone's life is far more immediately accessible to analytic treatment.

What is it that Freud refers to as Ernst's illness as an adult (he was just a few months shy of 30 when he first went to see Freud)? Despite the importance of rats in his neurosis and in one of his severest (yet short-lived) crises, it is open to debate whether it was the specific crisis related to the "cruel captain" and rats that drove Ernst to see Freud; for, although Ernst refers to it as "the experience that was the immediate occasion" of his going to see Freud (SE X, p. 165), it should be noted that the crisis occurred in August 1907, whereas Ernst seems to have first contacted Freud only two months later.[8] The illness—what perhaps truly brought him to see Freud, or at least what gave him the impetus to stay once the acute stage of the crisis had passed—was identified by the patient himself as his curious inability to study and get ahead in his chosen profession; "he had wasted years" (p. 158) not being able to work, he told Freud at their very first meeting, despite no apparent lack of intellectual acumen.

When did it begin? This is a vitally important question, and yet it is not easy to answer. In his session with Freud on October 5, 1907, Ernst indicated that his ability to work became seriously compromised a year and a half after his father died, thus around May 1901 (S. Freud, 2000, p. 65). On October 7, Ernst told Freud that starting in early 1903, he would have episodes of distressing thoughts lasting eight to ten days at a time, but that more recently, such thoughts had become constant (p. 73). And at the next session, he claimed that awful thoughts about his father had plagued him for a while at age 12, then again at age 20, and that they had assailed him incessantly since the age of 22 (p. 81), distracting him from his studies.[9]

If we read what Freud tells us carefully, establishing—as it seems Freud himself did—a timeline of the main events and crucial turning points in the Rat Man's life (SE X, p. 195), we find that Ernst's difficulties working began at the time, "after his father's death" in 1899 (p. 198), at which his mother told him that she and a relative of the family that had raised her (the Saborskys) had discussed the possibility of Ernst marrying one of the Saborskys' daughters, a "lovely, rich, and well-connected" (p. 198) girl. (Her name may have been Lizzie [see S. Freud, 2000, p. 181]; she was reportedly 17 in 1907 [p. 179], and was thus only around 10 or 11 when the match was first proposed, he being around 22).[10] The relative was prepared, his mother told him, to approve such a marriage *once the patient completed his education*. On telling Freud about this, Ernst had no sense that he was bringing forward something of importance, but he had certainly never forgotten it. Freud noticed, however, that although the patient had been making at least some progress in his studies up until that point, he suddenly became incapable of working and failed one examination after another.

Let us note that, as is so often the case, the patient was unaware that the beginning of his heightened difficulty concentrating on his studies coincided exactly with his learning that his relative would allow Ernst to marry his daughter *as soon as he completed his law degree*; whereas patients rarely pay attention to the precise moment at which their troubles begin, Freud seems to have always paid close attention to such details, attempting to establish a timeline in his head (if not on paper) in order to grasp what events might have led to what troubles in his patients' lives (for another example, see his dating of Dora's "appendicitis" in SE VII, pp. 87–88). Establishing such a timeline is often quite crucial for determining the cause and origin of symptoms, yet few clinicians today seem to devote much time and effort to doing so. And this is true despite the ease with which we can ask our analysands, regarding specific events, "About how old were you at the time?" or "Do you recall when that occurred?"; and despite our obvious ability to write down their major life events and turning points, as we hear about them little by little in the course of the analysis, and put them in order, adding to them as new ones come to light (in my experience, this takes all of about five minutes per month for each case).

Why did Ernst suddenly become incapable of working? What was it about this particular proposal made by his mother and the relative of the Saborskys that paralyzed him? Two facts are crucial here: (a) For most of the preceding decade, the Rat Man had been more or less in love with a woman by the name of Gisa Adler (S. Freud, 2000, p. 127), whom he almost always referred to in sessions as his "lady" (he refused to tell Freud her name for about two months, and Freud gave her name in the published case history as Gisela),[11] and had even directly asked her to marry him on at least one occasion; Gisa had little in the way of social status or financial resources, whereas the Saborskys' daughter was well-connected and well-off.

Having to choose between two such potential mates might have been difficult for almost anyone, but matters were complicated by a second fact: (b) The patient had heard that his father, prior to having married the patient's mother—who herself was from a well-to-do and relatively high-status family, according to the published case history, but who, according to Freud's notes, was of "modest condition" (most likely what today we would call "middle class") and was in fact *the father's first cousin* (S. Freud, 2000, p. 165)[12]—had been inclined to marry a butcher's daughter, a girl of few means and connections ("a pretty but penniless girl of humble birth"; SE X, p. 198).

The Rat Man's father, Heinrich Langer, had thus married not so much for love but for money, and perhaps for social status as well, his family members seeming to have believed that only Langers and their immediate relatives were worthy people (S. Freud, 2000, pp. 165 and 193). Although the father and mother's marriage was purportedly "an extremely happy one" (SE X, p. 198), the father had made a somewhat self-interested and "mercenary" choice—for which the Rat Man could hardly in good con-science fault him, as he himself would never have come into the world had the father not made that choice—and the Rat Man found himself on the horns of a dilemma: He was faced with an almost identical choice between "a poor but deserving" older woman and a beautiful young girl whom he believed almost any man would be happy to marry (from the same family that had raised his mother).[13]

Complicating all of this were the facts that Gisa was often cold toward him, had already turned down his first marriage proposal in December 1900 and his second, vaguer proposal in 1903, and was disapproved of by his father when the father noticed that his son was spending a great deal of time with Gisa (SE X, p. 201). But what seems to have been most paralyzing to the patient was the sense that fate had put him in the exact same position as it had put his father, and that he was but the plaything of destiny. How did he respond to this predicament? By falling ill—not physically but mentally. What did that do for him? It served as *a solution to the problem*: It allowed him to never finish his studies and thereby never make a choice at all. By not finishing his studies, he could not marry Lizzie and thus was able to remain in a state of suspended animation, so to speak, indefinitely (SE X, p. 237). He also gave his rightful inheritance upon his father's death to his mother (asking only for regular pocket money from her), which likely made it impossible for him to marry either woman.[14]

The Paralyzing Effects of "Destiny"

Those who cannot remember the past are condemned to repeat it.
　　　　　　　　　　　　　　　　　—George Santayana

Although one might be inclined to think this a highly unusual predicament in which to find oneself, I myself have worked with at least a half-dozen men whose hesitations and uncertainties regarding whether to marry and whom to marry involved the almost exact repetition of the situation in which their fathers or mothers found themselves with regard to their own marital status. I have described one such case in detail (in Fink, 2014b, Chapter 11), it having been panic over being on the verge of asking someone to marry him whom his parents had often said he should marry that first brought the patient to see me. In cases in which the patient identified more thoroughly with the mother than the father, the mother's marital predicament and the subsequent playing out of her marriage seemed central to the patient's difficulties in his long-term relationship with a partner as an adult.

And as in the case of the Rat Man, in none of the cases I have treated have the patients themselves been aware of the almost exact repetition in their lives of what I will call the "symbolic coordinates" of their parent's predicament. An almost identical scenario had developed as if through no action or will of their own and seemed to be poisoning their lives, they knew not why. Lacan (*Écrits*, pp. 249–250) suggests that Freud was able to sniff out this repeating scenario in the case of the Rat Man at least in part owing to having once found himself in a similar predicament, presumably as regards his own decision about whom to marry.[15] Although many people seem to wish for a sense that they are destined to marry a certain person and no one else, lamenting their uncertainty and their feeling that there is something arbitrary about their choice, we find in many cases that feeling compelled to marry a specific person is experienced as nightmarish.

Freud does not tell us that the Rat Man became freed from such repetition by being made *conscious* of the fact that he was repeating his father's predicament, insinuating instead that it was by exploring and articulating all of the parameters of the father's situation and decision and their parallels with the Rat Man's own that his condition improved and he was able to work again (this might be termed a *working through* of the symptom). We do not know what became of him as regards his love life (we do not know for sure, for example, whether he ended up marrying Lizzie or Gisa or neither),[16] but it does seem that he was able to get beyond the paralysis that brought him into analysis in the first place.

I suspect that few analysts today are on the lookout for such unwitting repetition (which is curious insofar as repetition is presumably one of the key concepts of psychoanalysis),[17] since they seem to pay less and less attention to their patients' pasts. Yet such repetition compulsions are clearly at work in a great many people's love and work relationships—they unknowingly reproducing the kinds of relationships they have either heard about or witnessed firsthand in their parents' lives—and a great deal of what they do and say can neither be grasped nor impacted without tracing out and articulating these relationships. All of this must be put into speech for it to stop running their lives unbeknownst to them.

What Was He Doing Instead of Working?

> *Resistance is the surest sign of conflict. There must be a force here that is seeking to express something and another that is striving to prevent its expression.*
>
> —Freud, SE XXII, p. 14

> *I want to lock horns with you, butt heads with you.*
>
> —An analysand

Let us turn now to what it was that was making it impossible for the Rat Man to work, as that is what was at the forefront of his mind when he went to see Freud. Freud was, I think, right to see the inability to work complained of by the patient as the primary illness or symptom, and the specific thoughts that were assailing him when he was supposed to be working as secondary, in a sense, for the latter became particularly intense only because of the necessity of the former. He had been plagued by intrusive thoughts for much of his life (since age 6, most likely), without them ever having taken on the overwhelming dimensions they took on later.

As we saw above, it was important for him not to work—because if he did, he would finish his studies and then be eligible to marry the Saborskys' daughter. What he did instead of working is secondary, to some degree, insofar as *he could have been doing any of a vast number of things*. In contemporary life and clinical practice, we encounter, for example, people who feel compelled:

- to keep up with every detail of the news (or some specific kind of news), checking the front pages or websites of certain papers or magazines constantly—often telling themselves that they will get to work after they have done so—in search of they know not what (news, for example, of some catastrophe or of some ill that has befallen someone they know and hate?);
- to watch television, it often not mattering what, just so long as they are watching something, even flipping between 10 different channels (some tell themselves they are just relaxing for a few minutes before getting down to work, and some even tell themselves that they are engaging in important sociological study);
- to play video games (sometimes convincing themselves that they are learning useful skills from them that will help them in their subsequent work);
- to survey various kinds of social media, whether Facebook, Twitter, or what have you, in search of they know not what (again, news of some ill that has befallen someone they know and hate or envy?);
- to read all of some author's work that is only very tangentially related to their own before they can start studying the field they are supposed to be studying or writing the paper they are supposed to be writing;
- to masturbate, often multiple times (again, they may tell themselves that it is a good way of relieving tension or burning off excess energy and will allow them to concentrate better afterward); etc.

The Rat Man engaged in some form of the last of these, especially late at night, which just so happens to have coincided with the main time of day at which he studied, having chosen such hours as if to convince himself and his father (who incidentally had been dead already for a number of years at that point, and who had died right around that same time of night) that he was truly "burning the midnight oil"—in other words, working hard at his studies into the wee hours of the morning.[18]

All such procrastinative activities as those listed above constitute forms of rebellion, rebellion against someone or some set of people that the procrastinator feels is wanting him to work or making him work. But why, he asks himself, would he do what such people want or order him to do when they are responsible for having deprived him of so many of his early pleasures in life? Ernst considered his father and his mother to be killjoys, in many ways, and spent far more of his time and energy thinking about flouting their demands and imagining them dead or even suffering in the afterlife (above all in the case of his father) than he did studying to achieve the goals they set out for him (see, for example, S. Freud, 2000, p. 145).[19]

But when he caught himself imagining his father dead or suffering, he would then feel compelled to punish himself by making himself pray that God preserve his father's soul, by swearing off all masturbation (S. Freud, 2000, pp. 97–99), and even by giving his mother the money his father had bequeathed him (because, as we saw, he had wished his father dead so that he would have enough money to marry Gisa, whom his father disapproved of). *The more he wanted his father dead* (for example, at age 12, because he thought it would make a girl he was interested in feel sorry for him), *the more he would force himself to ensure his father's safety and continued health.* He did the same with other people whom he both loved and hated—for example, Gisa (the more he wished harm would come to her, for being cold to him and turning down his marriage proposals, the more he would have to pray for her well-being, and the more likely it was that some word would intrude into his prayers, transforming them into curses). Indeed, it is quite clear that he recognized at some level that he himself posed the greatest danger to them and that they primarily needed to be protected from him!

The Structure of Obsessive Symptoms

> *Whatever one tries to fend off will always eventually infiltrate the very means one is using to fend it off.*
>
> —Freud, SE X, p. 225

Let us consider Ernst's symptoms in the terms we discussed in Chapter 1. His early urges to see females naked obviously qualify as a sexual drive (*scopophilia*—literally, "loving to look"), and his wish to have his father permanently out of the way so that he could satisfy such urges obviously qualifies as an aggressive drive. Both can be considered to be elements of Force 1, the force associated with the "bad self" (the libido or id), whereas the self-punishing impulses that would appear—either as soon as he felt the sexual or aggressive impulses, or shortly after he had at least in part satisfied them—can be associated with Force 2: his moral sense, his "good self," or what Freud later refers to as the "superego."[20]

$$\text{Force 1} \Rightarrow \text{Symptom} \Leftarrow \text{Force 2}$$

$$\text{"Bad self"} \Rightarrow \text{Symptom} \Leftarrow \text{"Good self"}$$

Id   Superego

We noted that in hysteria, the conflict between Forces 1 and 2 (that is, between the id and the superego) led to a compromise formation: a single symptom (such as a nervous cough or an inability to drink water) that combined both impulses or wrapped them up into something quite unrecognizable either to the person with the symptom or to that person's entourage. In the case of the Rat Man, however, what we find instead is an oscillation between Force 1 and Force 2: a cycling back and forth from one to the other. A sexual or aggressive urge would appear, he would mentally punish himself for it (intrapsychically uttering a "sanction" or "command" to himself, and feeling a *compulsion* to cut his own throat, for example), the same urge would return or another urge would appear, and he would then punish himself for that one as well (see Appendix III for a detailed account of the structure of the symptom that led him into analysis, the one involving the payment he owed for his new pince-nez).

His sexual and aggressive urges were generally obvious to him, which was at least one of the reasons why he considered himself to be a criminal. In hysteria, we saw that such sexual and aggressive urges are so disguised in the symptom as to be unrecognizable to the patient; in obsession, the patient is often painfully aware of his sexual and aggressive impulses, even if when he first presents them to an analyst, he couches them in negative formulations like the ones we saw in Chapter 2—for example, "It's not that I'd prefer my father were dead, it's just that . . ."—and even if he himself is often unaware of the why and wherefore of his urges. At times, however, obsessives, although aware of their *sexual* urges, can only become aware of their *aggressive* urges in a disguised form, the very form we see in the Rat Man's fully formed obsession at age 6, which might be schematized as follows:

1. He had a wish to see a girl naked (sexual urge);
2. he recollected his father's prohibition of sexual behavior (a reference to a childhood scene discussed further on);

3. he wanted to kill his father (this remained unconscious and was disguised as number 4);

4. he was afraid that his father would die (this is what became conscious);

5. he engaged in protective measures to ward off the harm that might come to his father (SE X, p. 163).

In such cases, the obsessive is conscious only of his *fear* that something terrible will happen to someone he ostensibly loves (and of the steps he feels compelled to take in order to ensure that this does not happen). It is noteworthy that it was in his write-up of a case of obsession that Freud first categorically stated that every fear covers over a repressed wish (SE X, p. 180).

Patients often have thoughts like, "Were anything to happen to my children, I would kill myself," and are fooled by the form of the thoughts into thinking that they simply express concern. They do not realize that *the thought of something bad happening to someone is far more important and telling than the way in which it is clothed or couched.*[21] Nor do they realize that several steps have been left out of such thoughts (as in the rhetorical trope of ellipsis), and that when they are restored, things become clearer. Consider, for example, what was elided from the Rat Man's intrusive thought or obsession, "If I marry my lady, some misfortune will befall my father." Freud (SE X) tells us:

> If we insert the intermediate steps, which had been skipped but were known to us from the analysis, we find the following train of thought: "If my father were still alive, he would be as furious at me for intending to marry Gisa as he was in the childhood scene [when I bit my nurse]; that would get me enraged at him again and I would wish him every possible harm; and owing to the omnipotence of my wishes such harm would be bound to come to him." (p. 226)

Had all these intermediate thoughts been available to the Rat Man, he could hardly have found such intrusive thoughts unintelligible.[22] We see here that *one of the many ways in which repression works is by ellipsis, by eliding connecting thoughts.*

Note that the cycle between Force 1 and Force 2, in the case of the Rat Man, did not always involve self-punishment; sometimes it involved an attempt to undo what he had done, as for example when he tried "to undo the fact of his father's death" (SE X, pp. 235–236), something patently impossible. We might say that one element of the cycle involves hatred, and the other love; and rather than being condensed into one and the same activity or symptom, as in hysteria, one force momentar- ily gets the upper hand and expresses itself, and then the other returns with a vengeance (p. 192). Consider, for example, what the Rat Man did one day when he knew that Gisa would soon be traveling along a par- ticular road in a carriage: Stubbing his toe on a stone in the road, he immediately imagined her carriage hitting it and moved the stone out of the way so that she could not be injured by it; but then he thought better of this and put the stone back in its original place. The first action demonstrated love and care (even if the fact that he imagined her car- riage hitting the stone may have been malicious), the second anger and aggression (p. 190), each undoing what the other had done. First one impulse (loving) was satisfied, then the other (hateful).

undoing

Not every case of obsession plays out in exactly this way, naturally. In many cases, the different warring forces are equally strong much of the time, leading to situations in which nothing at all happens for long stretches. As we saw in Chapter 2, people who are at war with themselves end up expending huge quantities of energy fighting their own tendencies, and to outside observers often seem quite dead, as if devoid of emotion (contemporary clinicians often characterize them as having "flat affect," overlooking the considerable affective forces that are warring within them). They are shocked when one force suddenly gets the upper hand and gives rise to an abrupt, seemingly incommensurate action—whether a marriage proposal (made out of the blue, on the spur of the moment, when nothing up until that time in the relationship sug- gested such an eventuality) or an outburst of violence (which is often immediately regretted and overcompensated for in the attempt to "undo it"). The more evenly matched the libidinal and prohibiting forces are, the more extreme the sudden action is likely to be when it finally comes. Hence Ernst's "fear of the violence of his own rage" (SE X, p. 206).

In cases of obsession where the libidinal and prohibiting forces are quite evenly matched, and no decision about anything important in patients' love or work lives can be made, *everything is left to fate:* One job will be accepted as opposed to another if it magically falls into the patient's lap through no doing of his own; and one relationship will be preferred to another if he himself need play no part in getting it started or solidified. Any choice that he is forced to make will be left to the toss of a coin, a "sign" from above (however superstitious it may seem), or other people's suggestions; in many cases, however, he will simply defer making a choice for so long that one of the two choices will no longer be available and there will no longer be any choice to be made at all! *Avoidance is, after all, a defining feature of neurosis:* Obsessives avoid making choices and decisions (telling us, for example,

avoidance

that they are inclined to do *x*, but that *y* might be the better choice, but then again maybe *x* would be best, and so on *ad infinitum*); phobics avoid situations and/or animals or insects that are anxiety provoking; and hysterics avoid recognizing what they themselves want.

The obsessive's mental landscape is dominated by doubt, doubt which "is, in reality, a doubt of his own love" (SE X, p. 241), a doubt that goes on to color or pervade his whole world, ending up with "an ever-increasing degree of indecision, loss of energy, and restriction of freedom" (SE XVI, p. 260). What should be the most certain is not, and therefore everything else is thrown into question. Everything he thinks he knows and remembers becomes open to question: "Did I lock the door?" "Did I remember to turn off the gas?" (He then has to check over and over again.) Through a longer or shorter series of missing intermediate thoughts, these questions almost always concern the person whom he both loves and hates (e.g., "Did I remember to turn off the gas? If not, the next person to go in my apartment might be my 'beloved,' and if she lights a candle or a cigarette, she might go up in smoke"; he keeps wanting, at some level, to have left the gas on so that she will die in the explosion).

In cases where the loving and hateful impulses are of equal strength, Forces 1 and 2 always remain at the level of thought, never being able to be put into action. And insofar as each of those forces brings a great deal of cathexis—that is, energy or excitation—with it, the thinking process itself becomes highly cathected, and indeed "libidinized" or sexualized. The constant cycling back and forth between alternatives ("I love her, I hate her, I love her, I hate her," as one of my analysands put it) turns into a kind of "mental masturbation" that is often characterized as painful or torturous, and yet that seems to bring with it some kind of satisfaction of its own (satisfaction that is a substitute for the kind of satisfaction action would more typically provide).

Jouissance in Obsession

I remarked [to Ernst Langer] that we were well aware that those who are ill derive a certain satisfaction from their suffering, such that they all, in fact, resist their own recovery to some degree.
—Freud, SE X, pp. 183–184

This should remind us of something Freud notices when Ernst tells him about the specific kind of torture practiced in certain Eastern countries (involving hungry rats burrowing into someone's anus), as it was recounted to him by Captain Nemeczek, the captain who is referred to in the published case history as the "cruel captain" (SE X):

> At all the more important moments while he was telling his story, his face took on a very strange, composite expression. I could only interpret it as one of *horror at pleasure of his own of which he himself was unaware.* He proceeded with the greatest difficulty: "At that moment the idea flashed through my mind that this [rat torture] was happening to a person who was very dear to me." (pp. 166–167; Freud's emphasis)

The Rat Man was obviously taking a kind of pleasure in imagining this horrible form of torture being carried out on Gisa (it turns out that he imagined it being carried out on his father, too), and yet he could not allow himself to recognize this pleasure as his own. It was precisely what the French would term *jouissance*—the satisfaction (in thought) of an aggressive drive that was simultaneously unbearable (even in thought), it being unpalatable to his moral conscience to even think such a thing. It was clearly exciting to him to imagine such a thing happening to someone dear to him, and yet at the same time he was horrified at his own pleasure ("These thoughts were entirely alien and repugnant to me," he said; SE X, p. 167).[23]

As extreme as this example may be, we often observe that patients smile, smirk, or even laugh as they tell us about all kinds of supposedly horrible things that have happened either to themselves or to others, their smiling, smirking, or laughter tipping us off that more is going on than meets the eye and that wishes are being revealed to us that are simultaneously repudiated by these patients. They are unwittingly informing us that Force 1 is finding some satisfaction in the story even as Force 2 (in the form of conscience here) is trying to keep a straight face or maintain a respectable countenance. The composite tone of voice with which they recount the story, and their labile facial expressions, speak of their contradictory feelings about it. The terms they use to describe their states characterized by jouissance vary considerably, running the gamut from "what really got me worked up" (or "revved up," "amped up," "riled up," "geared up," "jacked up," "jazzed," "jumped up," "all hot and bothered," "in a lather," or "my blood boiling") to "what really got me annoyed" ("pissed off," "bothered," "under my skin," "my dander up," and so on); what ultimately counts is not whether they describe the experience as positive or negative, but the amount of charge (or libido) that is attached to it.

The Rat Man seems to have been conflicted about virtually all sensations related to his anus, partly because he often had worms as a child, and also partly, no doubt, because of the beatings he suffered at his father's hands. Corporal punishment often leads to a kind of bodily closeness and aggressive passion between the beating and beaten parties that is not so distantly related to sexuality; and such punishment often targets the buttocks. Ernst's father would get very worked up when punishing his children—he would sometimes get carried away, no longer know what he was doing, get out of control, and go too far ("His father had had a passionate temper, and sometimes in his violence had not known where to stop"; SE X, p. 209)—and children are often excited ✦ by their ability to inspire such passion in their parents. There is something compelling to them about it. Here we see why Freud says that love and hate are so often inseparable. Even just being berated or criticized by one's parent can take on passionate, sexual overtones, and a child may well begin to find ways to bring on the parent's wrath in order to feel that passion again and again, especially in the absence of other parental attentions. Adolescents often repeatedly do things they know their parents will punish them for, especially when negative attention is the only kind of attention they feel they can get from their parents.

What such corporal punishment led to in the case of the Rat Man is that much, if not all, of his sexuality became tied up with his father. Popular culture prefers to depict cases in which it is the mother who gets wrapped up in her son's sexuality—consider Woody Allen in *Oedipus Rex*, where his mother appears in the New York City sky as if she were God when he is about to make love to his fiancée, and the movie entitled *Genie*, where the main character is just starting to make love to a woman he has been trying to get together with, and instead of her face he suddenly sees his mother's face. In such cases, having sex with a member of the opposite sex becomes a betrayal of one's mother, and this is fodder for comedy. Rarely, however, do we find depictions of the father entering the picture; yet they do so frequently in the love lives and fantasies of myriad obsessives. For the Rat Man, having sex meant betraying his father; note that the first time he had intercourse he said to himself, *"This is glorious, one might murder one's father for this!"* (SE X, p. 201; my emphasis).[24]

The Rat Man's Childhood Neurosis

I've outsourced my sexuality to masturbation.
—An analysand

When did Ernst's hateful thoughts involving his father begin? Around age 6, to the best of his recollection, he told Freud. Prior to that time, he seemed to have been able to express his affection toward the women in the household quite openly, but by age 6 his urges to see girls naked were always accompanied by the thought that something terrible would happen to his father, a thought that was itself accompanied by some form of self-punishment. Freud hypothesizes that something must obviously have happened in the interim—that is, between, say, ages 3 and 6. Yet the Rat Man was unable to recall anything that might have happened, until Freud made a quite specific hypothesis or "construction": The boy must have been beaten by his father for some "sexual misdemeanor connected with masturbation" (SE X, p. 205). This, Freud conjectured, "put an end to his masturbating, but . . . left behind an ineradicable grudge against his father."

Freud's construction seems to have been corroborated, at least in part, by the patient, who then recollected something his mother had repeatedly described to him: an incident in which he had bitten someone and was then brutally beaten by his father for it. While being beaten, "he had flown into a terrible rage and had hurled abuse at his father"—yelling things like, "You lamp! You towel! You plate!"—not having any truly insulting words at his disposal at that tender age, and perhaps thinking that it would be insulting to someone to be called by the name of such ordinary household items (SE X, p. 205).[25] Although the patient himself did not recall the incident directly, he seemed aware that he had become a coward from that moment on, "out of fear of the violence of his own rage"—in other words, as if he had suddenly come to feel that he could destroy someone with his angry words and that he had better protect them from his rage (pp. 205–206).

I suspect that few contemporary analysts make such hypotheses even when such an obvious transition in a patient's disposition or character calls for it. One might deliberately wait for such explanatory events to come out in the course of the analysis (and it might be argued that Freud did not wait anywhere near long enough), but in my experience, when no such explanations are forthcoming for quite some time, it is worth hazarding an incorrect hypothesis or construction in order to encourage the analysand to correct us. For example, in a case in which a man could not understand his own reaction to a traumatic incident in his childhood (seeing his uncle fighting with his mother, without intervening), I proposed that he in some sense felt his mother deserved the punishment and that he thus did not want to help her (he had often complained bitterly of things she had made him do); this turned out to be overly simplistic, but it led to a great deal of analytic work on the analysand's part. In the case of Ernst, Freud seems to have been wrong in assuming the child must have been engaged in some kind of *masturbatory* activity (he was perhaps led to hypothesize this because of the virtual non-existence of masturbation in the Rat Man's adolescence and adult life, and his various resolutions and vows not to masturbate), but the biting, *which had probably involved his "nurse," may well have been sexual as well as aggressive* (SE X, p. 206). In other words, although Freud may have been barking up the wrong tree, he was at least barking, and in the right general neighborhood.

Transference and Transferences

This leads us to the topic of Freud's technique at the time, which remained extremely active despite his claim that, in his work with the Rat Man, he for the first time truly followed the method of free association, allowing the patient a free rein in how to begin sessions and what to talk about in the course of them.[26] For we see that Freud took it upon himself to solve certain of the analysand's problems as they arose and in the order in which they arose, rather than allowing early childhood events, stories recounted by family members, and facts about loved ones to come out gradually over the course of a long period of work; the latter obviously poses a challenge to the analyst, who must remember what he does and does not yet know, and most likely keep a detailed record of incidents that come to light at points in time that are very distant from each other in order to fill in a more complete picture of the analysand's life.

Let us consider what this gave rise to as regards the transference. Ernst began to tell Freud about the severe crisis that started during the military training exercises he was part of in August 1907, and mentioned Captain Nemeczek (S. Freud, 2000, p. 55), whose story about the form of torture involving rats had such a big impact on him. But at one point in the story (SE X), the following happened:

> Here the patient broke off, got up from the sofa, and begged me to spare him the recital of the details. *I assured him that I myself had no taste whatsoever for cruelty, and certainly had no desire to torment him,* but that naturally *I could not grant him something that was beyond my power.* He might just as well ask me to give him the sun and the moon. The overcoming of resistances was *the law of psychoanalytic treatment,* and on no consideration could be dispensed with. . . . I went on to say that I would do all I could, nevertheless, to guess the full meaning of any hints he gave me. (p. 166; my emphasis)

Freud's first "guess" involves impalement and his second the anus. One of the immediate results of Freud's insistence on knowing what the patient was finding it so difficult to say aloud was that Ernst began calling Freud "Captain" during the very same session (SE X, p. 169), presumably having found rather cruel Freud's insistence on his overcoming his resistance so early on in the treatment! Freud's disclaimer—"I assure you, I have no taste for cruelty"—was belied by his insistence, proving to be a typically untrustworthy negation (S. Freud, 2000, p. 43).[27] The patient was undoubtedly aware that Freud could have waited a week or a month before learning the exact nature of the torture, and that the supposed "law" to which Freud professed to be submitting was actually a law of his own making (Ernst had, after all, read some of Freud's work).

Freud, at this point in his work, refers to moments like the one in which Ernst calls him "Captain" as individual "transferences" (S. Freud, 2000, p. 187), emphasizing their momentary nature, arising as they did at specific moments of the treatment. Nevertheless, there were so many such moments in the course of the analysis—for example, Freud's request that Ernst bring in a photograph of his lady and his insistence that Ernst tell Freud her name—that Freud quite enduringly became associated in the patient's mind with the "cruel captain" and with the patient's own punishing father.

The upshot of this was several periods in which, rather than remembering what had happened to him in his past, the Rat Man transferred onto Freud all kinds of negative feelings that he had had about his father (and other people who had interfered in his pleasures), and heaped abuse on Freud, his daughter, his wife, and every other member of his family whom he thought he knew about! He would walk around the office during sessions, keeping his distance from Freud as though he were expecting to be beaten at any moment by him for saying all manner of horrible things about him and his family (SE X, p. 209), and thus it was along the painful path of transference that many things came to light, rather than along the more time-consuming yet more bearable pathway of memory. As Freud tells us in his later work, what cannot be remembered is eventually repeated in the treatment—in the form of transference and acting out—and certain experiences, especially very early childhood experiences, can perhaps never come out in any other way. Yet it is clearly preferable to both the analysand (even though it requires a great deal of patience on his part) and the analyst when early experiences are recalled in connection with fantasies, dreams, and other topics, rather than through transferences that threaten to jeopardize the continuation of the analysis altogether.

Postmortem

The scientific results of psychoanalysis are at present only a byprod-
uct of its therapeutic aims, which is why it is often in the very cases
in which treatment fails that the most discoveries are made.
                                        —Freud, SE X, p. 208 n

Freud tells us that the treatment lasted most of a year (SE X, p. 155), and
we are aware that Freud generally saw his patients six times a week, suggesting that there were about 300 sessions in all. Few analysts are willing to work six days a week anymore, and the majority of patients are
unable to afford that many sessions per week given the fees most analysts request today; but we can see that Ernst and Freud were able to
accomplish quite a lot in a short space of time, even if Freud indicates
that he felt that Ernst's improved ability to work (SE X, pp. 220 and
249 n) led him to leave the analysis before a number of the threads of
his neurosis could be fully elucidated.

In this case, as in others, the quickly achieved relief brought on by the
therapy (which Freud worked so hard at) probably inclined the patient
to leave treatment before a number of other longstanding problems
could be addressed. In other words, short-term success got in the way
of longer-term success; or, as we might put it, too much relief early on
meant that the patient did not have the motivation necessary to go all the
way in his analysis, insofar as there is such a thing as "going all the way."

We might also suspect that the patient would have stayed longer had
Freud not badgered him for information at so many points in the therapy,
or insisted that something Ernst could not remember must have been
the case, despite his explicit goal of allowing the patient to take the lead
in each session and free-associate. Freud's attempt to convince Ernst to
bring a great many things out into the open quickly, and shed light on
obscure episodes from his past, may well have taken the reins of the
analysis out of the patient's hands, Ernst (like Dora, as we shall see in
the next chapter) *having come to feel it was Freud's analysis, not his own*.
Although this may have sped up the resolution of certain problems (like
the "rat complex"; SE X, p. 220), it was not conducive to the resolution
of others. Attempting to elucidate a specific problem quickly can be very
helpful to a patient during an acute crisis or anxiety attack, allowing him
or her to calm down, get some rest, and move forward in the remainder
of the analysis, but is ultimately counterproductive when adopted as a
regular strategy for every analysis and every session.[28]

On the plus side, we can say that Ernst's childhood trauma, stemming from the early conflict with his father owing to his having bitten someone, was drawn into relation with other experiences, thoughts, and events in his life. This was achieved, at least in part, by his reliving the conflict with Freud, berating him, heaping abuse upon Freud and his family, and expecting punishment from him. The Rat Man was able to express and articulate his rage against his father via Freud in the safe environment of the analytic setting, Freud neither being destroyed by his rage nor viciously retaliating against Ernst. In the transference, the conflict in Ernst between the id (aggression) and the superego (moral condemnation of aggressive feelings) was redirected from the symptom related to his father onto Freud, with whom the conflict was at least in part worked through. Within a year, the Rat Man presumably found that he no longer needed to repress his hateful tendencies as he had before. In many contemporary cases, far more time seems to be required to achieve as much. . . .

Some Forms Taken by Obsession Today: Doing Nothing and "Nothing Doing!"

> *I'm fed up with flushing my life away.*
>
> —An analysand

> *I will NOT invest in this life!*
>
> —An analysand

Turning now to the ways in which obsession often presents itself today, let us note that we have a tendency in everyday speech to talk about people as being "obsessed" in a work context, above all, whether that involves study, cooking, art, music, building, writing, planning, or any other kind of intense and perhaps detail-oriented activity. We talk about people who devote countless hours to such work as obsessed with their projects and their outcome, whereas in certain cases they are perhaps more *passionate* about them than truly "obsessed." Nevertheless, in contemporary common parlance, such people are often referred to as *anal* or *obsessive-compulsive*.

There is perhaps a category of people who could more aptly be thought of in terms of obsession, and the Rat Man was one of them: people who are diligently "doing nothing," who are occupied and preoccupied all day long with "not working." As an analysand of mine once put it, "Not working is a full-time job for me," a beautifully paradoxical claim that indicates that *not working is something that is often done* in our times (indeed, some work hard at not working!), not because one is a man or woman of leisure who was raised in the lap of luxury, has never had to make a living, and enjoys doing plenty of things that have no connection with paid work (think Bertie Wooster of P. G. Wodehouse fame), but rather *as a protest* against something, a statement, or the product of some kind of conflict. For some, saying no is a way of life—a career choice, even.[29]

Another analysand of mine once declared, "Making a living is not high on my list of things to do," and later amended that by saying, "In fact, making a living is not on my list of things to do at all; it's on my list of things NEVER to do." Indeed, it seemed quite clear that he was determined *not* to make a living, not to make anything of himself, and was dead set on sending the following message to his parents[30] and to anyone else who expected great things of him: *"Nothing doing!"* (As we shall see in Chapter 6, the vast majority of symptoms are secretly or unwittingly "designed" to send a message to one or more people, usually one's parents.) He was, in short, saying that there was no way he was going to let them have their way, no way that he was going to give in to their wishes that he become a great writer, stockbroker, professor, or anything else they had mentioned over the years. He was permanently on strike, as it were, and was actively on strike, deliberately doing anything other than what might even remotely smack of work—such as paying his bills, cleaning his house, or studying something that might one day lead to paid work. The analysand mentioned in the previous paragraph (who said, "Not working is a full-time job for me") once reported that one of his partners used to complain that he made her do all the work during sex; he went on to say, "My penis has no work ethic," insofar as it refused to function in such a way as to give his sexual partners pleasure, adding that *his penis was "on strike"* (which is nicely indicative of the subjective component we often find in so-called erectile dysfunction).[31]

Let us keep in mind that, for all of us, our primary caretakers (usually our parents or close relatives) act as killjoys at various moments in our lives (often one parent is perceived to be more of a killjoy than the other, when there are two parental figures involved in our upbringing). If we are breastfed as infants, we are eventually weaned, and weaning is a difficult experience for many of us, especially given (a) that breastfeeding is our primary source of early nourishment and often of comfort as well (this is true of bottle-feeding, too, given the closeness to the parent that typically accompanies it), and (b) that weaning tends to occur when we are still quite young in many Western cultures today, whereas in other cultures and eras it would last two to five years. If we begin to suck our thumbs or other fingers as a substitute for the breast or bottle, we eventually get grief for it from our parents, and there is often a struggle around giving it up, along with the tickle blanket (or "blankie"), stuffed animal, or other piece of soft fabric that generally accompanies it; some parents even go so far as to put red-hot pepper on their children's fingers or slap them whenever they put their fingers in their mouths. Breast- or bottle-feeding and weaning obviously correspond to what Freud called the "oral stage" of libidinal development, where the mouth is a primary source of satisfaction for the infant and then a considerable source of conflict between parent and child.

And toilet training is well-known to be a realm in which a great deal of conflict between children and their parents occurs, parents often attempting to initiate potty training too early (before children have much control over their sphincters) and children often getting the sense that it is more important to their parents that they be toilet-trained than virtually anything else. Kids sometimes get the impression that cleaning up their urine and excrement is considered by their caretakers to be such a huge pain in the neck that they will impose virtually any kind of training on their children that promises to put an end to it—including scare tactics, shaming, and enemas. Toilet training obviously corresponds to what Freud called the "anal stage" of libidinal development, during which control over the bowels may lead to considerable struggle between parent and child.

Note that in most psychology textbooks, Freud's oral, anal, and genital stages are mentioned with little or no discussion of the conflicts that develop between parents and children over them; in other words, they are presented as though they were stages of the child's biological development alone, corresponding to nothing as regards socialization and/or parental demands and desires.[32] Lacan emphasizes the complex relations between parents and children concerning the oral and anal stages in numerous seminars (see, especially, Seminar VIII, Chapters 14 and 15), indicating the degree to which they involve a potentially fraught and damaging dance between parents' and children's wishes.

Parents also stop us from running around naked in front of friends and family, as most of us are inclined to do when we are little, and often prohibit any signs of masturbatory activity they detect (sometimes in scathingly derogatory terms, sometimes just by telling us to only do that in private). At some point, they generally begin to make it more difficult for us to hang all over or even hang around a good deal with the one parent who has long been the greatest object of our affections (i.e., they initiate the *Oedipus complex*). And they often manage to interrupt sexual exploration we engage in as children (playing "doctor" and other such games) and vehemently criticize as unsuitable the children or adolescents we choose as our first girlfriends or boyfriends (masturbation and sexual exploration correspond to some degree to what Freud called the *genital stage* of libidinal development). Without even counting the hundreds of things they make us do or not do day in and day out (wake up at certain times, get dressed, brush our teeth, eat this and not that, hold our forks one way and our knives another, sit still, sit up straight, cover our mouths when we yawn or cough, not pass gas in public, go to school, do our homework, dress, look, talk, listen, and stand in specific ways—the list goes on and on), it is no stretch to say that our parents make us do a plethora of things we do not want to do, and prohibit us from doing a great many enjoyable things that we really want to do.

They impose upon us, therefore, a true sacrifice or loss of enjoyment—that is, jouissance—and we often come to bitterly resent them for it forever thereafter (I am speaking here about those who actually make the sacrifice, not about those who refuse to make one or more of those early sacrifices—never becoming potty trained, never speaking at all or in the way our parents require us to, eating as little as possible and certainly not what our parents tried to make us eat, etc.). Despite having given in to so many of their demands, and having sacrificed so many of our early enjoyments, many of us feel that we have received very little in return—in terms of love and/or recognition—and certainly not enough to have made it worth our while. We feel we have been treated most unfairly, shortchanged, cheated, gypped, ripped off, duped, bamboozled, and had our most precious objects wrenched from us (e.g., mother's breasts, our thumbs, and our blankies). And a number of us decide to draw the line somewhere, to take a stand and agree to go no further. "Enough sacrifices already!" we seem to yell. Now you want us to study hard instead of partying; keep our noses to the grindstone instead of lounging around, drinking, or smoking; go into a profession which does not interest us in the slightest—"Nothing doing!" "God forbid we should give you such pleasure and allow you to feel you have been good parents!" "Anything but that!"

I have depicted things here as though this were a conscious process—that is, as though we were aware that we had decided to draw the line here and knew exactly what we were protesting against—yet this is certainly not always the case. Some of us are unwitting protesters, believing that we actually want to work but have an *inability* to work ("having" so-called ADHD, OCD, or dyslexia, for example), some kind of a constitutional incapacity for work. Yet we, too, unconsciously wish to defeat or foil the very people who we feel have deprived us of a great deal and have imposed so many sacrifices and unpleasant activities upon us. Like the Rat Man, by "worrying" about the health of our loved ones, masturbating, and making a show of working (e.g., sitting in front of our schoolbooks, reading the same sentence over and over again, or simply daydreaming), we foil their career and marital hopes for us, waste their tuition dollars, and torpedo their best-laid plans. What could be more rewarding to us than that?! (One of my analysands referred to his refusal to toe the line as his "nuclear no," feeling that it was the most powerful weapon he possessed.)

Little do we care that we waste our lives in the process, that we "throw them away" or "flush them down the toilet," because our primary goal—whether we know it or not—is to deprive our parents of what we think they want from us. (Ernst Langer, for example, believed his mother wanted him to marry Lizzie, and his response to her was, "No way! Better to never finish my law degree and never marry than do your bidding!") No matter how debilitating such stances become for our own lives, *we derive more satisfaction from them than from anything else.* Which does not stop us from complaining about our lack of progress in life, or our making nothing of ourselves, owing to our supposed disabilities—genetic inadequacies, hormonal imbalances, neurotransmitter deficiencies, and the like—which medical science kindly allows us currently to blame on our parents' defective genes and/or our mother's less-than-ideal physiological condition during our intrauterine growth. Complaining about all of this and pitying ourselves become pleasures in their own right, little in life seeming as sweet in comparison. Certain of my obsessive patients have described to me in great detail the delectable delights they have at times derived from self-pity![33]

Going Through the Motions: Doing Something as if One Did Not Want To

> *I stay up late at night to try to get a little extra something for myself.*
> —An analysand

Not all obsessives are constantly on strike—some engage in a form of "work slowdown." Just as striking employees at times continue to provide some limited services (this is perhaps especially common in parts of Europe) but thwart the smooth functioning of their operations—whether subway, bus, train, garbage removal, snow removal, or any other form of service—certain obsessives continue to go through the motions of work but do so in a way that they themselves know to be inefficient, downright ineffective, or even counterproductive. Often, in the supposed interest of increased speed, they skip steps that experience has repeatedly taught them are crucial, which then requires them to go back later and complete those omitted steps, rendering a good part of their initial work useless. In this way they do and undo and then redo a great many things, *as if they felt compelled to carry out a certain project and yet not carry it out at the same time.* Completion of the work is put off, sometimes almost indefinitely. The explicit excuse often given is that it is not yet "perfect" (such people are referred to at times in common parlance as *perfectionistic* or *anal-retentive*).

This is a bit different than the kind of procrastination discussed in the previous section, for true procrastination is such that one never really begins to work at all. The one blurs into the other, however, to the degree to which those who perform work as though they do not want to often ostensibly work at parts of a project that are actually superfluous, which is ultimately just as counterproductive as watching TV or looking at social media instead of working. In both cases, the conflict between wanting to do something (or at least acting like one wants to) and refusing to do it is quite clear. In one case, it leads to doing nothing at all, in the other to doing plenty, but nothing conducive to getting the job done.

In the latter case, too, people often feel that they are living for others, doing everything for the significant others in their lives (spouses, children, bosses, etc.), and find themselves trying to sneak in a little bit of "illicit jouissance" for themselves late at night or during an extended lunch hour. Whether it involves drugs, pornography, alcohol, or just surfing the Net, it often compromises their ability to work in the afternoon or the next day; yet they feel compelled to squeeze a little bit of jouissance out of the day or night "just for themselves," not for others (they generally feel they are living almost exclusively for the Other, *à l'heure de l'Autre,* as Lacan calls it in Seminar VI: on the Other's watch, so to speak, or marching to the Other's drum).[34]

Obsessives are certainly not alone in refusing to do what parental figures (whether parents themselves, teachers, bosses, or other authorities) explicitly ask or obviously want them to do. Phobics may thwart parents' travel plans by developing a fear of flying; hysterics may binge eat or become anorexic in order not to look the part their parents want them to play in life ("the lovely, model daughter," for example), or as a protest against parental wishes that they become beauty pageant winners, models, actors, singers, or the like; psychotics may be understood to make a more radical and far-reaching rejection (Lacan calls it a "foreclosure") of their parents' prohibitions and punishments; and some children who are categorized as autistic may go so far as to even refuse the language in which parental injunctions and prohibitions are enunciated (note that what psychoanalysts like Bettelheim, 1967, refer to as autism does not necessarily correspond to what the *DSM-5* [APA, 2013] characterizes as "autistic spectrum disorder"). All of these refusals and protests can be understood to be self-defeating in certain ways, and as destructive of certain vital components of the refusing party's life, and yet they are engaged in at least initially as self-protective measures. Nevertheless, the "self" they are designed to protect often ends up being extremely limited.

Nothing Else Matters

I only want what I can't have.

—An analysand

Is this my life? This is not my life.

—An analysand

The protest, as we see it in obsession, for example, seems to imply that what we lost (for example, the breast as the "lost object" of early satisfaction, or the freedom to urinate or defecate whenever and wherever we chose)[35] was so much better than anything we could possibly get now that it is not even worth our while to try to ever get anything again. The pittance we could possibly get for ourselves today is worth nothing next to what those horrible people (our parents, teachers, etc.) made us give up. Any and every effort we might make to attain or achieve something would be doomed in advance, for we would never get back the object (for example, mom) or the comfort, warmth, and jouissance that we feel we were deprived of. Something is forever after rotten in the state of Denmark, and we have the radical sense that something is wrong, that something is missing in our lives, and that there is no hope of ever making things right.

This is fundamentally true. We can't go home again, we cannot have our primary caretaker and love object the way we believed we once had her or him (that is, with the sense of there having been no distinction between us, no boundary where one of us left off and the other began)—once we have come into being as individuals or subjects in our own right, such a sense of fullness, completeness, and blissful merger with another is no longer possible (except, perhaps, with the help of certain psychedelic drugs); henceforward we are doomed to always feel separate, incomplete, or lacking in some regard. Psychoanalysis can attenuate the intensity of this feeling, but can never eradicate it altogether (in the best of cases, it gives us the sense that such incompleteness is no longer of any interest or concern, other things we are doing being so much more compelling).

Although none of us can return to a state prior to separation from our parent(s), some of us feel (even without undergoing analysis) that what we received by way of love and recognition from our parents for our willingness to be weaned, toilet-trained, and socialized in myriad other ways was not so incredibly awful, overall, and that life seems to promise us some perhaps never entirely sufficient, but at least necessary satisfactions (even if we, to paraphrase Mick Jagger, can't always get what we want, if we try sometimes we just might find we get what we need). All of us continue to feel all of our lives that something is missing, that there is always still something that we have not obtained, attained, or achieved, and this keeps us shifting from one field of study or endeavor to another, from one set of friends to another, from one favorite author or director to another, from one lover to another, from one gadget to another, and so on. The gap we feel between the pricelessness of what we lost and the only relative value of each thing that we find keeps us forever in search of something more, something new and different that might be closer in value to that of the lost object; this Lacan (*Écrits*, p. 534) refers to as the "metonymy of desire" (metonymy here in the sense of desire's continual slippage or movement from one object to another related object), insofar as we keep looking for something new and different in our endless quest to close that gap.

But among extreme obsessives, one of the most commonly heard complaints is, "What's the point?" They are convinced in advance that they could never find any satisfaction that could in any way be commensurate with what they feel they lost, that could in any way make the endless quest known as life worthwhile. It avails little for the analyst to try to tell them that they might manage to find something worthwhile, if only they tried. It is as if it were always already too late for them! Whatever they might find now, whatever they might be able to achieve now, whether they are currently 20, 30, 40, 50, 60, or 70, would never be sufficient, since they are *so many years behind* where they would have been had they begun to try earlier (when, exactly, is always rather vague). They will never be able to "catch up," so what is the point of even trying? The obsessive is always behind schedule, behind everyone else, late to the party—so late, indeed, that there's no point even showing up.[36]

At its worst, such a stance leads to the impotent wish for a "do-over" (like little kids say when, in a game or sport, they have made a false start, slipped, or made a mistake), as if the hands of time could be turned back and the game started over again from zero. One of my analysands repeatedly expressed his demand for a "replacement life," a new life that would begin where he felt his went terribly wrong. Analysands like him—and there are many!—never feel they can truly be as old as it says on their birth certificates, as they have never really inhabited any age they have reached since some particular age—often their teenage years when they first began to be so disaffected. They often feel that the life they are living is not their "real life," and that their real life must be waiting for them somewhere else. Sometimes this is accompanied— and Freud (SE IX, pp. 237–241) pointed this out already, but not just for obsessives—by the sense that the parents who raised them must not be their real parents: They must have far better, more socially elevated parents somewhere (this is part and parcel of the "family romance," the novelistic rewriting of their history).

A man in his mid-fifties came to me complaining that he could not manage to be an adult—to grow up and act his age (this was not his only complaint). Although an accomplished professional in his chosen field, he felt he could not play the role that he had been entrusted with, could not assume a position of authority with any degree of serious- ness. He felt for some years in the analysis that he was still a child at heart—and not in a positive sense—and it was only after several years that he started to feel he could actually be as old as he was and begin to age gracefully and take on the roles assigned to older individuals in his native culture.

One of my obsessive patients indicated that if he didn't engage in life activities and compete with others for recognition, it was because that way (a) he could not lose, and (b) the winner could never feel sure he was better than the patient because the latter might have beaten him had he competed. The patient thereby took some of the wind out of the sails of all those he perceived to be winners, feeling in this way somewhat victorious over them.

It is their obsession with or fixation on early losses that leads such patients to put their lives on hold indefinitely. Their fundamental sense of having been shortchanged by their families and by the world at large must be worked through before they are able to move on in life and try to obtain the satisfactions that *are* available to them. Cognitive-behavioral therapy (CBT) is currently considered by many to be the "therapy of choice" for those suffering from so-called obsessive-compulsive disor- der. Yet CBT, with its focus on the present and on changing current thoughts, tends not to even broach the deeper roots of the problems suffered by those considered to be obsessive in psychoanalytic terms: the basic sense of having been ripped off, of having been deprived of the only thing worthwhile.

CHAPTER 5

Hysteria and the Case of Dora
(Ida Bauer)

> *Cases that are devoted from the outset to scientific purposes and are*
> *treated accordingly suffer in their outcome; the most successful cases*
> *are those in which one proceeds, as it were, without any purpose*
> *in view, allows oneself to be taken by surprise by any new turn in*
> *them, and always meets them with an open mind, free from any*
> *presuppositions.*
>
> —Freud, SE XII, p. 114

A S MUCH AS the case of the Rat Man has inclined generations of readers of psychoanalysis to become analysands themselves, Freud's
work with 18-year-old Dora has put people off and led them to steer
clear of analytic treatment. (I address a number of the critiques that
have been made of Freud's work with Dora in Appendix I, since readers
who have heard such critiques may think them so damning as to be
disinclined to study the case at all; I would encourage them to peruse
that appendix before continuing on here.) Freud's work with Dora represented an early form of analytic technique, which he later rejected quite
adamantly in his 1911–1915 *Papers on Technique* ("Unfortunate results
led me to abandon earlier methods"; SE XII, p. 111), and which he even
claimed to reject at the time he was working with Dora, whose real
name was Ida Bauer and whom I shall refer to as Ida throughout this
chapter.[1] It is nevertheless clear that Freud found it difficult to break certain of his own bad habits: that of trying to *figure everything out himself*
as quickly as possible, in any given case, and that of very much *wanting
to be right*, even if it did the patient precious little good.

Having played the part of an infallible, masterful figure in his work as
a hypnotist—which was probably not that different from the role played

by many physicians and psychiatrists (the "neurologists" or "nerve specialists") of his time, regardless of how inadequate their medical knowledge was, and no matter how often the advice of doctors was ridiculed by novelists (e.g., Dumas) and playwrights (e.g., Molière), especially the fact that no two of them could ever agree with each other—Freud continued to endeavor to play the role of a *perfect master of knowledge* for years in his early "analytic" practice. We saw some examples of this in the previous chapter regarding his work with the Rat Man (1907–1908), which proves that this approach to practice lingered on far longer in his consulting room than Freud would, at some level, have liked it to.

Let us consider what he says in his "Prefatory Remarks" to the Dora case study (SE VII):

> Readers who are familiar with the technique of analysis as it was expounded in the *Studies on Hysteria* will perhaps be surprised that it should not have been possible in three months [the approximate length of Dora's treatment] to find a complete solution at least for those of Dora's symptoms that were broached. This will become intelligible when I explain that psychoanalytic technique has been completely revolutionized since then [1895]. At that time, the work of analysis started out from the symptoms and aimed at clearing them up one by one. I subsequently abandoned that technique, because I found it totally inadequate for dealing with the finer structure of a neurosis. I now let the patient himself choose the subject of the day's work, and in this way I start out from whatever surface his unconscious happens to be presenting to his notice at the moment. But on this plan everything that has to do with the clearing-up of a particular symptom emerges piecemeal, woven into various contexts, and distributed over widely separated periods of time. In spite of this apparent disadvantage, the new technique is far superior to the old, and indeed there can be no doubt that it is the only possible one. (p. 12)

Despite this declaration, we find instance upon instance in which Freud appears to have *directed* Ida to continue talking about a dream (for example, one they had already discussed at some length in the previous session) and interpreted virtually every aspect of it for her instead of encouraging her to free-associate to it and interpret it herself;[2] asked her to tell him about a letter she had been reading in his waiting room before he opened the door for her, without pausing to see if she would tell him herself (p. 78); and did anything but wait patiently for keys to a particular symptom to emerge "piecemeal, woven into various contexts, and distributed over widely separated periods of time." Instead, he seems at times to have more or less kicked open locked doors, pushed Ida to make revelations as if she were in a confessional (pp. 74–76), and jumped to conclusions which he then tried to compel her to confirm (pp. 58–59 and 69–70).

When we compare his approach to working with her—as it is conveyed in his case write-up, at least—with a comment he makes later in the *Papers on Technique*, to the effect that *the analyst should not make an interpretation until the analysand is but "one short step away" from drawing the same conclusion herself* (SE XII, p. 140; my emphasis), we see that by 1913 he had realized the folly of his earlier ways. The interpretations he arrived at of Ida's predicament, as brilliant or off the mark as they may have been, had only a moderate effect on Ida's mental health (as far as we know) because she had not arrived at and articulated virtually any of those conclusions herself—or so I will argue.

It should be kept in mind that whatever Freud recommends we *not* do in the *Papers on Technique*, he himself did at one time or another! He learned, to some degree, by trial and error, and explored numerous different avenues before hitting upon the approach he presents to us in those *Papers*. And as is true of all moralists, the warnings contained in those texts were often addressed to himself, because they are precisely the sorts of things that he (and others like him) were constantly tempted to do. He essentially asks us to "do as I say, not as I do." Recall that there is no need to issue warnings or rules about something that no one is tempted to do. If practitioners never became romantically or sexually involved with their analysands, for example, there would be no reason to stipulate that therapists must never get romantically or sexually involved with their patients![3]

The result of Freud's way of practicing in 1900 was that Ida's analysis became not so much Ida's as it was Freud's. This is indicated by the following:

- He refers to her treatment as "my treatment" (SE VII, p. 120) at one point, and mentions "my conclusions" (p. 95) and the fact that he informed Ida "of the conclusions [he] had reached" (p. 100).
- He says that he "determined to make an especially careful investigation" of her first dream, and that his "expectations from the clearing-up of that dream were naturally heightened . . . , but [he] wanted to discover first what had been the exciting cause of its recent recurrence" (p. 64); this obviously implies that he had his own agenda, which was to prove, in the context of an actual clinical case, the theories he had expounded in *The Interpretation of*

Dreams, such as that all dreams fulfill wishes, and that they fulfill childhood wishes as well (pp. 68 and 71).

- He tells us that he wanted "to give a complete explanation of this case of *petite hystérie*" (p. 24); and yet he tells us that he could not as it was broken off too soon to have been considered a complete analysis, and so its gaps had to be filled in based on "other cases that were subject to thorough analysis" (p. 85), making us wonder why he wrote up this case and not the others (the answer ostensibly having to do with the two dreams that he analyzed in it, but perhaps having at least as much to do with other factors that we will turn to later).[4]

- He expressed to Ida his "satisfaction" at the end of what he believed to have been a particularly fruitful session (this is especially significant in light of the fact that Ida broke off the analysis at the very next session; p. 105).

- And at the end of the case study, where we learn that she came back to see him 15 months later to restart her analysis, Freud, instead of resuming the work with her under different auspices, was instantaneously convinced "she was not in earnest" (p. 121) and indicated that he "promised to forgive her for having deprived [him] of the satisfaction of affording her a far more radical cure for her troubles" (p. 122)—in other words, for having dashed his hopes of arriving at a complete explanation of everything in her life and bringing the analysis to a glorious end "just when [his] hopes of a successful termination of the treatment were at their highest" (p. 109).

It was obviously far too important to Freud at the time to show the world, through Ida's analysis, that his psychotherapeutic method was simply marvelous, and demonstrate that his approach to interpreting dreams as found in *The Interpretation of Dreams* contained the gospel truth.

Despite later claims that analysis should not be subordinated to "scientific purposes" (e.g., SE XII, p. 114), it seems quite clear that he subordinated Ida's treatment, at least the last several weeks of it, to a demonstration of his dream theory; indeed, he had initially intended to entitle this case study "Dreams and Hysteria" (SE VII, p. 10). It is, after all, hard to believe that Ida would have spontaneously devoted two or three full sessions in a row to the discussion of a dream if Freud had not strongly encouraged her to.[5] Note, too, that Freud withheld this case study from publication for five years, initially perhaps because it was rejected by the publisher he sent it to (Brodmann, the editor of the *Journal für Psychologie und Neurologie*) as containing too much personal or identifying information, but perhaps also because of certain qualms he had about the work he had done with Ida (see pp. 7 and 322). Otherwise it is hard to account for the fact that, although it was soon accepted for inclusion in a different journal, Freud withdrew it and waited another four years before finally publishing it.[6]

Synopsis of Ida's Situation

Like the living works of literature that they are, the material [Freud's case histories] contain is always richer than the original analysis and interpretation that accompany it.[7]
—Marcus, 1975/1990, p. 310

After such a preamble, let us turn to a brief summary of Ida's situation. Ida's father contracted syphilis (or a syphilitic-type illness) prior to his marriage to Ida's mother, and was thought to have transmitted "luetic" (i.e., syphilitic) symptoms to his wife, and possibly to his daughter as well (including, it seems, vaginal discharges that they found quite unpleasant and shameful; SE VII, pp. 83–84). When Ida was around 12 years of age, her father—who had already suffered from quite a few ailments, including labored breathing (dyspnoea), since she was about 6—was again doing badly and consulted Freud, who recognized the sexually transmitted disease and managed to help him when other physicians had been unable to (p. 19).

Relations between Ida's father and mother had not been good for many years (the mother may have developed what Freud refers to as "housewife's psychosis," perhaps having become obsessed with cleaning the family home owing to her "dirty" syphilitic secretions [SE VII, pp. 20 and 90], or because it was the only part of her life she felt she had any control over). And although the father was supposedly sexually impotent, he seemed to have been carrying on a romantic and sexual relationship with the female half of a couple, the Ks, that Ida's family had met while they were living, owing to the father's tuberculosis, in a small town that Freud refers to as B— (they moved to this Alpine resort, now known to be Merano in present-day Italy, when Dora was around six; p. 19).

Ida and Frau K had become intimate friends and indeed confidants for each other, sleeping in the same bedroom at night during visits and discussing details of sexual techniques—perhaps the kind used when a man has what has come to be known as "erectile dysfunction" (cunnilingus and fellatio?).[8] Frau K and her husband did not get along, had

considered getting divorced, but had thus far stayed together purportedly because of their children; and Ida had apparently served as Frau K's
"adviser in all the difficulties of her married life" (SE VII, p. 61).

Ida's "Entry" into Analysis

⌈*The structure of a neurosis is essentially a question [that the subject
⌊asks herself].*

—Lacan, Seminar III, p. 174

An issue of overriding concern to any practitioner would, I believe, be
the fact that Ida, who was still a teenager, *did not come to see Freud of
her own volition,* and indeed did not want to talk to anyone about her
predicament. She had seen dozens of doctors since she was a little girl
for a wide variety of ailments (labored breathing, migraine headaches,
nervous coughing, and loss of voice, among others), and had learned to
laugh at their futile efforts to cure her of any of them.[9] She had no faith
in physicians, and it was only at her father's insistence and owing to his
"authority" that, "in spite of her reluctance," she went to see Freud (SE
VII, pp. 22–23).

Worse still, perhaps, is that Ida herself expressed no interest in changing! *It was her father who wanted her to change.* He wanted her to change
because he was incredibly bothered by her ever more negative attitude
toward what he referred to as his innocent "friendship" with Frau K
(the wife of his good friend Herr K), a woman who had taken devoted
care of him during a number of his illnesses spanning quite a few years.
Ida had formerly been quite close to Frau K (beginning perhaps as early
as age 6, when Ida's family first moved to Merano, and continuing up
to age 16; SE VII, p. 19) and had initially taken no exception to Frau K
spending vast quantities of time with her father. But starting at age 16,
after an event to which we will turn shortly, her attitude changed and
she became disappointed with Frau K and furious with her father.

Moreover, it was Ida's father who contacted Freud, supposedly on
Ida's behalf, and he tried to convince Freud of his version of what was
going on between himself and Frau K, and of what had "really happened" between Frau K's husband, Herr K, and Ida. At age 16, Ida had
complained to her family that Herr K had propositioned her; when her
father and uncle looked into this, Herr K denied it vehemently (the vehe-
mence of his denial could easily have been understood by Ida's father as
a telltale sign of lying, but the father was certainly no psychologist and
preferred to believe that no such proposition had ever been made; SE

VII, pp. 25–26). To make matters still worse, Herr K claimed that Ida had been reading all kinds of books about sex (like Mantegazza's *Physiology of Love*) they had at their lake house and that she had obviously imagined the whole thing (p. 26). Now, the only way he could have known that Ida had been devouring such literature was if Frau K had told her husband about what she and Ida had discussed in private—in other words, it was clear to Ida that Frau K had betrayed her trust (SE VII, p. 62), having conveyed some or all of what she had told Frau K in confidence to Herr K (a man Frau K had often professed to wish to divorce). Ida's father was only too happy to believe that the "indecent proposal" had transpired in Ida's head alone, and wished to confide to Freud the task of convincing Ida that she had made up the whole scene!

Just about any clinician will, I suspect, concur that these are terrible auspices under which to begin psychotherapeutic work with someone. The patient had no interest in changing and no faith in therapy; she was being forced to see a practitioner because her father wanted that practitioner to convince her that all was hunky-dory: that his relationship with this "other woman" was not an affair of the heart or body, that his friend Herr K had never propositioned Ida, that they had made no sort of arrangement (whether explicit or tacit) whereby the father would receive Frau K in exchange for Herr K receiving Ida, and that all was thus well in the best of all possible worlds, there being no reason for the father to give up Frau K.

Freud obviously refused to take on the task proposed by Ida's father, but he agreed to meet with the girl herself to talk.[10]

The first task the clinician is faced with in such a situation is to *see if there is a way to intrigue the patient such that she finds a reason of her own to wish to engage in treatment.* Therapy that is done in order to please or appease someone else—put differently, to find favor with someone or get him off one's back—is doomed to go nowhere, and thus a patient who comes because someone else wants her to will get precious little out of the work if she does not quickly become inspired by it. Some may be initially intrigued by the relationship with the therapist as a new person in their lives, finding the therapist good-looking, witty, sympathetic, caring, or interesting in some other way, and this may, for a while, fuel their willingness to physically show up for sessions. But if the clinician is unable to find a way to inspire in the patient a curiosity of her own about how she wound up in the situation in which she now finds herself (her curiosity may grow out of the encounter with the practitioner's curiosity about her, and the practitioner should consider highlighting contradictions and paradoxes in what she says, for they may incite in her an interest in exploring her own history and figuring out what is going on), the therapy cannot but founder, since genuine therapeutic work is always fueled by the patient's own desire to discover something, to figure something out, or to find a new way forward. In psychoanalysis, it is the analysand's desire that serves as the ultimate motor force of the analysis (as Freud puts it, "the patient's desire for recovery, which has induced him to take part with us in our joint work"; SE XVI, p. 437). And whereas the analyst's desire must prop up and sustain the analysand's desire at times (and occasionally even stand in for it when the analysand has temporarily lost enthusiasm for the analytic project), there is no analysis strictly speaking if no desire on the analysand's part to explore and move on in her life ever comes to the fore. The analysand, if she stays at all, ends up simply "going through the motions."[11]

In this sense, we might view it as somewhat astonishing that Freud managed to keep Ida at least somewhat involved in the project for three months, for a total of around 70 sessions. There are even a few hints in Freud's case write-up that Ida had begun to raise questions of her own: He tells us (a) that, regarding the suicide note she wrote when she could no longer stand the relationship between her father and Frau K and had entertained the idea of ending it all, she wondered how her parents could possibly have found the letter since she had locked it in her desk (p. 23 n. 1); (b) that, prior to the first dream, she had been wondering why she had fallen ill and (without Freud's help) had concluded that her father was to blame for having passed his illness on to her (SE VII, p. 75);[12] and (c) that, prior to the second dream, "Dora herself had been raising a number of questions about the connection between some of her actions and the motives which presumably underlay them" (p. 95), especially regarding why she did not immediately tell her parents about Herr K's proposal (he was perhaps going to propose that he leave his wife and marry Ida, but Ida slapped him and did not allow him to finish speaking) by the lake in the town of L— (a proposal that highly offended her), and regarding why she then suddenly told them about it some time later (see also p. 104 n. 2, and p. 107, where we see that this question persisted in her thoughts right up until the end of the treatment).

The reader of the case write-up receives the impression, however, that, rather than fostering such self-questioning on Ida's part—and, insofar as desire (as Lacan tells us) is a question, rather than nurturing Ida's desire—rather than giving her room to run with her own ponderings and follow up her own lines of thought, Freud keeps bringing her back to what *he* considers to be the task at hand, which he seems to formulate at the time as getting her to divulge all of her deepest, most hidden motives and machinations *to him*.

It was rare at that point in time for Freud to work with anyone for more than a year at a stretch, and he already seems to have felt the need to temper the belief of the intended readers of his case history that he should have been able to cure Ida of everything that ailed her in three short months (SE VII, p. 12). Later, once Freud began to work with people for several years at a time, and occasionally even many years, he perhaps began to see things a bit differently, realizing that it was far more important to cultivate in the analysand a self-sustaining desire to figure something out—a somewhat autonomous desire that the analyst could simply accompany—than to work toward immediate "full confessions" of what Freud was convinced was the case (e.g., that Ida had wet her bed long after the usual age, had masturbated as a child [pp. 75–79], and was in love with Herr K and had sought to take revenge on him [p. 95])[13] and toward exhaustive explanations.

One consequence of Freud's single-minded goal is that he seems to have been working way too hard! Rather than inviting Ida to begin sessions as she pleased, wander off in this direction and that, and put things together at her own pace, his mind seems to have been in overdrive day after day as he attempted to figure everything out with as little help from her as possible (he even tells us that on one occasion his brainpower was at a rather "low ebb," because he had failed to immediately grasp something, and "let her go on talking," which led to her putting two and two together herself; SE VII, p. 59). We might say that all this brilliance was wasted by his insistence on getting to the bottom of it all on his own and of being infallibly right (p. 66). What good could Freud being right possibly do anyone if Ida wasn't helped by his interpretations (see p. 99)? And how could we even possibly know he was right if Ida wasn't helped by them? Isn't a patient being helped the only ultimate proof of an interpretation being on the mark?[14]

Whereas obsessive patients would often prefer to do all the interpretative work themselves, without any input whatsoever from the analyst (they may ignore what the analyst says, feign not to have heard it, belittle it, or bulldoze right over it), hysteric patients often end up in situations where their analyst is doing virtually all the work, whether because hysterics present themselves as incapable of doing the work—that is, as needing help—or because analysts themselves fall into the trap of seeing them that way (or both).[15] Whereas an analyst must ensure that obsessive patients actually stop talking long enough to take cognizance of things the analyst has said (and analysts must at times somewhat forcefully interrupt obsessives' monologues rather than accept to be silenced and sit back and do nothing), the analyst must try to find a way to ensure that hysterics do the lion's share of the work in analysis. I suspect that most psychoanalytic supervisors today would consider Freud to have been overly invested in the treatment, excessively hurt by what he took to be Ida's "unmistakable act of vengeance" directed at him (p. 109), and working far too hard throughout the analysis, attempting to impress Ida with the brilliance of his deductions, à la Sherlock Holmes (see, especially, his account of their last session together, in which it seems like he could not shut up and simply allow her to talk; p. 108).

Much of what Freud ends up deducing—regarding Ida's early childhood masturbation, her love for her father, her love for Frau K, the meaning of her dreams (pp. 66, 69), and so on—is ultimately quite useless insofar as he deduces it himself instead of bringing her to do so in a way that would be convincing to her and have an impact upon her life (see, for example, p. 82). Indeed, he badgers her at times, trying to force her to admit he is right about things that she does not agree with (e.g., about the reticule or purse she brings with her to a session one day, regarding which he appears to be policing her behavior; p. 69). Consider how much simpler it would have been if Freud had simply asked Ida if *Schmuck-kästchen* ("jewelry box" or "jewel-case")—the word she used to describe an object in her first dream which her mother was keen on saving from a house that was on fire—had any other meaning or connotation for her, or made her think of anything else, instead of immediately telling her he was sure she knew *Schmuckkästchen* was "a favorite expression" for the female genitalia! As it turned out, she did know the expression and would probably have found it far more convincing to make the connection herself than to have Freud "shove it down her throat," as it were.

The Unfolding of Ida's Analysis

It is striking that heretofore no one has stressed that the case of Dora is laid out by Freud in the form of a series of dialectical reversals.[16]
—Lacan, *Écrits*, p. 178

A string of reproaches against other people leads one to suspect the existence of a string of self-*reproaches with the same content.*
—Freud, SE VII, p. 35

Ida did not initially provide much information to Freud about the history and development of her relationships with Frau K and Herr K, as *her concern* (insofar as she had one) *at the outset of the treatment was to complain of the relationship between her father and Frau K.* It is always useful to consider what a patient's complaint is at the beginning of treatment, especially when the patient has not come to therapy of her own accord; and whereas Ida's father made it amply clear to Freud what his complaint was—that Ida was acting angrily toward him all the time and trying to get him to break things off with Frau K—it is the *patient's complaint* (not the parent's) *that can potentially become the motor force of the analysis*. Ida's complaint was that she had been thrust into an odious situation—which was more complex than a love triangle, being something more like a quadrangle or a still more complex geometrical figure (see Figure 5.1, where the lines with the double bar in them indicate a blocked or failed relationship), wherein she was being given by her father to Herr K in exchange for the latter's willingness to turn a blind eye to the father's affair with Frau K—and was no more than a pawn in it (Ida was aware no *explicit* pact had been made between the two men, as Herr K sometimes even complained of the relationship between his wife and Ida's father to Ida's mother). Freud, hearing Ida's complaint, had the sense that Ida's conclusion after seeing him a couple of times was that she was faced with a *fait accompli:* "You see, that's the way it is. How am I supposed to change anything? I can't do anything about it" (SE VII, p. 35; my paraphrase).[17]   *~Based on reality, not my own will~*

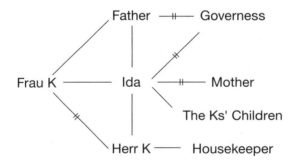

FIGURE 5.1.   Ida's Position in the Middle

It was only as Ida discussed the details of the situation with Freud that it came out that for years Ida had in fact aided and abetted the relationship between her father and Frau K. When the families were out on walks together, Ida's father and Frau K would generally find ways to dawdle behind the others so they could talk privately, and Ida would then often find herself alone with Herr K. She began to take a very lively interest in his children and became "almost a mother to them" (SE VII, p. 25), which led to the striking up of a rather close bond between herself and Herr K. Occasionally, when she would notice that her father and Frau K were off somewhere together, Ida would deliberately take the Ks' children in hand and lead them off in a direction where they would be sure not to disturb her father and Frau K's trysts. And she would never try to visit Frau K when she believed her father was with her (p. 36).

Even before we inquire into why Ida did these things, it should be pointed out that *this implies a radical change in perspective*. Did these details spill out spontaneously, or did Freud solicit them because (as Lacan hypothesizes) he held the view that although people (especially hysterics) often speak at the outset as though everything that is wrong in their lives is the fault of other people around them[18]—they themselves are pure, innocent, "beautiful souls" living in a low-class family, hick town, or cruel world that is unworthy of them—they have usually contributed in at least some way to the mess they find themselves in? We will probably never know, as Freud does not indicate whether he encouraged Ida to go into all the details because he was suspecting some such contribution on her part or simply because he was trying to get a fuller picture of the situation; nor do we know exactly when and how these details came out. But Freud does make it clear he felt there was likely more to the story than she initially implied (p. 35)—and isn't there always? Doesn't even popular wisdom recognize this with the expression "There are two sides to every story"?

Lacan suggests that Freud was inspired by Hegel's discussions of the "beautiful soul" in *The Phenomenology of Spirit* to suspect that Ida had played some role in bringing about her own misery; but it strikes me as at least equally likely that Freud came up with the idea that reproaches directed to others are often indicative of *self*-reproaches from his work on paranoia and from his own "self-analysis." He indicates in many places in his work that when people reproach someone for something, they often have good reason to reproach themselves for the same thing (and I know of no place where he explicitly professes to know anything more about Hegel than the fact that Hegel influenced Marx; SE XXII, pp. 176–177).[19]

In any case, even if we will never know whether this radically new perspective came out because Freud deliberately "turned the tables" on Ida, it is, I believe, an important move to keep in mind: We should always suspect that patients have played some not entirely passive role in getting into the mess in which they find themselves (whether in a specific dream or in their lives in general) and of which they complain, often bitterly, at the outset of the treatment. We should never turn this into an accusation (e.g., "So what did you do to get into this fix?"), but this suspicion should inform the practitioner's questions and punctuations.[20] Schematically we might represent this as follows (what is conscious being represented on top, and what is unconscious on the bottom, the question mark indicating that we do not yet know what might be unconscious here):

> Others are to blame for this sorry state of affairs.
> ───────────────────────────────────────
> ?

The "dialectical move" here is simply to assume that there is more to the story than meets the eye, and that there is some further material or motive that is hiding behind the conscious story being told, the conscious story taking the form of blame cast upon others.[21] What we often find is that the question mark can be replaced more or less as follows:

> Others are to blame.
> ───────────────────────────────
> I am to blame.

Here, as we already saw in Chapter 2, the unconscious thought, "I am to blame," is the exact opposite of the conscious thought, "Others are to blame" (a simpler way of formulating the opposite of the conscious thought would be "Others are *not* to blame," which would then raise the question, "Then who is to blame?").[22]

The new information that came out about how Ida fostered the relationship between her father and Frau K (Lacan refers to it as a "development of truth"; *Écrits*, p. 179) leads us to see that, rather than having been a pawn, Ida had been the willing *linchpin* of their relationship, the very person who had made their trysts possible. Without her, their relationship might have foundered or disintegrated quite quickly. She was complicit in allowing the foursome, including Herr K, to function as it did; she even accepted gifts from Herr K, seeing them perhaps as tokens of his esteem, and from her father, perhaps viewing his gifts as payment for the services she rendered to all three of the other parties to the dance.

Her self-reproach was thus presumably related to the fact that she allowed herself to play such a role and perhaps even enjoyed some aspects of it—for example, the extra attention she received from Herr K (which may have made up, in part, for the loss of her father's attention when her father began to court Frau K) and the intimacy that developed with Frau K, a kind of intimacy Ida had apparently never known with her own mother, or at least not for quite some time, their relations having "been unfriendly for years" (SE VII, p. 20).[23]

The Why and Wherefore of Ida's Accusation

In former years I often had occasion to find that the premature communication of a solution brought the treatment to an untimely end.
—Freud, SE XII, p. 140

Something then obviously happened that <u>shook up the stability</u> of this quartet and led Ida to first accuse Herr K of openly courting her, and then her father of having a love affair with Frau K. What happened?

The obvious event that occurred was Herr K's lakeside proposal or proposition, which Ida did not even allow him to finish before giving him a slap in the face (SE VII, pp. 25–26, 37–38, and 98). Note that for quite some time Freud appears to have been perplexed about her reaction to this proposal: Freud had met Herr K and, having found him to be young, affable, and good-looking—which may possibly have been how Freud liked to think of himself at the time—Freud believed his proposal to be an honorably intentioned one, indeed, no doubt a proposal to divorce his wife and marry Ida. And according to Freud, this must have been precisely what Ida had wanted all along! "How," he writes (p. 38 n. 2), "could a girl who was in love feel insulted by a proposal which was made in a manner neither tactless nor offensive?" (Recall that Freud was the one who kept claiming that Ida had been and probably still was in love with Herr K, a claim she never confirmed with any real conviction [pp. 37–38, 58, and elsewhere], and that he was the one who believed the proposal was "neither tactless nor offensive," which as we shall see was quite wrongheaded.)

What Freud did not realize—because even though he had heard about Herr K's lakeside proposal right at the outset of the treatment, *he failed to inquire* into the details of it until the last three sessions, when it was already too late (SE VII, pp. 98–99)—was the significance of what Herr K had said to Ida by the lake that day, the nuances of which are not necessarily that easy to render in English. In the preamble to his proposal, Herr K had said: *Ich habe nichts an meiner Frau.* Strachey renders it as "I get nothing out of my wife" (pp. 26 and 98),[24] and Anthea Bell translates it as "You know that there is nothing between me and my wife now" (S. Freud, 2013, pp. 21 and 90) and "You know I get no satisfaction from my wife" (p. 84); in all of these renditions, the implication seems to be that Herr K has gotten no love or sexual gratification from his wife in a long time, an interpretation of the German that is confirmed by Freud's footnote (p. 98); Lacan renders it as, "My wife is (or means) nothing to me," where the emphasis seems to be less on sex than on his general lack of esteem or love for her, as if he were saying, "I couldn't care less about my wife" or "My wife is worthless."[25]

This last rendition was destined to trouble a girl who had taken Herr K's wife as a model and indeed as an idol! Ida greatly admired Frau K for her "beauty" (SE VII, p. 32), her "adorable white body" (p. 61), her ability to attract her father, her knowledge and experience in love and sexual matters, and so on. Thus to hear her characterized as worthless, or as undeserving of esteem or love, would naturally be upsetting. And to a young woman for whom a third term or triangular structure was necessary to sustain her desire, to hear this idealized third party labeled as useless was to threaten the very structure of her desire with collapse (see Lacan, Seminar IV, pp. 143–146).[26] We might also imagine that Ida was suddenly confronted with an allusion to sexual desire on Herr K's part, whereas prior to that his attentions had almost always been situated solely at the level of romantic love, he having given her gifts and sent her flowers every day for a whole year (SE VII, p. 35).

Only once before had she been faced with his sexual desire—at age 14 when he ardently kissed her in his shop—and (as discussed in Appendix I, under the heading "Preconceived Ideas") that had led to disgust on her part. Love and desire are often two rather separate registers (see Fink, 2016, Chapters 1 and 2), which may or may not alight upon the same object or person (indeed, in Ida's case, we might hypothesize that she loved one member of the K couple and desired the other, although she perhaps both loved and desired Frau K);[27] and something that Ida may have admired and yet wondered at in Frau K was that she seemed comfortable being situated as the object of her father's love *and* desire.[28] Frau K may have represented to her one answer to the question, "What does it mean to be a woman who is both loved and desired by a man?" (Nevertheless, insofar as Ida's father was sexually impotent, Ida perhaps admired instead the solution Frau K had found to what Ida considered to be distasteful in a man's sexual desire, by having found a man who could not "take" her sexually, even if he could "pleasure her.")[29]

But instead of immediately asking Ida what she understood by Herr K's comment—*Ich habe nichts an meiner Frau*—and why it had such an effect on her, Freud seems to move on in his attempt to get clearer about what happened that day with Herr K by the lake. And thus it is not until the very last session he has with her that the true significance of Herr K's comment emerges! It turns out that shortly before Herr K made his proposal to Ida, Ida had heard the following from a young governess at the Ks' house (SE VII):

> Herr K had made advances to her [the governess] at a time when
> his wife was away for several weeks; he had courted her insistently
> and had implored her to yield to his entreaties, saying that he got
> nothing from his wife, and so on. (pp. 105–106)

Freud then remarked, "Why, those are the very words he used after-
wards, when he made his proposal to you and you gave him the slap in
his face." Ida went on, "Yes. She [the governess] had given in, but after a
little while he had ceased to care for her, and since then she hated him."
Freud queried, "And this governess had given notice?" (He asked this
because Ida had told him just minutes before that she had decided two
weeks ago that this session would be their last, and he had quipped that
it sounded "just like a maidservant or a governess giving two weeks'
notice"; SE VII, p. 105.) Ida replied:

> No. She meant to give notice. She told me that as soon as she felt
> she had been dumped she told her parents what had happened.
> They were respectable people living somewhere in Germany. Her
> parents said that she must leave the house instantly; and, since she
> failed to do so, they wrote to her saying that they would have noth-
> ing more to do with her, and that she was never to come home
> again. . . . She told me she meant to wait a little longer [before leav-
> ing], to see if there might not be some change in Herr K. She could
> not bear living like that anymore, she said, and if she saw no change
> she would give notice and leave. (p. 106)

Here we have material that is clearly germane to the way in which Ida
reacted to Herr K's proposal! Whereas Freud—who obviously identified
with Herr K (they were both, he felt, still somewhat young, good-looking,
and smokers whom Ida might wish to be kissed by)—considered Herr
K's proposal to be serious, honorable, and not lacking in tact, Ida knew
full well that Herr K had made a very similar proposal to a servant in
his household—including the exact same disparaging comment about
his wife as he subsequently made to Ida by the lake—had had sex with
the girl for a while, and then abandoned her instead of leaving his wife
for her (SE VII, pp. 106–107). Herr K was thus hardly singling Ida out as
his "one and only," as the unique, precious object of his undying love; to
him she might well have been just one in a series of fungible mistresses.[30]
Now, rather than allowing Ida to draw out the consequences of this
story herself, Freud (pp. 106–107) seems to have seized upon the information to inundate Ida with interpretations that must have lasted the
better part of 10 minutes: regarding her jealousy of the governess (and

her identification with the governess, too); anger at Herr K for treating her like a servant; only alerting her parents to what had happened by the lake after *two weeks* had gone by, having hoped in the interim that Herr K would recontact her and prove that his proposal to her was more serious than the one he had made to the governess; that Ida really did want to marry Herr K and believed he wanted to marry her; that Ida had facilitated the relationship between her father and Frau K so that Frau K would all the more certainly consent to get divorced; and that Ida was disappointed when Herr K, instead of renewing his proposal when she told her parents about it, denied everything and slandered her, saying that she had invented the whole story.

The fact that Ida "listened to [Freud] without any of her usual contradictions" and "seemed moved" (SE VII, pp. 108–109) by this incredibly detailed speech does not, in reality, tell us much. She may have been tired of contradicting him, since he apparently lent little credence to her contradictions, or simply did not bother because she had already decided it was going to be their last session. And she may have been moved by the simple fact that Freud was so interested in her, or at least in her case, that he was racking his brains trying to put everything she had ever told him together into a giant, coherent story. The fact that she was moved and did not try to contradict him is certainly no proof of the story's veracity. Nor is it proof of the contrary, for it could mean a number of different things.

Further Mysteries

I have never yet conducted a single psychoanalysis of a man or a woman without having to take into account a very considerable current of homosexuality.

—Freud, SE VII, p. 60

We have now seen that it was only in the last session that Freud came to grasp why Ida responded to Herr K's proposal as she did and waited before telling her parents about it. She was probably furious at Herr K for propositioning her in much the same way he had propositioned a simple governess in his household, and for having failed to prove his abiding interest in Ida by declaring to her parents that he was willing to make her an honest marriage proposal. Although, when questioned by mail by Ida's father as to what had happened between Ida and himself by the lake, Herr K had at first expressed "sentiments of the highest esteem" for Ida and proposed to come to the town where Ida's family was "to clear up every misunderstanding" (SE VII, p. 62), when he spoke with Ida's parents a few weeks later, he slandered Ida and told them he

knew she had discussed "forbidden topics" and read the sort of "indecent" literature that poisons the mind, inclining her to concoct the whole
situation in fantasy. As we have seen, this was information that he could
have received from but one source—namely, from Frau K, who had thus
obviously betrayed Ida's trust.

But strangely enough, *Ida was angry with everyone except Frau K!*
She was furious with Herr K for the reasons just mentioned (although
she "admitted that she found it impossible to be as angry with Herr K as
he deserved"; SE VII, p. 59); and she was furious with her father because
he preferred to believe Herr K instead of his own daughter (this then
led her to be furious with her father about his ongoing love affair with
Frau K). But she never seems to have blamed or attacked Frau K directly
for not keeping her secrets and for having accused Ida of lying—that is,
of making up the whole story of the "indecent proposal." Why didn't she?

Freud presents this as something of a mystery and as a "complication"
that a writer of fiction would have left out of the tale (SE VII, p. 59). Ida,
in Freud's view, was suddenly confronted with the fact that "Frau K had
never loved Ida for her own sake but solely on account of her father. Frau
K had sacrificed her without a moment's hesitation so that her relations
with her father might not be disturbed" (p. 62). This strikes me as rather
simplistic thinking on Freud's part, for, given Frau K's intimacy with
Ida for so many years, it seems unlikely that Frau K had no genuinely
positive feelings for Ida and could throw her under the bus (as many say
today) "without a moment's hesitation"; it appears more probable that,
weighed in the balance of Frau K's affections and interests, Ida's father
had simply won out over Ida.

Now for Ida, this was reminiscent of something that had happened a
number of years earlier: Ida had had a governess of her own who had
shown a good deal of interest in Ida, becoming on "excellent terms"
with her, only, as it turned out, because she wished to get close to Ida's
father. Whenever the father was around she would be kind to and affect
interest in Ida, but whenever the father was out of town, this governess
"had no time to spare for her, would not go for walks with her, and took
no interest in her studies." As soon as Ida noticed the pattern, she had
the governess fired (SE VII, pp. 36–37 and 60–61).

The Frau K situation also resonated with another liaison in Ida's past:
Although Ida had long been close to one of her female cousins, "and
had shared all sorts of secrets with her" (SE VII, p. 61), Ida had grown
quite cold to her from the moment the cousin had accepted an invitation
to travel alone with Ida's father to Merano (where the Ks lived) after Ida
had refused to accompany him there owing to Herr K's unavowed proposal. We do not know whether the cousin had been informed of Ida's

accusation against Herr K, and thus whether Ida believed her cousin to be siding with her father (at whom Ida was furious) against her; but she likely viewed the cousin's willingness to travel to Merano alone with her father as a sign of special affection for him, perhaps as a sign of greater affection for him than for Ida herself. Whatever the case may be, Ida had thenceforth given her cousin the cold shoulder, not being able to give her the ouster as she had with her erstwhile governess.

What we find here are thus *three close friendships with women* that ended when the women evinced (or were taken to evince, in the case of the female cousin) a preference for Ida's father over Ida.

The mystery to Freud's mind was why Ida did not speak of Frau K as a hated rival (for her father's affections) to eliminate, if at all possible; Ida did not speak of Frau K in the same terms in which she spoke of the dismissed governess, for example, but rather "in accents more typical of a lover than a defeated rival" (SE VII, p. 61). She praised Frau K's "adorable white body," recognized her good taste in certain gifts Ida had received from her father, and, as Freud put it, "never spoke a harsh or angry word against the lady, although from the point of view of her supervalent thought she should have regarded her as the prime author of her misfortunes" (p. 62).

Her "supervalent train of thought," as Freud calls it (SE VII, p. 62),[31] the one she could not get out of her head—namely, the thought that *she could not forgive her father* for having sacrificed her in order to continue his secret love affair with Frau K (p. 63)—seemed to leave her feelings regarding Frau K out of the picture. Freud's conclusion was that things must not have been as he was initially convinced they were, he having believed that Ida was jealous of Frau K because *Frau K was receiving the attention from Ida's father that Ida wanted and had formerly received herself.* Freud had jumped to the wrong conclusion (as we usually do when we jump): It turned out that Ida wanted Frau K's love for herself (p. 63).

Yet, by betraying Ida (giving ammunition to her husband in the form of damning secrets the two females had shared in confidence), Frau K had shown that there was another (if not others, if we include her husband) she loved more than Ida. Ida was jealous, not of Frau K but of her father! She wanted to be first with Frau K, the one Frau K loved the most.

Lacan (*Écrits*, p. 179) refers to this as the "second dialectical reversal" in the case: Ida was jealous of her father, in the sense that "she begrudged her father Frau K's love" (SE VII, p. 63). She was not jealous of Frau K because her father preferred Frau K to her; she wanted Frau K for herself, she wanted Frau K to prefer Ida to Ida's father, and she wanted Frau K to ally with Ida against all accusers. What her apparent jealousy of the relationship between her father and Frau K concealed was *her desire for Frau K.*

Jealousy

Desire

Note that, although Freud ends Part 1 of the case write-up with this conclusion, he does little if anything with it in Part 2, except to tell us in a footnote (on p. 102, probably added in 1905) that the big mistake he made in the course of her treatment was that he failed to see how important Ida's love for Frau K was. In other words, he admits to thinking he failed to put to proper use the major conclusion at which he had arrived at the end of Part 1, which presumably takes us up to the time just before the first major dream—that is, up to about two weeks before the end of the treatment.

Why did Freud fail to follow up on his own apparent discovery? In the abovementioned footnote, Freud says, "Before I had recognized the importance of the homosexual current of feeling in neurotics, I was often brought to a standstill in the treatment of my cases or found myself in complete perplexity" (SE VII, p. 120 n). Lacan (*Écrits*) interprets this comment as follows:

> Freud admits that for a long time he was unable to face this homosexual tendency . . . without falling into a state of distress that rendered him incapable of dealing with it satisfactorily.
>
> I would say that this has to be ascribed to a bias, the very same bias that falsifies the conception of the Oedipus complex right from the outset, making Freud consider the predominance of the paternal figure to be natural, rather than normative. (p. 182)

What Freud, in his footnote, couches as a problem of inadequate knowledge—he had not yet "learnt the importance of the homosexual current of feeling in neurotics" and was left "perplexed"—Lacan views as owing to *subjective distress* on Freud's part, in other words, to something inadequately analyzed in Freud himself.

We certainly should not be surprised to find that Freud was inadequately analyzed, since he engaged only in self-analysis. Self-analysis (notwithstanding Karen Horney's [1942] assertions) is incapable of going very far for numerous reasons—we need someone else to call our precipitated and/or convenient conclusions into question, someone else to project our own doubts and self-critiques onto, someone to hear and repeat back to us our own slips and double entendres, and so on—and Freud, who could not possibly have had a real analysis in 1900 because he was the only analyst on the planet at the time, can nevertheless be taken to task for *never having done a proper analysis* with someone he himself (or one of his trainees) had trained when he did have the chance later on.[32] His own homosexual currents were patent enough in his by now much-publicized relationship with Wilhelm Fliess, and in his tendency to become quickly enamored of smart-sounding physicians who initially showed great interest in his work, and to then feel abandoned, betrayed, and jilted by them (much like Ida did by Frau K), as though they had been his lovers.[33] Whatever remains unanalyzed in the analyst is likely to remain a blind spot in his or her work with analysands (see SE XII, pp. 116–117)!

Not having adequately recognized his own homosexual attachments (presumably), Freud adopted the conventional belief (based on the supposed natural, biological attraction between females and males; SE VII, pp. 21 and 229) that a girl's *strongest affection* is always naturally for her father, and constantly looked for that in practice—in other words, in all of his cases.[34] And he thus considered Ida to be having difficulty transitioning from her father as her primary love object to another man like her father (which he later formulated as one of the major tasks facing girls).[35] His own subjective distress when it came to falling for members of his own sex led to a blindness when it came to theory, which manifested itself in a prejudice or bias that operated in his practice.

Ida presumably had some love for at least three of the people around her. She admitted to having doted on her father for many years (having nursed him during some of his illnesses, and having been made by him "his confidante while she was still a child"; SE VII, p. 57) and to having wished to have ever more of his attention—this leading, at least in part, to her very poor relations with her own mother, with whom it seems she had been on unfriendly terms for years (Freud mentions that Ida "had withdrawn completely from her mother's influence," which implies that they had perhaps once been on friendlier terms, but he may never have taken much trouble to explore Ida's earliest relations with her mother; SE VII, p. 20). Ida spent a great deal of time with Herr K, and as ill-timed and unrelenting as Freud's interpretations were, she probably *did* feel some love for Herr K, too (the fact that her appendicitis-like symptoms appeared nine months after Herr K's lakeside proposal does seem to point to some fantasies about him [pp. 102–103], and she at one point nodded assent to Freud's interpretation that she had waited two weeks before telling her parents about his proposal because she had been longing for Herr K to repeat it [p. 107]; for further interpretation of Ida's specific symptoms, see Appendix IV).[36]

More significant perhaps, however, was her love for Frau K, whether for its own sake or because it was the most repressed of them all; after all, when something is repressed, it becomes far more powerful than it might otherwise have been. "The affect attached to an unconscious idea operates more strongly . . . , since it cannot be inhibited, . . . than the affect attached to a conscious one" (SE VII, p. 49).[37]

Had Freud's subjective distress and the bias it led to not been operative, Lacan (*Écrits*) suggests that Freud might have been able to bring Ida to a

> *third dialectical reversal,* the one that would reveal to us the real value of the object that Frau K [was] for Dora. Frau K [was] not an individual, but a mystery, the mystery of Dora's own femininity, by which I mean her bodily femininity. (p. 180)

Ida seemed to admire Frau K for many reasons: the "adorable" whiteness of her body (SE VII, p. 61), her knowledge of sexual matters, her attractiveness to her father and other men[38]—in a word, her embodiment of femininity as such (and let us note that, unlike myriad commentators and Freud himself [SE VII, p. 221], Lacan never falls into the overly simplistic trap of equating femininity with hysteria; see, on this point, Soler, 2003/2006).[39] Ida's mother was a rather poor model for Ida of what it meant to be a woman, as it had obviously been years since Ida's father (or any other man or woman, apparently) had paid her much attention.[40] Frau K, on the other hand, had managed to attract both Herr K and her father, serving Ida thus as a model of how to be a success as a woman in their particular social and historical context. Ida admired her, identified with her insofar as she wanted to be desired the way Frau K was (and perhaps wanted to desire the way Frau K did), and wanted to be like her.

Femininity

The concepts of "masculinity" and "femininity," whose meaning seems so unambiguous to ordinary people, are among the most confused that occur in science.

—Freud, SE VII, p. 219 n

Femininity is, it seems, something of a mystery for most women. Whereas for most men, there is nothing terribly mysterious about masculinity, in the sense that everyone appears to know more or less what it is, the same is not true of femininity. Masculinity is generally defined in our culture as everything associated with power: physical strength, force of character, cocksureness, indomitability, social and economic success, self-assurance, and independence. It goes by names like having gumption or balls, or being bold, ballsy, brash, macho, gutsy, nervy, cheeky, or cocky, several of which make explicit reference to the male genitalia. In more technical jargon, masculinity is associated with the phallus—that is, with some sort of potent, phallic attribute. Boys may often not be able to feel or act like a man (courageously, forcefully, etc.), but the nature of masculinity itself is generally no secret to them—they see it represented all around them in the heroes of our age and of the last few millennia, heroes who share many of the same characteristics from one generation to the next.

It might be argued that femininity, on the other hand, can take on so many different forms that it long remains a mystery to many girls and young women. What is a real woman? What does it mean to be a woman?[41] Who, if anyone, was or is a real woman? Was Catherine from Shakespeare's *Taming of the Shrew*? Medea from Euripides' eponymous play? Mae West? Madonna? The Virgin Mary? (Consider Ida's two-hour rapt admiration of the *Sistine Madonna*, a painting by Raphael Sanzio, in an art museum in Dresden; SE VII, pp. 96, 100 n. 1, and 104 n. 2).[42] Is one a real woman if one is self-confident and perhaps even impertinently brash, or rather if one is like the stereotypical meek, unassuming, obedient, supportive, attentive wife celebrated in certain traditional cultures (like Amish culture)? (Consider the formerly canonical marriage vow, whereby a wife promised "to love, cherish, and obey," not to mention "honor.")

What sort of women do we celebrate in contemporary culture? The women we place center stage, in novels, movies, and TV shows, run the gamut from being outrageous, funny, irreverent, sexy, seductive, and teases, to being sweet, kind, caring, sentimental, and virginal—and just about everything in between. How is a girl to know how to be? Many are led to look for models outside of their homes, especially when their own mothers, like Ida's, have been less than successful in attracting much love and drawing much attention to themselves.

Many different kinds of women inspire girls and men, having what can only be referred to as a certain *je ne sais quoi* that makes them fascinating to others. As Lacan puts it in Seminar XX, "We can't talk about Woman" (p. 73) because there is no such thing as Woman with a capital W, no such thing as Woman *as such*; there are only women in the plural, with their considerable variety, and thus there is always something mysterious or opaque about femininity and womanhood. This should—but never seems to—be taken to imply that psychoanalysis does not have any business trying to *define* femininity, for it is not, strictly speaking, a psychoanalytic concept; the most psychoanalysis can say is that there seems to be no such definition possible. Another way Lacan puts this is to say that there is no specific signifier of Woman, whereas there is a single signifier for Man, as it were: the phallus (Φ).[43] This does not stop people from looking for such a signifier, definition, or model to follow anyway, however. For Ida, as a teenager at least, Frau K "incarnate[d] the question, 'What is a woman?'" (Lacan, Seminar VIII, p. 244); in other words, Ida looked to Frau K for an answer to the question "What is a woman?" and thus to the question "How can I be a woman?" or "What sort of woman should I be?" (She perhaps also looked to the *Sistine Madonna* for an answer.)

If Lacan is right that femininity is often experienced as something of a mystery by many girls and young women, his claim here can be understood to be that Ida might well have been less interested in Frau K herself than in the model of femininity Frau K seemed to embody, which Ida herself would, in turn, have liked to embrace and embody. To put it differently, Ida might well have been more interested in getting into Frau K's head than into her bed; Ida might have wanted to crawl into her skin and feel what it was like to *be* her, more than she wanted to sleep with her.[44] (Which does not mean that she had no interest whatsoever in sleeping with her, but that her motive for sleeping with her might also have been, at least in part, to get into her head and know what it was like to be in the world as she was.)

Then again, even if Lacan is right about femininity often being a mystery, he is not necessarily right about Ida. Freud's work with Ida did not go far enough for us to know very much about Ida's desires and motives. Indeed, for all Freud's supposedly brilliant deductions and interpretations, and for all Ida's seemingly complicated affections, the case of Ida seems, in Freud's account, to be far more straightforward than virtually any case of hysteria encountered by analysts today who generally work with their neurotic patients for 20 to 50 times longer than Freud worked with Ida. In analyses that are conducted today, we expect that we will have to take into account and explore hundreds if not thousands of events that marked the analysand and helped shape her into the person she is today. In his work with Ida, Freud only dealt with a couple of dozen early childhood experiences and memories; today we are accustomed to working with far more, and to finding the various threads of the analysand's loves, hates, attractions, and repulsions to be much more numerous and knotted together in ways that are often extremely difficult to tease apart. Things are rarely as simple as they may seem when we read a case history that covers only a few short months of treatment.

Lacan makes what I find to be an odd comment at one point in his discussion of the case of Ida, rhetorically asking: "Didn't all the keys always fall into Freud's hands, even in those cases that were broken off like this one?" (*Écrits*, p. 180); there Lacan is referring to Ida's early memory of sucking her thumb and tugging on her brother's ear (SE VII, p. 51), which Lacan believes to be the key to her fundamental fantasy and jouissance.[45] But how could Lacan possibly know that there were no other keys yet to be discovered? <u>We should assume instead, I think, that</u> <u>*we never have all the keys at our disposal*</u>. For even if we did, by some miracle, have them all, we could never actually know that we did!

Freud fell into the trap of believing himself to be master of the situation; and Lacan perhaps fell into the trap, in 1951, of thinking that (thanks to his dialectical model) he could see the totality of the situation where Freud could not. Other analysts fall into other traps—traps that are perhaps not so intimately connected with believing one has full knowledge of the situation[46]—for there are many potential pitfalls that analysts face, like wishing to be the patient's father, mother, best friend, preacher, coach, reformer, and so on (perhaps I, too, have fallen into one or more such traps here). None of these have anything to do with the analyst's proper role.

At the end of the Dora case write-up, Freud tells us that he failed to "master the transference" in time (p. 118). This seemingly humble admission dissimulates an overweening ambition (perhaps both theoretical and therapeutic, a *"furor sanandi"*; SE XII, p. 171), which is tantamount to an illusion, for (*one never masters the transference.*)There is no such thing as "mastering the transference," and it is a mistake to even adopt this as a goal.

Freud and other analytic figures of historical importance are not the only ones who have been seduced by the fantasy of being masters in their consulting rooms and in their write-ups of their work: *Virtually all therapists*, especially early on in their careers, *imagine they will figure things out and magically, majestically solve their patients' problems for them.* Some clinicians foolishly continue to entertain such fantasies for decades, believing in their "God given powers to intuit,"[47] thereby simplifying their analysands' troubles to fit their own preformed expectations and conceptualizations.

More realistic practitioners learn through long (and often painful) experience that they cannot jump ahead of their patients and anticipate where their problems lie and how to "fix" them, but <u>can merely follow</u> <u>along behind</u> their patients and try to grasp facets of <u>problems little by</u> <u>little</u>. We rarely see the forest from a bird's eye view, generally remaining mired among the individual trees, and almost always needing the help of colleagues and/or a qualified supervisor to help us think about things more broadly. Analysis—when practiced as it should be—is a humbling profession and we should be suspicious of clinicians who claim to have it all figured out and who profess that they can see the solutions long before their analysands do. Such clinicians end up hogging the ball, as it were, instead of putting it in their analysands' court where it should be: If there is a master of any kind at all in the analytic context (and there really isn't), it is the analysand's unconscious!

Transference Revisited and the Breaking Off of the Analysis

> *I prefer to leave the notion of transference its empirical totality, while stressing that it is polyvalent and that it involves several registers: the symbolic, the imaginary, and the real.*
>   —Lacan, Seminar I, pp. 112–113

What exactly is transference? I have discussed this extensively elsewhere (Fink, 2007, Chapter 7) because there seems to be so much confusion, even on the part of practicing psychoanalysts, regarding what transference is. According to many practitioners today, transference concerns the way the analysand *feels* about the analyst, above all when that feeling actually derives from the way the analysand feels (or at some point felt) about someone other than the analyst; the feeling has, in other words, been displaced from its original object onto the analyst.

This leads contemporary clinicians to talk most commonly about "mother transferences" and "father transferences," whereby patients project, displace, or transfer their current or former feelings about one of their parents (or grandparents or other relatives) onto the analyst—feeling, for example, that the analyst cannot be trusted or is seeking to seduce them, just like one (if not both) of their primary caretakers while growing up. Freud himself condones this way of thinking at times in Ida's case when he opines that Ida initially suspected that he would be as dishonest and dissimulating as her father was ("He always preferred secrecy and roundabout ways"; SE VII, p. 118), and that she later took revenge on Freud the way she would have liked to take revenge on Herr K (and perhaps on her father as well). Indeed, he postulates that it was his failure to perceive Ida's transference onto him of her anger at Herr K that led to the untimely termination of the analysis; yet it is possible that he had dimly perceived it and failed to "heed the warning" (pp. 118–119).[48]

There was undoubtedly some truth to Freud's view that there was some "unknown quantity in [him—that is, Freud] which reminded Ida of Herr K" (SE VII, p. 119), but there was, I will suggest, only *some* truth to it, for even by Freud's own definition of transference in 1905, the transferential situation was far more complicated than that. Owing to his age and sex, Freud could not help but be associated by Ida, at times, with her father and Herr K (p. 120); and given the two men's sexual involvement with younger women and their duplicity regarding such dalliances, it was all the more important for Freud to avoid associating himself with them. Instead, he encouraged Ida to think of him as like them—for example, in connection with her impression of there being a smell of smoke in the air when she awoke from the first dream, he proffered, "I'm a smoker," thereby placing himself in a series including her father and Herr K (p. 73). Moreover, he made it obvious to Ida that he sympathized with Herr K, considering him to be an honorable suitor and a fine match for Ida, and perhaps even commented that he believed Ida had wanted Freud to kiss her at some point during a session, just like Herr K had kissed her in his shop when she was 14 (p. 74).

Such remarks and beliefs on Freud's part could only incline Ida to suspect him of having ulterior motives—perhaps he, too, wanted to use or seduce her—and of dissimulating them. Freud was at pains, as he tells us early on in the case, not to fall into the trap of believing the stories told to him by Ida's father about what was "really" going on, and yet he did not take pains to set himself apart in other ways from the problematic men in her life.[49] In this way he perhaps became for her just another older man who evinced interest in her for some obscure reason.[50] (This is not to say that analysts should deliberately strive to differentiate themselves from hated figures in the analysand's life at every point in the analysis, as this, too, can be problematic—impeding projections that the analysand may need to make at certain times[51]—but they should at least avoid identifying with hypocritical and mendacious figures.)

In this sense, we might say that Freud simply became another actor in the merry-go-round—or ring-around-the-rosy, with Ida in the middle— that we saw earlier in Figure 5.1:

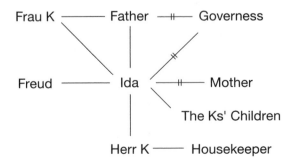

FIGURE 5.2.   Ida's Position in the Middle

The configuration[52] remained intact during the analysis and was only broken apart by Ida some time after the analysis ended, as we hear when she returned to see Freud 15 months later.[53] For at that point she indicated to Freud that she had seen the Ks some five months after the analysis ended (on the occasion of the death of one of the Ks' children), and had taken the opportunity to confront Herr K and force him to admit to what had happened, and to tell Frau K quite directly that she knew perfectly well that Frau K was having an affair with her father. She had then told her father of Herr K's admission and broken off all ties with the Ks (SE VII, p. 121).

We might see this, as Freud obviously wished to, as the kind of improvement that occurs in a patient's life—not during the analysis itself, but shortly after the treatment ends and the patient is no longer so wound up with the analyst as a person (p. 115).[54] For the analysis certainly brought many facets of Ida's situation into focus, and the fact that Freud took what she said seriously perhaps contributed to Ida's feeling that she could face down those around her who had cast aspersions on her. Freud also appears to have wished to view the fact that Ida went on to marry as a benefit she derived from the analysis, but this was quite speculative on his part.

Freud's Definition of Transference

The transference took me unawares.
—Freud, SE VII, p. 119

Freud is the person who first formulated the notion of transference, and he always defined it far more broadly than most practitioners do today: as *the reproduction of a whole situation or configuration*—perhaps not unlike the kind found in Figure 5.2—which includes one's position in a nexus of relationships and involves feelings, fantasies, thoughts, impulses, experiences, and so on.

"What are transferences?" he asks in his case study of Ida (SE VII).

> They are new editions or facsimiles of impulses and fantasies that are aroused and made conscious as the analysis proceeds; but they have this peculiarity, which is that they replace some earlier person by the physician. To put it another way: a whole series of psychical experiences are revived, not as belonging to the past, but as applying to the physician in the present. (p. 116)

Freud goes on to say that <u>some transferences are "simple reprints—</u>
that is, new, unchanged editions—of the <u>same story" while others are</u>
"<u>revised editions, not just reprints</u>" (p. 116). In other words, the reproduction of the situation may be only partial, rather than complete (that
is, it may not be identical to the earlier situation). It should be noted that
"<u>psychoanalytic treatment does not create transferences, it merely brings</u>
<u>them to light</u>" (SE VII, p. 117); transferences are found in many other life
contexts: in friendship and love relationships, in school, at work, in the
military, and so on. But for the most part, it is only in the psychoanalytic
context that they are recognized and explicitly worked with.

In 1914, Freud adds the following to his definition: "<u>Transference is</u>
<u>itself only a piece of repetition, and the repetition is a transference of</u>
<u>the forgotten past not only onto the doctor but also onto all the other</u>   *repetit*
<u>aspects of the current situation</u>" (SE XII, p. 151).[55] "The current situation"   *-ion*
is a very general notion, allowing us to imagine that someone's anxiety
upon walking into a college classroom might harken back to a humiliating experience that occurred in an elementary school classroom; and
that Ida could have been uncomfortable being alone with a man in his
"place of business" (e.g., a physician's consulting room), regardless of
his personality, age, or good or homely looks, owing to what happened
with Herr K at his "place of business" (as indicated in Appendix I, he had
duped Ida into believing others would be present there, and had then
ambushed her with a sudden, pressing kiss; SE VII, p. 28). Shock, disori-
entation, inability to think, and speechlessness are all possible manifestations of transference, not just positive or negative feelings.

How Can Transference Be Dealt With?

> *All the patient's impulses, including hostile ones, are aroused; they
> are then turned to account for the purposes of the analysis by being
> made conscious, and in this way the transference is constantly being
> destroyed. Transference, which seems ordained to be the greatest
> obstacle to psychoanalysis, becomes its most powerful ally, if its pres-
> ence can be detected each time and explained to the patient.*
> —Freud, SE VII, p. 117

For many years, if not until the end of his life, Freud seems to have
been under the misapprehension that it suffices to bring a particular
transference to the conscious attention of the patient in order to make
it disappear. As if it would be enough to simply tell a patient that she
distrusts us just like she distrusted her mother growing up for her to
stop distrusting us! Such comments may provide a certain amount of

temporary relief and clear the air in the session room momentarily, but they obviously do not dissipate longstanding mistrustfulness of others. If only it were that easy![56]

Indeed, such comments, as Lacan points out (*Écrits*, p. 591; Seminar V, p. 428), are generally heard by the patient as being uttered by the kind of person they already view us as owing to their transference—in this case, as someone who cannot be trusted—and thus as deceptive, untrustworthy assertions![57] The patient is likely to hear such an interpretation ("You distrust me just like you distrusted your mother growing up") as an attempt on our part to pull the wool over her eyes, just like her mother often did in order to dupe her into thinking that she could trust her mother. The transference interpretations we make are very often taken by patients to confirm their pre-existing view of us as untrustworthy, conniving, condescending, manipulative, and so on. They do not allow us to momentarily step outside of the transference and have a real "heart-to-heart" with each other, as some seem to think they do; rather, evidence shows they often make matters worse by reinforcing the patient's projections onto us.[58]

Freud offers us a more productive lead when he tells us that transferences must be handled, not by explicitly pointing them out to our patients, but "by tracing them back to their sources" (SE VII, p. 120)—that is, by attempting to pinpoint their historical antecedents, the earlier situations and relationships that are presumably being repeated in the present, whether inside or outside of the consulting room (and letting the analysand draw the connection between the past and the present analytic situation, assuming she is ready to do so).[59] Few analysts today seem to take the trouble to trace such transferences back to their sources, perhaps because this is often a difficult and laborious process, as there may well be multiple sources and a plethora of facets to each individual source. Nevertheless, a specific transference is likely to continue to appear and reappear at various points in the course of the analytic work until its sources have been exhaustively articulated (that is, worked through) by the analysand. (Insofar as interpretation plays a role in this process, it is interpretation of the *content* of the transference, not of the *fact* of transference.)

An analysand who feels that his analyst is trying to dominate, suffocate, and subject him to the analyst's will (as one of my analysands put it) can—if the analyst takes the time to explore who in the analysand's past was felt by the analysand to have wanted or tried to dominate him—often pinpoint the parent or other relative (sibling, uncle, aunt, grandparent, etc.) who first tried to subject the analysand to his or her will. Assuming the analyst has remained quite neutral in this regard, and has not attempted to dominate him (regarding scheduling, payment, and/or interpretations), much of the energy/libido tied up in such a transference—which can be quite trying for both parties to the therapy—will often dissipate once the connection with a prior figure in the analysand's life has been detected and discussed in depth. As simple as this is—requiring that the analyst begin with basic questions like, "Can you recall ever having felt this way about anyone before?" or "Have you ever had the impression before that someone wanted to subject you to his or her will?"—it is the most effective way to trace transferences back to their fountainheads and to begin the sometimes arduous task of working them through by exploring the analysand's relations with such prior figures in four-part harmony, including all possible details of their interactions.[60]

Shortcuts to this laborious process have been sought by clinicians in recent decades, and many analysts today view transferences simply as something to be brought to the patient's attention—presumably in the hope that her "observing ego" will integrate the analyst's observation and stop her from doing what she had been doing (e.g., distrusting the analyst). In order to bring transferences to the patient's attention, contemporary analysts often disclose their own countertransferential reaction to the patient's attitude and/or actions (and, indeed, such analysts often believe that their countertransference comes from the patient and has been "put into them" by the patient, which would imply that all analysts would inevitably end up responding or reacting to that patient in the same way, a notion that is patently false; see Fink, 2007, pp. 165–185).

Let us try to imagine what might have happened if Freud had, as he maintains he should have, brought to Ida's attention what he believed her transference to be. He writes,

> I ought to have said to her, "it is from Herr K that you have made a transference onto me. Have you noticed anything that leads you to suspect me of evil intentions similar . . . to Herr K's? Or have you been struck by anything about me or heard anything about me that has struck your fancy, inclining you to feel affection for me as you did for Herr K? (p. 118)

The questions Freud imagines he could have asked are extremely direct and might be understood as overly *leading*,[61] the kind that might well have put Ida off or made her feel that she had to say, No, she had never really noticed anything that made her suspect Freud of having evil intentions toward her. But Freud could have easily remedied this by simply asking whether he reminded her in any way of Herr K and, if she answered in the affirmative (which seems pretty likely, given that they at least had age, sex, and smoking in common), asking if she thought of Freud or felt about him in any of the same ways she thought of or felt about Herr K.

What Might Have Happened?

Instead of letting Dora appropriate her own story, Freud became the appropriator of it.

—Marcus, 1975/1990, p. 300

Let us assume, for the sake of argument, that Freud could have guided Ida to the realization that she had been viewing and treating him in some of the same ways that she viewed and treated (or would have liked to have treated) Herr K. What would the likely result of that have been? Ida might have come to believe that it was unfair of her to treat Freud as she had treated (or would have liked to have treated) Herr K, and from that point on, whenever she had an impulse to do so during a session, she might well have *suppressed* it. She might have begun to catch herself as she was just about to make a sarcastic comment or respond in some way to Freud as she might have wanted to address Herr K, and started forcing herself to speak or act in some other way. In other words, *the impulse to treat Freud as she treated Herr K would not have subsided or disappeared; she would simply have begun to suppress it whenever it arose.* Freud might thereby have felt better treated by her, less "unjustly" responded to as if he were someone else, but nothing would have fundamentally changed for Ida; and Freud would have lost access to information about her impulses that could have been crucial to the treatment.

Had Freud in any way let on that he felt hurt when treated by Ida as she had treated Herr K, Ida might well have begun to gauge virtually everything she told Freud in terms of whether or not he was likely to be hurt by what she was about to say, and thus to *censor* a great deal of what she might more spontaneously have spoken about so as not to even potentially hurt his feelings. The more a patient knows about her analyst's susceptibilities and emotional reactions, the more she is usually inclined to suppress certain topics and hold back certain ideas and impulses. *Nothing can ultimately have a more deleterious effect on the analysis than that!* And this is the typical result of all forms of self-disclosure, whether supposedly in the interest of bringing out something that is going on in the transference or not. This is also the typical result of analysts' attempts to bring their patients' supposed transferences to their conscious attention: Insofar as the patients accept the notion that they are indeed acting as the analyst says they are, they begin to con- sciously strive to act differently, deliberately withholding thoughts that cross their minds and suppressing impulses that arise within them.[62]

Freud seems to have believed that he could trace the source of Ida's negative transference (the decision she made two weeks before the end of 1900 to end the analysis on December 31st of that year, only telling Freud about it on December 31st)[63] to:

1. her wish at age 16 (after the lakeside proposal) to take revenge on Herr K for treating her like a maidservant in his home—indeed, like he had treated the young governess who worked for him and who was reluctant to give her two weeks' notice after he had seduced her but then grown cold toward her; and
2. her wish at age 16 to get away from Herr K, feeling she was unsafe as long as she stayed in his home, he having taken away the key that had formerly allowed her to lock the door of the guest bed- room when she was dressing, undressing, or napping (SE VII, pp. 66–69, 88, and 118) and having suddenly appeared in her room one day standing beside her while she slept.

Ida mentioned the danger she had sensed she was in at Herr K's house in the course of her discussion with Freud[64] of the first dream, which occurred about two or three weeks before the end of the treatment (p. 80) and thus more or less corresponded to the time at which she made the decision to end the treatment "a fortnight" later (p. 105).

The danger she had felt she was in of being raped if she remained in the Ks' house after Herr K removed that key may have in some way con- tributed to Ida's sense that to continue to see Freud was to put herself in danger (i.e., there may have been some transferential component to it). But it seems likely that Ida was as afraid of Freud's threat of *psychical* penetration as she had been of Herr K's threat of *physical* penetration two years earlier (SE VII, p. 93); we cannot know this for sure as Freud did not ask her what *fortnight* made her think of—it might have evoked in her mind their discussion of the previous dream or the two weeks she waited before telling her parents of Herr K's lakeside proposition (p. 107)—immediately averring instead that *it sounded to him* like a maid or a governess giving notice (p. 105). Freud later reproached himself for not having "heeded the warning" contained within the first dream (p. 118), which he thought of as a warning that she would soon leave the analysis (just as in the dream she needed to leave the house?). He appar- ently even told Ida more or less directly (p. 70 n. 2) that just as she had been afraid of the danger posed by Herr K and of her own temptation to yield to him, she was now afraid of something related to Freud and the treatment (her own temptation to yield to him?); and this is perhaps what first put the idea of breaking off the analysis in Ida's head!

Curiously enough, Freud never seems to have asked Ida to talk about the warning addressed to him that he was convinced was contained in the first dream, which would at least have brought out in the open any burgeoning intention on her part to leave therapy and allowed her to say why. Perhaps Freud did not want to know why. . . . If there was any sort of warning addressed to Freud in the dream, and it is not clear to me that there was, it was not a warning that she was transferring or projecting onto Freud either her sense of being in danger from Herr K or her desire to take revenge on Herr K (in other words, it was not about transference). It was a warning that Freud himself was acting in a threatening manner.

Ida was never given a chance, or so it seems in Freud's account, to analyze any part of the dream herself (SE VII, pp. 69–70). Freud presented himself there as a magician, dazzlingly turning everything into its opposite, bringing in everything he knew of her life that might be related, and creating an elaborate story. Curiously enough, he used the dream not to find something new, which is the whole point of discussing dreams in psychoanalysis, as he tells us elsewhere (SE XII, pp. 96 and 117),[65] but rather to confirm what he already firmly believed: namely, that Ida was hopelessly in love with Herr K (p. 70). Rather than letting her or encouraging her to free-associate to elements in her dreams, Freud mentions right away his own associations (p. 97), and jumps to some pretty outrageous-sounding conclusions (pp. 99–100). Although Freud tells us that his goal was to make the unconscious conscious (SE VII, p. 114),[66] this was clearly insufficient to bring about change (see Fink, 2014a, Chapter 1); *his attempt to make Ida's unconscious ideas conscious by telling her what he thought they were made her leave therapy, not get better.* If we are to maintain the goal of making the unconscious conscious, it must be the analysand who does the lion's share of that, and as I have indicated elsewhere, it is more important to bring the unconscious to speech than it is to bring it to consciousness.[67] Most important of all is not to hijack the analysis and make it one's own instead of the analysand's![68]

We see here how easy it is for analysts to draw the wrong conclusions: Ida's negative transference does not seem to have simply been a repetition with Freud of something that occurred (or that she wished had occurred) with Herr K. In Freud's attempt to "penetrate her secrets" (SE VII, p. 73 n. 1) in record time, Freud himself was inflicting a kind of violence on her—indeed, a form of mental rape. We could postulate that, like all patients, Ida was somewhat afraid to be cured, or unwilling to give up the jouissance she derived from her symptoms and predicament. But we could equally postulate that she was afraid of losing her ability to think for herself and of being steamrollered or brainwashed by a man who, as insightful as he no doubt was, professed that he knew her mind better than she herself did—which, as intriguing and thrilling as it may be at the outset, is generally rather scary in the long run. As Winnicott (1960) says,

> It is very important . . . that the analyst shall *not* know the answers except insofar as the patient gives the clues. The analyst gathers the clues and makes interpretations, and it often happens that patients fail to give the clues, making certain thereby that the analyst can do nothing. This limitation of the analyst's power is important to the patient. (pp. 50–51)

But Freud (SE VII) brags,

> When I set myself the task of bringing to light what human beings keep hidden within them, not by the compelling power of hypnosis, but by observing what they say and what they show, I thought the task was a harder one than it really is. He that has eyes to see and ears to hear may convince himself that no mortal can keep a secret.[69] If his lips are silent, he chatters with his finger-tips; betrayal oozes out of him at every pore. And thus the task of making conscious the most hidden recesses of the mind is one which it is quite possible to accomplish. (pp. 77–78)[70]

Freud's "penetrating" approach was such that he probably should not be considered to have been the victim of a particularly nasty negative transference on Ida's part from Herr K onto him. The analysis foundered more likely because he was practicing in an untoward manner that was not conducive to helping Ida solve her own problems. It is sometimes all too easy for practitioners to attribute to transference their own missteps in the analytic encounter and to "trace back" their patients' stances toward their therapists to something outside of the consulting room rather than to their own behavior inside it.

By his account, Freud fell into the very same trap that he believed Herr K fell into: He thought that Herr K should have pursued Ida after she slapped him and declared his honorable intentions to her and her family, for that might have allowed him to succeed in his suit and win Ida over (SE VII, p. 107). When Ida "slapped" Freud by telling him she had decided to terminate the analysis, Freud failed to clearly state that he himself wanted Ida to stay on. He justifies this in the case write-up with what smacks of rationalization, saying that he detested pretending or putting on an act, which would have involved "exaggerating . . . the importance to me of her staying on" (yet it was clearly of far too much importance to him that she stay on!), telling her instead that she was "free to stop the treatment at any time" (p. 105; see also p. 109). He claims, "There must be some limits set to the extent to which psychological influence may be used, and I respect as one of these limits the patient's own will and understanding."

In his *Papers on Technique* some eight years later, he tells us how important it is for the analyst to prevail upon patients to continue what is often difficult and laborious analytic work (SE XII, p. 130) by showing a "serious interest" in them (p. 139). Here, however, we get the sense that Freud was so hurt by Ida's decision to leave and perhaps troubled by his own disproportionate interest in the case—which would have inclined him to insist that she stay—that he overreacted by letting her go with no protest whatsoever, not even saying the kind of thing that is so classic today: "Well, why don't we at least talk about it once more next week?"

Here we see quite clearly that the primary resistance in therapy is the analyst's. Perhaps it was ultimately best that Freud did not insist that she continue, as he did not seem able to see the error of his ways at that point in time. Lacan adopts this point of view in 1951, but argues that Freud should have interpreted the transference (or what Freud believed to be the transference) not because that is the best way to proceed, but rather because it can at times be done as a last-ditch effort to break out of a deadlock or impasse in the treatment. When all else has failed, the analyst can attempt to proffer an interpretation of the transference; it will almost inevitably be incorrect or off target, but *it may nevertheless inspire the analysand to correct the analyst* (*Écrits*, p. 225).

Would Ida then have told Freud that he was barking up the wrong tree with his allusions to Herr K, because the real love of her life was Frau K? Would she have told him that she had decided to leave analysis because he was so clearly clueless about the true object of her affections? Recall that this is how Freud, in one of his 1905 footnotes to the Ida case, characterizes his mistake, saying that he failed to realize that Ida actually loved Frau K.

Let us note that *this is yet another attempt on Freud's part to define his failure, not at the level of his flawed, bullying technique, but strictly in terms of knowledge and insight.* Just as in 1900 he believed that he had failed to pick up on the fact that she was transferring her anger at Herr K onto him, in 1905 he postulated that he had overlooked the importance of her homosexual interest. Lacan in 1951 seems to accept Freud's 1905 conclusion, and opines that by interpreting the transference incorrectly Freud might have incited Ida to lead him in the right direction, which in Lacan's view is not so much Ida's love for Frau K herself but Ida's questions about her own femininity, which she had been exploring via Frau K. Both Freud and Lacan (in 1951)[71] thus construe Freud's problem in Ida's analysis in terms of accuracy: of getting something right at the level of knowledge. But we might argue instead that *if Freud had gotten his technique right*—more in line with his later *Papers on Technique*, where it is the analysand who does most of the work and the lion's share of the associating and interpreting—*accuracy would have taken care of itself.*

We would thus do well to take pains to avoid following Freud's example in the case of Ida, and to follow instead the advice he gave us with 10 to 15 years of further experience, in which he attempted to learn from his earlier mistakes. We can go quite far in psychoanalysis by embracing not Freud's personal example but his recommendations, he having arguably been far better at formulating a compelling theory of practice than at following it himself, far better as a theoretician than as a clinician, especially early on in his work (he, like most innovators, learned a great deal by trial and error).[72] As we saw in the case of the Rat Man, *psychoanalytic practice can go well beyond Freud the practitioner*, with all his biases and personal failings, and, thankfully, it often does.

Countertransference

No one who, like me, conjures up the most evil of those half-tamed demons that inhabit the human breast, and seeks to wrestle with them, can expect to come through the struggle unscathed.
—Freud, SE VII, p. 109

Many of the critiques that we have by now made of Freud's work with Ida (here and in Appendix I) can be grouped under the heading of Freud's countertransference. But this is so only if we do not restrict countertransference to being the simple counterpart of the reductionistic notion of transference mentioned earlier in this chapter, whereby transference is nothing more than how the patient *feels* about the analyst at any particular moment in time. Like transference, countertransference is a far more complicated animal, involving the repetition of earlier situations and configurations. Like transference, it could be said (if we substitute "analysand" for "analyst") to involve

> new editions or facsimiles of the impulses and fantasies that are aroused . . . as the analysis proceeds; but they have this peculiarity, which is that they replace some earlier person by the [analysand]. To put it another way: a whole series of psychical experiences are revived, not as belonging to the past, but as applying to the [analysand] in the present. (SE VII, p. 116)

In line with Freud's later definition of transference, we could add: Countertransference "is itself only a piece of repetition, and the repetition is a transference of the forgotten past not only onto the [analysand] but also onto all the other aspects of the current situation" (SE XII, p. 151).

Freud, as mentioned in Appendix I, was probably attracted to Ida, at least at the outset, both physically and owing to her intelligence and rather independent personality; and he was at other points annoyed at her uncooperativeness and refusal to answer a great many of his questions (not even making a show of trying to remember things he asked about, immediately replying instead, "I don't know") and confirm his interpretations. The fact that he took her uncooperativeness personally obviously says more about him than about her, for it was only her father's authority[73] that brought her to see him in the first place, and her uncooperativeness was only to be expected. What it says about Freud is not simply that he wanted to help Ida get better, but that he was anxious to solve her problems as part of his larger ambition to establish the veracity of his theories of hysteria and dream interpretation.[74] In other words, his annoyance with her—she obviously got under his skin, just as his account of her work has gotten under the skin of numerous commentators, especially in recent decades (see Appendix I)—was but one manifestation of his vast intellectual ambition to conquer the world, so to speak, with the brilliance and effectiveness of his newborn psychoanalytic technique; to be thwarted by her was thus to be thwarted as an all-knowing authority.[75]

Freud's psychobiographers would no doubt allude here to his sense of not having made much of a name for himself with his early medical/neurological writings, and his frustration at not being given a professorship at the university for so long; but in any case, we can see that at least some of his frustration with Ida had an origin that lay clearly outside of Ida as a living, breathing human being. His biographers—especially Jones, who was the only one to have seen the sum total of the letters

exchanged between Freud and his wife during their extended engagement, which involved them living in different cities for three years—
might also opine that Freud's relation to women up until he was 44
had repercussions on his work with Ida, he no doubt repeating certain
earlier relations with women with her in the consulting room, especially,
perhaps, via his identification with Herr K as a suitor whom Freud considered to be "unfairly treated" by Ida.

Regarding Freud's countertransferential stance toward Ida, let us now
consider Lacan's definition of countertransference. It is, he says, "the
sum total of the analyst's biases, passions, and difficulties, or even of
his inadequate information, at any given moment in the dialectical process" of an analysis (*Écrits*, p. 225; see also Lacan, Seminar I, p. 23). This
allows us to group under the heading of countertransference (a) Freud's
preconceived notions (i.e., biases) regarding what an adolescent girl
should or should not know and feel; (b) his determination (i.e., passion)
to always be right in his guesses and constructions; (c) his bewilderment
or distress (i.e., difficulty) when faced with homosexual impulses; and
even (d) his mistaken belief (i.e., inadequate information), owing to the
undeveloped state of medical knowledge at his time, that Ida's father
could have transmitted a venereal disease to Ida. All of these things
contributed to skewing the treatment in certain directions, sometimes
subtly, sometimes blatantly.

We should also include under the heading of Freud's countertransference his silly notion that Herr K was a "good catch";[76] his ambition
to cure Ida, instead of helping her cure herself; his ambition for her to
marry (he hoped she would marry the engineer who wrote her from
Germany during the treatment, but she did not, eventually marrying
instead a ne'er-do-well musician by the name of Ernst Adler); and his
wish that her father would not give up Frau K for the sake of Ida's health
(SE VII, p. 42), as he felt it would lead Ida to use illness or suicide threats
as blackmail to get her way with other men in the future.

Practitioners whom I supervise often mention that they have wishes
or ambitions for their patients, all of which fall under the heading of
countertransference insofar as they deviate from the ideal of psychoanalytic "neutrality" (that is, from the ideal of allowing patients to explore
different options without expressing or imposing our own ideas about
what would be good for them), even when they coincide to one degree
or another with the patient's own wishes or ambitions. When practitioners find that they have secret or not so secret ambitions for their
patients—hopes that they will get this or that job, marry or divorce their
current partner, and so on—they would do well to discuss these with

supervisors or trusted colleagues, as they are bound to get conveyed to their patients in subtle or not-so-subtle ways and tend to influence their patients (whether they endorse or reject their analysts' ideas about what would be in their best interests), the latter often feeling pressured by their therapists to do one thing or another, and resenting their therapists if such actions do not work out well. This is a far cry from the analytic ideal of allowing analysands to find their own way and make their own decisions and choices in life.

Freud, as we have seen, had several such ambitions for Ida. In addition, he had ambitions for himself related to his work with her and his subsequent write-up of the case; in particular, he wanted:

- to show the world how interpreting dreams can be useful in treatment;
- to "stimulate interest" in hysteria, for "no one, I believe, can have had any true conception of the complexity of the psychological events in a case of hysteria" prior to this; and
- to show that sexuality "provides the motor force for every single symptom" of hysteria (SE VII, pp. 114–115).

These ambitions of his were crushed "just when [his] hopes of a successful termination of the treatment were at their highest" (p. 109). Freud was obviously very hurt by Ida's departure and perhaps decided to write up her case at least in part as a way to figure out what went wrong and to find a way to get over her. He may have written this case study not so much because it contained good material regarding dream interpretation, for let us note that in the end Ida's two main dreams were not that thoroughly interpreted during the analysis itself, the proof of which is that Freud appended long footnotes to the end of the analysis of each dream to try to provide some sort of synthesis, which he admitted he still could not supply for the second dream (p. 110 n). We thus get the impression that just as Freud claimed that he had worked with other hysterics whose analyses were more complete, he had worked with other hysterics' dreams the analysis of which was more complete. Why, then, did he write up *this* case?

Was it simply untrue, as some critics have argued, that he had worked with other hysterics whose cases had been resolved (so this was the best he had to offer)? Or did he write up Ida's case to help grieve the loss of an intelligent, attractive patient on whom he had at least in part staked his reputation, a young woman with whom he was taken but who was not so taken with him?

Relevance and Conclusions

The case of Dora is first and last an extraordinary piece of writ-
ing. . . . For it is a case history, a kind or genre of writing—a par-
ticular way of conceiving and constructing human experience and
written language—which in Freud's hands became something that
it never was before.[77]

—Marcus, 1975/1990, p. 264

Nothing is more literary . . . than the disavowal of all literary inten-
tions.

—Marcus, 1975/1990, p. 272

Hysteria continues to be widespread at the present point in time, although it currently goes by many new and different names (Showalter, 1997; Mitchell, 2000; and Gherovici, 2003). Its demise was prematurely announced by psychiatrists (e.g., Veith, 1965) and psychologists alike (Satow, 1979) who, *confusing symptoms with structure,*[78] viewed the decline (not the total disappearance)[79] in attention-grabbing symptoms like psychosomatic paralysis, limping, muteness, and blindness that were characteristic of hysteria in the 19th century as a death knell. Assuming we remember that a structure like hysteria (a specific way of dealing with conflict) can manifest itself in myriad ways, one could argue that hysteria is at the core of numerous cases of what gets classified in clinics today as anorexia nervosa, bulimia nervosa, chronic fatigue syndrome, somatic symptom disorder, conversion disorder, fibromyalgia, PTSD (including Gulf War Syndrome and the Puerto Rican Syndrome; an older term was *shell shock*), depression, vaginismus, bipolar disorder (formerly manic depression), borderline personality disorder, agoraphobia, generalized anxiety disorder, social anxiety disorder, dissociative identity disorder (formerly known as multiple personality disorder), histrionic personality disorder, dependent personality disorder, and perhaps others as well that I have overlooked in this laundry list (see Appendix V).[80] Whereas obsession has at least remained present in our most recent diagnostic manuals in the truncated form of OCD, the latter being defined exclusively in terms of symptomatology instead of structure (which means that certain cases of hysteria end up included in it),[81] hysteria was excised from the *DSM* already in 1980, at least in part perhaps owing to the headache that it continued—and often continues today—to give clinicians, being multiform and protean, new bodily symptoms appearing, for example, almost as soon as old ones are articulated and disappear.

Remnants of hysteria live on in the many disorders just mentioned in my laundry list, but none of these diagnoses give, I would suggest, much guidance to practitioners. The hope on the part of the diagnostic manual writers was perhaps that by dividing, one could conquer—in other words, that by parceling out different hysterical symptoms into different diagnostic categories, subgroups could be found that might be less resistant to certain forms of psychotherapeutic or psychopharmacological treatment (note that much of the research conducted by the majority of those manual writers was and still is today funded by drug companies, and that not a single one of the writers of the *DSM-5* was a practicing clinician). To the best of my knowledge, this has never happened, no matter how many new subcategories have been added.

In this chapter, we have discussed at least as much what not to do when it comes to the treatment of hysteria (or of any other neurosis, for that matter) as what to do. First and foremost, we have seen that we must never immediately assume that something we suspect is going on in an analysis is based on transference; it might be, but then again it might be based on something we ourselves are doing. (We must not assume, like Freud does, that it is about Herr K when it is about us.) When we base this suspicion on something we ourselves are feeling—whether we feel pressured, cornered, helpless, impotent, empty, anxious, or whatever—we should look first to our own experience, past and present, to see if:

- We have ever felt this way before, and if so, when and under what circumstances. Does the analysand perhaps remind us in some way (e.g., appearance, attitude, intelligence, style of dress, voice, gaze, etc.) of someone else and thus of things that happened with that person?
- We feel the same way with a number of our patients, or just this one. If more than one, perhaps it says more about how *we* respond to certain types of people or to a certain attribute some people have than about the particular analysand in front of us.

It may be necessary to discuss such questions about *our* experience with our own analysts, supervisors, or colleagues in order to really explore them fruitfully—it should never be forgotten how important it is to talk about ourselves with *other* people, given how easy it is to content *ourselves* with the first explanation that comes to mind (pointing, once again, to the general uselessness of self-analysis). Frank discussions with others may help bring into focus our own characteristic ways of responding to certain kinds of people (people that we find, say, intimidating, seductive, or infuriating), which are related to our own "biases, passions, and difficulties," and even our own "inadequate information."

Supervision that includes both (a) discussion of patients' histories and what is going on in the treatment, and (b) an open forum in which to reveal our countertransferential feelings about patients—including our wishes for and frustrations with patients, our sense of not knowing what is going on, feeling backed into a corner, or stymied in all our endeavors, for example—should be seen as crucial throughout one's analytic career, not something that lasts a couple of years and then becomes superfluous. When analysts feel boxed in, sense that the treatment is going nowhere, or are bothered by patients' erotic or negative transference, supervision is an essential element for getting an outside and hopefully broader perspective on cases. If it should prove inadequate, analysts should seriously consider going back into analysis themselves; I have worked with many clinicians who have ended up doing so after undergoing supervision with me for a year or two in the hope that supervision would suffice for dealing with the difficulties that had been arising for them in their daily practice. They realized that hearing another person's perspective was not enough to break them of certain ingrained habits and allow them to stop experiencing certain chronic reactions to their analysands.

In this chapter we have also seen that, as Freud (SE XII) concludes some 10 years after the end of his work with Ida, *the analyst should not make an interpretation until the analysand is but "one short step away" from drawing the same conclusion him- or herself:*

> [We must condemn] any line of behavior that would lead us to give the patient a translation of his symptoms as soon as we have guessed it ourselves, or lead us to regard it as a special triumph to fling these "solutions" in his face at the first meeting. It is not difficult for a skilled analyst to read the patient's secret wishes plainly between the lines of his complaints and the story of his illness; but what a measure of self-complacency and thoughtlessness must be possessed by anyone who can, on the shortest acquaintance, inform a stranger who is entirely ignorant of all the tenets of analysis that he is attached to his mother by incestuous ties, that he harbors wishes for the death of his wife whom he appears to love, that he conceals an intention of betraying his superior, and so on! I have heard that there are analysts who pride themselves on making these kinds of lightning diagnoses and "express" treatments, but I must warn everyone against following such examples. Behavior of this sort will completely discredit oneself and the treatment in the patient's eyes and will arouse the most violent opposition in him,

whether one's guess has been true or not; indeed, the truer the guess the more violent will be the resistance.

As a rule the therapeutic effect will be nil; but the deterring of the patient from analysis will be final. Even in the later stages of analysis one must be careful not to give a patient the solution of a symptom or the translation of a wish until he is already so close to it that he has only one short step more to take in order to get hold of the explanation for himself. In former years I often had occasion to find that the premature communication of a solution brought the treatment to an untimely end, on account not only of the resistances that it thus suddenly awakened but also of the relief that the solution brought with it. (p. 140)[82]

The "untimely end" of Ida's analysis is perhaps being hinted at here, but there were no doubt other patients who fled before Freud's interpretative blitzkrieg. The method whereby Freud glimpsed, guessed, and relentlessly interpreted what was repressed (i.e., what lay beneath the bar, as I depicted the repressed in the section entitled "The Unfolding of Ida's Analysis") gave way in later years to one in which he, in theory at least, left it more and more up to the analysand to say what lay under the bar. (Note, however, that in 1912 Freud continued to hubristically speak as though he knew what was truly going on for even brand-new patients, but realized that, for pragmatic reasons, he had to wait before telling them what it was.)

We see a sure sign of excessive interpretation on analysts' parts when they find themselves spending a great deal of time outside of sessions thinking up interpretations they can make to a patient at the next session. And hysterical patients are the kind who most often inspire this kind of disproportionate cogitation in analysts, leading their analysts to try to solve their problems instead of bringing the analysands to discern their own role in creating the mess in which they find themselves, realize what they have been getting out of it, and solve their own problems. Just as students generally work harder in classes in which professors don't provide all the answers, analysands usually do far more of the interpretative work themselves when analysts refrain from answering all questions and interpreting every bit of the material brought up in the course of the analysis.

One consequence of leaving it more up to the patient to do the work is that *analysis takes longer!* Now that analysts have, for the most part, stopped intellectually "penetrating" patients (at least in the way that Freud seems to have at times), certain patients now complain that we fleece them, the process of analysis having become still more expensive owing to its length.

You can't win 'em all . . .[83]

How might we characterize the critiques of Freud's work with Ida that I have proposed here (and in Appendix I) in terms of Lacan's three registers: imaginary, symbolic, and real? Some of them might be understood to be situated at the symbolic level, insofar as they involve a change in theoretical perspective that grows out of Freud's self-critique or auto-critique, as it were, in his *Papers on Technique*; for there he comes to see that analysands' *engagement in the therapeutic work* (and feeling that the analysis is their own) must take precedence over any attempt on the analyst's part to bring them to make full and immediate confessions, to resolve any one specific symptom they suffer from, and to demonstrate brilliant "insight" into analysands' dreams, fantasies, parapraxes, and lives. Not abdicating all "directing of the treatment," the analyst must stop "directing the patient" (as Lacan put it in *Écrits*, p. 490), and ensure that the ball remains essentially in the analysand's court.

Other critiques I have proposed here might be understood to be situated at the imaginary level—for example, insofar as Freud saw himself in or identified with Herr K (or even with Ida herself or her father), and acted in the therapy like someone who seemed to need to feel he was *master* of or in control of the situation. Still others involve the "real," which is defined by Lacan, in this context, not as so-called reality, but as concerning psychical and/or bodily satisfactions (or jouissances). Here we would be speculating about the satisfactions Freud seems to have derived from his work with Ida. This is a delicate subject in many ways, the satisfaction or satisfactions that analysts derive from their work with patients rarely being discussed in the literature, to the best of my knowledge, even though it is clear that few analysts would probably say that their only gratification in working with patients is the money they receive for their services. We hear of cases in which especially talkative analysts seem to be attempting to cure themselves and solve their own problems while they are ostensibly treating patients, the analysts' own neuroses taking precedence over their patients' neuroses—an obvious travesty. And at least the majority of psychoanalysts would, I suspect, look down on clinicians who take a great deal of satisfaction in having directed their patients to do the very things that those clinicians believe they should do—for example, break up with certain partners, marry others, have children, pursue specific degrees or professions, become psychoanalysts, and so on. For in such cases, the jouissance such analysts seem to get from working with analysands is akin to the narcissistic self-satisfaction that pushy parents derive from steering their recalcitrant children toward parental goals (a far cry from psychoanalytic "neutrality"), whereas the aim in psychoanalysis is to help analysands arrive at their own goals and get beyond their neurotic obstacles to pursuing those goals.

Freud, it would seem, adopted a role with Ida that I would characterize as a cross between that of a parent and that of a suitor (who eventually became a lover scorned). Like a parent, he wanted Ida to stop thinking all men were "detestable" (lying and hypocritical like her father and Herr K), marry, and have children. And like a suitor, he seemed to want to dazzle her with his brilliance, his insight into what made her tick, and his ready cultural references that he suspected they shared. Having failed to win her over, it would seem that he began to derive satisfaction from badgering her to confess to things, from always believing himself to be right (an impoverished form of what we might call "phallic jouissance"), and from bullying her into confirming his views or at least acquiescing to them.

The kind of satisfaction involved in jouissance is not always pretty. Freud appears to have felt like a jilted lover, especially at the end of his work with Ida, and—as many of us have known at one time or another—to feel jilted is a significant emotional experience that may include anger, hatred, self-pity, a deep narcissistic wound, a wish for revenge, and so on. None of these are emotions that we would hope to find in psychoanalysts as they work with their analysands.

CHAPTER 6

Symptom Formation

I used to think I knew what I was about and what I was up to. Now I realize something else is running my life. I'm certainly not running my life—I really don't know what I'm doing.

—An analysand

Symptoms speak even to those who do not know how to hear them. Nor do they tell the whole story even to those who do.

—Lacan (cited in Fink, 2013, p. 1)

IN EARLIER CHAPTERS we discussed a number of different characteristics of neurotic symptoms, from their origin in conflicting impulses—one of which is usually sexual or aggressive, the other attempting to suppress the first, whether for moralistic, practical, or self-preservative reasons—to the curious form of dissatisfying satisfaction, satisfaction in the guise of suffering, or satisfaction in dissatisfaction they provide, all of which can be included under the heading of jouissance.[1] We will explore these and other characteristics in greater detail in this chapter, but first I want to reiterate that everything we "have said here about repression and the formation and meaning of symptoms is based on three forms of neurosis—anxiety hysteria [corresponding to phobia],[2] conversion hysteria, and obsession—and that it is valid for these forms alone" (SE XVI, p. 299).[3]

It is, I believe, important to underscore this, for what are sometimes referred to as "symptoms" of psychosis—for example, hallucinations, delusions, and "concrete" thinking (which might be better termed *non-metaphorical* thinking)—are not structured in the same way as the more "classical" psychoanalytic symptoms. Lacan refers to hallucinations and delusions not as symptoms but, rather, as the "elementary phenomena" of psychosis.[4] Put in somewhat more technical terms, whereas neurotic symptoms are a product of the negating mechanism known as repression ("Repression is the operative mechanism for the development of the neuroses"; SE VIII, p. 233), psychotic phenomena result from a different negating mechanism, which Freud termed *Verwerfung*—that is, foreclosure.[5] We will not go into the why and wherefore of foreclosure in this book, as it would take us too far afield and as I have done so elsewhere (Fink, 1997, Chapter 7, and 2007, Chapter 10). We will thus confine our attention here—as Freud himself did for the most part—to neurotic symptoms.

This should not be taken to imply that our discussion of symptom formation will have no bearing whatsoever on the symptoms presented by those who are so commonly diagnosed in our times as borderline, narcissistic, or bipolar. Diagnosis in the contemporary psychotherapeutic world has largely given up any vestige of the structural model briefly touched upon in Chapters 4 and 5, a model that distinguishes between neurosis, perversion, and psychosis insofar as each of these three clinical structures is characterized by a different negating mechanism—repression in neurosis, disavowal (what Freud called *Verleugnung*) in perversion,[6] and foreclosure in psychosis. Diagnosis, as laid out in the standardized manuals used in most offices, clinics, and hospitals today, is based almost exclusively on descriptive criteria whereby one is diagnosed as borderline, for example, if for a certain minimum period of time, one fits at least five out of a rather extensive checklist of "criteria" which are considered to constitute the "clinical entity" known as borderline personality disorder. This implies that diagnosis is now determined by supposedly significant "groupings" or "constellations" of what clinicians believe to be symptoms, which may change over time, meaning that one may be diagnosed as borderline at one point, as bipolar a couple of years later, and with generalized anxiety disorder still further on in time (seemingly fitting only two out of five criteria of a particular diagnosis at one doctor's visit and all of them later), when one is not given two out of three of those diagnoses at the same time. Indeed, more and more patients show up at practitioners' offices or treatment facilities today with a psychiatric file including half a dozen or more different diagnoses (a number of which have even been proposed by different clinicians seeing the patient within a few days of each other, disagreeing, as they do, with each other about which criteria the patient most closely and enduringly fits). This is not surprising given that the predominant manual, the *DSM*, which started out 130 pages long in 1952 and included about 106 mental disorders, has grown in its latest iteration to about 1,000 pages and includes about 265 disorders,[7] many of which obviously overlap (compare this to psychoanalysis, which generally includes less than a dozen different clinical structures; see Appendix V).

Above and beyond the fact that psychiatric nomenclature like this, which is based on such vague "clinical entities," is often of dubious value to practitioners hoping to learn how to direct the treatment with different patient populations (are there really that many different disorders for which we must adopt different treatment approaches?),[8] let me mention once again that psychoanalysts—when they are actually functioning as psychoanalysts and not as psychiatrists, clinical psychologists, or social workers—do not profess to decide what qualifies as a symptom for any particular person: In psychoanalysis, *a symptom is whatever someone complains of.* People behave in myriad ways that bother their entourage no end, and that their partners, relatives, friends, and coworkers believe to be highly symptomatic (saying such things as, "You never listen to anyone else," "You can't take criticism," "You do the exact opposite of what I tell you I want," and so on); and yet, as I mentioned in Chapter 3, none of these are considered to constitute symptoms from a psychoanalytic standpoint. *Something is a symptom and potentially accessible to analytic treatment only when it is the patient him- or herself who complains of it* and considers it to be problematic, not when those around the patient do. Analysts have no business telling patients what they think is symptomatic in their patients' behavior; they should instead allow patients to formulate what they themselves find problematic in their lives.[9] Simple questions—like "So what brings you here?" "What led you to contact me?" or "What would you like to talk about (or work on)?"—usually suffice to bring out a first sketch of what patients consider symptomatic in their own lives. The latter is often referred to as the "presenting problem," as it is what patients are willing to own up to at the outset, fuller sketches only emerging over the course of time. The majority of patients call more and more aspects of their lives into question all by themselves as in-depth therapy proceeds.

The Structural Viewpoint

Psychoanalytic research finds no fundamental, but only a quantitative, distinction between normal and neurotic life.
—Freud, SE V, p. 373

The borderline between normal and abnormal in nervous matters is a fluid one; we are all [at least] a little neurotic.
— Freud, SE VI, p. 278

> *If you take up a theoretical point of view and disregard the question of quantity, you may quite well say that we are all ill—that is, neurotic—since the preconditions for the formation of symptoms can also be observed in normal people.*
>
> —Freud, SE XVI, p. 358

It should not be thought that analysts thus believe that people who do not complain about anything that they think, feel, or do are symptom-free and thus "normal." *There is no such thing as normality, psychoanalytically speaking,* "since the preconditions for the formation of symptoms" are found in everyone, and not just the preconditions: Even "a healthy person is virtually a neurotic," and if "one subjects his waking life to a closer examination, one discovers . . . that this ostensibly healthy life is interspersed with a great number of symptoms" (SE XVI, p. 457).[10] Symptoms come into being as soon as repression occurs—that is, as soon as the unconscious comes into being. "There is no distinction between conscious and unconscious" in newborns (SE XVI, p. 409), but when the unconscious forms, the very process of its formation inevitably gives rise to one or more symptoms.

As soon as someone comes into being in the usual neurotic way—in other words, by having given up a certain number of pleasures and having set aside (that is, repressed)[11] the wishes associated with them—something that we can refer to as a symptom forms as part of the endeavor to get some of those pleasures back, albeit in a disguised or unrecognizable manner. As Freud tells us, people have a very hard time giving up their pleasures and constantly seek roundabout ways of obtaining at least some satisfaction for the very same wishes they have repressed: "Man is a 'tireless pleasure-seeker' . . . and any renunciation of a pleasure he has once enjoyed comes hard to him" (SE VIII, p. 126);[12] and, "Men have always found it hard to give up pleasure; they cannot bring themselves to do it without some kind of compensation" (SE XVI, p. 371).

The people who do not complain about their symptom (or symptoms) are often those whose ways of trying to obtain such compensation fit in well with the culture or subculture in which they operate and live. For example, a male who has suppressed his fury at his father (for any number of possible things his father did or was believed by him to have done) will find no shortage of outlets for his fury in a culture where football, boxing, and other such combative sports are widely accepted (not to mention warfare). A female who has repressed rivalry with her mother for her father's attentions may channel all of her energy into surpassing her mother in a plethora of ways her father might have been proud of or that scores of other men might admire: education, artistic accomplishments, beauty, fashion, humor, success in business, and so on. Workaholics, as destructive as they may be to themselves in some ways, often achieve high social status in the Western world; and compulsively restricting one's own food intake may help catapult one to supermodel stardom in a world in which, for the time being at least, "one can never be too thin or too rich," as the Duchess of Windsor is reported to have said. Those who find compensations like money, status, fame, and quasi-universal admiration—which, at times, win them fawning, courting, attention, and even love from others—are obviously less likely to complain of what they are unwittingly doing (e.g., still trying to best Dad or Mom, or still trying to take revenge on them).[13]

To be "symptom free" thus means one of at least two possible things: One does not suffer from typically neurotic symptoms (one may then be perverse or psychotic), or one is not especially bothered by the specific way in which one unknowingly tries to recover some of the enjoyment one ostensibly renounced when one was a child. Analysts may believe they detect such symptomatic enjoyment recovery strategies (i.e. symptoms) in their analysands, but do well to refrain from mentioning them until the analysands themselves complain of them.

How Symptoms Form

We seek not merely to describe and to classify phenomena, but to understand them as signs of an interplay of forces in the mind, as a manifestation of purposeful intentions working concurrently or in mutual opposition. We are concerned with a dynamic view of mental phenomena.[14]

—Freud, SE XV, p. 67

Turning now to those who *do* complain about their thoughts, actions, and feelings, let us recall that neurotic symptoms usually form owing to a conflict between two competing forces, which we have called Force 1 and Force 2. Recall the patient I mentioned in Chapter 2 who suffered from sensations of coldness that could not be alleviated by drinking hot beverages or taking long, steaming baths, a symptom that we traced back to a night on which she heard noises coming from her parents' bedroom, went out into the hallway, and, while standing on the cold tile floor, saw her father on top of her mother on their bed, his penis erect. In this particular symptom of coldness, as in any number of her other physical symptoms (like tightness in her chest), she seemed to identify with her mother and wish to be in her mother's place in that scene in bed with her father. We can think of that wish as Force 1, for it was an urge to be as important to her father as her mother was and to oust her mother from that pre-eminent role for her father. Force 2 could then be understood as the moral qualms she had with that wish insofar as it was both incestuous and involved a betrayal of her (at least somewhat beloved) mother.

In this obvious repetition of an experience from the past—and the reader may recall that this woman's sensations of coldness arose in the course of the analysis itself—conflicting forces were at work. Tracing this repetition back to its source, which was the night she witnessed her parents having sex, led to the demise of the symptom, but not to the end of the conflict itself; the conflict continued to produce other symptoms until many of the analysand's wishes and urges related to her father (whom she initially claimed to simply loathe) were spelled out and much of her anger at and rivalry with her mother (whom she initially claimed to absolutely adore) were articulated. The result of this was that Force 1 diminished considerably, meaning that it no longer had to be strenuously countered by Force 2.[15]

The symptoms presented by 21st-century analysands can be understood on the basis of such a "conflict model" just as easily as the symptoms suffered by Freud's analysands could be. In another case, a male analysand of mine would pursue women whom he considered to be at least as beautiful as his mother had been, and as soon as he had gotten them totally committed to him he would break up with them, only to do everything imaginable thereafter to convince them to come back to him (which, when successful, started the whole process over again). He was at a loss to comprehend why he did this, and, needless to say, his partners were highly distressed by it. It turned out that he felt that he had an overly close relationship with his mother, she and his father having divorced early on in his life and he being her only surviving child. There had been something thrilling and yet troubling to him about his virtually unlimited access to his mother, and he came to think—based on a few remarks and hints his father made—that his father disapproved of this closeness with his mother, commenting that his mother was "bad news" and the like.

What resulted was not a compromise symptom, like we saw in the earlier example of sensations of coldness, but rather an *alternating symptom* in which his urge to be with a woman whom he considered to be as beautiful as his mother (Force 1) would initially get the upper hand, and in which his sense of needing to heed his father's warning (Force 2) would take center stage afterward, in an endless cycling back and forth between the one and the other. With certain women later on in his life, the cycle would be shortened to such a degree that he would not even be able to take the first step of getting involved with a woman he thought beautiful, because he would almost immediately feel he was "not allowed" to have such a woman.[16]

In yet another case, a man with a highly active mind never put into action any of the myriad projects he would conceive of, and would complain bitterly that he was wasting his life doing nothing. He had long been fixated on his mother, whom he felt he had lost to his younger brother at the latter's birth; this patient seemed early in life to have alighted upon a policy of resentment: If his mother was going to withhold from him the love he wanted, he was certainly never going to do anything she in any way, shape, or form hinted at that she wanted from him or for him. This remained his lifelong policy: Never do anything his mother might want him to do or approve of; never achieve anything she might potentially enjoy vicariously. As long as his wish for her love (Force 1) remained unabated, it was accompanied by an urge for revenge (Force 2), which led to total paralysis in his life at the level of work and career. In his sexual fantasies, he would imagine a woman initially resisting his overtures, but then giving in to his charms, indicating the degree to which he was still fantasizing about winning his mother back.

This "policy"—like so many policies neurotics alight upon, whether deliberately or not—turned out to be "a bad deal" for the patient, he himself feeling he was paying "too dearly for an alleviation of the conflict" (SE XVI, p. 383). Some of the anxiety generated by the conflict between Forces 1 and 2 is generally "bound" or alleviated by the adoption of a policy (i.e., by formation of a symptom)—symptoms form, after all, "to escape an otherwise unavoidable generating of anxiety" (p. 404)—but the price paid by the person over the course of his lifetime far outweighs this escape from anxiety (which, moreover, often returns in other arenas).

The "Sense" of Symptoms

I don't have sex, I have psoriasis.

—An analysand

In the later chapters of his *Introductory Lectures on Psychoanalysis*, Freud reminds us of several other facets of symptoms that he had laid out in his earlier works. Like dreams, symptoms are not "random" events or occurrences in someone's life, but are, instead, meaningful (SE XVI, pp. 257–258). Moreover, *it is not just the symptom as a whole that is meaningful, but every single aspect of it.*

We saw in the case of Anna O, for example, that for six weeks she was unable to drink water. She was able to take liquids in other forms and eat fruit, but she could not drink water from a glass. This, let us recall, resulted from the fact that she had seen her lady companion's dog drink water out of that same lady's glass one day. Had it been wine in the lady's glass, Anna O might well have been able to drink anything but wine, and have had no trouble with water; and had the water been in a bowl (such as a washbasin) instead of a glass, Anna O might have become unable to wash her hands in such a bowl, but would have had no trouble drinking water from a glass. In short, each detail of the scene she witnessed played an important role in the exact symptom that eventually formed.[17] Clinicians must thus ask about every possible detail of a symptom: if a patient binges and then vomits, for example, it is important to inquire about what brings on the binging, what she binges on (usually sweets, but not always), and when and how the vomiting comes on (is it self-induced or spontaneous? does she vomit in the toilet, or in glass jars that she then hides in her closet where a parent might well find them?). All of these things must be gone into if we are to have an impact on the symptom; practitioners who fail to inquire into the minutiae of symptoms will find they acquire precious little purchase on them.

Now when Freud discusses the meaning or "sense" (*Sinn*) of a symptom, he includes two things under that heading: "its 'whence' and its 'whither' or 'what for'—that is, the impressions and experiences from which it arose and the intentions it serves" (SE XVI, p. 284). Anna O's inability to drink water from a glass resulted from witnessing the dog drinking from her lady companion's glass—in other words, that was its "whence," that was where it came from. The "whither" or "what for" of a symptom introduces a different issue: What purpose does the symptom serve? The popular mind tends to embrace the sufferer's view that her symptom serves no purpose whatsoever, insofar as it constitutes an obstacle to so many of her conscious aims and purposes. Indeed, she is likely to believe that it is a sheer aberration and is altogether "dysfunctional." Yet psychoanalysts might hypothesize in this case that it served to hide from Anna O's own consciousness her hateful impulses toward her lady companion (and possibly toward her mother)—that was its *raison d'être*.

Let us consider a more complicated example, one that we discussed in Chapter 1. Recall that in attempting to take total and flawless care of her father, Anna O became exhausted to the point that she had to take to her bed for about four months. If the main conflict in her life at that time can be understood as one between her filial duty and her desire to have a life of her own, we could hypothesize that she found a way to renege on her filial duty by falling ill. Her "state of weakness, anemia, and distaste for food became so bad that, to her great dismay, she was no longer allowed to continue nursing the patient" (SE II, p. 23); this particular "solution" to her conflict had the advantage of medical authority, it having been her doctors who informed the family that she could no longer look after her father—she did not have to refuse to do so herself. We might understand this result to have been a "secondary gain" from her illness, or perhaps to have even been its primary, albeit unconscious, aim. (As we saw in the case of Anna's nervous cough, we might say that in many instances what is effectively achieved by a symptom—drowning out rhythmic music that would remind her of her desire to go dancing—is not just a random function that gets served by the symptom but its very purpose.) Anna's deteriorated state presumably forced Anna's mother to take over the lion's share of the nursing during the final four months of her husband's life, which Anna might also have been wishing for at some level.

In this sense, we can often grasp at least some of the meaning of a symptom by looking at what it actually accomplishes—that is, the state of affairs that it manages to bring about. Here we can postulate that Anna's attempt to care for her father perfectly was designed to send a message to her mother—"Mom, this is what you should be doing"—and that her subsequent breakdown was at least in part designed to try to *force* her mother to do what Anna felt her mother should have been doing all along. In cases like this, we can see that *symptoms are often designed in such a way as to directly or indirectly send a message to some particular person or persons,* a message that is usually sent at great personal expense to the sender. To send such a message to her mother may well have been more important to Anna than her own health.[18]

How does one get at the purpose of a symptom? By asking the analysand what her symptom led to in her own life and in the lives of those around her, and by asking what she might have expected or even hoped it would lead to. This aspect of symptoms is, however, often woefully overlooked by clinicians, who then find it difficult to understand why a symptom does not disappear even though its historical origins have been extensively examined.

Symptoms Involve Wishes

The theory governing all psychoneurotic symptoms culminates in a single proposition, which asserts that they too are to be regarded as fulfillments of unconscious wishes. . . . *One portion of the symptom corresponds to the unconscious wish-fulfillment and another to the mental structure reacting against the wish.*
—Freud, SE V, p. 569 and n. 1

Nothing in life is as costly as illness—and stupidity.
—Freud, SE VII, p. 133

Freud also postulates that *wishes are at work in symptom formation:* They present us with the realization of a wish in the present tense (SE XVI, p. 263). We postulated that every time Anna O tried to drink water

from a glass she was reminded of her thoughts about diseases transmitted by dogs and of her hateful wishes toward her lady companion
(and/or mother). A wish that something bad would happen to this lady
seems to have been at the crux of this symptom, and she endeavored
to put this wish as far out of mind as possible, which implies the existence of a counterwish. In other words, *for a symptom to develop, there
must always be at least two different wishes that are at odds,* if not at
war. Recall here the Rat Man's short-lived symptom (a compulsive act)
of removing a stone from the road his ladylove would soon be taking
so that she would not be injured by it as her carriage traveled along
that byway, but then putting it back in its original place. The first action
demonstrated a wish for her well-being, the second a wish for her to be
harmed (SE X, p. 190).

[handwritten margin note: 2 wishes at odds]

Symptoms Involve Repetition, but with a Twist

> *If what neurotics long for the most intensely in their fantasies is pre-
> sented to them in reality, they nonetheless flee from it; and they give
> themselves over to their fantasies most readily when they need no
> longer fear they might be realized.*
>
> —Freud, SE VII, p. 110

In order to illustrate some of Freud's other claims about symptoms, let
us examine the case of a supposedly obsessive woman that Freud discusses in Chapter 17 of his *Introductory Lectures* (SE XVI, pp. 261–264).
This 30-year-old woman performed the following action many times a
day: "She ran from her room into the next room, stationed herself in a
specific spot next to a table that stood in the middle of that room, rang
the bell for her housemaid, sent her on some trivial errand or let her go
without one, and then ran back into her own room" (p. 261). The meaning of this repetitive ritual was opaque to both Freud and herself until
she discussed her wedding night some 10 years earlier when her much
older husband had run back and forth numerous times from his room
to hers in the attempt to have intercourse with her, but had ultimately
proved impotent. The next morning he had told her that he "would feel
ashamed in front of the housemaid when she made the bed" (p. 262) that
there was no blood on the sheets, and he poured red ink on the sheets,
creating a stain in what she felt to be the wrong place.

Lo and behold, there was a highly visible stain on the tablecloth of
the table she stood next to numerous times a day as she performed her
bewildering ritual 10 years later, a stain she felt her housemaid could

not fail to notice. Thus, thanks to a few displacements (e.g., from bed to table, from bedsheet to tablecloth, and from blood to some other type of stain), she was in a sense *correcting* what had happened on her wedding night: It was as if she were showing the housemaid that her husband had in fact been able to perform, and that she herself was therefore no longer a virgin. We see here that her ritual repeated what was obviously to her a somewhat traumatic experience from her past, the twist being that it was not a simple repetition but also what we might call a rectification—that is, something that would symbolically undo or redeem the fiasco of her wedding night, something that would make it as if the trauma had never occurred. As Freud puts it, its purpose was to correct "a distressing portion of the past" (SE XVI, p. 277).

Symptoms may thus at times repeat distressing or even traumatic experiences from the past (symptoms result from "an experience whose affective coloring was excessively powerful" [SE XVI, p. 275], and might therefore often be best understood as echoing or repeating an early traumatic encounter with jouissance),[19] without the repetition being immediately obvious either to the patient or to her entourage because certain distortions or displacements have occurred. Clinicians should, however, be on the lookout for such repetitions, given how common they are in people's lives, and should not fail to bring them to their patients' attention, encouraging them to think about their whence and wherefore (or "whither"). A ritualized action may therefore serve as a representation of an earlier scene even though the connection with that scene remains unrecognizable to its performer. And some satisfaction may be obtained through the performance of the ritual, without the performer having any idea what she is doing. The satisfaction in this case was multifaceted: (a) On the one hand, she preserved her husband's reputation (and it should be noted that they had remained married throughout those 10 years even though they lived apart, and that even after 10 years she could not decide whether to get divorced or not); (b) she seemed to spare herself a certain modicum of ridicule for having married such an old and impotent man; and (c) we might postulate that, in keeping her attention and libido focused on her husband, it prevented her from remarrying and perhaps having to confront a new and different husband who might be closer to her own age and far from impotent.[20]

We do not know why she had agreed in the first place to marry a man who was so much older than herself—he was presumably around her father's age—but we might well imagine that she had idealized her own father and was seeking some sort of father figure or fatherly love object as a life partner, something that is rarely altogether compatible with sexual passion. This is not to say that she was devoid of all interest in sexuality—Freud certainly does not tell us enough to in any way deduce that—but it does not strike me as too much of a stretch to suggest that by remaining fixated in this way on her estranged husband, she had found a way to create for herself *an unsatisfied desire*, a desire that she felt could not be satisfied without tarnishing her husband's reputation; simultaneously, it was a desire that she perhaps was somewhat afraid of in herself and that she found easier or safer to maintain as a simple fantasy, rather than as something to be actively pursued.

Divorce was clearly legal in Vienna at that time, and although we do not know of any religious scruples she might have had on the subject, we do know that she at least contemplated divorce, meaning that it was not entirely unthinkable to her. Yet for a decade, she seems to have preferred to remain legally bound to him, all the while living apart. We might be tempted to view this as some form of asceticism or self-punishment on her part, from which she could not possibly derive any satisfaction for herself. But we might alternatively consider the possibility that she derived some satisfaction from keeping alive in herself a desire or longing for something, without having to face the reality of a new partner who might turn out to be just as disappointing as her first husband, or who might turn out to arouse sexual passion in her, which might then bring all kinds of anxiety and/or self-reproaches in its wake.[21]

hysteric's maintenance of unsatisfied desire

A Symptom Is Not Equivalent to a Structure

> *The two forces that have fallen out meet once again in the symptom and are reconciled, as it were, by the compromise that is constructed through the symptom. It is for this reason, too, that the symptom is so resistant: it is supported from both sides.*
>
> —Freud, SE XVI, pp. 358–359

> *The language of an obsessional neurosis—the means by which it expresses its secret thoughts—is, as it were, only a dialect of the language of hysteria.*
>
> —Freud, SE X, pp. 156–157

Freud points out that in her repetitive ritual, the woman was playing the part of her husband, who ran back and forth from one room to the other on their wedding night. And Lacan points out that hysterics often play the part of a man (*"l'hystérique fait l'homme"*; Seminar XVI, p. 387, and Seminar XX, p. 85), owing to identification, in certain cases, or to their feeling that the male in their lives does not play it adequately or needs to be shown how to do it properly. This—taken in conjunction with what

I just mentioned regarding the desire Freud's patient perhaps preferred not to satisfy, as well as in conjunction with the fact that she seemed quite concerned with protecting her husband's image, as if she felt he were too weak to maintain a respectable social position by himself (i.e., propping him up was more or less equivalent in her mind to propping up her own father, whom she may have seen as rather weak)—would suggest that Freud's patient was in fact an hysteric, not an obsessive, as he claims.[22]

We might say that Freud here confused an obsessive-looking symptom with an overall diagnosis of obsession, as so many practitioners do in our own times. He seems to have been overly focused on the ritualistic aspect of the symptom rather than on the second component of the "sense" of the patient's symptom—namely, its "whither": the purpose it served, which was to keep a new relationship and perhaps sexuality itself at bay (the first component of its "sense," the "whence," was obviously her wedding night). We should not be misled by the outward appearance of a symptom—that is, the degree to which it seems typically hysterical (e.g., vomiting)[23] or obsessive (e.g., repetitive rituals)—but should, in attempting to determine the patient's most profound clinical structure, take our bearings from what holds the symptom in place. This is, indeed, a most important facet of its "sense."[24]

One and the same symptom can be found in people with different clinical structures. This was brought home to me very clearly one day in a graduate course on case formulation that I taught for many years at Duquesne University in Pittsburgh. In that particular class, two Ph.D. students presented different female patients of theirs, one in the first half of the class, and the other in the second, and both patients engaged in what the therapists-in-training referred to as "obsessive" surveillance of their eating as regarded calorie intake. Both students were inclined to diagnose their patients as obsessive owing to the compulsive nature of their rituals around eating, not having yet realized that *virtually all symptomatology involves compulsion,* whether it be a compulsion to do or not do something. Terms like *obsession-compulsion* and *obsessive-compulsive disorder* confuse the issue by making people associate compulsive behavior with obsessive structure, whereas hysterics often feel compelled to do any number of things, whether eat, vomit, or cough, and feel compelled not to do any number of other things, like talk, nourish themselves, or enjoy sex. In the specific class that I mentioned, it was by looking beyond the behaviors the patients engaged in to their radically different reasons for engaging in them (their sense—that is, their whence and whither) that we were able to conclude that one of the patients was likely obsessive while the other was likely hysteric.

A clinical structure like obsession is capable of producing a wide variety of symptoms—some mental, some psychosomatic—and the structure persists even when one or all of the previously visible symptoms are cleared up. As Freud (SE XVI) tells us,

> To laymen, the symptoms constitute the essence of a disease and its cure consists in the removal of the symptoms. Physicians attach importance to distinguishing the symptoms from the disease and declare that getting rid of the symptoms does not amount to curing the disease. But the only tangible thing left of the disease after the symptoms have been got rid of is its capacity to form new symptoms. (p. 358)

A number of medical conditions, including certain staph infections and sexually transmitted diseases, may persist in the body even when all outward signs of them have disappeared, and go on to produce new symptoms months or even years later. Similarly, one's clinical structure is generally permanent beyond a certain age (perhaps 6 to 9 years of age), and it may give rise to highly varied symptoms over the course of one's lifetime. One and the same conflict in a girl's life may manifest itself in the form of vomiting as a child, anorexia in her teenage years, shoplifting in her early twenties, and high-stress, high-volume trading as a stockbroker in her later years.

Freud at times confuses structure and symptom, as for example when he says that "it is typical symptoms that give us our bearings when we make our diagnosis" (SE XVI, p. 271). He guides us more surely when he indicates that "analytic therapy does not make it its first task to remove the symptoms" (SE XVI, p. 436), its first task being to look to their causes—that is, to the conflict that is giving rise to the symptoms in the first place. Contemporary psychotherapy's obsession with "symptom reduction," "symptom removal," and "symptom alleviation," although perhaps initially well-intentioned, has a tendency to overlook the forest (the fundamental conflict between warring forces in a patient's psyche) for the trees (the individual symptoms he complains of). This is not to say that contemporary psychoanalysis' obsession with insight and understanding, sometimes at the expense of symptom reduction, is necessarily any better oriented. Both would do well to work toward impacting the warring forces such that the conflict abates, rather than striving to "understand" the conflict or to remove specific symptoms generated by the conflict.

As we have already seen, one way to impact those forces is to explore the wellsprings of the forces—often lustful or aggressive forces—that patients find so distasteful in themselves; this usually leads to a diminishing of the strength or intensity of such forces. Another way is to explore the self-condemnation—usually morality- or superego-related—that arises because of the aggressive forces, and call into question the quintessentially American notion that all aggressive feelings and thoughts are unacceptable and have to be squelched, as well as the more widespread social condemnation of many of our lustful impulses. (They can be called into question by making queries—let us assume we are addressing Freud's patient with the ritual related to her wedding night—as simple as "What is so terrible about wishing your husband might have been more of a man?" or "What is so awful about wishing he were out of your life, now that you have been separated for 10 years?" or "Are such wishes so reprehensible after all you have been through?")

One fairly widespread symptom that is found in several different clinical structures is the fear of flying. Phobics are often afraid of the confined space within the airline cabin, just as they may be of other confined spaces. Hysterics are often afraid the plane will crash, whether in the ocean or not, leading one or more significant others in their lives to lose them—that is, to be separated from them, something they often ardently wish for even as they dread it! Obsessives may well complain that they are not in control of the plane and find it very unsettling to have to hand over control of almost any conveyance to another person. I am not suggesting that these are the most profound reasons why certain phobics, hysterics, and obsessives have a fear of flying, but we can already see at least superficial ways in which "the same fear," as it were, has a different root cause and functions differently for them. This simple example will hopefully illustrate sufficiently that *a symptom does not a structure make:* The fact that someone is afraid of flying does not mean he is fundamentally phobic.

Nor does the fact that someone works through a phobia mean that he is no longer structurally phobic (assuming he was at the outset): The alleviation of a symptom does not make one's diagnostic structure as a whole change, for that structure may produce new symptoms later on.[25] One's overriding "subjective position" in life as an obsessive, say, as in the case of the Rat Man, and one's "fundamental fantasy," may remain largely the same despite the dissolution of something like the "rat complex." Then again, if the symptom that was alleviated was one's major symptom in life and a longstanding one as well, it may be accompanied by a significant change in one's subjective position and fundamental fantasy (on these, see Fink, 2014a, Chapter 1), even if it does not change one's clinical diagnosis: One becomes less obsessive, not something other than obsessive (such as "normal").

Although Freud attempts at different times to distinguish hysterical symptoms from obsessive symptoms by indicating that in hysteria Force 1 and Force 2 become condensed into one and the same cough or pain, for example, whereas in obsession, Force 1 first manages to find expression and then Force 2 does, the binge-purge cycle we often see in bulimia (in which one first binges on food and then vomits) would seem to be an exception to this rule of thumb, bulimia being fairly widely viewed as an hysterical symptom. We might say much the same thing of Freud's attempt to distinguish hysterical symptoms from obsessive symptoms by indicating that in hysteria highly charged early events are usually forgotten (leading to "amnesia"), the affect related to them going into the body, forming psychosomatic symptoms (SE VII, pp. 40–41), whereas in obsession, highly charged early events are not forgotten, but the affect related to them does not go into the body but is displaced within the mental realm. This oftentimes useful rule of thumb is nevertheless belied by the multiple psychosomatic symptoms we find among obsessives today, including irritable bowel disorder, acid reflux, and so on, some of which were simply grouped together under the term *indigestion* in earlier times. In short, *we must be careful not to too closely associate a certain type of symptom with a specific clinical structural or psychoanalytic diagnosis.*[26]

Symptoms Bring Jouissance with Them

> *The kind of satisfaction that a symptom brings has much that is strange about it. . . . The subject experiences the alleged satisfaction as suffering and complains of it.*
>
> —Freud, SE XVI, pp. 365–366

> *I define the symptom as the way in which each person gets off on the unconscious.*
>
> —Lacan, Seminar XXI, class given on February 18, 1975

Freud postulates that symptoms provide us with a form of satisfaction, which we generally experience as suffering instead of satisfaction. Following Lacan, I have referred to this type of satisfaction as *jouissance.* Freud suggests, furthermore, that the jouissance symptoms bring is a substitute satisfaction: We may not have much, if any, other satisfaction in our lives, but we manage to obtain some from our symptoms (SE XVI, p. 299). It is well-known, for example, that certain people love to complain; we might say that complaining is their greatest enjoyment in life.

In this sense, we could say that the popular mind acknowledges that kvetching, nagging, arguing, and fighting bring certain people the little satisfaction they manage to find in life (indeed, it seems to keep numerous couples going more or less indefinitely); it is clear to many of those around them that they are deriving satisfaction from situations that they themselves characterize as blocked or impossible to change. Clinicians must always be on the lookout for what patients may be getting out of situations that they complain of and say they cannot modify in any imaginable way, for perhaps something in them ultimately does not want to imagine a way out of them.

Freud goes a step further when he hypothesizes that the kind of satisfaction symptoms bring us is quite specifically a substitute for *sexual satisfaction,* which many of us feel is lacking in our lives. The way in which people get worked up in certain situations is certainly suggestive of sexual excitation at times; consider, for example, what people often say happens to them in the course of what used to be known as "hysterical fits" and now more often go by the name of "panic attacks" or even "seizures": Their hearts begin to race, their breathing accelerates (even if it is often shallow), they feel they are about to burst or explode in some way, and so on. In Freud's era, close observers often noticed that hysterical fits looked, at times, astonishingly like sexual excitation ("the labored [or heavy] breathing and palpitations that occur in hysteria and anxiety neurosis are only detached fragments of the act of copulation"; SE VII, p. 80);[27] and in our own time one can occasionally even hear analysands admit that their attacks or seizures end in orgasm.

In most cases, however, people experience such fits, attacks, or seizures as frightening and painful, above all, the counterintuitive form of enjoyment they may be getting out of them being disguised to them, even as it may be somewhat or even blatantly apparent to certain onlookers. Freud complicates his account of the enjoyment symptoms bring when he says that "symptoms aim either at a sexual satisfaction or at fending it off, and that on the whole the positive, wish-fulfilling character prevails in hysteria and the negative, ascetic one in obsession" (SE XVI, p. 301). He also opines that "most hysterical symptoms, once they have developed fully, represent a fantasy of a sexual situation—such as a scene of sexual intercourse, pregnancy, childbirth, confinement, or some other such scene" (SE VII, p. 103 n).

It does not seem overly far-fetched to say that *at least some symptoms bring with them a satisfaction that serves as a substitute for sexual satisfaction,* which individuals often have precious little of in their everyday lives. But does that mean that *all* symptoms do? Freud even goes so far as to claim that when people have regular sexual satisfaction in their lives, they do not develop symptoms—which seems to me to be contradicted by much of my clinical experience, and which seems to contradict the idea that upon close examination, all of us have at least some symptoms (at least those of us who are neurotic), as we saw above. Freud also suggests that children cannot form symptoms prior to acquiring knowledge of sexuality, which again is going quite far in establishing an intimate, "biunivocal" or exclusive link between sex and symptoms, at least in hysteria: "Where there is no knowledge of sexual processes even in the unconscious, no hysterical symptom can arise" (SE VII, p. 49).[28]

Yet, insofar as Freud elsewhere considers libido to have two different components—sex and aggression (or, put more mythologically, Eros and Thanatos)[29]—we might well wonder what would stop symptoms from providing a substitute for aggression. And, indeed, it would seem that the kinds of nervous tics, twitchings, and jerky or spasmodic movements we discussed in Chapter 2, which develop in children who seem to have suppressed tremendous anger at one or more of their primary caretakers, "speak of" such anger, that anger being expressed in a distorted or displaced manner, which often involves it being turned against the children themselves. This happens in adults as well, of course, where we find much the same urge to strike out at someone and a simultaneous attempt to suppress that urge (for moral, practical, or other reasons), leading to the buildup of tension within themselves that can, as I put it in Chapter 2, "be quite self-destructive, leading to high blood pressure, muscular and skeletal problems, and . . . the grinding of teeth."

Symptoms other than tics can provide us with substitute satisfactions for our aggressive urges, too, by leading us to engage in acts in which our aggression toward others appears in a disguised form, whether that be excessive solicitude or concern, klutziness, accidents, ineptitude, forgetting appointments or dates, or a wide variety of other things. In such cases, we attempt to hide from ourselves and from others the fact that we are deliberately harming specific people by clothing the aggression in a veil of good intentions that ever so unexpectedly leads to calamitous unintended consequences. Such symptoms provide us an *indirect* satisfaction of certain of our aggressive impulses.

Clinicians can try to uncover potentially aggressive impulses in failures to act—such as forgetting to do something or show up somewhere when one has committed to—by asking patients whether something in them did not really want to go to that meeting, was dreading seeing someone at that lunch date, or preferred to be somewhere else at that time. And they can seek to unearth potentially aggressive impulses in "klutzy," accidental acts by asking patients if in fact something in them was not angry at that person and in a way happy to stain his or her jacket, ruin his or her vacation, or worry or even physically hurt him or her. (These are not the kind of questions we should generally ask early on in the treatment, but only once patients have come to trust us, as such questions may otherwise be taken as accusations instead of as well-intentioned queries.)

Symptoms Are Overdetermined

I'm now able to get so much more enjoyment out of things.
—An analysand (after a good deal of analysis)

Freud also points out that many symptoms are "overdetermined" (SE XVI, p. 269) in the sense that a number of different events or relationships have contributed to their formation—in other words, there are multiple reasons why they formed (their "why" or "whence" is multifaceted) and they have, perhaps over time, come to serve several different functions (their "whither" is many-sided).[30] Symptoms can, moreover, be reinforced by other reasons (whys) and purposes (whithers) over the course of time—"In the course of years, a symptom can change its meaning or its chief meaning, or the leading role can pass from one meaning to another"—which need not "be compatible with each other, that is, fit together into a coherent whole" (SE VII, p. 53; see also p. 83). This is one of the reasons why longstanding symptoms in a person's life often take a huge amount of analytic work to alleviate, so many different threads having connected up with the symptom over the course of time, all of which have to be traced out and fully articulated.

The Rat Man's "rat complex" had many different determinants (which we did not take the time to explore in Chapter 4); and, as discussed in Appendix III, the symptom that apparently brought him into analysis with Freud—all the crazy-seeming goings-on related to the money he owed for his new pair of glasses ("pince-nez")—was perhaps even more complex and overdetermined than the "rat complex" (I attempt in that appendix to clarify the confusing jumble of the multiple determinants of the "pince-nez" episode).

A young woman once entered analysis with me complaining of longstanding and ever-worsening claustrophobia, which arose in all kinds of enclosed spaces (including airline cabins), but above all in elevators. It took many years to unravel the myriad different threads that had become woven into the fabric of her symptom, threads that involved at least three different important figures in her life from three different familial generations: (a) an excessively anxious mother who warned her not to take elevators in which she could not reach the emergency call button in case the elevator got blocked between floors, and not to take them alone with men who were not family members; (b) a sister who refused to heed those same warnings by that same mother, and whom the patient decided to distinguish herself from by taking the stairs instead, even though the stairs could be quite dark and deserted (moreover, her father's apartment building had no elevator, only stairs); (c) an older relative with whom she often took elevators, who allowed her to playfully push certain buttons to delay their return to his apartment where they would find themselves anew in the presence of his wife, whom the patient felt to be a competitor in a number of ways.

One can well imagine that she associated elevators with enjoyable experiences with the older relative (even as these were fraught with certain Oedipal rivalries), which were then tainted by her mother's anxious concerns about her being alone with a man. Indeed, the mother's possibly realistic concern about her daughter being raped or molested was overshadowed by the excessive jouissance she expressed in her tone of voice and bodily postures when issuing such warnings to her daughter (and overshadowed by the fact that she claimed it was the superintendent of their building who did not want youngsters too short to reach the alarm bell taking the elevator, the daughter knowing full well that he had never said any such thing). To take the elevator was thus, the daughter felt, to almost literally kill her mother (with worry and anxiety), something she would unconsciously have liked to do at that point in time, but she instead turned that against herself and panicked in elevators as if she herself were disintegrating and falling apart. Add to that a complex relationship to a younger sister whom she was expected to look after, but who flouted their mother's admonitions by asserting her own will, and it becomes understandable that this analysand's early life history and most intimate relationships had to be explored at great length and in exhaustive detail in order for the incredibly intertwined threads, which had for so long constituted the fabric of the symptom, to be untangled.

Symptoms Signal the Return of the Repressed

I was always happy being unhappy.
—An analysand

We saw in earlier chapters that, although repression allows a child to solve a certain kind of conflict within herself or between herself and her caretakers, repression does not mean the complete and definitive disappearance from her life of such amorous or aggressive thoughts or wishes: Such thoughts or wishes virtually always return (we refer to this as the "return of the repressed") in a disguised form, interfering in her life in ways that often seem far worse than the initial conflict, and generating incomprehensible symptoms that may well last a lifetime. As we have seen, there is something fundamentally dysfunctional or excessive about repression, insofar as it often gives rise to problems that seem incommensurate with the conflict that occasioned them, problems that never go away. Repression can become crippling: "Although it served a useful purpose to begin with, repression ultimately leads to a damaging loss of inhibition [of one's impulses] and mental control" (SE V, p. 617).

As mentioned above, symptoms form "to escape an otherwise unavoidable generating of anxiety" (SE XVI, p. 404), anxiety that arises from the conflict within the child herself or between herself and her loved ones. That anxiety may be temporarily bound or alleviated by the formation of a symptom—for example, a fear of elevators may temporarily help a child forget about certain conflicts in her life insofar as it is not that difficult in most cases to simply avoid taking elevators. Nevertheless, what tends to happen is that the fear of elevators begins to broaden into a fear of all kinds of enclosed spaces, and so on. In other words, the anxiety that the child initially escaped from often returns little by little after symptom formation has occurred.

This can be seen quite clearly in the case of "little Hans," a child whose father was an admirer of Freud's work and who tried to treat his own son by following what he felt he had understood in Freud's writings in addition to some direct advice Freud provided. Freud, having seen the young boy but once in the course of this so-called treatment, wrote up an extensive case study of little Hans (SE X, pp. 5–149). In Freud's account, it seems quite clear that Hans, who had been highly conflicted over his incestuous feelings for his mother and his love for his not-at-all-authoritarian father, achieved a significant reduction in his anxiety when his phobia of horses first developed. His anxiety became, we might say, "bound" or isolated through the formation of this symptom—in other words, he was no longer anxious all the time but only when he was out of the house and encountered horses that wore blinders (reminiscent of his father's glasses) and had something black, perhaps part of a harness or muzzle, around the mouth (reminiscent of his father's mustache), thinking they might bite him (pp. 41–42). This was not necessarily the most convenient symptom to form at a time in history when cities were full of horses pulling carts, but as long as the boy stayed home (with his mother), he did not become anxious. Nevertheless, as

time went on, he began to think about such horses even when he was
at home, and became fearful of more and more things related to horses
(of them starting up suddenly from a stationary position, trotting fast,
rounding corners, and falling down, and of wagons, too; pp. 51 and 59
n. 2) and even to railways. Hence, although the horse phobia initially
accomplished a certain amount of work for him, leading to a binding of
anxiety and a seeming elimination of the lion's share of his discomfort in
most daily circumstances, he eventually became phobic about so many
things that his life was seriously hemmed in by his symptom. What had
been repressed by Hans ineluctably returned in the form of anxiety,
which seeped into ever more facets of his everyday life.

The Psychical Cause of Symptoms

*Parapraxes are the outcome of a compromise: they constitute a
half-success and a half-failure for each of the two intentions involved.*
—Freud, SE XV, p. 66

In *Studies on Hysteria*, Freud and Breuer talked about a new kind of
relationship between a symptom ("the pathological phenomenon") and
its precipitating cause, a relationship the likes of which had never been
seen in the "natural sciences": a symbolic relationship (SE II, p. 5). West-
erners generally believe, for example, that thinking goes on in the brain,
and people sometimes develop headaches (often referred to as *neuralgia* in medical parlance) when they are experiencing mental anguish—
struggling, say, over a difficult decision where a great many factors have
to be taken into account, or where two important strands have to be
weighed and neither one easily wins out over the other (we learn about
these different factors and strands by asking patients what they are
thinking or worrying about when their headaches come on). Many of us
have had the experience with friends or family of bringing up a subject
they are loath to discuss, and when they get to the point where they do
not want to think or talk about it anymore, they get a headache. Here
there is an association of ideas: Their circuits are overloading or they
feel a kind of conceptual torture occurring, and it manifests itself as a
headache. Since, in countries like South Korea, thinking is thought to go
on in the heart, native Korean speakers would be unlikely to have headaches in such circumstances, as they would not associate mental torture
with cranial neuralgia.

Similarly, when someone is brokenhearted, as we say metaphorically
in English, he or she may feel chest pains or heart palpitations. And when

someone cannot swallow, as the idiom goes in English and French, the kind of treatment a boss or spouse is dishing out, she or he may have the sense of tightening in the throat or a choking or gagging sensation. Such bodily symptoms (albeit short-lived, for the most part) can only develop as they do owing to specific *ideas*—which are obviously psychical—the sufferer has about where thought occurs in the body, where love springs from, and by what orifice one takes in ill-treatment. And such ideas often differ from one country to another and from one language group to another. (Those who are genuinely bilingual may, naturally, develop symptoms typical of those who speak both of their mother tongues, as well as hybrid symptoms.)

Freud gives us a striking example of "the psychical cause" of a symptom in *Studies on Hysteria* (SE II), in his discussion of his work with Frau Cäcilie:

> We came at last to the reappearance of her facial neuralgia. . . . I was curious to discover whether this, too, would turn out to have a psychical cause. When I began to call up the traumatic scene [during which her facial pain first appeared], the patient recalled a period of great mental irritation at her husband. She described a conversation she had had with him in which he had made a remark that she had found terribly insulting. Suddenly she put her hand on her cheek, gave a loud cry of pain, and said, "It was like a slap in the face." With this her pain and her attack evaporated. (p. 178)

Such a symptom—facial neuralgia—would obviously not have been a possible outcome of the heated conversation with her husband had Frau Cäcilie not spoken a language in which insults are sometimes characterized figuratively as a "slap in the face." Another symptom might have formed based on an idiom in a different mother tongue, but not pain in her cheek.

In a 21st-century case of mine, a man spent a couple of sessions talking about his somewhat recent "obsession with UNIX," the computer operating system. When I eventually commented that the sound of the word *UNIX* could be spelled differently, he laughed hysterically—obviously having suddenly realized it could be spelled like *eunuchs*—and at the next session told me that I had "killed" his obsession with learning computer languages. UNIX, the computer operating system, was consciously foremost in his mind as an object of compulsive study, but the motive for such study seemed to be its unconscious resonance or association with *emasculation* (I have discussed this case at length in Fink, 2014b, Chapter 11). Had he not been familiar with the word *eunuch* and the role of eunuchs in certain earlier cultures, no such obsession would probably have formed at that point in his life; I commented that the sound of the word UNIX could be spelled differently because I knew full well of his knowledge of such cultures.

We never find such symbolic, linguistic cause-and-effect relations in the natural or animal world; they are obviously related to the fact that we are speaking beings, and that our thoughts and wishes are made of the stuff of language, and that many of our feelings are similarly colored, if not outright created, by idiomatic expressions (like "feeling blue," "being heartbroken," or "feeling thrown for a loop"). As I mentioned above, the connection between mental anguish and headaches is a linguistic connection in certain languages, not a physiological connection. Other languages do not have the same expressions and may not facilitate the same connections or links. Each language thus has a propensity to generate symptoms in its own way. The French, for example, experience anxiety above all in their throats; they have a plethora of idiomatic expressions that indicate this (including *ça me prend à la gorge, j'ai la gorge nouée, ça m'est resté en travers de la gorge, j'ai une boule dans la gorge*, and *j'ai les boules*).[31] Americans, by contrast, experience anxiety above all in their midsections, tending to get knots in their stomachs, butterflies, acid reflux, heartburn, or diarrhea. In short, the same sort of mental distress or conflict suffered by two people whose mother tongues are different may get expressed in different bodily symptoms.

Psychology thus has its own unique form of cause-and-effect relations. Freud and Breuer initially underestimated the importance of their discovery in 1895 that there is such a thing as "psychical causality," linguistic/ideational causality, or symbolic causality. Rather than realizing that they had stumbled upon the symbolic cause of symptoms, they continued to view such linguistic connections as epiphenomenal, as mere psychical correlates of underlying biological processes. But one could argue that, as time went on, Freud came to see that psychical changes—such as acquiring new knowledge, or learning new ideas—can lead to biological changes, that speech and ideas affect the body, that form affects matter, and that symbols and idioms affect our jouissance.

Freud continued to occasionally pay lip service to the idea that science would someday discover the physiological substratum of all human ideation and affect—for example, psychoanalysis "will one day have to be set upon its organic foundation" (SE XVI, p. 389)—but it may well have been no more than that: lip service. It is possible that Freud occasionally viewed biology as a last-ditch explanation of seemingly inexplicable clinical facts (he often evokes "constitutional factors" to explain why some people's drives seem stronger or less controllable than others'), and/or that he sometimes pandered to medical colleagues by giving them the impression that he believed in many of the same things they did.

Freud nevertheless indicates in several places that he strove to formulate the basic concepts of psychoanalysis, not on the knowledge of biology or chemistry that was accepted as his time, but "independent of the findings of biology" (SE VII, p. 131). He attempted to describe the psyche as he encountered it in his analytic work, relying as little as possible on his prior knowledge of neurology and physiology.[32] From our vantage point a hundred years later, we can say that Freud was smart to do so, for despite an additional century of medical research, and "a vast investment in basic neuroscience research, we have," in the words of Richard A. Friedman (2015), professor of clinical psychiatry at Weill Cornell Medical College, "little to show for it on the treatment front." As he puts it,

> The doubling down on basic neuroscience research seems to reflect the premise that if we can unravel the function of the brain, we will have a definitive understanding of the mind and the causes of major psychiatric disorders. Indeed, an editorial in May [Ross, Travis, and Arbuckle, 2015] in one of the most respected journals in our field, *JAMA Psychiatry*, echoed this view: "The diseases that we treat are diseases of the brain," the authors wrote.
>
> Even if this premise were true—and many would consider it reductionist and simplistic—an undertaking as ambitious as unraveling the function of the brain would most likely take many years [or even centuries]. . . . Anyone who thinks otherwise should remember the Decade of the Brain, which ended 15 years ago without yielding a significant clue about the underlying causes of psychiatric illnesses. . . .
>
> More fundamentally, the fact that all feelings, thoughts and behavior require brain activity to happen does not mean that the only or best way to change—or understand—them is with medicine. We know, for instance, that not all psychiatric disorders can be adequately treated with biological therapy. [Many disorders] are generally poorly responsive to psychotropic drugs, but are very treatable with various forms of psychotherapy. (p. 9)

Friedman goes on to say that "psychotherapy has been shown in scores of well-controlled clinical trials to be as effective as psychotropic medication for very common psychiatric illnesses like major depression and anxiety disorders," and that, secondly, "a majority of Americans clearly prefer psychotherapy to taking medication." Friedman points furthermore to results indicating that, according to certain studies (especially one that appeared in the *American Journal of Psychiatry*; Markowitz et al., 2015), PTSD showed about a two-thirds response rate to psychotherapy, which is higher than that of any other currently known treatment. And, as Shedler (2010, p. 100) reports, the "effect size" (or effectiveness) of most well-known psychotropic medications (including Prozac, Zoloft, Celexa, Lexapro, and Cymbalta) is far lower than that of psychodynamic psychotherapies.

All of which suggests that the mind and body can, in a great many cases, be quite adequately treated by talking with someone. And if speech can cure what ails us, perhaps it is not overly far-fetched to hypothesize that *the cause of many mental and bodily symptoms is* not so-called "chemical imbalances in the brain" but, rather, *speech itself*—whether that be speech we hear from others or things we ourselves say (or even just think).

On Other So-Called Neuroses

> *It is true that psychiatry, as a part of medicine, sets about describing the mental disorders it observes and collecting them into clinical entities; but at favorable moments the psychiatrists themselves have doubts as to whether their purely descriptive hypotheses deserve the name of a science. Nothing is known of the origin, mechanism, or mutual relations of the symptoms of which these clinical entities are composed; there are either no observable changes in the brain that correspond to them, or changes that shed no light on them. These mental disorders are only accessible to therapeutic influence when they turn out to be subsidiary effects of an organic illness.*
>
> *This is the gap psychoanalysis seeks to fill. It tries to give psychiatry its missing psychological foundation. It hopes to discover the common ground on the basis of which the convergence of physical and mental disorders will become intelligible. With this aim in view, psychoanalysis must keep itself free from any hypothesis that is alien to it, whether of an anatomical, chemical, or physiological kind, and must operate with psychological ideas alone.*
>
> —Freud, SE XV, pp. 20–21

A few comments may be helpful here about Freud's somewhat archaic use of terms having to do with neurosis. The word *neurosis* itself comes from the Greek term for "nerve," and thus originally referred to *everything* that was thought to come under the heading of "nervous disorders"—that is, disorders of the central nervous system—regardless of their cause. Especially early on in his work, Freud was led to distinguish between two different types of nervous disorders:

- what he called "psychoneuroses" and sometimes "neuropsychoses" (SE III, pp. 45–61), nervous disorders whose cause was psychological,
- and what he called "actual neuroses," nervous disorders whose cause was *not* psychological.[33]

The adjective *actual* in *actual neuroses* is something of a misnomer, insofar as the German *aktual*, like the French *actuel*, does not mean "actual" in English, but rather "current" or "contemporary." The German adjective *aktual* thus suggests that such nervous disorders arise owing to something that is currently happening in someone's life, such as ongoing exhaustion owing to a physical illness, use of drugs (whether prescription or nonprescription), overwork, or tension-generating sexual practices like coitus interruptus. There may well be psychological reasons why the person is working so hard or engaging in such frustrating sexual practices, but it is the physical state that results from such practices (whether nervous exhaustion or jumpiness) that most directly gives rise to the nervous disorder in question.

Such a nervous disorder may resemble a psychoneurosis outwardly, but neither its cause nor its possible treatment lies within the psychical realm. Freud, for example, classifies "anxiety neurosis," which involves generalized or "free-floating anxiety" (perhaps corresponding to what is today called *generalized anxiety disorder*) as an "actual neurosis" (SE XVI, p. 398), and it may outwardly appear not that different from certain anxiety states that we find at times in hysteria or phobia. Yet, insofar as its cause (a particular behavioral practice like abstinence or coitus interruptus) is physical, it is not *"amenable to psychotherapy"* (SE III, p. 97; emphasis in the original). It involves *"a deflection of somatic sexual excitation from the psychical sphere, and a consequent abnormal employment of that excitation"* (p. 108; emphasis in the original).[34] Once the practice ceases—for example, once the person stops engaging in a sexual practice (or nonpractice) that does not allow for the discharge of sexual tension, leading instead to a buildup of tension in the person— the so-called anxiety neurosis ceases. Once a person stops working herself to the point of exhaustion, her actual neurosis ceases.

This is what led Freud to say that the actual neuroses are not accessible to psychoanalytic treatment per se (SE XVI, p. 389). They may be accessible to persuasion by those around the person who has become exhausted or exceedingly tense—in other words, she may take the advice of those around her or even of a doctor to slow down, take a vacation, or find a different method of birth control; and when she does her problem disappears. She might then benefit from an exploration of why she went to such extremes in the first place, but such exploration would be designed to prevent a recurrence of the problem, not to solve the problem in the first place.

Virtually no one today refers to such conditions as *neuroses*; insofar as they are discussed at all, they are likely to be referred to as *nervous states*, *nervous conditions*, and/or as resulting from a *nervous breakdown* or *burnout*, where it is understood that none of these terms are terribly precise. I am mentioning this because certain psychoanalysts (e.g., Verhaeghe, 2004, and Vanheule, 2014) have recently attempted to revive the term *actual neurosis* in the analytic literature, and thus I feel it is important that the reader not be confused as to its meaning.[35]

Freud introduced another potentially confusing term: the "narcissistic neuroses." What is confusing about it is that he included dementia praecox (the early term for what we now generally refer to as schizophrenia) and paranoia among these so-called neuroses, even though schizophrenia and paranoia are widely recognized psychoses.[36] He also sometimes placed melancholia under the heading of the narcissistic neuroses, despite the fact that melancholia is quite often a form of psychosis (SE XVI, Lecture 26).

As for what he refers to as the "transference neuroses," these include hysteria and obsession (SE XIV, p. 124); in other words, we might say that these correspond to neurosis proper.

For Freud, the term *neurosis* simply meant nervous disorder, and he accordingly classified virtually every kind of nervous disorder (excepting, it seems, perversions) under the neuroses. The following reconstruction of the meaning of Freud's early terms as compared to more contemporary psychoanalytic diagnostic labels may help certain readers as they grapple with Freud's work directly:

- the "transference neuroses": hysteria and obsession (perhaps phobia as well), which we today consider to be neurosis proper;[37]
- the "narcissistic neuroses": paranoia, schizophrenia, and melancholia, which today are grouped under the psychoses;
- the "actual neuroses": anxiety neurosis and neurasthenia (which in our times are given no specific designation, and may be referred to at times simply as nervous states or conditions) and certain trauma states, which are sometimes classified today under PTSD.[38]

CHAPTER 7

Beyond Freud?

Everything that has to do with the unconscious is easily forgotten.
—Lacan, Seminar VI, p. 79

I T WOULD BE IMPOSSIBLE to mention here everything thought and done in psychoanalysis today that purports to go beyond Freud. Many analytic practitioners and schools believe they have corrected and amended certain facets of Freud's approach, and we shall turn to some of those facets in a moment. But let us first consider the views and claims of those nonanalysts who have been most loudly proclaiming for several decades now that they have gone well beyond Freud.

Psychiatry Prematurely Rings the Death Knell of Psychoanalysis

Neither speculative philosophy, nor descriptive psychology, nor what is called experimental psychology . . . is in a position to tell you anything serviceable about the relation between body and mind or to give you the key to understanding possible disturbances of mental functioning.
—Freud, SE XV, p. 20

Psychiatry unofficially declared its overthrow of psychoanalysis in the late 1960s and early 1970s by ceasing, at many training programs, to hire experienced analysts as faculty members (letting older analysts retire without replacing them). And it officially declared war against every form of psychotherapy with its repeated claims that all psychological problems were biologically based and that medical science would very soon isolate the genes, neural networks in the brain, and "imbalances" in neurotransmitters responsible for every psychical and behavioral "abnormality" (a claim still being repeated by the authors of the *DSM-5* some 50 years later).

Without going into the current state of genetics and neuroscience and their at least current inability to locate the vast majority of psychological or behavioral phenomena in any particular place on the genome or in specific neural networks, let me just say a word about the so-called cures for mental troubles that medical science has thus far made available. A careful review of the effectiveness of the majority of psychotropic medications currently prescribed by doctors, when such a review is carried out *not* by those whose research is largely funded by drug companies (which obviously have a vested interest in having their products appear to the world to be effective, and let us not forget that the research conducted by the majority of the authors of the *DSM-5* is funded, at least in part, by "Big Pharma"—that is, the largest drug companies),[1] shows the following:

- Not many of these medications can claim greater effectiveness than placebos—in other words, they help through the power of suggestion, much like hypnosis did (Menand, 2010).
- The medications that can claim some effectiveness are often only helpful for a couple of weeks, after which the body and brain find a new equilibrium that nullifies the palliative effects of the drugs.
- The side effects of the medications are often worse than the disease, short-term side effects often including "decreased libido"—which, more plainly put, means loss of one's interest in life, sex drive, and will to live—decreased energy, and (thus not surprisingly) increased suicidality. Long-term side effects often include tardive dyskinesia and a progressive decline in general motor and brain functioning, leading to premature dementia (see, for example, Whitaker, 2002, 2010; Whitaker & Cosgrove, 2015).

Such results hardly seem to justify the sweeping claims made by physicians and pharmacologists. It should be noted, moreover, that when a particular medication does help patients, that medication often needs to be taken for the rest of their lives, suggesting that we are not talking about an actual cure—since a cure is generally understood to be something that eventually frees patients from the form of therapy employed.

The obvious goal of virtually every form of psychotherapy is to take patients far enough that they no longer need to come back to psychotherapy, or at least not for a great many years. As Freud (SE XVI) put it,

> Psychoanalytic treatment demands from both doctor and patient the accomplishment of serious work, which is employed in lifting

internal resistances. Through the overcoming of these resistances the patient's mental life is permanently changed, is raised to a high level of development, and remains protected against fresh possibilities of falling ill. (p. 451)

Whether or not any form of psychotherapy has a good track record for bringing patients this far is an open question, but it at least remains a goal (however distant). A treatment (like lifelong psychotropic drug usage) that has to constantly be engaged in or periodically resumed is obviously inferior in quality and far less than we might hope for. When Freud recommended that analysts go back into analysis themselves every "five years or so" (SE XXIII, p. 249), it was in recognition of the unusual demands made on them by their intense work with analysands, not something applicable to all analysands; and it must be understood in a context in which training analyses lasted about six months in all, rather than four to fifteen years, which is far more common today.

Despite the rather paltry and short-lived benefits of current drug treatments, psychiatry's victory over psychoanalysis has often been announced with great fanfare. The director of the powerful National Institute of Mental Health in Washington asserted, for example, in July 1990 that the medical establishment was likely to "conquer" virtually all mental illness by the year 2000 (as reported in *The San Diego Union*, July 12, 1990), an instance of hubris if ever there was one, making analysts' occasionally exaggerated claims regarding the effectiveness of psychoanalysis pale in comparison. The public was brazenly told that scientists and physicians would find effective chemical or other cures for every form of mental illness in very short order. The fact that such claims have never panned out does not stop physicians and scientists from averring that even if their earlier pronouncements were perhaps a bit premature, the next decades will infallibly bear them out. Hope (or is it, rather, delusion?) springs eternal. . . .

Psychoanalytic Schools: Beyond Freud?

Reading Freud in itself trains us.
—Lacan, 1977/1984, p. 11

We noted in Chapter 5 that Freud's own approach to psychoanalytic practice rarely if ever seems to have caught up with his own *theory of practice*. Although stipulating that the analyst must be no more than a mirror, showing the patient only what the patient has shown the analyst, Freud seems to have been unable at many points to stop himself from bringing himself into his work with patients as someone with his own personality, biases, preferences, and cultural references. And despite his recommendation that analysts not make interpretations until their patients are but one short step from arriving at the same interpretations themselves, it is clear from clinical material that Freud presents in 1915–1916 that he was still interpreting a great deal to his patients long before they were prepared to hear and assimilate what he had to say.[2]

As I am unaware of accounts of analyses with Freud written by ordinary patients of his (with one soon-to-be-published exception),[3] I will comment briefly here on what we can glean from some of the curious accounts of their brief analyses with Freud written by doctors, psychiatrists, and analysts-in-training, each for his own reasons, no doubt, and none of them including much about their own psychological makeup, as if they were more concerned with presenting and testifying to Freud's life and approach than to their own psychoanalytic adventure.

If Joseph Wortis, in his 1954 account of his supposed "didactic analysis" with Freud over the course of four months in 1934–1935, can be believed (he tells us he took extensive notes after each "session" with Freud), Freud at least sometimes (a) took the bait cast at him by intellectualizing patients and spent long hours debating with them about psychoanalytic theory, social, economic, and political questions, medicine, literature, opera, music, marriage, and the nature of American women (not to mention gossiping about people they knew in common),[4] resisting the analysis as much as his patients were by failing to get them to actually talk about themselves and by even talking about himself at times ("I have had three or four phobias myself," he purportedly told Wortis; 1954, p. 38); (b) lapsed into making direct judgments about their intellectual abilities and personal character (judgments that were at times flattering, at times hurtful, but in all cases damaging to their analyses, generating more resistance in his patients than had already been present; see, for example, pp. 58 and 75), and judgments about whether a certain dream they told was important (p. 33) and whether patients had done good work or not during a particular session (p. 67); and (c) seems to have been more concerned with the "truth," as he understood it, and the pithiness of his remarks to his analysands than with the likely effect the revelation of "truth" and such pointed remarks would have on them (see, for example, p. 24). Freud fortunately made it clear to Wortis that he considered Wortis unprepared to work as an analyst himself after such a short training period (suggesting that two to three years of analysis, plus classes, and seeing patients under supervision were necessary; p. 128), but if that was the kind of brief training many of the first American analysts received, it is no wonder they were woefully unprepared to work with analysands.[5]

Smiley Blanton's (1971) book about his analysis with Freud suggests much the same thing, although he claims to have gotten a great deal out of his work with Freud ("It was the most helpful thing—as far as personal understanding—that ever happened to me"; p. 62) and found Freud rather easygoing and "undominating" (p. 31), allowing Blanton to do most of the talking at times, but talking up a storm himself at others (pp. 34 and 43). Freud's technique with analysts-in-training may well have differed considerably from the technique he employed with other patients, and he perhaps even broke certain of his own rules in order to show such trainees the kinds of problems rule breaking leads to (although perhaps he simply couldn't help himself and tried after the fact to turn his mistakes into lessons for his analysands).[6] For example, he at one point made a gift of some of his books to Blanton, which then led to a difficulty in the transference (p. 42).[7] And he interpreted the fact that Blanton had repeatedly looked at his watch in the previous session as a sign of boredom or as a concern that Freud was not giving him a full hour until Blanton explained that his watch had stopped during the session; at that point Freud commented, "You see how difficult it is for me to understand the meaning of things unless I have the associations. They may have so many meanings" (p. 69). To his credit, he purportedly told Blanton that technique cannot be learned from books and that analysts "must learn to develop their own technique" (p. 48); he opined further that Blanton seemed overly anxious about his patients and needed to learn to "let them drift. Let them work out their own salvation" (p. 76).

All in all, it seems to me that, when it comes to clinical work with neurotics (and analysts-in-training), Freud can hardly serve us as a model therapist, he perhaps having rarely practiced what he preached.[8] This should not be taken to imply that later psychoanalysts have always striven to put more rigorously into practice the techniques that Freud recommended or have necessarily improved upon his suggested techniques. Indeed, we may well wonder whether later generations of psychoanalysts, in the guise of enhancing or "updating" psychoanalysis, did not in fact often throw the baby out with the bathwater.

Ego psychologists, for example, began in the 1940s and 1950s to focus more directly on the defenses ("the analysis of defense") as something that needed to be done *before* the unconscious could be broached; but their actual clinical practice often suggests that they became so obsessed with the defenses that they essentially forgot about the unconscious (see Jacoby, 1975).

Kleinians, relationalists, and intersubjectivists began (to oversimplistically lump them together, and to the best of my admittedly limited knowledge of their work) to focus intensely on the "here and now" of the analytic relationship, attempting to draw everything patients talked about into the transferential relationship with the analyst. It might be argued that they were simply taking seriously Freud's model whereby the redirecting of problems with others in the patient's life and from the patient's past onto the analyst transforms the patient's pre-existing neurosis into a "transference neurosis" (SE XII, p. 154; SE XVI, p. 445); the latter supposedly allows analysts to "get hold of all the libido that has been withdrawn from the ego's dominance by attracting a portion of it onto ourselves by means of the transference" (SE XVI, p. 455; see also pp. 444 and 454) and to resolve the struggle between the libido and the ego (Forces 1 and 2) on the "battlefield" of the transference (p. 456; note the military metaphor).[9]

Yet it would seem that they simultaneously jettisoned (a) Freud's recommendation that analysts act as much as possible like a mirror, instead of directly or indirectly disclosing a great deal about themselves,[10] and (b) his notion that in the course of an analysis, the holes or gaps in the patient's memory of the past should be progressively filled in (SE XVI, p. 435). For many in these newer schools of psychoanalysis, the past is passé, so to speak; it is now considered to be largely irrelevant. They seem, in fact, to believe that everything that could possibly be of importance from the past will get played out in the here and now of the transferential relationship, and that they have found more effective ways of working with the transference than Freud did (we saw that Freud sometimes had trouble even simply recognizing the transference, much less working with it). The latter often involves the belief that both they and their analysands can momentarily step outside of the transference in order to examine it together, as if they could temporarily become "objective outside observers" of what had been going on in the transference (for a critique of this belief, see Lacan, *Écrits*, p. 591, Seminar XV, class given on November 29, 1967, Seminar V, p. 428; and Fink, 2007, pp. 140–145).

One of contemporary analysts' most prized innovations related to transference is something they refer to as *projective identification*, whereby—to oversimplify to some degree, as there are at least several different formulations of it extant in the literature[11]—virtually anything analysts think, feel, or experience in the course of a consultation is considered to have been "put into" them by their patients. No comprehensible or satisfactory explanation for how this could possibly happen (i.e., the transmission mechanism) has ever been provided, to the best of my knowledge, and analysts' belief in it seems to verge on a belief in extrasensory perception (or some sort of "grokking," à la Robert Heinlein in *Stranger in a Strange Land*). It would, in my view, be interesting and useful to see if an empirical study could be designed and carried out in which analysts who believe in projective identification conduct sessions with volunteers, in which they would *refrain* from conveying to the volunteers what they believe the volunteers have projected into them at various points during the session. The analysts and volunteers would then be interviewed *separately* about what they recall they were feeling and thinking at various points during the consultation (perhaps replaying the session with the help of audio or video recordings), and then the separate accounts would be compared.

Although the practical details of such a study would be difficult to get right, I suspect that we would find little correspondence between what analysts said was being projected into them and what volunteers said they were feeling and thinking. There might turn out to be a higher correspondence between analysts' and patients' accounts when they have been working together for some time, but this might be better explained by analysts' *familiarity* with such patients owing to a great many actual cues given by them—including speech, nonverbal sounds, rhythm of speech, posture, body language, and so on—than by "projective identification."

The focus in these newer schools of psychoanalysis on the here and now of the transference relationship might be understood to privilege acting out over remembering; analysts have even gone so far as to coin the term *acting in* to indicate that this goes on "in" session as well as outside of the consulting room. Freud had already indicated that what cannot be remembered by patients gets played out—that is, gets repeated—in the transference (as well as in their everyday lives), but he cautioned that although occasional instances of acting out are inevitable in the course of an analysis (as, for example, when patients forget about sessions, show up at the wrong time or on the wrong day, call their analysts when they meant to call their mothers, or forget to pay for their therapy), more serious forms of acting out can be quite damaging, as such repetitions are generally harder for both patients and analysts to deal with. In other words, to Freud's way of thinking, *it is far preferable to foster remembering than repeating.* Lacan echoed Freud's viewpoint when he opined that acting out on the patient's part implies that the analyst needs to adopt a different stance or position in the treatment (e.g., stop playing the part of a parent or a suitor, as Freud arguably did in his work with Dora).

Many in the contemporary psychoanalytic world seem to have inverted this recommendation, practicing as though it were more desirable for patients to repeat than to remember. Should this be considered a way of going beyond Freud or simply of forgetting Freud? That is for the reader to decide. . . .

Psychoanalytic Approaches to Working with Psychosis

Numerous schools of psychoanalysis have undoubtedly improved upon the psychoanalytic treatment of psychoses, Freud having believed "that paranoia and dementia praecox [his term for what is now more commonly termed schizophrenia] in strongly marked forms are inaccessible" to analytic therapy (SE XVI, p. 458; see also pp. 438-39) owing to the absence in them of what he recognized as transference.[12] Freud had a tendency, in his practice, to view anyone who was intelligent and mostly successful in life when judged according to rather conventional standards (the term used today is *high functioning*) as neurotic and therefore capable of doing depthful interpretive work in analysis. This tendency is still found in all too many clinicians today, even though there is no known correlation between one's so-called intelligence and one's diagnostic category or clinical structure. Freud often failed to realize that many intelligent, successful people are in fact not neurotically structured but rather psychotically structured,[13] and that the attempt to get at the unconscious in one's work with them has a profoundly destabilizing effect on them. As we saw in Chapter 6, he often used the term *narcissistic neuroses* in referring to paranoia, schizophrenia, and melancholia, which is misleading in that it may give the impression that they are simply more-difficult-to-treat subsets of neurosis (the easier ones being obsession, hysteria, and phobia), rather than something fundamentally different; and he claimed that certain processes operating in schizophrenia were "almost identical to those of repression" (SE XVI, p. 421), which seems quite implausible.

Elsewhere, however, Freud hypothesized that in schizophrenia the unconscious is decathected (SE XIV, p. 235) and that, "as regards schizophrenia, . . . a doubt must occur to us whether the process here termed 'repression' has anything at all in common with the repression that takes place in the transference neuroses" (p. 203). In his early work, Lacan, taking this a step further, says, "My starting point is as follows: the unconscious is present in psychosis, *but it does not function*" (Seminar III, p. 143; emphasis added). Some 20 years later, he speaks of a "rejection of the unconscious" in psychosis (Lacan, 1974/1990, p. 22),[14] using this expression as something of a synonym for the act or process of what he calls foreclosure. He also refers to James Joyce as, in a manner of speaking, "having cancelled his subscription to the unconscious" or as being "unsubscribed to the unconscious" (*désabonné à l'inconscient*; Seminar XXIII, p. 164). I myself put this more categorically than either Freud or Lacan did: Strictly speaking, there is no unconscious in psychosis and this fundamentally alters how we must practice in our work with psychotics (see Fink, 2007, Chapter 10).

A well-known example of Freud's failure to recognize psychosis in a patient is that of the Wolf Man (SE XVII, pp. 7–122); after four years of analysis with Freud, the Wolf Man went on to work with Ruth Mack Brunswick, one of Freud's closest associates at the time, and Muriel Gardiner, and they attest to what is clearly a psychotic structure (see Gardiner, 1971, pp. 263–307 and 311–366). A less well-known example is that of Horace Frink, an American physician who had been referred to Freud by Abraham Brill (the first American psychoanalyst) after Brill had worked with Frink for some time in "once-a-week 'psychoanalysis'" (Warner, 1994, p. 140). Freud seems to have assumed that since Brill thought Frink was a good candidate for training analysis with Freud (at that point in time, 1921–1922, Freud considered six months to be adequate), and since he seemed intelligent and coherent at the outset, he must be a typical obsessive neurotic. Yet Frink had already suffered severe depressions in 1908 and 1918, and had had to take time off from his professional activities in New York to undergo "rehabilitation" on a ranch in New Mexico for what he called his "toxic headaches" (the expression itself should have raised a red flag). Frink may not have mentioned these experiences to Freud, hoping to make a good impression and get in his good graces—which worked, since Freud went on to recommend that Frink become "the new leader of the New York Psychoanalytic Society"—and Freud failed to see the signs of Frink's fragility and longstanding psychosis. Their work together led to "decompensation" on Frink's part, and to a life that was at least as difficult after working with Freud as it had been before (see Warner, 1994).[15]

Analysts today have improved upon Freud's work with psychotics in two rather different ways: Non-Lacanians have often adopted an approach to psychoanalytic technique that they use with both neurotics and psychotics. Indeed, they often do not distinguish terribly much between the two, their favorite diagnoses being borderline personality disorder and narcissistic personality disorder, which tend to blur the distinction between neurosis and psychosis, as does their belief that one can be psychotic at certain moments and then go back to being neurotic, which is anything but a structural viewpoint. This new approach, in focusing on the here and now and often verging on supportive psychotherapy, in many cases ends up leaving the unconscious to one side. This is less than auspicious in work with neurotics, but is precisely what is called for in work with psychotics.

Lacanians, on the other hand, have become very adept at detecting psychosis even when there are no obvious signs of it (such as hallucinations, delusions, "concrete thinking," and so on). They have even in more recent years formulated the notion of "ordinary psychosis" (IRMA, 2005a), wherein no flamboyant or blatant signs may ever appear and yet it is nevertheless clear that the patient does not have an unconscious that operates in the usual neurotic way (IRMA, 2005b, 2005c). Lacanians have formulated a whole different approach to technique for psychotics than for neurotics, continuing to probe the unconscious with neurotics, but working in a very different way with psychotics.

It would thus be fair to say that both Lacanian and non-Lacanian psychoanalysts today generally have more success working with psychotics than Freud did, even when they do not recognize them to be psychotic.

Beyond Freud's Biases in the Realm of Sexuality

Analysts of many ilks would claim to have gone beyond Freud's bias regarding the "natural" attraction between the sexes (realizing the full extent to which attraction is very much a product of family environment, education, and culture), and his view of activity and passivity as the basis of masculinity and femininity, respectively, despite his repeated claims that such notions are inadequate. We would be wrong to think that these are merely theoretical considerations that have little impact on how analysts actually practice. Theoretical biases often have a subtle but insidious effect on what practitioners actually do in the consulting room.

Lacanians would, in the same vein, say that they have gone beyond Freud's conventional notion (welcomed with open arms in Hollywood) that love, desire, and sexual satisfaction should always eventually converge on the same object, and that every relationship should lead to some kind of harmonious "genital-to-genital" connection (see, for example, Lacan, Seminar XX, and *Écrits*). In other words, Lacanians reject Freud's belief in the unification of the partial drives (e.g., oral and anal), in the course of "normal" human development, under the "tyranny" of the genital drive (SE XVI, p. 323).

Beyond Understanding

I no longer have to be Superman; I just have to do my best.
— An analysand

Lacanians would say, furthermore, that they have recognized something that Freud himself recognized, but was never able to truly move beyond: the sterility of the concern with "conscious understanding" of one's problems. Freud long believed that curative effects were guaranteed by the passage of thoughts from the unconscious to the conscious, but in many texts he admitted that patients' conscious recognition of past and present wishes, desires, and urges did not necessarily make them disappear, much less the symptoms linked to them. Freud came to realize that a powerful economic factor was at play, and that it often took more than "understanding" a connection between past and present, for example, for the libido (or jouissance) attached to a symptom to become unfixated and freed up for other life purposes. Lacanians would contend that they have attempted to move beyond understanding and have shifted their approach to interpretation such that it bypasses comprehension and aims to have an effect that is not at the level of the ego or consciousness, but that more directly targets the unconscious and jouissance. They refer to this as *analytic action* (*l'acte analytique*), and the kind of action they have in mind includes punctuation, oracular interpretation, and scansion (for a discussion of these, see Fink, 2007, Chapters 3–5).

"Self-Analysis"

True self-analysis is impossible; otherwise there would be no [neurotic] illness.
— S. Freud, 1985, p. 281

Although Freud occasionally recommended that the physicians who came to see him from afar, for a "training analysis" lasting just a few months, continue the work they had done together by engaging in self-analysis, he often recognized the severe limitations of self-analysis. And anyone (including myself) who has tried analyzing him- or herself, and has then undergone analysis with a living, breathing analyst, can tell you that self-analysis does not go terribly far. As Freud put it, "In self-analysis the danger of incompleteness is particularly great. One is too soon satisfied with a partial explanation, behind which resistance may easily be keeping back something that is more important" (SE XXII, p. 234). Freud himself did not have the luxury of doing an analysis with someone else at the outset, and thus had no other option; but for most people today, analysts to work with can be found, whether close by, or via phone or video-chat.

To insist in our times that one can analyze oneself boils down to avoidance: avoidance of the encounter with the unconscious that can only occur by working with someone else. Avoidance being one of the defining features of neurosis, one must muster courage to overcome it. As Freud indicates, "moral courage" is important in facing the wishes and impulses that inhabit us, and "moral cowardice" plays a part in symptom formation (SE II, p. 123); Lacan (1974/1990) echoes this in *Television*, indicating that it requires moral courage to be willing to find one's way about in the unconscious (p. 22).

The Analytic Couch

> *A particularly large number of patients object to being asked to lie down, while the doctor sits out of sight behind them. They ask to be allowed to go through the treatment in some other position, for the most part because they do not want to be deprived of a view of the doctor. Permission is regularly refused.*
>
> —Freud, SE XII, p. 139

Having patients lie on the couch was a remnant of the hypnotic method of treatment Freud had experimented with in the 1880s and 1890s, but he continued to use the couch in psychoanalysis for his own personal reasons: "I cannot put up with being stared at by other people for eight hours a day (or more)" (SE XII, p. 134). He would even put brand-new analysands on the couch right at the very first session (see, for example, Wortis, 1954, p. 20; and Blanton, 1971, p. 50). Still, he never declared that everyone else should do as he did. Yet, like Freud, many analysts today direct even patients who are totally new to analysis to the couch immediately, despite the fact that few patients find it tolerable to begin to work with someone in such an unfamiliar way, feeling they need visual cues from their interlocutor before being able to go on with what they are saying, and before they are willing to reveal things that are difficult for them to discuss.

Patients who are immediately put on the couch often end up sitting up instead of lying down, twisting around to look at the analyst, or requesting to move to the chair now and then; and this can lead to a confusing situation for both parties, wherein neither knows where the analysand is going to be on any specific day.

Certain contemporary analysts seem to think that the main differences between psychoanalysis and psychotherapy are the frequency of sessions (some claiming that four or more times a week is analysis, fewer is therapy) and the position in which the patient sits (on the couch is analysis, in the armchair is therapy). This implies *a confusion between certain external trappings of the situation and psychoanalysis proper.* It would seem more sensible to define psychoanalysis (at least with neurotics) as involving a kind of work in which one focuses on the unconscious, regardless of how many times per week analyst and analysand meet (it is admittedly harder, although not impossible, to work with the unconscious at a frequency of only one session per week), and regardless of whether the analysand is sitting up or lying down.

Lacanians have, for the most part, stopped using the couch altogether with psychotics (because the inability to see the analyst may bring out paranoid thoughts about what he or she is up to "back there" and may make the analyst into a threateningly abstract other to the patient), and have adopted the policy that all new analysands begin their psychoanalytic work sitting in an armchair facing the analyst. They may stay in the armchair indefinitely, if the analyst remains unconvinced they are neurotic. But it is not enough that the analyst be convinced they *are* neurotic to automatically move them to the couch. Lacanians generally wait until they feel that their analysands have formulated a question for themselves that will drive the analysis, that they have come up with an autonomous desire to explore their dreams, daydreams, and fantasies, rather than asking the analyst what he or she wants them to talk about at each session. It is only once analysands begin to consistently pick up the thread from prior sessions and take up the exploration of their own psyches without constant help and/or approval from the analyst (whether in the form of verbal or visual encouragement) that they are directed to the couch. Lacanians often talk about these face-to-face sessions using Freud's term "preliminary meetings" (or "preliminary interviews," as they are sometimes called; SE XII, pp. 124–125), and they may last up to a year or more, even at a frequency of five sessions a week.

Such a policy has, in my experience, the advantage of obviating the kinds of shifting back and forth between the armchair and the couch that I have seen occur time and again when analysts too quickly direct their patients to the couch. And it leads to a sense on analysands' part of having taken a decisive step in their analyses (some even refer to it as "graduating to the couch"), a step they rarely wish to take back in the opposite direction. This policy can, moreover, temper the kind of trou-

blesome erotic transference that sometimes arises when patients are very
quickly directed to the couch, leading some to immediately construe the
analytic situation as a sort of seduction scene rather than a professional
encounter between two people.

Scheduling and Cancellation Policies

Whatever interrupts the progress of analytic work is a resistance.
—Freud, SE V, p. 517

*Each patient is allotted a particular hour of my available working
day; it belongs to him and he is liable for it, even if he does not make
use of it. . . . People will be likely to object that many accidents may
prevent the patient from attending every day at the same hour and
they will expect me to make some allowance for the numerous intervening ailments that may occur in the course of a longish analysis.
But my answer is: no other way is practicable. With a less stringent
policy, the "occasional" missed sessions increase so greatly that the
doctor finds his material existence threatened; whereas when the
arrangement is adhered to, it turns out that accidental hindrances
do not occur at all and disruptive illnesses only very seldom. . . .
Nothing brings home to one so strongly the significance of the psycho-
genic factor in the daily life of men, the frequency of malingering,
and the non-existence of chance as a few years' practice of psychoanalysis on the strict principle of leasing by the hour.*
—Freud, SE XII, p. 127

Although Freud charged his patients for sessions they missed when they
were ill, and noted that by doing so his patients missed very few sessions owing to illness, he never claimed that everyone should do so.
Nor did he ever say that analysts should charge patients when they
take vacations that do not overlap with the analyst's vacations. Curiously
enough, however, many psychoanalysts seem to have adopted a rather
odd cancellation policy that seems to hark back to the 1960s when the
majority of New York City analysts, at least, took off the whole month
of August and perhaps a week or two at Christmas time, but expected
their patients to pay for any missed sessions owing to vacation time they
took at any other period of the year. This practice seems to have been
designed at that time to compensate medically trained psychoanalysts
(and the American Psychoanalytic Association, unlike the International
Psychoanalytic Association, refused for many years to allow anyone but
physicians to train and practice as analysts) for the lower incomes they
earned than their colleagues who had decided to stay in medicine; it

gave them a more or less guaranteed fixed income that did not vary based on patients' potentially erratic vacation schedules. It was clearly designed to serve the analysts' interests and not their analysands'.

Almost no one takes a full month off at a time in the United States today, and people's vacations are often few and far between, amounting to at most two or three full weeks per year. Americans generally take vacations when their jobs permit, and those with children often try to coordinate their vacations with school vacations that vary from one part of the country to another, and sometimes even from one school district to another within the same city. Most psychoanalysts I know are happy to take time off when it pleases them to do so, as well as when they attend conferences, are ill themselves, or have family emergencies or other obligations. I find it hard to understand what could lead them, then, to penalize their analysands for doing the same, apart from simple greed. It seems to me rather heavy-handed (a rather obvious power play) to tell analysands they have to either coordinate their vacations with their analyst's or pay the difference.

It occasionally happens, of course, that a particular analysand takes so many vacations that the analytic work is being regularly interrupted and the analyst is forced to keep an opening in his or her schedule for some-one who is missing a significant percentage of sessions; this becomes especially problematic when, owing to either the analysand's schedule and commitments or the analyst's, they are unable to make up the missed sessions before and/or after the vacations. In most other cases, however, a modicum of flexibility on the analyst's part would generally seem to make the most sense. And given that more and more people today are led to take occasional and sometimes even frequent business trips for work, a lack of flexibility on analysts' parts is likely to make it impossi-ble for a great many potential patients to undergo analysis at all. In my experience, patients are often able to have sessions by phone when they are away on business; and although there is considerable debate in the analytic community about the effectiveness of phone sessions, virtually every analyst I have ever met has come to the conclusion that they are helpful and often necessary to keep the analytic work moving forward (see, on this point, Fink, 2007, Chapter 8).

Regarding sessions that analysands miss owing to illness, there are obviously times when it is preferable for analysands to stay home rather than spread their potentially infectious conditions to all and sundry, including the analyst, and times when they are so ill as to be unable to leave the house or even talk coherently on the phone. This is not always easy for analysts to gauge, but I would recommend that they not take an especially hard line in forcing patients to pay for sessions missed owing to alleged illness unless a pattern of missed sessions sets in; the analysand seems perfectly fine the very next day (or perhaps unwittingly reports having gone out to do other things on the day of the session missed owing to purported illness); the analysand always seems to cancel right after something important comes up in the therapy; the analysand reports a history of faking illness at school and/or work; or something else occurs that raises a red flag. It is one thing to convey to analysands our desire for them to make their sessions and engage as fully as possible in the analytic work; it is another thing to penalize them for missing sessions, when we ourselves might well have cancelled a day's work had we been feeling as ill as they were. Even though anything that "interrupts the progress of analytic work" can theoretically be considered to be a resistance (SE V, p. 517), *not everything need automatically be treated as resistance.*

Although most analysts try to see their analysands regularly—whether two, three, four, or five times a week—more or less at the same time on the same days every week, some analysands' work and life schedules may make this difficult if not impossible. Analysts thus either have to adapt or turn away large numbers of students, artists, musicians, physicians, and businesspeople. Most practitioners ask patients to pay for their sessions daily, weekly, or monthly, but I have heard in recent years about some odd-sounding "innovations" on the part of analysts, whereby they ask their patients to pay the same fee monthly regardless of how many sessions were missed by either the patient or the practitioner during any one month; and I have even heard about an analyst who told a wealthy patient of hers that he could come in seven days a week within a three-hour window (e.g., 8 to 11 a.m.) and *stay as long as he liked*, she charging him an incredibly high flat monthly rate regardless of the number of sessions or length of the sessions he had. Such arrangements seem to suggest the analyst is more concerned with the steadiness of his or her income stream than with the analysand actually coming to sessions and working. Session length has become a hotly debated topic since Lacan introduced what has become known as the *variable-length session* in the 1950s, but as the above example shows, there are many analysts who vary session length (sometimes by just a few minutes, sometimes by hours; the famous American analyst Ralph Greenson, for example, sometimes held four-hour sessions with Marilyn Monroe; see Spoto, 1993). Freud himself indicated that "one occasionally encounters patients to whom one must give more than the average time of one hour a day, because the better part of an hour is gone before they begin to open up and become communicative at all" (SE XII, pp. 127–128).[16]

A widespread practice among clinicians is to charge patients for sessions that are cancelled (usually for nonmedical emergencies) less than 24 hours in advance. But some analysts—perhaps those with especially fixed schedules—have a 48-hour cancellation policy, and others still longer. Their analysands often bridle at this, especially in the early years of their work together, feeling their analysts are lording this over them as few other service providers do (even if a few MDs now charge patients a partial fee for not giving 24-hours' notice for an appointment cancellation; medical offices often try to forestall such conflicts with patients by giving them appointment reminder calls a day or two in advance). Such strict policies can work just fine as long as the analysts who enforce them do not take time off without giving their analysands at least as much notice, which, in the case of illness, car trouble, and family emergencies, is often impossible. Analysts should thus be careful not to hold their patients to a higher standard than the one to which they themselves can be held.

If it is to remain a vital form of practice, psychoanalysis must thus adapt to the changing world of analysands. This does not mean analysts should allow their analysands to take and make calls in their offices or constantly consult their electronic devices during sessions, but that they should make allowances for analysands' changing work and social lives. Freud never said everyone should practice as he did and certainly could not have predicted what the world would look like a hundred years after his death!

APPENDIX I

Addressing Some of Freud's Critics

"Freud Bashing"

I have not entered in this book into recent debates (Borch-Jacobsen, 1996; Borch-Jacobsen & Shamdasani, 2012; Onfray, 2010) about whether Freud actually cured his patients or not, debates that seem undecidable given that most of the treatments occurred a century or more ago. It is not clear to me why Freud should be considered less trustworthy in his reports on his successes and failures than contemporary therapists of various ilks, virtually all of whom have a vested interest in emphasizing their successes and downplaying their failures. It seems to me that we have ample evidence from both practitioners and patients since Freud's time that clinicians practicing in an analytic manner have greatly assisted numerous people (see, for example, Baldwin, 2015; Bettelheim, 1950, 1961, 1967; Cardinal, 1975/1983; Fink, 1997, 2007, 2014a, 2014b; Gherovici, 2003; Gunn, 2002; Miller, 2011; Rogers, 2006; Swales, 2012). We have reports, too, naturally, of people who have not been helped or have even been harmed by unskilled or unscrupulous therapists, just as we have reports of patients who have been irreparably harmed in the course of routine medical operations by ignorant and/or inept physicians.

As in any profession, whether medicine, psychoanalysis, or plumbing, there are able and responsible practitioners and there are bumbling, irresponsible ones. The existence of incompetent plumbers does not imply, it seems to me, that the entire field of indoor plumbing need be considered fraudulent or a hoax! Even if Freud himself was not the most capable clinician, psychoanalysis as a whole need not be impugned or damned. In any case, the onus is upon those who maintain that Freud was ineffectual to explain how he managed to acquire a reputation in Vienna for doing good work, for surely it was neither his flashy four-color ad in the yellow pages nor his professionally designed website (neither of which yet existed, obviously)—nor even his "bestselling" books (*The Interpretation of Dreams* sold some 351 copies in the first six years it was on the market, and *Studies on Hysteria* sold about 48 copies a year from 1895 to 1908)[1]—that reeled in the patients who eventually filled his waiting room. Accounts of the positive effect of his work with patients have been provided by certain analysts he trained (such as Blanton, 1971)—indeed, we might wonder why anyone in his right mind would become an analyst if he had not been at least in some way helped by his training analysis—and by people he worked with from all walks of life (see, for example, Lohser & Newton, 1996).[2]

Most analysts I know are quite modest as regards their success with analysands, especially given the number of analysands who leave analysis prematurely, claiming financial difficulties, allowing spouses and/or other family members to disrupt the treatment, or simply being frustrated with the slow progress virtually endemic to all forms of the talking cure.[3] But many practitioners can point to successes they have had with analysands who had been unable to find help in any other quarter, having tried multiple medications, other forms of talk therapy, acupuncture, hypnosis, meditation, palmistry, chakras, and/or crystals before seeking out a psychoanalyst. Indeed, the literature is full of such examples. The fact that treatment is not always able to fulfill all of an analysand's (or therapist's) expectations hardly means that it is utterly and completely useless. If a physician is able to clear up only three quarters of a patient's acne or skin rash, is that a valid reason to reject all such treatment? A teenager suffering from acute acne is likely, I suspect, to prefer the 75% solution to none at all.[4] Numerous studies have, in any case, shown that long-term psychodynamic psychotherapy is as effective, if not more effective, than other so-called evidence-based or empirically validated therapies (see, for example, Shedler, 2010; Leichsenring & Rabung, 2008, 2011; and Angus, Watson, Elliott, Schneider, & Timulak, 2015, for studies of related treatment approaches), as well as having more enduring positive effects (see, for example, Bateman & Fonagy, 2008).[5] And a survey of 4,000 participants conducted by *Consumer Reports* (1995) found that most respondents said they were helped by psychotherapists they consulted, above all those respondents who stuck with the treatment for a prolonged period: "People who stayed in treatment for more than two years reported the best outcomes of all" (p. 739), and "the longer people stayed in therapy, the more they improved" (p. 734).

Let me very briefly address a number of other criticisms often made of psychoanalysis. Should analytic forms of treatment be condemned because they take a long time? So does maintaining a healthy lifestyle, involving a balanced diet and physical activity. Because they are expensive? The slightest surgical operation necessitated by excessive stress, obesity, undue concern with one's looks, alcoholism, or other addictions easily costs as much as several if not many years of intensive psychotherapy! Psychoanalysis should hardly be condemned for being "hopelessly bourgeois" when we live in a world in which individuals and insurance companies are willing to pay astronomical sums for surgical procedures that could have been avoided by laying out half as much to talk with someone several times a week for a few years; and rehab centers regularly charge alcoholics and drug addicts prices for a few weeks of treatment (that often does not work) that would pay for years of intensive psychoanalysis. One often hears people say that they cannot "afford to" go into psychoanalysis; one might counter that, in terms of their suffering and life trajectory, they cannot "afford not to."

There are undoubtedly analysts whose fees are beyond the realm of possibility for all but the top one percent of earners, but there are plenty of others who are more accommodating; and let us bear in mind Freud's claim that "nothing in life is as expensive as illness" (SE XII, p. 133), neurotic illness in particular. In my experience, people are often quite willing to spend tens of thousands of dollars more on cars than is necessary for reliable transportation (or on kitchens, bathrooms, and many other items that are not truly indispensable), rather than devote the additional money to their mental health or that of their supposed loved ones.

Regarding Scathing Critiques of Freud's Work with Dora

I will address here a number of the critiques that have been made of Freud's work with Ida Bauer (aka Dora), since readers who have heard such critiques may think them so damning as to be disinclined to study the case at all, which would, I think, be unfortunate. To grasp the import of these critiques, some knowledge of Ida's situation at age 18 prior to beginning analysis with Freud is required, and so for those who may not yet have read Chapter 5 above or be familiar with the case history itself, I will recommend reading the brief section entitled "Synopsis of Ida's Situation" near the beginning of Chapter 5.

"A Fragment . . ."

A great deal of venomous ink has been spilled regarding this case study, especially over the last several decades. These critiques can, in my view, be grouped into a number of different categories—above all, there are those that have been made at what Lacan refers to as the imaginary level, wherein critics imitate and repeat toward Freud himself the very same gestures and moves they accuse Freud of (in a kind of mimicry), and others at what Lacan calls the symbolic level, wherein critics bring a different theoretical perspective to bear on the case[6]—but one fact that many of them seem to overlook is that Freud entitles his case study "A *Fragment* of an Analysis of a Case of Hysteria" (my emphasis; in German, *Bruchstück einer Hysterie-Analyse*): He presents his work with Ida as a "fragment from the history of the treatment of an hysterical girl" (SE VII, p. 15), not as any sort of complete presentation. He even goes on to say that "it is incomplete to a far greater degree than its title might lead one to expect" (p. 112). Note that the 2013 retranslation of the case by Anthea Bell for Oxford University Press reinforces the forgetting of this incompleteness by reducing the title to *A Case of Hysteria* (S. Freud, 2013), whereas Freud explicitly indicates that he omitted "a number of the results of the analysis . . . because at the time when work was broken off they had either not been established with sufficient certainty or required further study," and that he considered it quite impossible to illustrate the actual technique he employed alongside the conclusions and dream analysis that he presented (especially regarding "the internal structure of a case of hysteria"; p. 112).[7]

What he tells us he left out of his account of his work with Ida was precisely the questions he himself asked and Ida's responses and associations; as he puts it, what we have before us is not "the raw material of the patient's associations" (SE VII, p. 112) or "the process of . . . the patient's associations and communications . . . , only the results" (p. 12). In other words, all the back-and-forth between the two of them, which probably constituted the main substance of the sessions, has been left out; and almost none of the specific terms and idiomatic expressions she used have been included (except for rare instances, like when she repeatedly characterized her father as *"ein vermögender Mann,"* which means both "a man of means" and "a potent man"—that is, a man who does *not* suffer from sexual impotence; p. 47).[8] The unfortunate upshot of this is that we get the impression that Freud did the lion's share of the talking—and perhaps he did, which would certainly have been regrettable and a far cry from the approach that he recommends in his later work—and that he interpreted a mile a minute, so to speak, providing far more interpretations than any analysand could possibly absorb and respond to (as Steven Marcus puts it, in the Dora case, "the demon of interpretation [was] riding him"; 1975/1990, p. 302).[9] It appears that Freud did not, at least in many instances, give Ida the time to free-associate to certain elements in her dreams or other things that came to mind in the course of sessions, or allow her to ponder for any length of time what they might be connected with or what they might mean, instead inter-jecting almost immediately what *came to mind for him* (see SE VII, pp. 97 and 99–100). We might nevertheless consider giving Freud the benefit of the doubt by assuming that he at least occasionally followed his own precepts and gave Ida more opportunities to free-associate and arrive at conclusions of her own than we see evidence of in the case study as he wrote it up; but this seems to imply more generosity than many com-mentators on the case have been willing to extend him.

Among the critiques of Freud's work with Ida that have been made and/or published since 1905, but especially in more recent decades, we find those related to Freud's personal likes and dislikes, Freud's sexism, and Freud's bourgeois attitudes, for starters. I shall summarize what I consider to be the gist of a number of them and then discuss their broader import.

Good Looks: He Must Have Found Her A-Dora-ble

Freud often indicated that one or another of his patients was especially good-looking, intelligent, or charming, as if these were relevant pieces of information for us to know as students of psychoanalysis. I am always surprised when the clinicians I supervise tell me that one of their cli-ents is terribly attractive, as if they felt that I should know that as I discuss the case with them; they perhaps think this bit of "factual information" relevant to the patient's success or lack thereof in amorous matters (yet isn't attractiveness in the eye of the beholder, at least to some degree?), but I generally take such comments as an indication that the therapist is attracted—indeed, perhaps a little too attracted—to the patient and that this may be giving rise to difficulties in the treatment, even (and perhaps especially) when the therapist expresses particular pleasure in seeing and working with this patient. Freud tells us that Ida at 18 was "in the first bloom of youth" and "a girl of intelligent and engaging looks" (SE VII, p. 23), and certain commentators have suspected that Freud must have been dazzled by Ida, and felt his own hands tied in relation to her as he was so smitten by her charms.[10] If this is true, it would likely have posed a problem for Freud at almost any stage of the development of his technique, whether in 1900, 1913, 1920, or even at the very end of his life, given that he never underwent a proper analysis of his own.

It seems, for example, to have had a considerable impact on his treat-ment of another 18-year-old who was sent to Freud by her parents in around 1920 (written up in "The Psychogenesis of a Case of Homosex-uality in a Woman," SE XVIII, pp. 147–172); Freud seems to have found that patient too attractive for *his* own good, and made many mistakes with her—some of them akin to those he made with Ida, some quite different (see Lacan, Seminar IV, Chapter 8; and Fink, 2004, Chapter 2). As I have indicated elsewhere (Fink, 2016, pp. 127–129), beauty has a paralyzing effect on certain people, and Freud may well have been one of them. We see this commonly enough in parents, grandparents, educators, and babysitters who find certain children adorable and end up spoiling them, feeling unable to lay down the law with them or force them to make certain sacrifices that they know full well everyone must learn to make at some point. And the cuter they find those kids, the more often they feel their hands to be tied in their dealings with them, and the more exceptions and excuses they make for them. They wind up acting very differently with children they find beautiful than with others.

It is one thing to appreciate, in a somewhat abstract manner, the good looks of one's patients when one is an analyst, and quite another thing to be captivated and even paralyzed in certain ways by their looks, such that one wittingly or unwittingly ends up working with them in ways that are very different from the ways one works with other patients. The latter is most likely to happen when there are difficulties in the therapist's own love life (which is hardly uncommon), and when the therapist has not pretty thoroughly worked through his or her own "imaginary captivation" by certain features found in other people that recall features of his or her earliest love objects (mother, father, sister, brother, etc.). In such cases, practitioners often do best to refer such entrancing patients to colleagues who might be less susceptible to their physical and other personal charms, the second-best choice being to immediately begin discussing such cases with their supervisors to ensure that the therapists keep their eye on the analytic ball, as it were, instead of on the patient's charms. If it is true that Freud was infatuated with Ida owing to her looks, intelligence, and personality, we can say in his defense that he had no such referral or supervisory possibilities at his disposal: He was the only game in town at the time—indeed, the only practicing psychoanalyst in the world. Whatever the case may be, attraction to one's analysands owing to their looks, intelligence, or charm falls under the analyst's imaginary and/or symbolic countertransference (countertransference is discussed at some length in Chapter 5).

Preconceived Ideas

Freud seems to have had some rather fixed ideas about what 14-, 16-, and 18-year-old girls know, feel, and should feel about sexual matters, leading him to make curious assumptions as to Ida's "reversal of affect"—for example, her reacting in the opposite of the "normal" way when a male friend of her father's, a man at least twice her age (Herr K), suddenly clasped and kissed her at age 14, after having lured her into his shop under false pretenses, having claimed they would be meeting his wife there to watch together a religious procession that was to occur in the square below his shop windows (SE VII, p. 28).[11] "A healthy girl," Freud tells us, would have been sexually aroused by the kiss (p. 29), instead of being disgusted by it as Ida was, regardless of the fact that it came from a married friend of her father's, was quite forcible, and took her totally by surprise. It is, naturally, conceivable that Ida was already attracted to Herr K (as a substitute for her father, for example, whom she was quite enamored with for many years)—Freud, who knew Herr K, even tells us that he was "still young and of prepossessing appearance" (i.e., hand-some; p. 29 n. 3), which obviously tells us more about Freud's views than about Ida's!—and that she found the unexpectedness of the kiss exciting, but there seem to have been fairly obvious reasons to consider the situ-ation to have been more confusing than arousing.[12]

Freud also opines that "a normal girl" would have been able to deal with the proposal/proposition that Herr K made to her at age 16 (dis-cussed in some detail in Chapter 5) all by herself instead of complaining about it to her family, as Ida did (SE VII, p. 95). And Freud even seems to think that at age 18 a young woman would obviously know that the best way to help a man get to sleep at night is to have sex with him (p. 98 and 98 n. 1; Freud clearly assumes this to be true).[13] Ida may have heard some such thing from Frau K, but then again she may not have; and if she did not, this hardly seems to be the kind of thing that Ida would have read in romantic novels or encyclopedia articles about sex.

Contemporary critics (e.g., Erikson, 1962; Lear, 2005; and Paul, 2006) tend to put forward their own somewhat fixed notions as to what is normal and what is not normal for adolescent girls and young women (such as a "phase-appropriate quest for an extra-domestic embodiment of ideals," "harnessing a healthy idealism with a healthy narcissism," a desire "for good containment," and "age-appropriate idealism and search for validation of her experience" [Mahony, 1990, pp. 39 and 73], notions that, in my view, cross over into pop psychology), normalizing notions that are simply different from the ones that Freud held at the time. What needs, in my view, to be emphasized is that notions of what it is normal or abnormal for girls to know and/or feel at different ages are really quite useless in psychoanalytic work, for we come across girls (like "the Piggle"; see Winnicott, 1978) who begin masturbating already at age 2 and who seem to know quite a bit about sexual intercourse as early as age 2 or 3 (often from having witnessed parents or others engaging in it), and we encounter other girls who manage to arrive at adulthood knowing precious little about their own physiology, much less about sexual matters. *In psychoanalysis we are concerned with individuals,* and individuals tend to fall outside of any set notion of what is "normal for" or "typical of" infants, children, adolescents, or adults—in other words, they fall far from the middle of the nice little bell curves plotted by psychologists, often by a considerable number of "standard deviations." It is of no help to clinicians to know that their patients are not "normal" by current societal (or by the American Psychiatric Association's) standards—we take people as they are and work with what they present, with no concern for assessing them as "abnormal" or making them "normal" by anyone's standards.[14] When Freud said, "I would think that a normal girl would deal with such matters [Herr K's proposal by the lake] herself" instead of turning to her parents, or that "a healthy girl" would have become sexually excited at age 14 when kissed by a middle-aged man, he was merely expressing a bias or prejudice of his own, which was of little to no use whatsoever to Ida. Such ideational biases can be classified under Freud's symbolic countertransference.

Do unto Freud As . . .

As he was valiant, I honor him. But, as he was ambitious, I slew him.
—Shakespeare, *Julius Caesar* III:2

A rather large number of critics in recent years have adopted the surprising strategy of doing unto Freud as they believe Freud did unto Ida. Whatever injustices they feel Freud subjected Ida to, they subject Freud to. If they believe that Freud acted paternalistically toward Ida, they act paternalistically toward Freud, claiming to know the truths that Freud failed to grasp, averring that they know better than Freud did. If Freud played the part of a master of knowledge with Ida, they play the part of masters of knowledge too: They write as though they are absolutely sure of what was going on for Ida, just as Freud seemed sure that he knew what was going on for her (e.g., Paul, 2006). And just as Freud flattered himself in thinking he was endowed with some sort of "second sight"—thinking he knew from experience and through his penetrating insight that bed-wetting, for example, is always associated with early childhood masturbation and that *Ida must therefore have been a masturbator* (SE VII, pp. 72–73),[15] that she must have suppressed her love for Herr K and was actually "still in love with him" (note that he later concluded that he had been barking up the wrong tree with this "unavoidable assumption"; p. 58), and that all of his guesses and deductions went straight to the truth even if Ida never confirmed them—these critics flatter themselves that they are endowed with some sort of "third sight," in a game of one-upmanship. In the end, we might say that they fall into the same imaginary trap that Freud himself fell into of thinking themselves all-knowing; they put themselves in Freud's shoes and tell us what they believe to be the absolute truth about Ida.

Not to mention the absolute truth about Freud! A whole generation of literary critics seems to have become self-designated psychoanalysts of Freud (e.g., Moi, 1990, p. 184; Kahane, 1990, p. 23), telling us all about Freud's unconscious and everything Freud imagined and felt, as if they had—via the English version of Freud's case write-up—all the keys to understanding Freud himself. Many of them (e.g., Bernheimer, 1990),[16] in telling us what they believe Freud projected onto the case, wind up projecting all kinds of ideas, quirks, and perhaps even pathologies of their own onto the case, and we end up caught in a whirlwind of imaginary reflections, whereby one author says, as it were, "If you don't like what I'm saying, it must be because you have your own hang-ups. If you can't see what I see so clearly in the text, it must be because of your own blindness." Each such critic seems to imply that he or she is weighed down far less by prejudices, fantasies, and neuroses than Freud himself was, which is why they can perceive the situation so much more clearly than he could.

Sprengnether (1990), for example, uses all kinds of psychoanalytic concepts invented by Freud to criticize Freud. She reads every denial Freud makes as an avowal, and every reproach he makes to Ida as a self-reproach (pp. 261–263). This may be legitimate enough, but if one's aim is to shoot the messenger for being so horrendous, how can one then justify one's own use of his theory? Is the idea that his theory was great but that absolutely every facet of his practice was awful? Although Freud violates Ida in a number of ways, it would seem that Sprengnether repeats his traumatic violation by violating Freud. Every statement Freud makes is used against him, just as Freud used certain statements of Ida's "against her" (SE VII, p. 59).[17]

Mahony, in his book-length attack on Freud's work with Ida, far from viewing Freud as overly captivated by Ida, makes the bald-faced claim that Freud abhorred Ida: "He did not like her, period" (1996, pp. 39–40), and instead saw her as "a vengeful little bitch" (p. 42; see also pp. 35 and 143). Although it seems quite clear that Ida frustrated Freud's attempts to plumb the depths of her psyche and "cure her," Mahony attempts to show us a Freud who literally *hates* his patient; and this apparently gives Mahony license to hate Freud as much as he believes Freud hated Ida. So much so that we might wonder what Freud ever did to Mahony to make him detest Freud to such a degree! (Mahony could, instead, have simply said Freud was wrong, shown why he was wrong, and then moved on.) Mahony's tone is the kind we might expect had Ida been his daughter, niece, wife, or mother, but not one that we can easily comprehend in an analyst discussing another analyst's work.[18] Did Mahony, like Michel Onfray (the recent ultra-harsh French critic of psychoanalysis), feel he was mistreated by an analyst he consulted and decide to take it out on Freud?[19] Or should we hypothesize that critics like Mahony try to get into Freud's head because they think that with his writings he tried to get into their heads and they resent the implications of his work about their psychical makeup? Is it, in other words, that they dislike what Freud might have had to say about them and take it out on him personally rather than on his theory?

As a psychoanalyst reading such impassioned critiques, I often cannot help but think of little children who, when one calls another a liar, the other replies, "You're a bigger liar," "Takes one to know one," or "I know you are, but what am I?" (see SE VII, p. 35; Freud calls it the "*tu quoque* mechanism used by children" in SE XII, p. 52). One imitates one's interlocutor, mimicking his accusations, being just as blind and hateful as one perceives him to be, which is obviously a response at the imaginary level (as we often see it in spiteful countertransferential reactions on the part of analysts). There seems to be some sort of contest here over who is most blinded by their neuroses. People are, of course, blinded by their neuroses, but when nonanalysts and even many practicing analysts profess to see what was going on so much more clearly than Freud himself did—and I have undoubtedly been guilty of some of this myself in Chapter 5—we might imagine Freud retorting, "That's easy to say, but then you weren't there when she told me what she told me and did what she did."

Given the vast quantity of pages devoted by a plethora of authors to analyzing Freud—through a close examination of his letters, texts, and hearsay from other psychoanalysts—one might easily get the impression that to such authors Freud, the man, is truly *the only case worth analyzing,* or at least the most important one to analyze.[20] Are we to understand that all of psychoanalysis itself is to be impugned by Freud's own character flaws? (And if so, why do we even bother to keep talking about psychoanalysis?) Or that we will learn more about how to conduct psychoanalyses in the best possible way by endlessly uncovering every hidden thread of Freud's personality? This seems positively implausible! There is ample evidence that, even if Freud was far from a model practitioner of the approach he invented, psychoanalysis works when practiced by a great many other clinicians.

One is led to wonder why, rather than spending weeks, months, or even years piecing together what often seem to amount to wild speculations about Freud's own character and motives, the analysts who have critiqued Freud have not devoted more time to *presenting full-length case studies of their work with their own analysands* to show how analysis should be conducted and to counterbalance Freud's flawed work. And yet, curiously enough, few analysts have taken up the gauntlet; precious few have taken upon themselves the challenge to show the world their own approach to psychotherapeutic work in detail. Are they afraid to expose themselves to the same kind of critique to which they have so pitilessly subjected Freud?! Perhaps one of his most severe critics was onto something when he said, "Being published made Freud feel vulnerable in the hands of the specialist and predominately male reader; being read meant resembling an analysand,[21] being a passive object, a woman. Freud struggled against that identification, against feeling passive with the reader and being mistreated by him" (Mahony, 1996, pp. 124–125). Might not the same be said of all those analysts who have devoted far more time to critiquing Freud's work with Ida than to presenting to the world their own cases?

A Change of Frame

We are obliged to pay as much attention in our case histories to the purely human and social circumstances of our patients as to the somatic data and the symptoms.
—Freud, SE VII, p. 18

Other literary and cultural critics base their beef with Freud upon a frame of reference or perspective that is different from that of psychoanalysis, whether that be Marxism, feminism, or both. They tax Freud with having been insensitive to questions of social and economic class, the oppression of women, the suffocating roles imposed on daughters in families at the time, and the subordinate and often sexual role of governesses, housemaids, nurses, and cooks in the bourgeois households of the time (e.g., Gallop, 1990; Cixous & Clément, 1990; Moi, 1990). Historical perspectives on the roles played by women in late 19th-century Viennese society can enlighten us as to the place of and possibilities that existed for women at the time, compared to now; and Freud can be taken to task for having been a man of his own time who may not have believed in the importance of the liberation of women from the limited range of options available to them (but then one might have to explain why his own daughter, Anna, became, with his encouragement and support, a renowned psychoanalyst in her own right), and for not having seen some of Ida's difficulties as being those of virtually any young woman in her position at the time.[22] Each frame of reference allows us to see certain things, while blinding us to others, and clinicians always do well to endeavor to take into account numerous frames of reference, viewing each case from a number of different points of view.

Marxist/feminist critics point out, for example, that whereas Ida had the sense that she was a pawn or object of exchange between her own father and Herr K (feeling that "she had been handed over to Herr K as the price of his tolerating the relations between her father and his wife" in a sort of "I'll give you mine if you give me yours"; SE VII, pp. 34 and 86),[23] this was the typical destiny of many daughters for centuries, daughters being married off to this person or that person to serve their fathers' own personal quests for ever greater social, political, or economic power. Girls were married to specific men not because it was thought that such men would make them good husbands or that the couples were good matches for each other, but because such men brought property, capital, or influence to the girls' fathers.

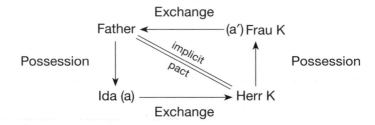

FIGURE A.I.1.   Ida as an Object of Exchange

As undeniably true as this may be, from the practitioner's perspective it is not entirely clear how useful this fact could have been to Freud or to Ida. For what turned out to be most important in their work together (insofar as there was *something* therapeutic about it) was that—as we see in Chapter 5—whereas Ida first claimed to be a mere pawn in her father and his friend's machinations, it turned out that she herself greatly contributed to the situation in which she was an object of exchange between the two men. In other words, yes, she was "a victim of circumstance"; yes, she was an object of exchange (like so many other women for centuries); but more importantly for her analysis, she seems to have aided and abetted her being placed and kept by her father and Herr K in such a position—that is, she seems to have actively worked her way into such a position. To have made her aware of her oppression by the male-dominated society around her might have led to a form of women's liberation activism on her part (which she was, in fact, led to later in life), but would most likely have left the question of her own subjective position and positioning within that society out of the picture (unless it focused, too, on her complicity in her own oppression).[24] Some might argue that even Ida's subjective positioning was *dictated* to her by her social/cultural position, as it was only by getting in the middle of things that a woman could obtain anything she wanted at that point in time; but some women did not play the game as Ida did—they refused this particular option and chose other paths among the admittedly limited number available to them. Regardless of how much we attribute to ambient social/political forces, we must not, in my view, overlook the role of the unconscious in how people position themselves in any particular form of society.

Freud was, like everyone else, a product of his own socioeconomic class, some referring to him as "bourgeois" (Lacan),[25] others as a conventional Viennese bourgeois (André Breton), and yet he seems quite liberated at times from bourgeois social and moral conventions (see, for example, SE VII, pp. 48–49, and SE XVI, p. 434).[26] Nevertheless, as many critics have pointed out, the almost complete absence of Ida's mother in Freud's case write-up is quite glaring, as is that of the Rat Man's mother in the case history Freud devoted to him; and Freud seems incapable of imagining that Ida could be interested in Frau K in any way other than via identification on Ida's part with a man, as if it were unthinkable to him at the time that she could be a woman interested in a woman. As we see in Chapter 5, some of this may have been attributable to his own psychological makeup, and some to an inadequate symbolic frame of reference.

A Change of Clinical and Historical Frame: Hysteria Is Not an Illness

The most important change of frame we can supply when it comes to hysteria is, to my mind, to emphasize that, like obsession, *hysteria is not an illness but rather a structure*. Insofar as a large percentage of human beings are neurotic (as opposed to psychotic or perverse, neurosis, psychosis, and perversion being the three main clinical structures), and insofar as there are only three principal neuroses—obsession, hysteria, and phobia—each neurosis constitutes one of the ways in which vast swaths of the population operate in life when faced with psychical conflict. Different people can, of course, be more or less obsessive, hysterical, or phobic—there are differences of degree—but a great many of us are neurotic and the different neuroses correspond to permanent ways we deal with the world, each of which involves a different approach to repression—that is, a different solution to the problem of conflict as regards thought and affect. As Freud tells us already in 1889, the fact that we manage to resolve a particular hysterical symptom "does not mean that the hysteria is cured: in similar conditions it will provoke similar symptoms" (SE I, p. 100; see also SE II, p. 17). Neurosis, we might say, is not symptom specific; rather, it is a way of life.

The solution to conflict that is characteristic of obsession—whereby thought and affect become detached from each other, the affect connected to an experience being displaced onto some other experience or thought—is no more "rational" than the solution to conflict that is characteristic of hysteria, whereby the thought connected to an experience is repressed and the affect is found in an unrecognizable form in the body. Although generations of doctors have associated hysteria with irrationality, absurdity, overdramatization, excessive excitability, and even faking, and have often considered these things to be especially associated with women as opposed to men, hysteria is no more "irrational," "illogical," or "unreasonable" than obsession; each neurosis has its own rationality or logic, each has its own reasons for being, and these reasons and logics are simply different from each other. Obsessives are led to do things that are just as irrational-seeming, from an everyday perspective, as hysterics are.

As Mark Micale puts it, hysteria is "not a disease; rather, it is an alternative physical, verbal, and gestural language, an iconic social communication" (cited in Showalter, 1997, p. 7). In other words, hysteria constitutes a different way of manifesting and communicating one's psychical conflict and pain than obsession does, and we might recall here that Freud even refers to obsession as merely "a dialect of the language of hysteria" (SE X, p. 157)—that is, a variation on the solution to conflict that is offered by hysteria. We should recall, too, that hysteria "appears in the young as well as the old, in men as well as women, in blacks as well as whites" (Showalter, 1997, p. 7). Those who tax Freud and other psychoanalysts with having sanctioned the near equation in many clinicians' minds between women and hysteria overlook the fact that Freud was almost laughed out of the Vienna Society of Medicine when, in 1886, he gave a paper "On Male Hysteria," and was largely ignored when he presented a specific case of male hysteria later that same year (SE I, p. 24). Charcot himself is said to have treated some 90 male hysterics (Showalter, 1997, p. 33).

Hysteria was perhaps isolated earlier in history as a clinical entity than obsession was (perhaps already in early Egyptian times), but given its plasticity—appearing in the body, but in a body that is a social body, a body that is coded and overwritten with all the linguis-

tic, social, cultural, and religious connotations of each particular his- ✗
torical era—hysteria is forever changing in its manifestations. This has
misled a number of psychiatrists and psychologists into believing that
hysteria no longer exists because its better-known manifestations from
the 19th century—psychosomatic paralyses, blindness, deafness, aphonia, anesthesia, and so on—are rarely found among patients today. But
hysteria is far from dead! The same mechanism, whereby affect goes
into the body and is disconnected from the thought or memory that
gave rise to it, lives on. As Showalter puts it, hysteria "has simply been
relabeled for a new era" (p. 4); for a list of some of these new labels,
see the conclusion to Chapter 5 and Appendix V.

APPENDIX II

On Suggestion

WHEN SOMEONE AFFLICTED in some way goes to see a "medicine man," a "healer," or a "layer on of hands" with the expectation and will to be cured, the very desire to be cured and the willingness to submit to whatever form of treatment the healer prescribes makes the afflicted person suggestible. The healer need then but prescribe virtually anything, assuming it is not too much out of keeping with the individual's expectations—saying, "If you do *x*, *y*, and *z*, you will be cured"—for the desired cure to come about.

In a tribal context, the prescription may involve exposing oneself to the elements by way of expiation, accomplishing deeds to prove oneself worthy, or a drug experience under the guidance of an elder (e.g., eating an hallucinogenic mushroom and spending a week with the tribe's medicine man in the desert). In a modern medical context, the prescription to relieve headaches, insomnia, anxiety, and a host of other ailments may include placebos (pills containing no active ingredients) and encouraging words such as "Take one of these three times a day and you will feel much better." In medicine and psychiatry, suggestion is usually known today as the *placebo effect*. Patients are led to believe that they are receiving medication that will help them, and lo and behold, they are helped.

Suggestion obviously cannot cure all, but it plays a major part even today in exorcism, faith healing, and hypnosis. In the late 1700s, Franz Anton Mesmer (1734–1815) managed to become the talk of Paris by exploiting suggestion to its fullest. Though claiming that his miraculous cures resulted from righting imbalances of "animal magnetism"— an invisible fluid presumed to be present everywhere (like the "ether" thought to exist by many early scientists), but which could become unevenly distributed in the body, creating afflictions—Mesmer had an unerring sense of the spectacular, and carefully staged his treatments in an aura of mystery, mysticism, and initiation (beautifully captured in Alexandre Dumas' novel entitled *The Queen's Necklace*). His treatments became highly stylized, patients being cured 20 at a time in wooden "hot tubs" (equipped with iron rods intended to supercharge these early Jacuzzi-like devices with animal magnetism). Ceremoniously entering the room wearing a long cape, Mesmer would wave at one person after another with his magic wand, and one by one the patients would fall into a fit (referred to at the time as a *crisis*) from which they would emerge saying they were cured.

While Mesmer's claims regarding animal magnetism were ultimately discredited by the government commissions assigned to investigate them (which included such well-known figures as Benjamin Franklin and Lavoisier), his therapeutic success must be taken seriously. Of 100 patients questioned (presenting spleen infections, rheumatism, asthma, headaches, skin diseases, and nervous disorders)—all of whom had been treated by one of Mesmer's students—50 claimed they had been completely cured, and all but 6 claimed they had been partially cured. Though unrecognized by the medical establishment of his time, Mesmer's peculiar use of suggestion and spectacle ("mesmerizing" patients) indicates to us today that many supposedly medical problems can be at least partially cleared up through psychological means. Call it hocus-pocus if you like, but the fact remains that it often worked. Indeed, it often worked better—had a higher success rate—than many 21st-century medical techniques. It is likely, however, that only those who were already suggestible and willing to believe in animal magnetism came forward to be treated by Mesmer and his assistants—in other words, the patient population was not randomly sampled but self-selected.

Note that practitioners of suggestion need not believe in the technique they use, as the 1992 film *Leap of Faith* (starring Steve Martin) illustrates. Only the patients need have faith.

The Varied Uses of Suggestion

The "treatment modalities" that were tried before Freud's time were developed in the following order:

1. mesmerization (through dazzling) and suggestion (associated with Franz Anton Mesmer, 1734–1815);
2. hypnosis and suggestion (Jean-Martin Charcot, 1825–1893);
3. hypnosis and talk, leading to catharsis (Josef Breuer, 1842–1925).

We might think that Mesmer provided the first step in the development of medical treatment through suggestion, but this would be somewhat arbitrary, for the kings of France, for example, were thought for some 500 years to be able to cure certain diseases just by touching the afflicted, and exorcism has been practiced for millennia.

By Freud's time, suggestion used in conjunction with hypnosis (Step 2 above) had become a major technique for treating "nervous disorders." Charcot hypnotized patients presenting all kinds of paralyses and sensory disturbances, and showed that, in the more suggestible hypnotic state, these symptoms could be made to disappear—during hypnosis itself and for some time afterward through the use of posthypnotic suggestions (e.g., "When you awaken, your legs will feel perfectly fine and you will be able to walk again without assistance"). More striking still was the fact that, under hypnosis, paralyses and sensory symptoms could be made to appear in otherwise normal people—again, both during the hypnosis itself and after awakening, owing to posthypnotic suggestions.

In the late 1800s, a number of researchers in France and Austria (such as Hippolyte Bernheim and Pierre Janet) were using hypnosis to greater or lesser success to relieve a wide range of symptoms that were increasingly recognized to be psychosomatic in nature. Today it seems obvious to us that if Charcot could alleviate a paralysis of the lower limbs by simply hypnotizing a patient and commanding him to walk, the paralysis could not have been medical in origin; nevertheless, the British and Austrian medical establishments of the time dismissed such results as the work of charlatans and quacks. Charcot held beliefs that went against the grain of those held by the majority of physicians at the time.[1]

Though evincing some astonishing results, suggestion's successes tended to be short-lived. As Freud says about his use of suggestion with Emmy von N., "The therapeutic success on the whole was considerable; but it was not lasting" (SE II, p. 101). Suggestion generally provided only temporary relief and required frequent repetition of posthypnotic suggestions. This remains true today for patients who attempt to stop smoking, for example, by seeing a hypnotist. They hope hypnosis will have a permanent effect, yet it rarely does; people nevertheless continue to seek out hypnotists because hypnosis, unlike psychotherapy, is quick and requires no special effort on the patient's part.

Freud ultimately rejected hypnosis because many patients were, in his experience, not suggestible enough to be reliably hypnotized; and he rejected suggestion owing to "the lack of permanence in its successes" (SE XVI, p. 449).

The Difference Between Suggestion and
Psychoanalytic Interpretation

Let us note that suggestion aims to heal by *directly influencing* the afflicted person, regardless of the reason(s) for that person's affliction. And many therapists today continue to rely a great deal on suggestion, even if they do not employ hypnosis, by suggesting to their patients that they try out certain behaviors or engage in certain activities (sports, dieting, etc.), and even go so far as to suggest that the root of their problems is such and such, despite the fact that their patients have in no way indicated that this is the case. In this sense, they try to provide their patients with ideas or bits of "knowledge" the therapists have fabricated (or found in books), instead of encouraging their patients to find the root of the problem themselves.

This is the fundamental difference between suggestion and psychoanalytic interpretation: Although they cannot always be clearly differentiated, *psychoanalytic interpretation aims at analysands' own truth,* at something analysands come up with themselves and feel in their bones to be true, not something ready-made (e.g., something the analyst found in a manual or heard in a course) or fabricated based on the analyst's own pre-existing ideas. Psychoanalytic interpretation comes primarily from the analysand and seeks to heal by alighting upon or hitting the truth, not by adopting just any old thing that might work temporarily. In the best of cases, interpretations that come from the analyst do not tell analysands what to do or think or feel, or purport to explain why they do, think, or feel certain things; instead, they take one short step beyond what the analysand is already saying (Freud) or aim to shake up the analysand's way of seeing things (Lacan).

APPENDIX III

Toward an Elucidation of the Rat Man's Crisis

F OR READERS WHO may be confused by the specific crisis shortly after which the Rat Man first came to see Freud, I will attempt to articulate some of its parameters here.

Let me first mention that, despite the intensity and apparent madness of this crisis, Freud was not led to conclude that the patient, Ernst Langer, was psychotic. Nor was he led to do so when he detected something reminiscent of a delusional formation in Ernst's discourse (Freud also refers to it as a *delirium*, a term no longer in use in a psychiatric sense)—namely, the idea, which first occurred to Ernst when he was about 6, that his parents knew his thoughts even though he had never told his thoughts to them (SE X, p. 164).[1]

We see here that Freud implicitly distinguished between the *primary obsessive symptom*—which determined Ernst's diagnosis or clinical structure—and a broad range of secondary symptoms. These might be articulated as follows:

1. the primary symptom: oscillating obsessive thoughts, leading him to do nothing;
2. secondary symptoms such as paranoia.[2]

The Rat Man's Presenting Problem

What patients initially present to the analyst as their reason for coming to therapy is often a cover—that is, a problem they are willing to own up to, rather than the less palatable and more longstanding ones they suspect or even know exist. The analyst must never assume that the presenting problem—the event or series of events that, according to the patient, led the patient to seek therapy—is what actually brought the patient to therapy: Often it is something else altogether.

In Ernst's case, the presenting problem was clear: The events in August 1907 surrounding his glasses and the "cruel captain" (SE X, p. 165). The Rat Man had been on maneuvers as an officer in the army and, at one point, during a halt in the course of a forced march, he had mislaid his pince-nez (an old-fashioned sort of glasses that clipped onto one's nose and had no earpieces). Although he told Freud that it would have been easy to find the pince-nez, he did not pause to look because he did not want to delay his company. Why? Largely because he wanted to prove that he was as tough as the others were; as he put it, "I was keen to show the regular officers that people like me [glasses-wearing intellectuals] had not only learned a good deal but could stand a good deal too" (p. 165). Glasses were a sign of weakness to him, and it should be noted that the German term for pince-nez, *Kneifer*, also means "a cowardly person," someone who trembles or backs down when confronted (some of the colloquial meanings include chicken, yellow-belly, skiver, and shirker). Machismo was obviously involved here for Ernst: Was he going to show himself to be a man or a mouse?

He had never been much of a man in his own mind—indeed, he told Freud that he had been a coward since age 6. He had now lost another vestige of his manhood by losing his ability to see well, something that can obviously be quite important in the military. He was to some extent crippled without his glasses.[3]

Rather than take a few minutes and look for them, he wired his optician in Vienna to order a new pair and have them sent, cash on delivery (COD), to a town (that Freud refers to as Z—; see the map provided in SE X, p. 212 n) where he intended to go pick them up. During the same halt at which he lost his glasses (during a meal, perhaps), he sat next to a certain Captain Nemeczek (S. Freud, 2000, p. 55; Freud simply calls him Captain N. in the published case history, or the "cruel captain"; SE X, p. 169), a man who believed in corporal punishment and was quite vocal in defending its use in the military. Ernst "very sharply" disagreed with him in the course of their conversation, but Nemeczek went on to tell the officers about a particular form of torture used in the East (involving hungry rats being put in a pot under a man's backside and eating their way into his anus).

The Rat Man obviously began to associate Nemeczek with his own cruel father—who, as we saw in Chapter 4, also believed in corporal punishment and was inclined to get so caught up in beating his children that he sometimes did not know what he was doing—and as soon as he heard about this form of torture, "the idea flashed through [his] mind *that this was happening to a person who was very dear to [him]*," indeed, to two people: his lady and his father. In order to put such aggressive thoughts out of his mind (they must have struck him as absurd, too, since his father had died about eight years earlier), he repeated things to himself (as he did as a child of 6), such as, "Whatever are you thinking of?" He felt such ideas to be criminal and was inclined to punish himself for having had them. But how would he do so?

By forcing himself to do something really stupid and humiliating. He was told by another captain he had met (not the cruel captain) that his glasses had arrived in Z—, and that a woman who worked at the post office there had decided that, since he was a lieutenant, he must be trustworthy, and had taken it upon herself to pay the COD charges (SE X, p. 172). She figured there was little risk he would not pay her back, and he took that as a sign of favor: He believed he was in her good graces. Ernst was told this, by a captain who had himself been at the post office at the time the package arrived there, several hours before Ernst received his glasses.

A few hours later, the cruel captain, Nemeczek, handed Ernst his glasses (having received them from Lieutenant A, presumably, or possibly from the woman at the post office herself) and told Ernst that Lieutenant A (someone we never learn anything about in the case study) had paid the COD charges of 3.80 crowns and that therefore Ernst *had to pay Lieutenant A back* (SE X, p. 168). The cruel captain was mistaken about this and the Rat Man knew he was mistaken from the very moment the captain enunciated these words.

What went on in Ernst's mind at that point was quite complicated. To begin with, I will present Freud's interpretation of it in the published account. Here, at first glance, things break down as follows (SE X, pp. 217–218):

1. Nemeczek said, "You have to pay Lieutenant A 3.80 crowns," and Ernst experienced this as an *order*.
2. Ernst, who now associated Nemeczek with his father due to the torture story (and who probably wished something horrible would happen to both of them), inwardly retorted, "Like hell I will!" or "Kiss off!" What flashed through his mind was actually more complicated still: "I'll pay when hell freezes over!" or "I'm as likely to pay as my dead father is to have children!" (SE X, pp. 218; a similar thought involving his lady, who had been sterile since having an operation about six years earlier, ran through his mind as well). Freud qualified these thoughts as "derisive affirmations" or

ironic claims, involving "an absurd condition that could never be fulfilled." Here we see an element of _revolt_ on Ernst's part: a vow not to pay. (This might be viewed as an aggressive id impulse.)

3. Having revolted against his father (and his lady), Ernst then felt guilty: Such thoughts were criminal. He would have to punish himself for them by making himself look ridiculous (in front of Lieutenant A and yet another officer, Lieutenant B, for example) by fulfilling Nemeczek's erroneous order. Here we see a progression from revolt to guilt to a self-punishing command. (This might be understood as an action on the part of his superego.)

4. Ernst then resolved to follow to a tee the order made by Nemeczek. In Freud's account of this, it seems that punishment prevailed and that Ernst himself could get nothing out of the compulsion he experienced to execute the order: There was nothing in it for him except _self-punishment_.

Such an interpretation of the situation only goes so far, however, because _there was something in it for him,_ or so I would argue. In his several-hour-long vacillation over whether to go to Z— or back home to Vienna (involving a kind of mental masturbation, as we shall see), he was weighing in his mind a number of different factors:

1. Ernst was quite interested in meeting the trusting young lady at the post office whom he believed to be kindly disposed toward him without even knowing him; and he was also interested in seeing once again the pretty girl (the daughter of an innkeeper) in that same town who had flirted with him and with whom he had considered having a fling (SE X, p. 211). But to go see those women would mean slighting Gisa (his "lady"), and it would also involve going against his father's wish that he marry into money. In other words, to pay back the person to whom he knew he actually owed the money (the woman at the post office) would, in his imagination, harm both his lady and his father. (It would also have made him more like his father in one respect, repeating his father's dilemma of having to choose between two women—the innkeeper's daughter and the woman at the post office—and would be tantamount to giving in to his father's advice that he not be involved with Gisa. It would have simultaneously differentiated him from his father, for his father had never paid off a significant debt the father incurred while he was in the army.) These were some of the personal meanings for Ernst of the option of going to Z—.

2. He then vowed *not* to pay back the money, which was a form of *revolt* on his part.

3. But this, too, he felt to be a crime against his father (his father had never paid the debt he owed to a fellow soldier, and Ernst felt obliged to pay it for him, if only in a displaced manner) and his lady. Perhaps this was due to the ironic way in which the vow occurred to him: "I'm as likely to pay as my dead father or my lady is to have children!" He felt that he had insulted them by making this vow or resolution, which gave rise to *guilt*.

4. A *command* was then enunciated in his mind: "You *must* pay back the 3.80 crowns to Lieutenant A." You must bring Lieutenant A to the post office in Z— and betray both your father (by not marrying into money) and your lady (by visiting the two women there). This humiliating action would ostensibly constitute *self-punishment* for his having slighted his father and his lady; by this action he would honor or prop up the cruel captain/father who, like the king Freud mentions (SE X, p. 218), always has to be right.[4] *The solution he found in this short-lived symptom* (played out on the train back to Vienna and for a brief time thereafter) was one in which *he seemed to be obeying, vindicating, or exonerating his father figures* (paying his father's debt and executing the cruel captain's order even though it was misguided), and punishing himself by making himself look ridiculous (bringing Lieutenant A all the way to Z—, even though he knew full well Lieutenant A had nothing to do with his pince-nez), *but was at the same time disobeying* his father's deeper wishes for him to marry "the right kind of woman." The command he issued to himself was thus designed to allow him to *both obey and disobey his father*, it being a compromise or solution to his ambivalence. It also required him to go see two women he believed were interested in him, thereby abandoning Gisa.[5]

What all of this suggests is that *there may still be something in a command* (even an obviously absurd one) *for the obsessive, something he gets out of it.* Why else would he at least try to obey it? Even if the command was issued by the superego, in order to inflict punishment on Ernst, Ernst might still have been getting something out of it.

Lacan views the superego as issuing the imperative *"Jouis!"* meaning "Enjoy!" (*Écrits*, p. 696). In Ernst's case, it might be thought of as commanding him to "Enjoy those women!" The libidinal impulses that went into the command were multilayered and overdetermined, and carrying out the command might well have provided him a kick of some kind, it being *a command to obey his drives for a change* (note that he only seems to have had regular sexual relations with women after the treatment with Freud was well underway). We might say that there was something in the command for both agencies, for both the id and the superego, suggesting once again that symptoms (even short-lived ones like this) are compromise formations.

Let us not forget that *Ernst did not carry out the command*. Indeed, he never carried out *any* of the commands he gave himself, whether to slit his own throat or kill Gisa's grandmother (in the latter case, he fell down on the floor crying instead). For an obsessional neurotic like Ernst, there is a certain distance between himself and a self-imposed order or command. Psychotics, on the other hand, often believe such commands come from parties outside of themselves and take them far more seriously. Ernst apparently made a feeble attempt to obey his self-imposed command, but was not successful because Lieutenant A refused to accept the money. After that, Ernst went no further.

The Great Vacillation

In the following table I try to schematize the highly personal meanings to Ernst (reasons no one else could easily fathom) of going to Z— and of going instead to Vienna:

Reasons for going to Z—	**Reasons for going to Vienna**
Disobey father; harm his lady. Raises in his mind the conflict between Gisa, frowned upon by his father, and the Saborskys' daughter, Lizzie.	Avoid exonerating his father, by not paying the debt his father owed.
Attraction of starting an affair or two; attraction of repeating his father's marital choice based on money and social status. He flees this attraction, much as he falls ill later.	Avoidance of the problem. Go back to his lady and disobey his father.
Obey his father (in the guise of the cruel captain).	

His ultimate solution was to make no decision—and as noted in Chapter 4, avoidance (e.g., avoiding making decisions) *is a hallmark of neurosis*—and to leave his actions to fate. His thoughts regarding the train porter and his lunch car reservation, as well as those about feeling foolish in front of Lieutenant A, were mere rationalizations, in the end— that is, ad hoc reasons adopted to explain his more profound attractions and repulsions related to the women, the money versus status conflict, paying his father's debt, and so on. The scales in favor of Z— and Vienna were quite evenly balanced, and thus Ernst was too divided or ambivalent to decide. As obsessives so often do, he allowed fate to decide his course; and since it led him back to Vienna, he let a good friend of his in Vienna deal with the problem for him.

APPENDIX IV

A Freudian Interpretation of Dora's Specific Symptoms

DESPITE BEING AFFLICTED with a *"petite hystérie,"* as Freud puts it (SE VII, pp. 23–24), rather than a *"grande hystérie"* like Anna O's, we see that Dora (referred to hereafter by her real name, Ida) suffered from a plethora of problems, the majority of which were somatic. This contrasts sharply with the predicament of the Rat Man, whose problems were all in his head, so to speak—that is to say, primarily thought-related. In his case, wishes that harm would come to those he supposedly loved were repressed, returning in the form of conscious worries or fears of horrible things happening to them (these then led to some propitiatory, compulsive acts designed to ward off evil consequences). Stated somewhat too categorically, in obsession the repressed returns in the mind (SE III, pp. 51–52), whereas in hysteria it returns in the body.

As we saw in Chapter 1, Freud refers to the return of the repressed in the body as "conversion": the conversion of psychical conflict into chronic somatic symptoms (SE II, pp. 86, 147, 203–208; see also SE III, p. 49). In such instances, ideas connected with the conflict are usually forgotten, and when they are not forgotten, they become devoid of affect, the affect having gone into the body (SE II, p. 206–208); this might at least partially explain why Ida consciously remembered little of her past and seemed so unmoved by virtually everything she and Freud discussed.

Ida's most chronic somatic symptoms included nervous coughing, dyspnoea (labored or heavy breathing), asthma, aphonia, migraines, gastric pains, and foot dragging (a number of which persisted at least into middle age, according to Deutsch, 1957).[1] But we should also note that she had certain conscious ideas that were quite the opposite of her unconscious ones—for example, her "supervalent" thought, the one she could not get out of her mind (some might mistakenly call it an obsessive thought) about how her father had thrown her under the bus (i.e., handed her over to Herr K and then refused to believe his friend had propositioned her) in order to be able to continue his affair with Frau K, a thought that seemed to hide from herself her own interest in Frau K. In other words, not every symptom in hysteria is found in the body; similarly, not every symptom in obsession is found in the mind alone—consider the proliferation of digestive problems found among obsessives that go by names like irritable bowel disorder (or syndrome), indigestion, reflux, heartburn, gas, and all of the physical pains in the body related to the basket category currently in vogue: "stress."

Although Ida had one of the same somatic symptoms as Anna O, *tussis nervosa* (nervous cough)—supposedly owing to catarrh (or phlegm), which implies inflammation of the mucous membrane in the throat—it was not designed, in Ida's case, to cover over music and try to drive out of her mind the thought of going dancing, which conflicted so thoroughly with a sense of filial duty. We do not know for sure what Ida's cough was designed to do, since her work with Freud seems not to have eliminated it (even though her coughing stopped "shortly after she had tacitly accepted the explanation" that we shall discuss momentarily, Freud himself admitted that this was inconclusive as her cough "had so often before disappeared spontaneously"; SE VII, p. 40); and even if their work together had eliminated it, we might still remain somewhat in the dark as to exactly what the ultimate cause and purpose of the symptom was and exactly which part of their discussion led to its demise.[2] We can, nevertheless, hypothesize that Ida's coughing (usually for three to six weeks at a time, but once for several months; p. 22), like Anna O's, "spoke of" or came to signify the simultaneous existence of a wish and a reproach leading to the suppression of that wish. What wish and what reproach?

According to Freud, the *wish* would be to perform (or have Frau K perform) fellatio—on her father, presumably, and later to perform fellatio herself on Herr K (SE VII, pp. 47–48)—whereas Lacan (*Écrits*, p. 180) postulates that the wish would be, rather, to have cunnilingus performed (by herself or her father?) on Frau K. (Perhaps we should entertain the possibility that *both* were involved, if not simultaneously, then alternately.) The *reproach* would, in theory, have to do with the degree to which such things were not done in polite society with friends of one's parents, and especially not with another woman. The conflict for Ida between a sexual desire and the taboo surrounding sexual acts seems to have given rise in her, from about the age of 8 on, to a decreased ability to act in the world (which, as we saw in Chapter 5, disappeared at least in part within five months of the end of the analysis when she confronted both Frau K and Herr K, and began to devote herself more energetically to her studies). The cough could be understood as transforming the fantasized sexual sensation in her mouth and/or throat into something asexual (and, indeed, that led to her receiving *medical* attention), or possibly as an attempt to express disgust at the imagined act.[3] (The fact that her nervous cough began already at age 8 does, however, cast some doubt on this explanation, although it is possible she already knew a fair amount about sex by then.)

Freud hypothesizes that she had may have had an inflammation of the throat at some point owing to an ordinary cold or flu (SE VII, p. 82), or that the tickling in the throat may have been simply the revival of the sensation she had known for quite a few years as a thumb sucker, which then somehow took on meaning for her—perhaps retroactively—when she learned about oral sex.[4] This is the essence of what Freud calls "somatic compliance" (pp. 40–41 and 47–54), whereby a purely physical problem (e.g., a flu-related cough) takes on psychological meaning, which then sets it in stone as a psychosomatic symptom. It can, subsequently, take on further meanings, which then makes it resistant to alleviation when the first meaning alone is alighted upon.

We might understand Ida's periodic inability to speak or loss of voice (aphonia) for "three to six weeks" at a time in much the same way, especially insofar as it often resulted from or at least coincided with the coughing (SE VII, p. 39). Although Freud construes it as a lack of interest in speaking when her supposed beloved, Herr K, was away on business,[5] Lacan (*Écrits*, p. 180; Seminar III, p. 175) construes it as "the call of the oral drive"—in other words, as an urge to perform oral sex on Frau K—that would make itself heard when Herr K was out of town and Ida was alone with Frau K (perhaps especially at night, when they shared a bedroom at the Ks' house). This urge would then presumably have been countered in her or thwarted by thoughts regarding the moral reprehensibility of such a course of action, its unacceptability leaving her dumbfounded or speechless, it being an "unspeakable" act. Her inability to talk likely put a damper on her relations with Frau K while Herr K was away, their relationship having been structured around intimate discussions of a wide range of topics when he was around. Her loss of voice thus perhaps served the purpose of creating distance between them precisely when "the call of the oral drive" was at its height.[6]

Such a reconstruction of Ida's nervous cough and aphonia fits the model I proposed in Chapter 1:

Force 1 $\Rightarrow$ Symptom $\Leftarrow$ Force 2

"Bad self" $\Rightarrow$ Symptom $\Leftarrow$ "Good self"

On the left we have the impersonal force of the "it," and on the right the force of the "me" (or "ego"). Cast in later Freudian terms, we can characterize the conflict as that between the libido (or id) on the left and the forces of prohibition (or superego) on the right. This remains, however, no more than a theoretical reconstruction, for Freud's work with Ida never went so far as to permanently relieve her of either of those symptoms, as far as we know.

Note that her father had catarrh (or phlegm) too, probably owing to his smoking and tuberculosis, and that Ida's cough thus perhaps also spoke of an identification with him at the level of sexual desire;[7] as Freud puts it, it is as if the cough were saying, "It is from him that I got my evil passions, for which I am being punished by illness" (SE VII, p. 82). This identification, and not the later connection with the Ks (even if she had first met them in Merano when she was 6), could potentially explain the fact that her coughing and loss of voice had started already when she was 8 (p. 27), shortly after she had stopped—if Freud is to be believed—masturbating.

Ida claimed to have been a "wild creature" (*ein wildes Ding*—literally, a "wild thing," as in the eponymous song by The Troggs) up until the age of 8—and perhaps indulged her sexual urges by masturbating, although she never confirmed this construction on Freud's part—but then calmed down and became a "good girl" when she first became afflicted with labored or heavy breathing (like her father's, and perhaps especially like her father's, and perhaps mother's too, while they had sex in the bedroom next to Ida's, at a point at which the father was not yet impotent; SE VII, pp. 79–80),[8] asthma, coughing, and loss of voice. Such *turning points* in a person's life are crucial, as they *signal a major change of some kind*, but Freud devotes no more than a footnote to it. Freud writes, "She had in fact been a wild creature; but after the first attack of 'asthma' she became quiet and well-behaved. To her mind, that illness marked the boundary between two phases in her sexual life" (p. 82 n. 1).

We might hypothesize that her somatic symptoms formed as punishment for having masturbated while thinking about her father (presumably a crime against her mother), the symptoms preserving within themselves a connection to her father, inasmuch as he had some of the same symptoms, and involving a number of the zones associated by Ida with sex: the mouth, throat, and lungs (heavy breathing). Her symptoms thus *replaced* her childhood sexuality, or, as Freud puts it, her symptoms *were* her sexuality (speaking of it, as it were, while usurping its place): "The symptoms constitute the patient's sexual activity" (SE VII, p. 163), the implication being that patients derive a satisfaction or jouissance from their symptoms that is similar to the satisfaction they had previously obtained from masturbation.[9] He postulates that "hysterical symptoms hardly ever appear so long as children are masturbating, but only afterward, when a period of abstinence has set in; they form a substitute for masturbatory satisfaction" (p. 79).[10]

If it was true that her somatic symptoms formed as punishment for having committed a "crime" against her mother by masturbating while fantasizing about her father—which is, it should be recalled, no more than a theory, since it was never confirmed in Ida's case—the question that arises is why this happened at age 8. What was going on in her life at that point that led Force 2 to grow so strong as to be able to thoroughly counter Force 1? Perhaps we shall never know. . . .

We do know, however, that "a short time before the attack of nervous asthma in her eighth year" (SE VII, p. 103), she twisted her right foot when she slipped on a step while going down a flight of stairs. Her foot had become swollen and had to be bandaged, and she had had to lie in bed for a few weeks.[11] Had Ida been thinking of something in particular at the moment she slipped (fantasizing about her father, for example, or some other love interest) instead of watching where she was going? Did she come to think of the twisted foot as a punishment for her fantasies? Having to lie in bed for a few weeks would, presumably, have been quite burdensome for a "wild child," and this could possibly have been the "incubation period" leading to her crucial turning point from wild to well-behaved.

Again, all of this remains highly speculative. What is less so is that her foot injury led to no psychosomatic symptoms until around the age of 17 when, after an appendicitis-like attack (to which we will turn momentarily), she began dragging her right foot for no apparent reason (SE VII, p. 101). We also happen to know from Felix Deutsch that this foot dragging continued on into her middle adulthood, suggesting that if Freud had been right about this being related to the thought of having made a "false step" (SE VII, p. 103) or "misstep" in life by not having given in to Herr K's advances (or having wished that she had?), Freud telling her this had obviously been insufficient to alleviate the symptom. Here Freud would have done well to heed his own earlier rule of thumb to regard "as incomplete any story that brought about no improvement" (SE II, p. 79) and his later rule of thumb not to interpret until the analysand was but "one short step" (not "misstep") away from arriving at the same conclusion.

If Ida had in fact come to view her slipping on the stairs at age 8 as punishment for her sexual fantasies (whether accompanied by masturbation or not), perhaps something similar was involved at age 17 when she began dragging her right foot after her appendicitis-like attack. Recall that the attack purportedly occurred nine months after Herr K's lakeside proposal, making it suggestive of the labor pains of childbirth (pp. 102–103), which would imply a wish to be pregnant or have a child—we need not jump immediately to the conclusion that it reflected a wish to have had sex with Herr K. She may then have reproached herself for having had such an (unconscious) wish, as though that were only for other, older women—her mother and Frau K—as though the joys of motherhood were not for her.

I have left out of my account of Ida's symptoms some of the more isolated ones, owing to lack of detailed information: gastric pains (supposedly via identification with a female cousin who masturbated; SE VII, p. 38) and migraine headaches on one side of her head starting at age 12, then becoming less frequent, and ending at age 16 (p. 22). Had the analysis proceeded further, we might have discovered a similar wish and counterwish—Force 1 and Force 2—structure in them, but then again we might have discovered something else altogether.

APPENDIX V

Sample Correspondences Between Psychoanalytic and *DSM-5* Diagnoses

(*Nota bene*: not *everyone* currently diagnosed with these *DSM-5* disorders falls neatly into the corresponding psychoanalytic structures, and many *DSM-5* disorders can come under more than one psychoanalytic structure.)

Psychoanalytic	***DSM-5***
AUTISM[1]	Autism spectrum disorder (now includes autistic disorder and many earlier diagnoses, e.g., early infantile autism, childhood autism, Kanner's autism, high-functioning autism, atypical autism, pervasive developmental disorder, and childhood disintegrative disorder)
NEUROSIS	
Obsession	Tic disorders and Tourette's (now misleadingly included under motor disorders)
	Obsessive-compulsive disorder
	Obsessive-compulsive personality disorder
	Autism spectrum disorder (especially what used to be termed Asperger's)

Psychoanalytic	***DSM-5***
	Attention-deficit/hyperactivity disorder
	Avoidant personality disorder
Hysteria	Eating disorders (includes anorexia nervosa and bulimia nervosa)
	Somatic symptom and related disorders (includes conversion disorder)
	Histrionic personality disorder
	Dependent personality disorder
	Borderline personality disorder
	Dissociative identity disorder
	Panic disorder
	Social anxiety disorder (social phobia)
	Separation anxiety disorder
	Generalized anxiety disorder
	Major depressive disorder
Phobia	Anxiety disorders (including specific phobia and agoraphobia)
PERVERSION	Paraphilic disorders (including voyeuristic, exhibitionistic, frotteuristic, sexual masochism, sexual sadism, pedophilic, fetishistic, and transvestic disorders)
PSYCHOSIS	Brief psychotic disorder
	Delusional disorder
	Paranoid personality disorder
	Schizophrenia
	Schizoaffective disorder
	Délire à deux (no longer in the *DSM*, but referred to in earlier versions as shared psychotic disorder)
	Narcissistic personality disorder
	Bipolar and related disorders (formerly manic-depression)

Notes

Introduction

1. SE XIV, p. 16.

2. The expression "analysis of resistances" is used by Richard Sterba (1934, p. 117). Freud discusses myriad ways of overcoming resistances in SE II (see, especially, pp. 271 and 282–283). He critiques the attempt to simply "point out his resistance to the patient," indicating that "no change sets in; indeed, the resistance becomes all the stronger"; what we need to do, he suggests, is "discover the repressed urges that are feeding the resistance" (SE XII, p. 155).

3. See Anna Freud, 1936/1966; Anna Freud and Joseph Sandler, 1985.

4. See SE II, pp. 301–305, and SE VII, pp. 115–120. He does go on to say in the latter (the case of Dora) that "transference, which seems ordained to be the greatest obstacle to psychoanalysis, becomes its most powerful ally, if its presence can be detected each time and explained to the patient" (SE VII, p. 117). Yet his admission a few lines later—"I did not succeed in mastering the transference in time" (p. 118)—clearly indicates to what degree he found transference to be an obstacle, at least in that case. And his further admissions on the following pages (and especially in the footnote on page 120 regarding the "homosexual current" he had missed) suggest that transference is *always* an obstacle unless the analyst is smart enough, clairvoyant enough, and sensitive enough to guess what is going on at every single instant, which is patently impossible.

5. As Lacan (Seminar II) puts it, "Transference is both an obstacle to remembering and the rendering present of the closing up of the unconscious, which results from the failure to hit the spot at just the right moment" (p. 145); in other words, transference arises at the very moment at which the analysand finds himself unable to approach (with or without the analyst's assistance) the pathogenic nucleus of a symptom any more closely—unable to "hit the spot."

6. Russell Jacoby (1975) said something similar about 40 years ago.

7. Some might argue that the obstacle, when focused on, becomes its own way to the goal. Discussing the obstacle may, in certain cases, allow the patient to move past it toward the goal (exploring what seems so scary to the patient about discussing violent fantasies may, for example, allow the patient to then talk about those fantasies); but the focus on obstacles seems to have led many analysts to become more interested in the so-called defenses than in what they defend.

8. Lacan said this in Seminar XVI, p. 242.

9. Freud did too: He wrote to Fritz Wittels, "It seems to me that the public has no [reason to] concern [itself] with my personality, and can learn nothing from an account of it," and purportedly told Joseph Wortis, "People should interest themselves in psychoanalysis, not in me"; Wittels, 1924/1971, pp. 11–12; Wortis, 1954, p. 121.

10. Freud mentions his father's story in SE IV (p. 197). Here are a few examples of the glories of "psychobiography": Bruno Bettelheim (1990, pp. 9–10) suggests that the Emperor Franz Joseph's wife, Elizabeth, was one of the first nutty royal figures in Europe, inspiring Freud to think about madness and hysteria, whereas there had clearly been plenty of them before. Bettelheim tries to use the royal family as a model for Freud's theory of Oedipal conflict, despite the fact that Oedipal struggles between fathers, sons, uncles, and nephews, and so on were rife in many European courts for millennia and date back to our earliest texts (e.g., the Old Testament).

Bettelheim's further suggestion (1990, p. 12) that the fact that the emperor of Austria was not master in his own house led Freud to come up with the idea of the ego not being master in its own house is extremely far-fetched, since it has been true of a great many administrations throughout history (for just one example, consider certain *maires du palais* ["stewards of the king's house"] in the Merovingian period in France, in the seventh and eighth centuries, who often grew more powerful than their sovereigns), and therefore *one would have to explain why other thinkers did not come up with such an idea.* To try to find the source of all of someone's ideas in that person's life and times is quite foolhardy. We should instead ask the opposite question: *Given all the historical precedents, how come no one came up with this idea before?!*

11. James Strachey provides a great deal of useful material on Freud's intellectual development in his editor's introductions to each of Freud's works in the *Standard Edition* (SE I–XXIV).

12. For a brief discussion of this topic, see Appendix II.

13. Lear suggests that through analysis, analysands can become aware of all of their thoughts, and claims that "as analysands become increasingly aware of the flow of their self-conscious minds, they become increasingly able to change their minds directly through their own self-conscious activity" (p. xvi); this appeal to what the ego psychologists called the *observing ego* to bring about genuine change strikes me as a philosophical pipe dream (see my discussions of this in Fink, 2007, 2014a, 2014b).

14. See Low, 1935, p. 4.

15. See SE IV, p. 198, where he says, "The deeper one carries the analysis of a dream, the more often one comes upon the track of experiences in childhood which have played a part among the sources of that dream's latent content." "More often" implies "not always," and Freud discusses many dreams that are never traced back to childhood sources (see, for example, SE IV, pp. 248–250, and SE V, p. 510) and many dreams that are never interpreted as having anything to do with sexuality (see SE IV, pp. 127–130). Regarding sexuality, he says, "The majority of the dreams of adults deal with sexual material" (note, however, that he says little of sexual matters when he interprets his own dreams for us!) since "no other drive has been subjected since childhood to so much suppression as the sexual drive . . . ; from no other drive are so many and such powerful unconscious wishes left over, ready to produce dreams in a state of sleep"; nevertheless, "we should also, of course, avoid the exaggeration of attributing exclusive importance to them" (SE V, p. 396). He continues on the next page, in a passage added in 1919, "The assertion that all dreams require a sexual interpretation, against which critics rage so incessantly, occurs nowhere in my *Interpretation of Dreams*" (p. 397).

16. Those who believe in ESP might think there is more to intuition than

what I have said here; but they might find more profitable ways to employ their extrasensory powers than in the consulting room with patients!

17. Even if I do take Bruno Bettelheim's (1982) and Lacan's various critiques of the Strachey translations to heart.

Chapter 1: Tracing a Symptom Back to Its Origin

1. On missing out on an opportunity and "neglected opportunities," see SE IV, pp. 204 and 207. Note that such "cathartic experiences" do not alter anything fundamental within us, meaning that they must be repeated periodically; in other words, the *source* of the aggression or longing that is momentarily released through catharsis remains unchanged. Catharsis thus cannot stop new symptoms from forming (SE II, p. 261) because it is "a symptomatic therapy"—that is, a therapy that aims solely at symptom reduction (p. 264).

2. The German term *Verdrängung* is found in *Psychologie als Wissenschaft* by the early 19th-century psychologist J. F. Herbart (1824), a work known to some of Freud's teachers.

3. They seem to feel that there is a fundamental "incompatibility between the single idea that is to be repressed [the insult] and the dominant mass of ideas constituting the ego," that is, their overall sense of themselves (SE II, p. 116).

4. One sometimes hears the variant *Il n'y a que la vérité qui fache*—which one might render literally as "The truth alone can make you angry" or figuratively as "Nothing can piss you off quite like the truth can."

5. As Lacan (*Écrits*, pp. 24–25) says, "Like the man who withdrew to an island to forget—to forget what? he forgot—so the Minister, by not making use of the letter, comes to forget it. This is expressed by the persistence of his conduct. But the letter, no more than the neurotic's unconscious, does not forget him."

6. Lacan suggests in Seminar VII that guilt arises when we give up on our own desire (p. 319). He often indicates that it was a mistake to have translated Freud's term *Versagung* as "frustration," for it means *renunciation*, a kind of self-renunciation, a giving up on one's own wishes or desires (see, for example, *Écrits*, p. 385). Lacan argues that although post-Freudians believed they were following Freud in trying to relieve the patient's "frustration," they completely misunderstood what Freud was getting at, which was the moment at which people give up on or set aside what they want to say or do, thereby renouncing their own desire. (They do so for a variety of reasons.) For more on this point, see further on in this chapter and Chapter 5.

7. One might even liken isolation to the *partitioning* of a hard drive, as we shall see a bit further on.

8. See also SE I (p. 153 and elsewhere) for a description of the unconscious as a "second state of consciousness."

9. Note that Freud himself likens sets of memories to "files" (like the kind people keep in file cabinets or file drawers) in *Studies on Hysteria* (SE II, p. 289)—and even refers to "files of memories" (p. 295)—although I stumbled upon this long after coming up with the computing analogy. Breuer likens the psyche to an electrical distribution system (pp. 193–195, 203–204, and 207) and "abnormal facilitations" in it to short circuits (p. 203).

10. Note that what is repressed often disappears so thoroughly or becomes so completely unrecognizable that consciousness (or the ego) refuses to believe it even exists; we often consciously believe that we know all about ourselves and

deny that there are thoughts, memories, and wishes that inhabit us of which we are not aware. But the repressed nevertheless exerts pressure to gain expression, leading to the "return of the repressed" in the mind, body, or both.

Oneiromancers of bygone days tried to open up dream files, so to speak, but using their approach is like opening a file with one software program when it was created with another (e.g., opening a PDF file in Microsoft Word): All one may see is an incomprehensible jumble of symbols, and one can make of them whatever one wants.

11. Except perhaps in children in whom we believe there may be no repression whatsoever and who thus may be in danger of psychosis.

12. Freud (SE I) says,

> I myself have had not a few happy results from hypnotic treatment; but I do not venture to undertake some cures of the kind I witnessed under Liébeault and Bernheim in Nancy [France]. I know, too, that a good part of this success is due to the "suggestive atmosphere" which surrounds their clinic, to the milieu, and to the mood of the patients; (p. 100)

and,

> As soon as I tried to practice this art on my own patients, I discovered that *my* powers at least were subject to severe limits, and that if somnambulism [here I believe he simply means the kind of deep hypnosis seen in those who sleepwalk] were not brought about in the patient at the first three attempts, I had no means of inducing it. The percentage of cases amenable to somnambulism was very much lower in my experience than what Bernheim reported. (p. 108)

13. In the case of Frau Emmy von N., Freud (SE II) says that

> we see that even in a somnambulistic state she did not have access to the whole extent of her knowledge. Even then there was an actual and a potential consciousness. It used often to happen that when I asked her during her somnambulism, where this or that phenomenon was derived from, she would wrinkle her forehead, and after a pause would answer in a deprecatory tone: "I don't know." On such occasions I made it my practice to say, "Think a moment and it will come to mind directly"; and after a short reflection she would be able to give me the desired information. But it sometimes happened that nothing came to her mind and that I was obliged to leave her with the task of remembering it by the next day; and this never failed to occur. (p. 98)

14. On these different "treatment modalities," and on suggestion more generally (especially insofar as it differs from interpretation), see Appendix II.

15. Freud himself likened the isolated memory not to a virus but to "a 'provoking' crystal," something that leads other molecules in a solution to crystalize (SE II, pp. 123 and 264).

16. One of my patients once suddenly recalled a humiliating and embarrassing scene he had "forgotten" about for some 30 years; in his early teens, he had been taking a shower and at one point suddenly realized that his mother had

come into the bathroom and was watching him in the shower. He was so surprised and disconcerted that he felt unable to say anything to her, and promptly tried to simply forget the whole matter. This led him to forget a great many other related events as well.

In other instances, when one traumatic incident is repressed, another incident or scene—perhaps connected to the repressed one in time or place—is remembered with great intensity, even though it is more or less psychologically indifferent, not charged with energy or libido. Freud refers to such intensely remembered diversions as "screen memories" (see, especially, SE VI, pp. 43–52).

17. A "splitting of consciousness" can be theorized to occur in all of us who can be understood as neurotic as opposed to psychotic, that is, for I would argue, following Lacan, that if there is an unconscious in psychosis, it is quite different from and operates otherwise than the unconscious we are familiar with in neurosis (see Fink, 2007, Chapter 10).

18. With one of my analysands who was reluctant to say whatever came to his mind, I was led to say, "To *not* say the things you think you shouldn't be thinking ensures that you'll keep thinking them." I also opined that all his notions about what was "appropriate" and what wasn't "would not get [him] anywhere in psychoanalysis." This shocked him and eventually led to less self-censorship on his part.

19. One of my analysands told me she had surprised herself in the previous session when she had said that although she had felt very confident about her intelligence growing up, having been convinced by her father that she was like him and therefore especially bright, now she felt far less confident about it, despite having recently accomplished a great deal on her own (e.g., having been promoted to the highest possible rank in her profession). This constituted something of an enigma for her, suggesting the emergence of (or at least the alighting upon) something unconscious.

Note that Freud (SE X, p. 196) at one point talks about the feeling "of having always known" something as related to a form of repression, the form characteristic of obsession in which thought and affect have become dissociated, the thought thereby seeming devoid of significance as it brings no affective charge with it.

20. See Freud's somewhat detailed discussion of the distinction between latency and the unconscious in his 1912 "Note on the Unconscious in Psychoanalysis" (SE XII, pp. 260–266). He later confuses things somewhat when he talks about aspects of the ego and superego as being unconscious, when more strictly speaking he means that those aspects function outside of consciousness—they are, in other words, nonconscious or preconscious, which does not mean that they are repressed (SE XXII, pp. 69–72).

21. See, especially, SE III, pp. 304–309, and SE VI, pp. 45–52. On the indestructibility of such inscriptions, see, for example, SE V, p. 553 n.

22. The story Emmy von N. told Freud on that occasion turned out to be "incomplete" (SE II, p. 79), as stories told by patients usually are (whether they are told under hypnosis or not), and a great many more details needed to be told about that particular occasion (as well as about other occasions that had led to the reinforcement of the symptom) in order for the tic to disappear more enduringly. The fact that she fell ill again some years later is no doubt due to the fact that the conflicting forces that gave rise to it could never be worked through by the use of the "cathartic procedure" alone, without the assistance of interpretation (p. 75 n).

23. Breuer tells us that "a number of extremely obstinate whims were similarly removed after she had described the experiences that had given rise to them. . . . The hysterical phenomena disappeared as soon as the event that had given rise to them was reproduced [i.e., recounted in some detail] while she was under hypnosis" (SE II, p. 35).

24. "The only thing one can be guilty of," says Lacan, "is giving up on [or giving ground when it comes to] one's desire" (Seminar VII, p. 319).

25. For other people—and this may be true for many of the Amish among whom renunciation is considered to be a virtue—allowing another's will to prevail over one's own may be difficult but in the end highly satisfying. In Seminar VIII, Lacan comments that "_Versagung_ implies not making good on a promise, on a promise for which one has already given up everything" (p. 300); this promise may be a promise one has made to oneself. On renounced wishes, see SE IV, pp. 147–151.

26. Breuer mentions that for quite some time she would never eat bread, but never tells us why (SE II, pp. 27, 31).

27. In the case of Emmy von N., Freud tells us that the patient promised to stop being frightened by certain things "because you asked me to" (SE II, p. 72); and when he asked her to drink water and eat her dessert, she replied, "I'll do it because you asked me to" (p. 81); she was even sorry to have told Breuer that she was not yet completely well after two weeks of intensive treatment with Freud, feeling she had betrayed Freud (p. 65). Making certain gains out of love and affection for one's doctor was especially common when hypnosis and suggestion were used, since these techniques did not resolve the longstanding conflicting forces in the patient's life but merely identified painful memories, employed the cathartic method to discharge the affect attached to them, and (as Freud did in the case of Emmy von N.) instructed the patient not to bring those memories to mind ever again, even though they clearly persisted somewhere in the patient's memory. (On one occasion, Freud asked Emmy von N. where her stammer came from and she replied that she did not know, adding "Because I'm not allowed to," Freud himself having told her not to remember the troubling memories that had given rise to her stammer [p. 61].)

Freud indicates the role of (transference) love in another case: "A woman patient, whom I had repeatedly helped out of neurotic states by hypnosis, suddenly, during the treatment of an especially obstinate situation, threw her arms around my neck" (SE XVI, p. 450; see also SE XX, p. 27).

28. This version of the story comes from Freud and Ernest Jones (see Jones, 1953, pp. 222–226) and is repeated by Lacan; but some parts of it are contested by Breuer's biographer Albrecht Hirschmüller (1978/1989). Hirschmüller admits, however, that Jones had access to letters that he himself never saw, and his arguments strike me as generally quite weak. The only points he makes of relevance here that I find convincing are (a) that, whereas Jones claims that the result of the sudden second honeymoon in Venice that Breuer took his wife on as soon as he put an end to Anna O's treatment was the conception of Breuer's youngest daughter, Dora, she was actually born on March 11, 1882, thus three months *before* Anna O's treatment ended (she thus could not have been the product of the purported "second honeymoon"); and (b) that Dora committed suicide not in New York, as Jones (1953, p. 225) claims, but just before the arrival of the Gestapo in Vienna (Hirschmüller, 1978/1989, pp. 337–338 n. 194).

The fact that Breuer referred Pappenheim to Robert Binswanger (Ludwig's son) after breaking off the treatment is confirmed in Breuer's letters to Robert Binswanger (Hirschmüller, 1978/1989, pp. 293–296). Freud's letter of June 2, 1932, to Stefan Zweig asserts that Breuer told Freud that when Bertha's parents called him urgently back to her sickbed the day he broke off the treatment, he "found her confused and writhing in abdominal cramps. Asked what was wrong with her, she replied: 'Now Dr. B.'s child is coming!'" (E. L. Freud, 1960, letter 265, pp. 412–413). Breuer apparently did not confess to Freud that Bertha was having an hysterical pregnancy, but Freud put two and two together; he claims in the same letter that his deduction was confirmed by Breuer at a later date through his youngest daughter.

In what is perhaps the most tendentious take on the case of Anna O in print, Mikkel Borch-Jacobsen (1996) argues that the entire case is a sham and that Freud made up stories about it, sometimes getting Breuer to do so as well. Borch-Jacobsen argues the following: Pappenheim was not really ill—it was sheer simulation, encouraged by Breuer (he fails to explain why her family would have called in a well-known nerve specialist for "a lingering cough," the only symptom he acknowledges at the outset, apart from her suffocating "family atmosphere"; pp. 81, 83); there were no amorous, much less erotic, feelings between Breuer and Pappenheim (indeed, Borch-Jacobsen seems to think there never are between therapists and patients, making one wonder how he would account for the overwhelming evidence of affairs between them); there was no hysterical pregnancy and no trip to Venice (p. 32); Pappenheim did not remember events from the year before with remarkable accuracy; Pappenheim was in no way helped by her work with Breuer; there is no such thing as the unconscious or transference; the list goes on and on. His evidence is often sketchy, including portions of private letters shown to him by the notoriously unreliable historian Elisabeth Roudinesco and indirectly by Jeffrey Masson and Peter J. Swales. He assumes that Breuer would normally have written in his report to Binswanger all the same things—many of which Breuer believed to be crazy at the time—he said when discussing the case at great length with Freud, which any clinician referring a patient to another practitioner would find implausible, to say the least. And complex problems of the will (related to "faking," "simulation," and being dimly aware of what one is doing) are glossed over by him as though all mental illness were a matter of mere Sartrian bad faith.

Even if Borch-Jacobsen's facts were correct—and they would be very difficult to substantiate—his conclusions do not follow, for *psychoanalytic concepts like transference and the unconscious, and the benefits of talking, do not, in any way, collapse if one particular case was not what it was made out to be.* Even if Freud had been the unscrupulous confabulator and fabricator Borch-Jacobsen makes him out to be, the whole profession is not thereby damned, unless the sins of the father of psychoanalysis must inexorably be visited (by Borch-Jacobsen) upon the children of psychoanalysis until the seventh generation. The vast majority of my patients tell me how much they feel they have benefited from the treatment (having more energy, being less plagued by fantasies they find repulsive, being able to stand up for themselves, finally feeling they have a voice of their own, etc.), and one patient even offhandedly reported that his wife was very much in favor of his analysis, saying that it had "worked wonders" for their marriage.

29. In SE IV, p. 337, he refers to "conflict of will."

30. Freud contrasts this with what we see in obsession: symptoms residing

primarily in the mind, instead of crossing over into the body (SE III, p. 52; SE XVI, p. 258). Freud's notion of conversion lives on in the *DSM-5*'s so-called conversion disorder (see Appendix V).

31. A potentially traumatizing event like a car crash may also have a far greater or different psychological impact on someone who is three or four and whose psychical structure is still developing than on a teenager or adult with a more or less set psychical structure.

32. Freud does sometimes speak in topological terms like surface and depth (topology being, briefly stated, the study of geometric properties and spatial relations), especially when he uses his archeological metaphor for the mind— "This procedure was one of clearing away the pathogenic psychical material layer by layer, and we liked to compare it with the technique of excavating a buried city" (SE II, p. 139; see also SE VII, p. 12, and SE XXIII, p. 259)—but the term "depth psychology" is above all associated with Carl Jung. Breuer makes it clear that talking about the conscious versus the "subconscious" (a term rarely used by Freud, and later rejected outright by him; SE XX, pp. 197–198) involves employing a spatial metaphor—in other words, a kind of analogical thinking (p. 228). Freud primarily talks about relative distance from or proximity to "the pathogenic nucleus" or M1 (SE II, p. 289), but occasionally lapses into such figures of speech as "deeper strata" (p. 299).

33. Freud often uses the French term *double conscience*; see, for example, SE XI, p. 19.

34. For a concise, informative account of the superego, see SE XXII (pp. 57–68). Freud indicates the degree to which the divisions between such theoretical "entities" as the id, ego, and superego are provisional and somewhat fluid, and "subject to great variations in different individuals," on p. 79.

35. Freud later wrote that a neurotic must "employ a great deal of his available energy to keep his libido repressed and to ward off its assaults" (SE XVI, p. 454), which may result in "an extraordinary impoverishment of the subject as regards the mental energy available to him and in paralyzing him for all the important tasks of life" (p. 358).

36. Readers interested in knowing what became of Anna O (her life as a social worker, writer, feminist, and translator, for example) can find a synopsis of the most recent information on her life at https://en.wikipedia.org/wiki/Bertha_Pappenheim.

37. Breuer tells us that Anna O herself set the date for the last day of treatment so that it would coincide with "the anniversary of the day on which she was moved into the country" from her home in Vienna a year earlier (SE II, p. 40). I am unsure how this should be understood, given that others tell us that Breuer was the one who decided to break off the treatment.

38. Consider, too, the words from "Goosey Goosey Gander": "There I met an old man / Who wouldn't say his prayers, / So I took him by his left leg / And threw him down the stairs."

39. Lacan refers to what Freud called "ignorance or deliberate overlooking" (SE II, p. 68 n) and "not wanting to know" (p. 270) as *méconnaissance*, a kind of active or deliberate misrecognition (cf. Freud's comment that "Hysterics do not know what they do not *want* to know"; SE III, p. 296). Note that such trancelike states are often experienced by severely traumatized children.

40. Freud obviously heard many similar arguments in his own time, mentioning clinicians who believed hysterics made "chance connections" between

thoughts (SE II, p. 294). James Strachey, the main translator of Freud's work, made up the odd-sounding term *parapraxis* (whose Latin roots perhaps makes it sound more medical or scientific, just like *cathexis*) to purportedly render into English Freud's common, everyday German term *Fehlleistung* (literally "faulty act" or "faulty function"), less obscure translations of which include mistake, botch-up, mess-up, slipup, slip, and bungled action (see SE VI, p. xii; SE XV, p. 25 n.).

41. In 1895, Freud already indicated that he never really encountered patients (like Anna O) in whom such altered states arose spontaneously (SE II, pp. 285–286). And in 1905, he claimed to set little stock in the importance of hypnoid states, attributing his earlier concern with them to Breuer's influence (SE VII, p. 27 n. 1).

42. Events can, of course, also be remembered bodily and/or sensorially (whether through vision, sound, feel, or smell).

43. Consider the connection between the facial neuralgia of one of Freud's early patients (Frau Cäcilie M.) and what she relayed to him when he asked her about a traumatic scene (SE II):

> The patient saw herself back in a period of great mental irritability towards her husband. She described a conversation she had had with him and a remark of his which she had felt as a bitter insult. Suddenly she put her hand to her cheek, gave a loud cry of pain and said: "It was like a slap in the face." With this her pain and her attack were both at an end. (p. 178).

Lacan provides an example of something that occurred in a patient's childhood that became traumatic later when the boy learned something about its significance. His father was accused of being a thief, and he later learned that, according to the laws of the land governed by the Koran where he lived, the stipulated punishment was that his hand be cut off, a punishment he could not wrap his mind around. This gave rise in the son to "writer's cramp," through identification with his father; in other words, it was as if the son's hand had been cut off (Seminar II, pp. 129–130).

44. Her feelings of coldness went away after she recounted the scene to me, and another symptom—tightness or pain in the chest—went away when she added another detail to the scene she had witnessed: From the angle from which she observed the scene, it looked as if her "father had his knee on her [mother's] torso." These bodily sensations were, in her case, examples of repeating rather than remembering, living something out in the present, rather than recalling what had happened in the past (see SE XVIII, pp. 18–20).

45. At that point it was a product of the analysis itself, "joining in the conversation" (SE II, p. 296) between the woman and myself and bringing to light an essential element of her history that she had never before recalled.

46. Indeed, I have heard several young analysts express that they feel they benefitted little from their training analyses, leading them to have little confidence in their ability to help others.

Chapter 2: The Unconscious Is the Exact Opposite of the Conscious

1. Chaucer's retraction is the final section of *The Canterbury Tales* in which Chaucer asks for forgiveness for the vulgar and unworthy parts of this and other of his previous works, and seeks absolution for his sins.

2. As Freud puts it, "It is as though the patient had said [in response to a query who the woman in his dream was]: 'It's true that my mother came into my mind as I thought of this person, but I don't feel inclined to let the association count'" (SE XIX, p. 235).

3. Regarding judgment, he relies on the work of the philosopher Franz Brentano.

4. Even if a one-horned deer with a genetic anomaly was born in an Italian nature preserve in 2008.

5. See, for example, SE V, p. 613, SE XVI, p. 368.

6. Consider the following statement made by a rebellious winemaker in Napa Valley, Raj Parr, who has adopted methods quite different from those of his neighboring winemakers (primarily, it seems, in order to gain notoriety): "It's not a fight to take over the wine world" (Schoenfeld, 2015). But then, who had ever suggested that it was?

People often get lost in their negative formulations, especially when they include double or triple negatives, like "It's not that I don't think he's an idiot." Analysts must pay close attention to their grammar, for they often end up saying the exact opposite of what they consciously meant to say.

7. According to Freud, negation is "an *Aufhebung* of the repression" (see SE XIX, p. 236, where it is translated as "a lifting of the repression"): I negate the thought that it is my cousin in the dream, and yet I bring my cousin up in the discussion. I thereby conserve, suppress, and negate the thought of my cousin simultaneously.

8. Insofar as most patients are subject to repression and thus cannot remember certain things (or cannot remember what affect was associated with them), projection is an indispensable avenue to encouraging certain thoughts and feelings to come out in the open in analysis. When, however, the analyst is self-disclosing, the analyst becomes less of a "mirror" to project onto (as Freud recommends he or she be: "The analyst should be opaque to his patients and, like a mirror, show them nothing but what is shown to him"; SE XII, p. 118); analysands cannot as easily project certain thoughts and feelings of their own onto a person they actually know a fair amount about as onto a blank screen. The less they know about us, the more they can project.

9. In the South in the United States, it is apparently socially acceptable to say highly disobliging things about people, as long as one adds, "Bless his (or her) heart" just before or after them; for example, "He is dumb as a rock, bless his heart," or "Bless her heart, I just can't stand her."

10. Note that the "in" in "innocuous" is a kind of negative, serving to negate "nocuousness" or noxiousness.

11. One of my analysands had his mother visiting him for a week, and he told me that during her visit he "made a date" (this involved pretending he had one that he did not in fact have); he then lapsed into silence. "What was going through your mind?" I asked. "I don't know why, but the words 'to make her feel jealous' almost came out of my mouth." He was reluctant to speak them, since prior to that moment he had had no idea that he might have wanted to make his mother jealous, and the words thus made no sense to him.

But it is precisely with things that make no sense, and that the analysand is likely to characterize as stupid, irrelevant, or out of the blue, that we do analysis. We must be vigilantly on the lookout for such things, for it is the analysand's natural tendency to *not* bring them to speech since he does not understand them. Most neurotics have considerable self-censoring capacities and filter out a large number of things that come to mind that they consider ridiculous, unimportant, or downright stupid.

We need not view this as bad faith or resistance on the analysand's part: Social conventions in polite society dictate a certain amount of self-censorship, and it is up to us to break the analysand of the ingrained habit of not saying a vast number of the things that cross his mind. It is not enough to tell the analysand once or twice to try to say everything that occurs to him, and content ourselves that he will free-associate for the next five to ten years without any further prompting on our part. Free association is one of the hardest tasks imaginable, and it is our job to help the analysand associate as freely as possible. We do so by, for example, inquiring into what is going through his mind when he lapses into silence; picking up on bits of words or phrases that he clips as he articulates them and substitutes other words or expressions for them (as when he says he had "an arg— a discussion" with his partner, censoring the word "argument" even as it left his lips); and noting even brief pauses when he responds to questions, indicating that he is not telling us the first thing that popped into his mind. When we fail to help him free-associate, we ourselves are, in Lacan's view, resisting the therapeutic process.

12. See Austin (1962) and Searle (1969).

13. There are, of course, many other reasons why analysands are late for their sessions.

14. This does not mean that a formulation that contains any such words necessarily covers over a wish. Having been invited to a party you do not want to go to, you might, for example, respond, "I'm afraid I will be out of town at that time," a formulation that does not actually express fear. On the relation between worry and wishes, see, for example, SE IV, pp. 266–267.

15. For a Derridean account of repression in relation to translation, see Weber, 1982 (pp. 46–48). Derridean readings of many other aspects of Freudian theory can be found in the same book.

16. On so-called switch words, verbal bridges, or associative bridges, see also SE VI, pp. 49, 109, and 274; SE VII, pp. 65 n, 82, and 90; and SE X, p. 213.

17. Freud does, however, occasionally talk about an unconscious sense of guilt. Note that we already encountered displacement at least twice in our discussion of Anna O: the displacement (or transference) of her affection for her father onto Breuer, and her possible displacement of horror or disgust from her lady companion or the dog (that drank out of that lady's glass) to water. We can even see possible instances of displacement in the animal kingdom, as, for example, when two or more dogs begin barking furiously when a jogger or cyclist goes by their fenced-in yard and, since they cannot attack the passerby, begin to fight with each other instead. For a fine discussion of the separation between thought and affect, see Freud's 1894 paper entitled "The Neuropsychoses of Defense" (SE III, pp. 45–58).

18. This point seems to have so rarely been assimilated—even by authors like Quinodoz (2005) who claim that Freud accepted the notion of "unconscious feelings" later in his work—that I will cite the fuller (and later) passages in which Freud spells it out:

> In the first place, it may happen that an affective or emotional impulse is perceived but misconstrued. Owing to the repression of its proper representative it has been forced to become connected with another idea,

and is now regarded by consciousness as the manifestation of that idea. If we restore the true connection, we call the original affective impulse an "unconscious" one. Yet its affect was never unconscious; all that had happened was that its idea had undergone repression. In general, the use of the terms "unconscious affect" and "unconscious emotion" has reference to the vicissitudes undergone, in consequence of repression, by the quantitative factor in the instinctual impulse. We know that three such vicissitudes are possible: either the affect remains, wholly or in part, as it is; or it is transformed into a qualitatively different quota of affect, above all into anxiety; or it is suppressed, i.e., it is prevented from developing at all. (These possibilities may perhaps be studied even more easily in the dreamwork than in neuroses.) We know, too, that to suppress the development of affect is the true aim of repression and that its work is incomplete if this aim is not achieved. In every instance where repression has succeeded in inhibiting the development of affects, we term those affects (which we restore when we undo the work of repression) "unconscious." Thus it cannot be denied that the use of the terms in question is consistent; but in comparison with unconscious ideas there is the important difference that unconscious ideas continue to exist after repression as actual structures in the system Ucs. [i.e., the unconscious as a system], whereas all that corresponds in that system to unconscious affects is a potential beginning which is prevented from developing. Strictly speaking, then, and although no fault can be found with the linguistic usage, there are no unconscious affects as there are unconscious ideas. ("The Unconscious," SE XIV, pp. 177–178; see also p. 165 n)

It remains true, therefore, that sensations and feelings, too, only become conscious through reaching the system Pcpt. [i.e., the perceptual system]; if the way forward is barred, they do not come into being as sensations, although the "something" that corresponds to them in the course of excitation is the same as if they did. We then come to speak, in a condensed and not entirely correct manner, of "unconscious feelings," keeping up an analogy with unconscious ideas which is not altogether justifiable. (*The Ego and the Id*, 1923, SE XIX, pp. 22–23)

Patients do not easily believe us when we tell them about the unconscious sense of guilt. They know only too well by what torments—the pangs of conscience—a conscious sense of guilt, or a consciousness of guilt, expresses itself, and they therefore cannot admit that they could harbor exactly analogous impulses in themselves without being in the least aware of them. We may, I think, to some extent meet their objection if we give up the term "unconscious sense of guilt," which is in any case psychologically incorrect, and speak instead of a "need for punishment," which covers the observed state of affairs just as aptly. ("The Economic Problem of Masochism," 1924, SE XIX, p. 166)

It is ideas that are subjected to repression and that may be distorted to the point of being unrecognizable; but their quota of affect is regularly transformed into anxiety—and this is so regardless of the nature of the affect, whether it is aggressiveness or love. (*New Introductory Lectures on Psychoanalysis*, 1933, SE XXII, p. 83)

19. He says something quite similar about the Rat Man's feeling that he is guilty of being a criminal: The affect is justified, but the ostensible reason for it (having fallen asleep for an hour, after watching over his father on his deathbed, and his father having died during that exact time) is not the true reason—it has been displaced (SE X, pp. 174–176).

Chapter 3: Dreams

1. Lacanian institutes make no distinction between a personal analysis and a training analysis. On the enduring importance of dreams to analysands, see, for example, "La passe de B." (2005), Leray (2008), and Canedo (2006). Freud wrote, "The interpretation of dreams plays a large part in a psychoanalytic treatment, and in some cases it is over long periods the most important instrument of our work" (SE XVI, p. 456).

2. For more on this point, see the last section of the present chapter.

3. Consider the musician and composer Tartini (1692–1770), who purportedly dreamt he sold his soul to the devil, the devil then taking up a violin and playing a beautiful sonata, which Tartini promptly wrote down as much of as he could remember upon awakening; this gave rise to his famous *Trillo del Diavolo* (SE V, p. 613 n). Freud mentions that Goethe and Helmholtz indicated that much of their creative work came to them without any conscious "premeditation and as an almost ready-made whole," justifying Freud's expression "unconscious thinking," which is so paradoxical to many philosophers (p. 613); and Arthur Koestler (1964) recounts many other such instances of creative work while dreaming in his *Act of Creation*.

4. Freud wrote, "What has been called the dream we shall describe as 'the text of the dream' or 'the *manifest* dream'" (SE XXII, p. 9). Lacan sometimes refers to this text as the *"élaboration"* (elaboration or first revision); see *Écrits*, pp. 315 and 393.

5. To those who might object to what appears to be a theoretical assumption here on Freud's part, two points should be stressed: (a) If practicing on the basis of such a theoretical hypothesis leads to curative effects, it is worth making the hypothesis, even if it is not thereby proven to be absolutely true (recall that although empirical data can disprove theories, they can never conclusively prove them, for new data may eventually be unearthed that will disprove those theories); (b) Freud, in making this hypothesis, is being no more nor less theoretical than phenomenologists who might claim that a dream is a "phenomenon in itself" with no hidden cause. To refuse to accept that dreams (or fantasies or symptoms) are caused by something that is not immediately visible in them is to make just as big an assumption as to assume that they are.

6. In my experience, one of the most common slips of the tongue made by analysands when they discuss dreams is the substitution of the word *film* or *movie* for *dream* (e.g., "In the movie, I saw so-and-so"). Films and videos are also taking on increasing importance in analysands' associations to their dreams, given their ever greater accessibility in our culture and the fact that many an analysand now watches a visually rich movie almost every night before going to sleep. Some of the most common slips of the tongue made in general, in my experience, are the substitution of mother for wife, father for husband, and he, him, and his for she, her, and hers (and vice versa).

7. What is *suppressed* here is the urge to drink water; what is *repressed* here is the connection between the urge to drink and the wish that harm would come to her lady companion.

8. Certain humanistic psychologists and even cognitive-behavioral therapists sometimes talk about "clients" as "the experts" when it comes to their own experience, but often play the part of "masters of reality"—that is, of those who see "reality" better than their clients do—in actual clinical practice. It seems that many analysts and therapists are unable to practice what they preach . . .

9. Lacan suggests that we often wake up in the middle of a dream when it fulfills or satisfies our demand (as opposed to our desire), because the satisfaction of demand crushes desire and then we can no longer go on existing as desiring subjects: "It is, in any case, a fact of experience that when my dream begins to coincide with my demand (not with reality, as is improperly said, which can safeguard my sleep)—or with what proves to be equivalent to it here, the other's demand—I wake up" (*Écrits*, p. 624). In Seminar VIII, he says, "I awaken when the satisfaction of demand appears in my dream" (p. 377).

10. Bicyclists who participate in the grueling Race Across America (RAAM), who rarely take time to sleep, regularly end up hallucinating. Freud comments that "the wish to sleep . . . represents the conscious ego's contribution to dreaming" (p. 234), as do censorship and secondary revision.

11. This could, alternatively, be represented as follows:

Dreamwork:	Latent content	$\longrightarrow$	Manifest content
Psychoanalytic work:	Manifest content	$\longrightarrow$	Latent content

12. Freud comments that "if someone forgets a proper name that is usually familiar to him . . . it is plausible to suppose that he has something against the person who bears the name and prefers not to think of him" (SE XV, p. 52).

13. See, for example, SE IV, p. 105 n. 2. He even once admits, regarding an aspect of the dream of "Irma's injection," that "frankly, I had no desire to penetrate more deeply at this point" (p. 113). Lacan points out that, regarding this dream, Freud tells us quite a bit about his conscious (or preconscious) desires related to ambition and competition with his colleagues, but little if anything about his unconscious desires. Lacan highlights the horrific nature of what Freud sees when he looks down Irma's throat, referring to it as "the real" for Freud, a real no doubt associated with feminine sexuality (Seminar II, pp. 154 and 164).

14. Freud recommends, for example, that we ask the patient to relate the dream again right after the first telling, and that we then focus on the differences between the first and second telling; this is quite impractical when a dream is on the longish side, and may at times suggest to the patient that the analyst simply was not paying sufficient attention the first time through. He also recommends that we focus more on the indistinct and perhaps indifferent-seeming elements than on the very distinct and seemingly important ones (SE VII, p. 654). Thirdly, he suggests we emphasize the parts of a dream that are not recalled on a first telling but only come back to the patient later (SE VII, p. 100, n. 2) while associating to it, something that only happens occasionally, in my experience.

15. Even if in a psychoanalytic context an analysand may wonder about his own choice of that expression owing to the presence in it of the words *beat* and *bush*.

16. This case is discussed in detail in Fink, 2014b, Chapter 11.

17. Underscoring the degree to which sexuality so often plays a part in unconscious formations, she even mentioned that she had heard the word "tackle" used to characterize the male genitalia.

18. She may, of course, instead think of black eyes in the sense of "shiners," and go on to opine that she'd be happy if someone would punch her mother.

19. It is always possible that a further and possibly more profound interpretation will be found, since dreams are "overdetermined" (SE V, p. 523)—in other words, their construction generally involves the confluence of several different wishes.

20. Allegorical writing and poetry often employ the same forms of disguise, which, according to Lacan (*Écrits*, p. 425), go by the names of metaphor and metonymy in literature and rhetoric.

21. See Freud's comments on his wife's fears and wishes in his *Autodidasker* dream, SE IV, pp. 298–302, especially p. 301. See, too, his remark that the dreamer appears in each of the characters in a dream (SE IV, p. 267): We are in each of the characters in our dreams (pp. 322–323), just like a child is in each action figure or doll in a game it plays, and an author is in each character in a story he or she writes. It is, after all, the dreamer's/child's notion of what each character is like that makes the story, not the real people on whom the characters are based.

22. Lacan prefers the term "desire" to the English "wish" and the French *"voeu"* usually used to translate Freud's *"Wunsch,"* because "wish" and *"voeu"* sound somewhat weak and wishy-washy compared to *le désir* (see *Écrits*, p. 518).

23. *Cui bono* is usually used to suggest a hidden motive or to indicate that the party responsible for something may not be who it at first appears to be. The guilty party may be found among those who have something to gain, chiefly with an eye toward financial gain. The party who benefits may not always be obvious or may have successfully diverted attention to a scapegoat. Freud cites *"is fecit cui profuit"* (he did the deed who gained by it) in SE IV, p. 308.

24. See Lacan's discussion of the witty butcher's wife (*Écrits*, pp. 620–627) and my commentaries on it (Fink, 1997, pp. 125–127; 2004, pp. 20–23).

25. In Seminar XVI, Lacan indicates that the analysand's articulation to us of a dream leads to a "reconstituted sentence" (the reconstructed thought that underpinned the formation of the dream) and that we are looking for the gap or fault line in it where we see something fishy, something that does not seem quite right (*qui cloche*). "That's the desire" in the dream, he opines (p. 197).

26. Note that he also says that "a symptom is itself structured like a language" (*Écrits*, p. 223), and that the drives, too, "are structured in terms of language" (p. 390). Based on his later work, we might also propose that the unconscious, dreams, and symptoms are structured like *lalangue*, which we might understand here in a sense as "baby talk," language as we know it as children when we are conscious of the Saussurian "ribbon of sound" (Saussure, 1916/1959) long before we know how to divide that ribbon up into separate signifiers (such as *la* and *langue*), and enjoy the phonemes and syllables for their own sake, not for the meaning units they can constitute. Freud proves to be a fine precursor to Lacan's notion of *lalangue* in *Jokes and their Relation to the Unconscious*, when he refers to the "sense in nonsense" (SE VIII, p. 131) and especially to our "pleasure in nonsense," saying:

> During the period in which a child is learning how to handle the vocabulary of his mother-tongue, it gives him obvious pleasure to "experiment with it in play," to use [Karl] Groos' words [from *The Play of Man*, 1898/2007]. And he puts words together without regard to the condition

that they should make sense, in order to obtain from them the pleasurable effect of rhythm or rhyme. Little by little he is forbidden this enjoyment, until all that remains permitted to him are significant combinations of words. But when he is older attempts still emerge at disregarding the restrictions that have been learnt on the use of words. Words are disfigured by particular little additions being made to them, their forms are altered by certain manipulations (e.g., by reduplications or *'Zittersprache'*), or a private language may even be constructed for use among playmates [like "pig Latin"]. (p. 125)

Zittern = Tremble

Further on he adds,

infantile is source of unconscious

For the infantile is the source of the unconscious, and the unconscious thought-processes are none other than those—the one and only ones—produced in early childhood. The thought which, with the intention of constructing a joke, plunges into the unconscious is merely seeking there for the ancient dwelling-place of its former play with words. Thought is put back for a moment to the stage of childhood so as once more to gain possession of this childish source of pleasure. (p. 170)

Freud's comments in the same book on "significance" (p. 12) may have also inspired Lacan's notion of *signifiance*; and Freud seems to be thinking along the same lines as Saussure there when he says that "in a play on words, the word is but a sound-image to which one meaning or another is attached" (p. 46); in Saussure's work, a signifier is an *image acoustique*, sometimes rendered "sound-image" or "sound-pattern," with which various signifieds (i.e., meanings) may be associated.

27. Freud reiterated this point of view 25 years later when he wrote that "dream-interpretation . . . without reference to the dreamer's associations would, even in the most favorable of cases, remain a piece of unscientific virtuosity of very doubtful value" (SE XIX, p. 128).

28. To the best of my knowledge, Jungians continue to use some variation on the decoding method even today.

29. Does this really mean that any two analysts would be likely to agree about the meaning of someone's dream, after they have heard the full range of associations to it, and are aware of the full backdrop of the case? This would, in theory, be a useful experiment to try, even if it might be difficult to conduct in practice—why, after all, would any analysand tell exactly the same stories twice to two different analysts? We would perhaps have to make an audio recording of an analyst and an analysand discussing together a dream and the analysand's associations to the dream and then play the recording to a range of different analysts to ask how they might interpret the dream after having heard the same set of associations.

30. Freud explicitly mentions Wilhelm Stekel in this regard in his 1911 Preface to *The Interpretation of Dreams* (SE IV, p. xxvii).

31. He admits, nevertheless, that "a dream-symbolism of universal validity has only emerged in the case of a few subjects, on the basis of generally familiar allusions and verbal substitutes" (SE V, p. 345). In general, work with symbols is resorted to only when the dreamer has no associations to a part or the whole of a dream (p. 360 n. 1; p. 372), and such work remains "an auxiliary method"

(p. 360), not the primary method, which is that of relying on the dreamer's own associations.

32. According to Wortis' account of his analysis with Freud, Freud continued to appeal to universal symbols in interpreting dreams even as late as 1934, saying, for example, that "sitting in a theater always meant watching coitus" and "falling is a constant symbol for femininity, for giving birth, or being born" (1954, p. 85; see also pp. 82–83).

33. Things that have been used so often as phallic symbols in our culture (like the Empire State Building, the Washington Monument, and the Eiffel Tower) may no longer provide enough of a disguise to satisfy the censorship, and their appearance in dreams today may no longer allude to an erection the way they once may have. Similarly, fireworks displays were once so commonly used in films to indicate intercourse and orgasm that in someone's dream such a display might not prove adequate to disguise sexual wishes today, and often refers to something else altogether. In order to disguise sexual acts with, say, someone we feel we should not be involved with, some other ruse or cover might have to be found to successfully hide such wishes from our semiwaking consciousness in the dream so we do not wake up in shock or feeling anxious. For a detailed discussion of love and sex in Freud's work, see Fink, 2016, Chapters 1, 2, and 4.

34. He is even occasionally critical of interpretations he himself proposed of other people's dreams that were not grounded in their own associations. For example, regarding a dream reported by Simon that he had interpreted, he added a footnote in 1925 saying, "Incidentally, the interpretation given in the text, pointing to a reminiscence of *Gulliver's Travels*, is a good example of what an interpretation ought *not* to be. The interpreter of the dream should not give free rein to his own ingenuity and neglect the dreamer's associations" (SE IV, p. 30 n).

Freud surprisingly indicates that he cannot fully explain typical dreams of flying, which generally involve sensations of power, freedom, and joy; yet I suspect many languages have expressions similar to the following in English: "free as a bird," "get a bird's eye view," "fly the coop," "light as a feather," "on cloud nine," and so on.

35. I have discussed myriad 21st-century dreams recounted by my analysands in Fink, 2007, 2014a, and 2014b.

36. Or perhaps the child feels her mother is bereaved when she drops her off and feels required to make an even bigger show of feeling to stave off her mother's show of feeling—to cut it off at the pass, as it were.

37. Freud attempts to draw relations between the dream and what he calls the *psychical chain*—that is, conscious ideas the dreamer has regarding people, life events, and so on. Like a pathological idea in isolation from the rest of the thoughts (as we saw in Chapter 1), *a dream can be viewed as a symptom* (SE IV, p. 101) or a traumatic event that has to be associated with other ideas to become legible and at least partially understandable.

38. Similar meaning-making techniques are employed in interpreting difficult texts and translating them, especially when there are ambiguous grammatical constructions allowing for multiple meanings or signifiers with a plethora of signifieds. Context plays an especially important role in interpreting the Old Testament and many ancient Greek texts that include words and expressions found in no other extant texts, and which often have no certain punctuation.

39. As he puts it 25 years later, "The censorship has neglected its task, this

has been noticed too late, and the generation of anxiety is a substitute for the distortion that has been omitted" (SE XIX, p. 132).

40. Freud comments in a number of contexts that, paradoxically enough, "the more moral" someone is or behaves, "the more sensitive" or demanding his conscience or superego often is (see, for example, SE XIX, p. 134).

41. "The accumulation of excitation . . . is felt as unpleasure. . . . A current of this kind in the apparatus, starting from unpleasure and aiming at pleasure, we have termed a 'wish'; and we have asserted that only a wish is able to set the apparatus in motion" (SE V, p. 598). Twenty-five years later, he adds, "What is [generally referred to as utilitarian or] useful is itself (as is well known) only a circuitous path to pleasurable satisfaction" (SE XIX, p. 127).

42. In *Beyond the Pleasure Principle*, Freud attempts to provide several different explanations for why "it is not in the service of that principle that the dreams of patients suffering from traumatic neuroses lead them back with such regularity to the situation in which the trauma occurred" (SE XVIII, p. 32). The psyche, he suggests, strives:

- to master the situation—that is, it repeats the experience in order to become the active agent instead of the passive victim of the traumatic event;
- to insert anxiety, in the form of preparedness, "back" into an experience, as if that could be done retroactively, so that one would have been better prepared for it;
- to bind (in order to contain) an overload of stimuli; this involves a different approach to mastering stimuli (different than the pleasure principle's approach involving discharge) by cutting them off or isolating them (like a soldier might try to ignore the pain he feels after being wounded in battle in order to be able to save his own life and/or that of his fellow soldiers).

His theoretical discussion in that text is quite complex, and he even goes so far as to qualify the repetitive reliving of trauma as a pure expression of the "death drive."

43. For video footage of animals dreaming, see https://www.youtube.com/watch?v=Js50Orx94iM.

44. As Freud says, in the case of Dora, "Experience shows that people often assert that they have had the same dream, when as a matter of fact the separate appearances of the recurrent dream have differed from one another in numerous details and other respects that were of no small importance" (SE VII, pp. 92–93). The same is true of "recurrent" daydreams and masturbation fantasies as well.

45. Regarding affect in dreams, recall that, according to Freud, the affect in a dream is attached to the latent content, not the manifest content, and that at least four different things happen to affect in dreams (SE V, pp. 460–487): It is

- suppressed to protect sleep;
- displaced (e.g., from one Bob to another);
- reversed into its opposite (e.g., from hatred into love);
- exaggerated (having been bottled up, it all comes out as soon as there is an excuse to do so); see, especially, SE V, p. 479.

46. Or, as Henry Fielding (1749/1979) said of his heroine,

> Notwithstanding the nicest guard which Sophia endeavored to set on her
> behavior, she could not avoid letting some appearances now and then slip
> forth: for love may again be likened to a disease in this, that when it is
> denied a vent in one part, it will certainly break out in another. What her
> lips, therefore, concealed, her eyes, her blushes, and many little involun-
> tary actions, betrayed. (p. 149)

47. Among these phenomena, only fantasies sometimes go beyond the pleasure principle, reenacting or restaging traumatic experiences.

48. Jokes too are, according to Freud, structured like symptoms, there being
two opposing urges involved in them (at least in what he calls "tendentious
jokes"; SE VIII, p. 135). And he suggests that "joke-work and dreamwork must,
at least in some essential respect, be identical" (p. 165).

49. On this point, see Freud's discussion in SE XV, pp. 31–32.

50. Many clinicians have trouble paying the kind of "evenly hovering" or
"free-floating" attention to their patients that is the counterpart of the analysand's free association, and that is necessary if we are to hear slips of the tongue
and notice many forms of parapraxes. They are often too focused on the meaning of what their patients are saying and find it hard to pay attention to meaning
and listen carefully to patients' words at the same time; yet they often hear their
own slips without any trouble. Evenly hovering or free-floating attention are just
as difficult to achieve for the practitioner as free association is for the patient;
both constitute ideals that we aim at but rarely live up to fully. I suggested some
ways of learning to pay attention in this way earlier in the present chapter.

51. It might be said that a Lacanian perspective would have us look not simply for wishes/desires in dreams, but also for jouissance, which would assist us
in discerning the dreamer's "fundamental fantasy" and "subjective position" in
life (on these latter, see Fink, 2014a, Chapter 1). Freud occasionally points to the
libidinal charge or jouissance dreams provide, as for example in his discussion
of Dora's second dream, where he mentions that "cruel and sadistic tendencies
find satisfaction in this dream" (SE VII, p. 111; see Chapter 5 below). Jouissance
is also implied by his claim that dreams unfold in the present tense (SE V, p. 535)
as we seem to seek some sort of satisfaction here and now in them. Although
sleep can be thought of as involving a "shutting-out of the external world" (p.
544) and as a time when we are generally cut off from our bodily jouissance (not
noticing, for example, aches and pains we suffer from while awake), at times we
certainly enjoy or abhor things that occur in our dreams.

A simple way to explore the jouissance dreams bring is by asking a patient
who has had a seemingly anxiety-ridden or disturbing dream, or a dream in
which the opposite of what the patient professes to want to happen comes to
pass, "Why have this kind of dream in the first place if it's precisely what you
don't want?" "What's in it for you?" "Why dream this, of all things?" "What does
it do for you?" "What could you possibly be getting out of it?"

As Lacan (Seminar XVI) puts it,

> What guides us when we interpret a dream is certainly not the question
> "What does that mean?" Nor is it "What does [the analysand] want in say-

ing that?" Rather it is, "What, in speaking, does it [or id] want?" It apparently does not know what it wants. (p. 198)

52. See Freud's further comments on the only relative "etiological importance" of actual seduction or sexual trauma during childhood for the generation of a neurosis in SE III, p. 168 n. 1 (added in 1924).

Chapter 4: Obsession and the Case of the Rat Man (Ernst Langer)

1. There is some debate about the Rat Man's true identity, Patrick Mahony (1986, p. 2) claiming it was Ernst Lanzer ("Paul Lorenz" is the pseudonym Freud uses for him in the published case history). I have relied here on the recent, extremely well-documented bilingual German/French edition of Freud's daily notes taken on the case found in *L'homme aux rats : journal d'une analyse* (S. Freud, 2000). This includes the only sample we have of the notes Freud took every evening after seeing patients all day. In every other instance, he seems to have destroyed his notes after he wrote up a case; here, however, we have his complete notes from the first four months of the treatment, with the real names of the protagonists included. The "Original Record of the Case" in Volume X of the *Standard Edition* includes much, although not all, of the same material; it disguises some of the names of the people mentioned, as Freud himself did in the published case history, and seems to misread or misinterpret some of Freud's handwriting. The name Langer is found in the German/French edition on p. 31 and Ernst on p. 65; Freud's handwriting might possibly have made it difficult to distinguish between Langer and Lanzer. Note that although Freud gave numerous oral presentations on his work with Langer while the case was unfolding, he only wrote up the case history a year after it ended (see Jones, 1955, p. 263).

Mahony (1986) reads the name as Lanzer and provides a list of all the other real names of those mentioned in the case history and notes (p. 3 n). He does not cite his sources for much of the chronology he claims to have established (pp. 24–27), some of which does not coincide with my own. And when he does cite his sources (pp. 33–35), his reconstruction of the chronology of Langer's life strikes me as quite speculative, hardly constituting grounds for criticizing as he does Freud's formulation of the case. For more on Mahony's readings of Freud's cases, see Chapter 5 and Appendix I.

2. While the *DSM-5*'s criteria for OCD (APA, 2013, pp. 235–237) bear some resemblance to the psychoanalytic diagnosis of obsession, its criteria for obsessive-compulsive personality disorder bear less. Criteria of the latter are said to include orderliness, perfectionism, inflexibility, and rigidity; and those who are afflicted with this disorder are said to be characterized by such traits as having one's "sense of self derived predominantly from work or productivity" (whereas, as we shall see at the end of this chapter, many of those with obsessive structure flee work like the plague, and when they do work achieve little); "constricted experience and expression of strong emotion" (whereas many of those with obsessive structure are subject to sudden, uncontrolled outbursts of anger); and "difficulty understanding and appreciating the ideas, feelings, or behaviors of others" (whereas many obsessives understand others' ideas and feelings so well that they feel dominated by, submerged in, and even annihilated by them; these citations are from the "Alternative *DSM-5* Model for Personality Disorders," APA,

2013, p. 768). For some comparisons between psychoanalytic diagnoses and the *DSM*, see Appendix V.

Note that certain analysts prefer the term "obsessive character" to that of "obsessive structure," and that of "hysterical character" to "hysterical structure."

3. Intrusive thoughts are often experienced as coming not from me but from elsewhere. I do not recognize them as mine—hence they must be someone (or something) else's.

4. Ernst was 12 years of age at the time, and the girl was the sister of a friend of his (S. Freud, 2000, p. 73). The father of Gisa (a different girl who was later to become Ernst's "lady") had died a number of years before that (when she was 6; pp. 145–147; this contradicts what the editors of the *Standard Edition* conclude, which is that her father died in 1887, when she was at least 9, if not 10 or 11; SE X, p. 256, "Chronological Data"), which may be what gave Ernst the idea in the first place: Perhaps he first really noticed Gisa when he heard that her father had died. Although he claims to have fallen in love with her when he was 20, he could hardly have failed to have met her much earlier in life, as she was his first cousin.

5. Interestingly, although I have often heard from my male analysands that, as boys, they asked their mothers about their erections, I have never once heard of boys asking their fathers about them, as if they sensed that their erections had something to do with their mothers.

6. Jones (1955, pp. 263–264) tells us that Freud spent about a month writing up this case study.

7. The "trees" in this case are far more numerous than in the case of Dora, for example, whose treatment only lasted about three months. The Rat Man's treatment lasted four times as long, and is the only example of a case of Freud's for which we have his daily notes (at least for the first four months of the treatment). It is a difficult task for any clinician to find a coherent way of presenting and summarizing material when a case lasts for more than several months; imagine how difficult it must have been for Freud in the case of the Wolf Man, whose treatment lasted four years. Now imagine what contemporary analysts are faced with, given that treatments regularly last a decade or more in our times! On the many challenges presented by the preparation of case histories, see the Preface to Fink, 2014b.

8. Freud tells us that Ernst decided "to consult a doctor" (to get a certificate that related to his complicated scenario to pay someone back for his pince-nez) and chanced upon Freud's *Psychopathology of Everyday Life* (SE X, p. 173). Did it take a month or two for the treatment to begin because Freud had no openings right away? Or could it be that this particular crisis passed without leading Ernst to contact Freud?

9. Note, however, that on December 23, 1907, Ernst tells Freud that "his father had *always* been upset that he was not industrious"—that is, by the fact that "he did not apply himself" in his studies (SE X, p. 300; S. Freud, 2000, pp. 201–203), suggesting that he had perhaps never been that great a student, even before his father's death.

10. In the published case study (SE X, p. 198), this relative is referred to as a "cousin." In the notes, Freud indicates that it was "a relative of the Saborskys" who proposed this match, the girl being "a daughter of the Saborskys" (SE X, p. 292; S. Freud, 2000, p. 179). In SE X (p. 293), her name is disguised as "Emmy." The name "Lizzie" in Freud's notes (S. Freud, 2000, p. 181) may possibly refer

to another girl mentioned in the same session (a seamstress or "dressmaker"; SE X, p. 292), but my sense is that it refers to the Saborskys' daughter, and I will use it here as if it did. The proposed match was accompanied by an offer to set him up in legal practice with Jakob Freundlich (note the similarity of his last name to Freud's; *freundlich* means kind or friendly), a cousin of his (brother to Lizzie?) who married Ernst's younger sister, Olga (note that Jakob himself had long vacillated between two women: Olga and one of Dr. Steinberger's daughters; Steinberger was the Langers' family doctor, and he himself had married one of the Saborskys' daughters). The Saborskys and the Langers were thus very closely intertwined.

The actual date at which the marriage proposal was made is never made very clear in the notes, but it obviously postdated his father's death and may well have been made in late 1902 or early 1903, which is precisely when Ernst's condition took a serious turn for the worse (S. Freud, 2000, p. 207).

11. Confusing matters somewhat, Gisa Adler was also a relative of Ernst's—indeed, his first cousin (like his mother was of his father). He had perhaps initially become interested in her when her paralytic father died when she was around 6. She may have been somewhat older than him, for he apparently believed at one point that she was too old for him (S. Freud, 2000, p. 153). Ernst was also aware, by the time his mother told him about the proposal of marriage to the Saborskys' daughter, that Gisa was sterile, having had both ovaries removed (SE X, pp. 216–217).

12. Freud told colleagues that he regretted that he had to change quite a few details when he published the case history in order to disguise the Rat Man's identity; the loss of details like this one may have seemed particularly unfortunate to him. The mother had been raised as an orphan by another family, the Saborskys (they were perhaps relatives of hers and were probably wealthy and well-connected), and the young, beautiful, well-to-do cousin (Lizzie) was from the Saborsky family. In the published case history, Freud tells us Ernst's father was immediately taken into the mother's family business and "thus by his marriage made himself a fairly comfortable position" (SE X, p. 198), but in his notes it is recorded that the father joked about how poor he and Ernst's mother were when they first married, even if he was exaggerating a little (S. Freud, 2000, p. 165).

13. The Rat Man later unwittingly turned this conflict into a transferential one: Having glimpsed someone whom he believed to be Freud's daughter in the stairwell at Freud's house one day, and imagining that Freud was only being nice to him because he wanted Ernst for his son-in-law, the Rat Man reformulated his conflict as one between marrying Gisa and marrying Freud's daughter (S. Freud, 2000, p. 165). He even went so far once as to imagine Freud's daughter with dirt balls, dung, or "cow pies" (*Dreckpatzen*) instead of eyes, as if to indicate that he would choose her for her money, not for her *"beaux yeux"* (beautiful eyes), Lizzie being said to have had lovely eyes (SE X, p. 200; S. Freud, 2000, p. 181).

Freud also notes that the choice between Gisa (who was older than him) and Lizzie (who was about 12 years younger than him) may have harked back to Ernst's relations (which seem at times to have been quite sexual) with his older and younger sisters (S. Freud, 2000, pp. 141, 151, 181, and 237–239). Let us observe, too, that his father was indebted, in a sense, to the Saborskys (he owed his being well-off in his adult years to them), and Ernst may have felt responsible for paying off his father's debt to them (like his gambling debt)—

perhaps by giving himself to their family (or would he then be incurring a still greater debt?).

14. He did so, he believed, in order to punish himself for having wished his father dead when, at about 20, he felt he was not financially well-off enough to marry Gisa and realized he would be if his father died and he were to collect his inheritance; the punishment he inflicted upon himself was designed to ensure that he would *never* financially benefit from his father's death (it was perhaps also designed to repay his mother for the money he once, at his father's instigation, stole out of her handbag). Ernst even briefly entertained the idea of getting baptized, which would have rendered marriage to Lizzie impossible, as she was from an observant Jewish family; Gisa Adler was perhaps Jewish too (S. Freud, 2000, p. 205).

15. Lacan is, presumably, thinking here of the fact that Freud's father and half-brother Emmanuel had, according to Jones (1953, p. 25), formed a plan to wean Sigmund "from his intellectual pursuits and replace them by more practical ones, after which he would settle in Manchester and marry his half-brother's daughter, Pauline, a playmate of early childhood." See Lacan's other comments on the Rat Man case (*Écrits*, pp. 239–241). It might be worth noting that Freud, in a letter to Jung, diagnosed himself to be of "the 'obsessional' type" as opposed to the "hysterical type" (S. Freud & Jung, 1974, p. 82).

16. Even if Mahony (1986) claims that about a year after the end of the analysis, Ernst became engaged to Gisa, and a year later they married (pp. 17 and 27), since it is not clear on the basis of what evidence Mahony makes this claim.

17. See, for example, Lacan, Seminar XI, where repetition figures as one of the "four fundamental concepts of psychoanalysis."

18. He repeatedly looked at his penis in the mirror, even if he was not exactly masturbating, and we might wonder what he was trying to see or check. Freud, in his notes, indicates that Ernst was concerned that his penis was too small (for what, we don't know); was he also concerned about something else, such as whether he had caught a sexually transmittable disease (S. Freud, 2000, p. 207)?

19. Although Freud says very little about the mother in the published case history, there are numerous indications in the notes that Ernst viewed his mother as a killjoy, and many indications of other important roles she played in his life as well (S. Freud, 2000, pp. 99, 145, 191, and 195).

20. Here he simply refers to the *Ich*, that is, the "ego" or "I" (SE X, pp. 162–163).

21. This is true of hysterics as well. Emmy von N., for example, had a great many "frightening ideas, such as that something might happen to her children, that they might fall ill or die, or that her brother, who was then on his honeymoon, might have an accident, or that his wife might die" (SE II, p. 72), and she clearly resented all of these people for a wide variety of reasons.

22. His belief that his thoughts could harm or kill others may possibly have originated with the death of his older sister, Camilla, when he was 3 or 4, if we assume he had had some rivalrous or aggressive thoughts about her.

23. Here we see that Freud, in a sense, says to himself, "This *unwitting display of enjoyment* tells me more about the patient's fundamental relation to pleasure and sex than most of what he has told me so far! This expression on his face is revealing an unconscious wish for this to happen to his father and to his lady." Certain readers may find it helpful to think of the following everyday experiences as related to jouissance: playing with a loose tooth, even though it is painful to do so; scratching mosquito bites or poison ivy, it feeling good

even as it feels bad; and harping on a nitpicky point or comment with a partner, even when you know no good will come of it, because you just can't leave well enough alone or can't help yourself.

One of my analysands described a very early experience of jouissance that involved rubbing dirt out from between her toes; she characterized the dirt as "wet, granular, and smelly," and professed that she would have liked there to be more dirt so she could go on rubbing and rubbing. In hindsight, she saw this rubbing as an early masturbatory pleasure that she hid from her mother, sensing that her mother would have heartily disapproved of it.

24. Note, too, that there are numerous allusions to homoeroticism in his case, as in virtually every other case, including his concern that his brother's penis had gone into his anus during play in the bathtub; his close relationship with the male friend who often relieved his mind when he was in crisis (SE X, p. 159); and his first great disappointment when a male tutor who he thought liked and thought well of him turned out to have been trying to ingratiate himself to Ernst simply to have the opportunity to be around Ernst's sister (p. 160).

25. See Soler, 2011/2015, p. 89.

26. According to Otto Rank's summary of a preliminary talk on the case of the Rat Man that Freud gave to the Vienna Psychoanalytic Society on October 30, 1907, just four weeks into the treatment, Freud indicated that "analytic technique has changed insofar as now the analyst no longer seeks what he himself is interested in, but instead allows the patient to follow the natural unfolding of his thoughts" (cited in S. Freud, 2000, p. x). As we shall see in the next chapter, he had said much the same thing about work with Dora seven years earlier, suggesting that such a principle was far easier for Freud to enunciate than to implement in his daily practice.

27. This was hardly Freud's only deviation from the approach to technique he laid out in his *Papers on Technique*, written not long after his work with the Rat Man. Mark Kanzer mentions "the guessing game," Freud's demand to know his lady's name and request to see a picture of her, and the fact that Freud sent Ernst a postcard at one point, lent him a book, and gave him a meal of herring one day when he was hungry (Kanzer & Glenn, 1980, p. 245).

28. It could, potentially, lead to analyses that solve certain important problems rather quickly (in a couple of years instead of in seven to ten), but would most likely leave analysands stuck as regards their main stance with respect to the Other, which it is a crucial goal of analysis to reconfigure (see Fink, 1995, 1997, 2007, 2014a, and 2014b). Freud's attempt to reassure Ernst at one point that he had formed a "good opinion" of him (SE X, p. 178) contributed to keeping Ernst dependent on Freud's recognition of him, and probably played some role in Ernst imagining that Freud wanted him as a son-in-law.

29. For an example of such a person, see "Bartleby, the scrivener: A story of Wall Street," by Herman Melville.

30. Even after one of them had died, as in the case of the Rat Man.

31. We see here that *both* workaholism and an allergy to work, which are usually considered to be diametrically opposed, can be indicative of obsession. Another variation, which Freud (SE XI, p. 67) suggests was the case for Leonardo da Vinci, is working a lot but never finishing anything—in particular, beginning a lot of ambitious projects but never bringing any of them to fruition (others may deem them complete, but their author does not). One of my own analysands put it thus: "I'm very good at not finishing things." He added that, since "the thing

finished won't be that great," why finish? Early on in the project he can imagine it will be great and works hard at it; once he perceives that it won't be as great as he had hoped, he becomes "good at wasting time." Another analysand of mine worked only at things that would bring him no income, feeling that the world somehow owed him a living. Yet others never do many of the things they think they should do because "the time is never right": It is, according to them, always "too early" or "too late" to do what they have in mind.

32. They are also discussed in such textbooks as if they occurred at predetermined times in a child's life, whereas in some cultures and in certain households toilet training precedes weaning, meaning that the anal stage comes to an end before the oral stage does.

33. I have written up a number of cases of obsession over the years; see, especially, Fink 1997 (Chapter 8), 2007 (Chapter 4), 2014a (Chapters 10 and 11), and 2014b (Chapters 1, 11, 12, and 13).

34. When such obsessives do actually attempt to give pleasure or jouissance to others, it is often in order to appear to be *morally superior* to them. Their reasoning seems to run as follows: "I don't want to, but I will do so anyway because I am better than them (or to prove I am better than them)."

35. On the *lost object*, see Freud, SE XIV, pp. 249–251, and Fink, 2010, "The Case of the Lost Object."

36. For a fictional character whose features are based on many of my obsessive patients, see Geoffrey in Fink (2014c).

Chapter 5: Hysteria and the Case of Dora (Ida Bauer)

1. In German, *Bauer* means peasant or farmer, but also birdcage and what we call a pawn in the game of chess; it can also be used in the slang expression *"den kalten Bauer aufwärmen,"* which means to practice fellatio (see translator's note to S. Freud, 2013, p. 109 n. 89), *Bauer* having been a slang term in Viennese dialect for sperm. *Kalter Bauer* apparently also means to ejaculate, as during a wet dream or masturbation (Appignanesi & Forrester, 1992).

It might be said that we know *all too much* about Dora's "real identity," to the point of knowing her entire family and many intimate details of their lives (see, for example, Mahony, 1996, pp. 2–21). A great deal has been written about her, based on more or less reliable research, and much of it is summarized in Mahony's (1996) tendentious, book-length study entitled *Freud's Dora* (Mahony writes as though he has managed to reconstruct the gospel truth regarding factual matters—dates and ages—from numerous conflicting accounts, which strikes me as a bit far-fetched). Felix Deutsch, an analyst who was asked to see her by a physician in 1922, wrote an article in 1957 about her; Rogow (1978) added to it; as did Loewenberg (1983), Decker (1991), and Roazen (2001, pp. 366–369). And these are just the historical studies—that is, the tip of the iceberg! More analytic/critical studies include Erikson (1962), Seidenberg and Papathomopoulos (1962), Blos (1972), Muslin & Gill (1978), Lewin (1973), Lindon (1969), Rieff (1971), Kanzer (1966), Major (1974), David (1974), and numerous others included in Kanzer and Glenn (1980); many more still can be found in the bibliographies of each of these works.

We know, more or less for certain, that her parents were Philipp (or Philip) and Katharina (or Käthe, for short) Bauer, and their friends, the Ks, were Hans and Peppina Zellenka (see S. Freud, 2013, pp. viii–x). Freud discusses how it came about that he chose the pseudonym Dora (which means "gift" in Greek) in SE VI, pp. 240–241; Marcus (1975/1990, p. 309 n. 26) suggests that Freud named her Dora for different reasons—that is, for the first love and wife of David Copperfield in Freud's favorite novel by Dickens—and others have seen fit to construe Freud's choice of the pseudonym based on other "evidence" (see Mahony, 1996, p. 43 n. 2). Oddly enough, little has been written in French on Dora since the 1970s.

2. Moreover, he almost always interpreted apodictically (see, for example, SE VII, p. 66), rather than tentatively or in the form of a question like, "Do you think it might be such and such?"

3. The same holds true for recommendations I have made in other texts and make here as well: I have no doubt done at one time or another virtually everything I counsel people not to do, and have failed to do at times what I recommend that people do.

4. Later he admits that "even the most exhaustive analysis has gaps in its data and is insufficiently documented" (SE XXI, p. 107).

5. Note that, during the session in which Ida told Freud the first dream, he "promised to communicate [a further interpretation of the first dream] to Dora at the next session" (SE VII, p. 71), obviously conveying to her that he felt they should keep talking about it; but then after the second session devoted to it, he felt that "the interpretation of the dream [was now] complete" (p. 73) even though Dora had more to say about it! Two full sessions seem to have been devoted to the second dream as well (p. 105), and at the third "sitting" Dora broke off the treatment. Years later Freud (SE XII) wrote,

> The amount of interpretation [of a dream] that can be achieved in one session should be considered sufficient and it is not to be regarded as a loss if the content of the dream is not fully discovered. On the following day, the interpretation of the dream should not be returned to unless it becomes clear that nothing else has forced its way into the foreground of the patient's thoughts in the meantime. (p. 92)

In other words, the general progress of the analysis should take precedence over the interpretation of any one dream (which is, in any case, "incapable of complete solution"; p. 93). Freud went on to say, "We may rest assured that every wishful impulse that creates a dream today will reappear in other dreams as long as it has not been understood" (p. 94).

6. Jones' accounts of this vary. In 1953 (Vol. 1, p. 362 n. i), he says, "On May 8, 1901, [Freud] expressed his hesitation about publishing it ["I have not yet made up my mind to send off the other essay"; see S. Freud, 1985, p. 441; this was perhaps because of Oscar Rie's unenthusiastic reception of it], but on June 7 he sent it to Ziehen (one of the editors of the *Monatsschrift für Psychiatrie und Neurologie* where it ultimately appeared) ["'Dreams and Hysteria' has been sent off"; S. Freud, 1985, p. 442]. Shortly after, however, he again changed his mind and retrieved the manuscript, to keep it in his desk for another four years." In 1955, Jones indicates that further details have since come to light:

> In 1909 Freud told Ferenczi that Brodmann, the editor of the *Journal für Psychologie und Neurologie*, had refused to publish the Dora case. We know that when in January 1901, he offered the paper to Ziehen and

Wernicke . . . , it was immediately accepted, and when Freud sent them the manuscript in the following June it was with the expectation it would appear that autumn. He must then have asked for it back and kept it for another four years before he could bring himself to run the risk of being charged with professional indiscretion. It is entirely mysterious why he should have offered it to another periodical after it had already been accepted. The only suggestion that occurs to me is that he had doubts whether Ziehen and Wernicke, both severe critics of his work, would accept it after really reading the manuscript. (pp. 255–256)

Appignanesi and Forrester propose that Freud decided to publish the case once he heard that Dora had become a mother on April 2, 1905, having moved past the concerns that vexed the girl he had treated, having "in Freud's eyes crossed the Rubicon that separates the girl from the woman" (1992, p. 164).

7. A case history worth its salt always contains more than the author intended to convey, allowing readers to come to interpretations of the material that differ significantly from and go well beyond what the author saw (on this and related points, see Fink, 2014b, pp. xiii–xvi).

8. Freud, when Ida confirms his suspicion that she is alluding to oral methods of giving someone sexual gratification (SE VII, pp. 47–48), assumes that Ida and Frau K talked about fellatio, which obviously implies the ability on the man's part to get an at least partial erection; and it is true that "erectile dysfunction" is often code in our times for the inability, not to get an erection in general, but to get and maintain an erection for the purposes of intercourse with a partner. Note, however, that Freud tells us Ida's father had (in addition to tuberculosis and syphilis) a heart condition, it thus being somewhat probable that he could not get an erection at all; therefore, as Lacan points out, Ida was more likely alluding to cunnilingus as the obvious oral act performed on a woman by a man in as poor health as Ida's father was (*Écrits*, p. 180). Freud jumped to the conclusion—for his own reasons, no doubt—that Ida must have imagined Frau K performing oral sex on Ida's father, whereas any and all forms of oral sex could have been involved.

9. For some possible interpretations of her specific symptoms, see Appendix IV.

10. It is always more complicated when the therapist knows a patient's family members and their perspectives on things, and it is worth pointing out that Freud knew virtually everyone in Ida's family except for her mother (SE VII, pp. 19–20).

11. Note that even her father's interest in the treatment waned once he realized Freud was not convincing Ida that he and Frau K were nothing more than friends (SE VII, p. 109).

12. The reference here is to the father's syphilis, which was believed by many at the time to be both hereditary and infectious (S. Freud, 2013, p. ix). The translation provided in the newer edition insinuates that her question was perhaps why she had fallen ill whereas her brother had not (p. 63).

13. It is not clear whether Freud tried to get Dora to admit that the thought had once crossed her mind during a session that she wanted Freud to kiss her, as he concluded it might have (SE VII, p. 74).

14. As Freud himself tells us, the fact that a patient initially disagrees with an interpretation does not necessarily mean that it is wrong, for the patient may

find the interpretation unpleasant or even insulting at the outset but later come to agree with it. But an interpretation that has neither an immediate nor a retroactive impact—that is, that does not change the patient sooner or later—must be rejected as false (see Freud, SE XXIII, p. 265).

15. If my experience supervising other analysts can be believed, it is not only male analysts who fall into this trap with female hysterics; male and female analysts often fall into the same trap with both male and female hysterics.

16. Lacan (*Écrits*) is quite complimentary to Freud here in 1951, for he continues:

> This is not a mere contrivance for presenting material whose emergence is left up to the patient, as Freud clearly states here. What is involved is a scansion of structures in which truth is transmuted for the subject, structures that affect not only her comprehension of things, but her very position as a subject, her "objects" being a function of that position. This means that the conception of the case history is *identical* to the progress of the subject, that is, to the reality of the treatment. (p. 178)

17. Or, as Lacan paraphrases it, "All of this is factual, being based on reality and not on my own will. What's to be done about it?" (*Écrits*, p. 179).

18. Obsessives, on the other hand, generally place the blame for everything on themselves, granting themselves far more power than they actually have in the world and misrecognizing their actual role in events and relationships (i.e., they blame themselves for the wrong things).

19. Hegel is also mentioned in passing in SE IV, p. 55.

20. On punctuation, see Fink, 2007, Chapter 3.

21. This approach is light-years from the approach taken by many a contemporary therapist, who would say: "Yes, that's right, you *are* being used here. Let's figure out whom you should confront and what else you can do about it." The problem encountered in such cases is that the patient may well not want to do anything about it, because she is getting something out of it and feeling guilty for that. Freud's assumption is that what is covered over by blaming everything on others is a self-accusation or self-reproach. *We often reproach others when we feel we ourselves are guilty of something:* This is known as projection. The therapist who agrees (saying, "Yes, you're right, they are blameworthy") is essentially conniving with the patient's *méconnaissance*—self-misrecognition—and allying or aligning with the conscious instead of the unconscious.

A "dialectical reversal" of perspective is something we see, for example, in Marx's work: The profit said to be created by the capitalist (à la Adam Smith) is actually surplus value created by the worker. This kind of change or flipping of perspective (or of the frame) is often fruitful in philosophy and in psychoanalytic technique as well. When some aspect of a dream seems to make no sense, one can try the opposite of an element in it ("I was in a crowd" can sometimes imply "I was all alone") when interpreting it to see if things then fall into place. Lacan often relies on reversals when reinterpreting Freud's work: He says, for example, that by the end of her analysis a woman does not have to accept her own castration (as Freud claimed)—since she is not castrated in the same way that a man is—but rather her partner's castration.

22. Yet another opposite would be, "Others are to be thanked," not blamed. See Freud's comments on unconscious thoughts being the "direct contrary"

of conscious ones in SE VII, p. 55, where he comments, "Repression is often achieved by means of an excessive reinforcement of the thought contrary to the one that is to be repressed."

23. Had Dora's relations with her mother in fact become unfriendly when her relationship with Frau K began when Dora was around 6? This may have also been the precise moment when the rift or "estrangement" between her mother and father occurred, supposedly owing to his illness (SE VII, p. 20), but perhaps more significantly owing to Frau K's presence in the town they moved to in order for him to obtain a cure.

24. Curiously enough, according to Freud's account, these are almost the exact same words used by Ida's father regarding his own wife when he first contacted Freud to ask Freud to treat Ida (SE VII, p. 26).

25. In Seminar VIII, Lacan says that Ida "casts [Herr K] into the abyss, into the darkest shadows, at the moment at which the beast says to her the only thing that he should not have said, 'My wife means nothing to me.' Namely, she doesn't excite me. [Ida's next thought is:] 'But if she doesn't get you hard, what good are you to me?'" (p. 245). In Seminar IV (pp. 136–147), Lacan argues that when Herr K said this to her, he destroyed a complex structure in which Ida felt she was part of a circuit of desire, her father loving in and through Ida what was beyond Ida, namely, Frau K; Herr K loving Ida in and through Frau K; and Ida desiring Frau K vicariously through Herr K, hysterics always desiring vicariously, according to Lacan, and not wishing to be the exclusive object of desire for someone (moreover, if Ida were the exclusive object of desire for Herr K, perhaps that meant that Frau K was the exclusive object of desire for Ida's father, an intolerable thought). What is perhaps Lacan's most profound commentary on Ida is found in Seminar VIII, pp. 244–245; there he explains why hysterics are led to prop up the Other—in this case, their weak (impotent) fathers.

26. This is related to Lacan's notion, which grows out of Freud's analysis of the dream recounted by the butcher's wife in *The Interpretation of Dreams* (SE IV, pp. 146–151), that *a hysteric's desire is for an unsatisfied desire*; desire must not go straight to an object (like Herr K), for if it does, it might be satisfied and then disappear. There must always be an intermediary and a beyond—there must always be something more to be desired (see Lacan, *Écrits*, pp. 518–522 and 571; and Fink, 1997, pp. 123–127, 2004, pp. 20–23). Just as Herr K annihilates what serves as an intermediary and a beyond for Ida (by saying he has no use for Frau K), Freud does much the same by repeatedly trying to convince Ida that she loved and still loves Herr K and Herr K alone.

27. Ida certainly seems to have enjoyed her intimate talks alone with Frau K (just as she had with her governess), in which they spoke of both love and sex. As Lacan says at one point, "To speak of love is in itself a jouissance" (Seminar XX, p. 83). If Freud is right that she nevertheless both loved and desired Herr K, we could perhaps say that she both loved and enjoyed Frau K—in other words, whereas she could have both love and desire with the one, she could have, or potentially could have had, both love and jouissance with the other.

28. In Seminar XVI, Lacan suggests that the hysteric "is captivated by and interested in—recall Dora here—Woman insofar as she believes that [a real] Woman knows what it takes to give enjoyment to a man" (*"elle croit que la femme est celle qui sait ce qu'il faut pour la jouissance de l'homme"*; p. 387).

29. In my own clinical practice I have encountered many a woman who preferred, with her life partner, to be pleasured than to be taken, even if in her

fantasies she seemed to enjoy being taken; and many a man who preferred to pleasure his female partner and get off on his own by masturbating to pornography. Taking and being taken are, it seems, quite problematic for many people, as is sexual desire and enjoyment (or jouissance) in general.

30. We might possibly characterize what Herr K thus did as conveying to Ida that she was not the "phallus" for him, assuming we conceptualize the phallus as the precious *je ne sais quoi* that we love someone for—e.g., looks, sense of humor, personality, wealth, style, drive, gumption, or passion—corresponding as it may to something in which we feel ourselves to be lacking (yet perhaps what we truly love in others is not what we think they have, but what we think they don't have). He had perhaps led her to believe she was the phallus for him with his daily bouquet of flowers and other expensive gifts, but it suddenly seemed she was, instead, just one in a series of girls who aroused his sexual desire (in other words, just *an* object for him, not the one object—Lacan's "object *a*"—that could put a stop to the metonymic slippage of his desire). Did Ida see Frau K as someone who could comfortably occupy both positions (that of the phallus—like the *Sistine Madonna?*—and of Lacan's nonfungible object *a*), insofar as she was both loved and desired by her father? See, on these points, Fink, 2016, Chapters 3 and 8.

31. "'I can think of nothing else,' she complained again and again" (SE VII, p. 54).

32. On the importance of undergoing analysis with someone else, instead of just doing "self-analysis," see Freud's comments in SE XII, pp. 116–117.

33. It might be worth noting here that we find homosexual tendencies in everyone, and that their presence has nothing to do with the current everyday notion of "being gay." Homosexuality is not a psychoanalytic diagnosis (nor is being gay, lesbian, or bisexual), but rather a type of sexual object choice that may be exclusive, yet is not necessarily so. Some people assume that the slightest interest in or crush on someone of the same sex automatically means that one is gay or lesbian, and this is often taken to be a description of one's essence as opposed to the simple labeling of some percentage of one's current sexual fantasies or practices.

34. By 1915, Freud had changed his tune, adding a footnote to the *Three Essays on the Theory of Sexuality* (1905): "The exclusive sexual interest felt by men for women is also a problem that needs elucidating and is not a self-evident fact based upon an attraction that is ultimately of a chemical nature" (SE VII, p. 146).

35. See Lecture 33, "Femininity," in the *New Introductory Lectures on Psychoanalysis* (SE XXII), and the article entitled "Female Sexuality" (SE XXI, pp. 225–243).

36. Lacan (Seminar IV, pp. 137 and 146) asserts that a close reading of the case suggests that it was not nine months but fifteen; he does not, however, explain how he arrives at that figure.

37. A number of writers have pointed out that Ida and Frau K reportedly stayed in contact later in life and became quite expert partners in the game of bridge, which "became hugely popular in Vienna between the two world wars" (Appignanesi & Forrester, 1992):

> It is as if, across the years, they had finally dispensed with the superfluous men who had previously been their partners in their complex social

games and contracts, and yet they had retained their love of those games whose skill lies in the secretive mutual understanding of open yet coded communications within and across a foursome. Ida, adept at keeping her hand secret, also knew when and how to play it.

Freud might well have been impressed by Ida's fidelity to her friend Frau Zellenka; it certainly would have reinforced in him his belated conviction that Ida's secret love for her had been the deepest current in her mental life. He might also have thought of Ida's choice of occupation as a bridge master as an example of that rarest of all skills, successful sublimation. (p. 167)

38. Ida perhaps identified with Frau K, feeling that *Ida somehow possessed her father via Frau K,* insofar as Frau K may have told her about her intimate relations with her father. *Better still, Ida believed she possessed them both:* she perhaps felt she had intimate relations with Frau K, as well as with her father vicariously through Frau K. And she perhaps felt that her father, in loving Frau K, loved Ida via Frau K, insofar as Ida was like Frau K and necessary to his continued relations with Frau K.

39. Earlier in history, hysteria had been considered to be a specifically female form of suffering. Hippocrites, for example, coined the term *"hysterikos"* (in about 400 B.C.), meaning "of the womb," to describe certain women's bad moods, seizures, and morbid thoughts, his theory being that their wombs had migrated in their bodies from their usual location and needed to be brought back to their original position. The world's oldest known medical document, the Kahun Gynaecological Papyrus (from about 1900 B.C.), apparently had already said much the same thing (Grose, 2016, p. xv). Galen, in the second century A.D., proposed that hysteria "was caused by an unsatisfactory sex life and pointed out that nuns, virgins, widows, and women with rotten husbands were particularly likely to suffer from it" (p. xvii).

40. Recall that in her second dream, Ida asked her mother repeatedly, "Where is the key?" Could it be the key to femininity she was after, the key to being a woman?

41. Lacan points to the importance of this question in Seminar III, pp. 171–175.

42. One might compare her adoration of the *Sistine Madonna* with Marie Cardinal's (1975/1983) complex feelings about the image of Jesus that hung above her bed at home.

43. This should not be taken to imply that psychoanalysis has any business trying to define masculinity either, since masculinity is defined conventionally by one's culture; masculinity is no more a psychoanalytic concept than femininity is. The fuller passage I am referring to by Lacan reads as follows: "'Woman' [*la*] is a signifier the crucial property of which is that it is the only one that cannot signify anything, and this is simply because it grounds woman's status in the fact that she is not-whole. That means we can't talk about Woman [*La femme*]" (Seminar XX, p. 73).

44. As I have put it elsewhere, "the hysteric ostensibly seeks to divine the reasons for her *own* man's interest in another woman, but is actually more interested in unearthing the secret of femininity through this other woman so that she can become like her, thereby becoming the very essence of Woman" (Fink, 2016, p. 14), she persisting in believing such an essence exists.

According to Lacan, Ida had to *first* "exhaust" what she was looking for in

Frau K (the mystery of her own femininity) *before* she could be flattered by a man's proposition—that is, by a man situating her as the object of his desire. Herr K certainly could not tell Ida that Frau K was nothing (to him) and expect Ida to fall into his arms. As Lacan (*Écrits*) puts it in 1951:

> As is true for all women, and for reasons which are at the very crux of the most elementary social exchanges (the very exchanges Dora names as the grounds for her revolt), the problem of her condition is fundamentally that of accepting herself as a man's object of desire, and this is the mystery that motivates Dora's idolization of Frau K. In her long meditation before the Madonna and in her recourse to the role of distant worshipper, this mystery drives Dora toward the solution Christianity offered for this subjective impasse by making woman the object of a divine desire or a transcendent object of desire, which amounts to the same thing. (p. 222)

Lacan is obviously assuming here that Ida was truly interested in men, but could not yet accept to be a man's object of desire. Frau K, on the other hand, above and beyond the desire we can imagine she may herself have had for Dora's father, accepted this position as the object of a man's desire, hence Ida's idolization of her. Yet Frau K was the object of an impotent man's desire, which perhaps made her into an object of love, not of jouissance (i.e., not an object from whom anyone obtained sexual gratification), and thus akin to the Madonna. By accepting this role, Frau K became a transcendental object, an object of "worship" (SE VII, p. 26).

45. Freud refers to it as "the complete form of self-gratification by sucking" (SE VII, p. 51). Lacan opines, "What we seem to have here is the imaginary mold in which all the situations orchestrated by Dora during her life came to be cast—a perfect illustration of the theory, yet to appear in Freud's work, of repetition automatisms [better known in English as *repetition compulsions*]. We can gauge in it what woman and man signify to her now" (*Écrits*, p. 180). Lacan emphasizes the importance of Ida's identification with her slightly older brother in Seminar III, pp. 175ff. On what Lacan refers to as the "fundamental fantasy," see Fink, 2014b, Chapters 3 and 13. It is something that develops in response to foundational, existential questions like "Who am I?" "Who or what am I to my parents?" and "What do people want from me?"

46. Recall Freud's later comment that "it is not the same thing whether the analyst knows something or the patient knows it" (SE XII, p. 96), and his realization that one does not cure someone through the communication of knowledge to him or her (p. 141). Elsewhere (SE XVI), he wrote:

> If the doctor transfers his knowledge to the patient as a piece of information, it has no result. [Or] it has that of setting the analysis in motion, of which the first signs are often expressions of denial. The patient knows after this what he did not know before—the sense of his symptom; yet he knows it just as little as he did before. Thus we learn that there is more than one kind of ignorance. . . . Knowledge must rest on an internal change in the patient. (pp. 280–281; see also p. 436)

Thus it is change that is important, not knowledge per se (see Fink, 2014a, Chapter 1).

47. The genial writers of the *Frasier* television series have the radio psychiatrist Frasier Crane boast about his "God-given gift to intuit," only to show him completely mistaken in his so-called intuitions on virtually every occasion (see, in particular, the episode entitled "Can't Buy Me Love").

48. As we saw earlier, he probably had come to believe that it was a different failure on his part that led to the demise of the analysis by 1905 when he finally published the case history, that being his failure to recognize Dora's love for Frau K.

49. Nor did he take pains to distinguish himself from the problematic women in Dora's life, including her governess and Frau K, who at least in part feigned interest in her in order to get closer to her father, and who thus ultimately betrayed her.

50. Her father was obviously paying for the analysis, and the money was perhaps not even passing through Dora's hands—Freud tells us nothing about the financial transaction. Had she been paying for the analysis herself, and putting the money directly into Freud's hands, she might at least have been made aware day after day that Freud was paying attention to her because he was being paid to do so, and that might have neutralized or at least tempered her suspicion regarding his other potential motives (see SE XII, pp. 131–133).

51. On this point, see Fink, 2007, pp. 192–194 n.

52. We might even imagine the configuration with Freud in the middle, insofar as he also had dealings with Dora's father and had met Herr K. We would have to add to the configuration his imagined medical audience and readership.

53. The date of her appointment with Freud, April 1, might give us pause for thought (assuming she herself chose the date); Valérie von Raffay has informed me that there was a form of April Fools' Day in Vienna at the time where people would play jokes on each other and "send each other into April."

54. As Freud (SE VII) put it,

> It is surprising, and might easily be misleading, to find that the patient's condition shows no noticeable alteration even though considerable progress has been made with the work of analysis. But in reality things are not as bad as they seem. It is true that the symptoms do not disappear while the work is proceeding; but they disappear a little while later, when the relations between patient and physician have been dissolved. The postponement of recovery or improvement is really only caused by the physician's own person. (p. 115)

55. Lacan adds, "I have always reminded you that we must begin with the fact that transference, in the final analysis, is repetition compulsion [*automatisme*]" (Seminar VIII, p. 172). This is not to say that transference and repetition should be equated; see, on this point, Seminar XI.

56. Bringing a particular transference to the conscious attention of the patient is what is often referred to today as "interpreting the transference," which is a rather specious use of the word *interpreting*, and is perhaps designed to make us forget that interpreting very often involves tracing something back to its source. What is clear is that this banal sort of "interpreting the transference" in no way allows one to dissipate the transference, for transference is not the sort of thing one can step outside of and render null and void by having a frank, honest dialogue with the "healthy part of the patient's ego" about it (see Fink, 2004, Chapter 1, and 2007, Chapter 7).

57. As Lacan (Seminar VIII) puts it in 1961,

> Under the normal conditions of analysis—in the case of neurosis, that
> is—transference is interpreted [by those analysts who try to interpret the
> transference] on the basis of and using the instrument of transference
> itself. It is thus impossible for the analyst not to analyze, interpret, and
> intervene in the transference from the position bestowed upon him by
> transference itself. (p. 173)

58. See Gill, 1982; Gill & Hoffman, 1982; and my discussion of their work in
Fink, 2007, pp. 143–145. As Lacan puts it, "Transference, no matter how much it is
interpreted, retains within itself a kind of irreducible limit" (Seminar VIII, p. 173).

59. "Instead of remembering, [the patient] repeats attitudes and emotional
impulses from his early life which can be used as a resistance to the doctor and
the treatment by means of what is known as 'transference'" (SE XVI, p. 290).

60. In my analysand's case, it was also germane to discuss the degree to
which he wanted to dominate, suffocate, and subject me to *his* will.

61. See my critique of asking such leading questions in Fink, 2007, Chapter 2.

62. Sadistic patients may, on the other hand, engage in more of what their
analysts disclose as hurtful behavior on their part, having now a clear view of
their analysts' Achilles' heels.

63. Freud even felt that by putting an abrupt end to the analysis, Dora had
metaphorically slapped him in the face and dashed his hopes of curing her at
the very moment at which his expectations were at their apex.

64. If it can be called a "discussion," given that Freud does so much of the
talking and concluding!

65. "The great majority of dreams forge ahead of the analysis; so that, after
subtraction of everything in them which is already known and understood,
there still remains a more or less clear hint at something that has hitherto been
hidden" (SE XII, p. 96). To forget that is to be "in danger of never finding anything but what one already knows" (p. 112).

66. Elsewhere he puts it as follows: "Our therapy works by transforming
what is unconscious into what is conscious" (SE XVI, p. 280) and by "*translating* what is unconscious into what is conscious" (p. 435; my emphasis).

67. See Fink, 2007, pp. 80–81. As Lacan (2001) says,

> It is false to think that an analysis comes to a successful *dénouement*
> because the analysand consciously realizes something. . . . What is at stake
> is not a move from an unconscious level, plunged in darkness, to the con-
> scious level, the seat of clarity, by some mysterious elevator. . . . What is at
> stake is not, in fact, a move to consciousness but, rather, to speech . . . and
> that speech must be heard by someone. (pp. 139–140)

68. As I have put it elsewhere (Fink, 2007),

> It is generally advisable to allow the analysand to take the lead in starting
> off sessions and bringing up different subjects to discuss instead of regu-
> larly directing the analysand to associate to a dream recounted in the previ-
> ous session (or to return to any particular topic the analyst found especially
> interesting or important in prior sessions). The analyst who worries that

a certain opening or crucial association may be lost if he fails to return to it in the next session may find that he has lost a lot more than that by usurping the analysand's role in the therapy: the analysand may well come to feel that she is there simply to answer the analyst's questions and follow his line of inquiry, as opposed to raising her own questions about her life and taking the reins of the analysis in her own hands. (p. 106)

69. Cf. Mark 4:9 and 8:18.

70. Insofar as this is true, it belies the notion of the unconscious as a "depth" of some kind, confirming instead Lacan's notion that the unconscious can be seen right on the surface in people's rhetoric and actions (see Fink, 2007, Chapter 3), the relationship between conscious and unconscious being likened by him to the two "sides" of a Möbius strip (Seminar IX).

71. Later, Lacan (Seminar XVII, p. 98) opines that it was a lucky thing that Freud did not insist by showing a "warm personal interest in Dora," presumably because Lacan thought other analysts were doing that sort of thing as part of their misguided attempt to replace analysands' mothers and "reparent" them.

72. Certain authors like to highlight how Freud actually practiced, as opposed to how he recommends we practice. For some, this seems to be done in an attempt to emphasize his "humanity" (e.g., Ernst Langer came to a session one day famished and Freud had a meal brought to him) as opposed to his supposedly cold, strict analytic stance; for others it seems to reflect a fascination with the kind of rule breaking they associate with "genius"—they believe that only true geniuses can succeed by breaking all the rules. This strikes me as no more founded than the romanticized 19th-century equation of creativity with madness, and as related to what I would term "the cult of personality"—namely, the notion that we should study and celebrate the specific *personality traits and quirks* of those who make major breakthroughs or do supposedly significant things (think Napoleon or Einstein) as if that could reveal to us the essence of genius. It leads to the absurd view that practitioners like Freud and Lacan could do no wrong *because* they were geniuses (or that any wrong they did should be excused because they were geniuses).

73. Or his "imperious words," as Mahony (1996, p. 20) translates the German, or his "putting his foot down," as we might say.

74. Later Freud (SE XII) concludes "that dream-interpretation should not be pursued in analytic treatment as an art for its own sake; its handling should be subject to those technical rules that govern the conduct of the treatment as a whole" (p. 94).

75. Calling such authority into question is part and parcel of what Lacan refers to as the *hysteric's discourse* (see, above all, Seminars XVII and XX).

76. Perhaps Freud would, at some level, have liked to give Herr K what Frau K refused him! See SE VII, p. 70.

77. It would not be a stretch, I think, to say that Freud *invented* the literary genre of detailed case studies with this "Fragment" (less detailed case histories had been written up by him in *Studies on Hysteria*), and that few other analysts have contributed much to the genre. Some of the strangeness of the Dora case is perhaps attributable to this first-of-its-kind status (Marcus refers to its "novelistic framing"; 1975/1990, p. 270).

78. The confusion of symptoms with structure will be discussed at length in Chapter 6.

79. For some recent cases of "old-time" hysteria, see Dominus, 2012.

80. Showalter (1997) goes much further in her discussion of new forms of mass hysteria: "The heroes and heroines of 1990s hysteria call themselves traumatists and ufologists, experiencers and abductees, survivors and survivalists" (pp. 5–8), adding conspiracy theorists of all ilks and those who believe they have "recovered memories" of past abuse. Bollas (1983) provides a very odd comment about what has become of the hysteria of the past: "In the contemporary hysteric it is not her body and self that is innervated but the analyst who is innervated in his countertransference" (p. 26); in other words, it would seem that, to Bollas, it is analysts themselves who now suffer from the symptoms that hysterics formerly suffered from!

81. Freud himself makes a similar mistake, I would suggest, in his *Introductory Lectures on Psychoanalysis* (SE XVI, Chapter 17, especially p. 258), where he diagnoses two cases of hysteria as obsession simply because they include obsessive (bedtime and other) rituals. He seems at times to have confused conversion with hysteria, whereas conversion can occur in a variety of clinical structures.

82. I have not delved into the complex relationship between resistance and transference here, as I have done so extensively elsewhere (Fink, 2007, Chapter 7).

83. Freud opines, "In the early years of my psychoanalytic practice I used to have the greatest difficulty prevailing upon my patients to continue their analyses. This difficulty has long since been shifted, and I now have to take the greatest pains to induce them to give them up" (SE XII, p. 130). Can you imagine following Freud's advice to make the patient "promise not to make any important decisions affecting his life during the time of his treatment" (SE XII, p. 153), whether they regard the "choice of a profession, business undertakings, marriage, or divorce" (SE XVI, p. 434), when his analysis is likely to last the better part of a decade?

Chapter 6: Symptom Formation

1. "A symptom brings with it a jouissance that satisfies even if it is not pleasurable. It is in this respect that symptoms are related to the real [as opposed to the imaginary and the symbolic], for they do not appeal to the [symbolic] Other" (Association mondiale de psychanalyse, 1994, p. 155). As Freud puts it, "We have every reason to believe that sensations of pain, like other unpleasurable sensations, verge on sexual excitation and produce a pleasurable condition, for the sake of which a subject will even willingly experience the unpleasure of pain" (SE XIV, p. 128).

2. Freud classes the phobias under "anxiety hysteria," or what he sometimes calls "anxiety neurosis" (SE XXII, p. 85). According to Freud, "anxiety neurosis" is a condition of "free-floating anxiety" often found prior to the formation of a phobia; the anxiety becomes pinned down and localized when a specific phobia forms (SE XVI, pp. 398–400).

3. Indeed, Freud felt that psychoanalysis was effective, at that point in time, only for neurotics: "These three disorders, which we are accustomed to group together as 'transference neuroses,' circumscribe the region in which psychoanalytic therapy can function" (SE XVI, p. 299). Elsewhere (SE XII) he adds the following:

I am aware that there are psychiatrists who hesitate less often in their differential diagnosis [than psychoanalysts], but I have become convinced that just as often they make mistakes. It is far more important to avoid making mistakes for the psychoanalyst than it is for the "clinical psychiatrist," as he is called. For the latter is not attempting to do anything that will be of use, whichever kind of case it may be. He merely runs the risk of making a theoretical mistake, and his diagnosis is of no more than academic interest. Where the psychoanalyst is concerned, however, if the case is unfavorable he has committed a practical error; he has been responsible for wasted expenditure and has discredited his method of treatment. He cannot fulfill his promise of cure if the patient is suffering, not from hysteria or obsessional neurosis, but from paraphrenia, and he therefore has particularly strong motives for avoiding mistakes in diagnosis. (pp. 124–125)

4. The late 19th- and early 20th-century psychiatrist Gaëtan Gatian de Clérambault, one of Lacan's professors in psychiatry, had used the term "mental automatisms" (or "mental compulsions") for many of the same phenomena.

5. Although neither the noun *foreclosure* nor its various verb forms (*to foreclose, forecloses,* and *foreclosed*) is used in the *Standard Edition* of Freud's work as translations for terms derived from the German *Verwerfung* (e.g., *verwarf* and *verworfen*), they could well have been used instead of "rejected" and "abominated" in SE XVII, pp. 84–85.

6. See "Fetishism" (SE XXI, pp. 152–157, especially p. 153), SE XIX, p. 143 n, and Fink, 1997, Chapter 9. On so-called perverse sexual acts, see SE VII, pp. 49–50, where the notion of what is normal is called into question. "The unconscious fantasies of neurotics show precisely the same content as the documentarily recorded actions of perverts. . . . Neuroses are, so to speak, the negative of perversions" (p. 50)—that is, neurotics fantasize about doing the very things perverts actually do.

7. The authors of the *DSM-5* apparently claim that it includes 157 truly distinct disorders (APA, 2013). The proliferation of disorders is at least partly due to the fabrication of new diseases based on the discovery of drugs that have a particular effect—for example, if a drug is shown to reduce anxiety in social situations, a disorder is created from what was previously just referred to as shyness, insecurity, or awkwardness: *social anxiety disorder*. In this sense, "the discovery of the remedy creates the disease" (Menand, 2010). Let us note, too, the degree to which politics, not science, is involved in the determination, on the part of the *DSM*'s authors, of what constitutes a disorder and what does not:

Homosexuality, originally labelled a sociopathic personality disorder, was eliminated from the *D.S.M.* in 1973, partly in response to lobbying by gay-rights groups. The manual then inserted the category "ego-dystonic homosexuality"—distress because of the presence of homosexual arousal or the absence of heterosexual arousal. Further lobbying eliminated this category as well. Post-traumatic stress disorder was lobbied for by veterans' organizations and resisted by the Veterans Administration, and got in, while self-defeating personality disorder was lobbied against by women's groups, and was deleted. (Menand, 2010)

8. Whereas it strikes me as implausible that *DSM-5* categories can be of use to most clinicians, the authors of that manual nevertheless claim that "until incontrovertible etiological or pathophysiological mechanisms are identified to fully validate specific disorders or disorder spectra, the most important standard for the *DSM-5* disorder criteria will be their *clinical utility* for the assessment of clinical course and treatment response of individuals grouped by a given set of diagnostic criteria" (APA, 2013, p. 20, my emphasis). Note, however, that "assessment of clinical course and treatment response" is hardly equivalent to guidance regarding how to direct the treatment. Yet the manual's authors also claim that "the primary purpose of *DSM-5* is to assist trained clinicians in the diagnosis of their patients' mental disorders as part of a case formulation assessment that leads to a fully informed treatment plan for each individual" (p. 19). They claim, too, that the criteria included under each disorder "are intended to summarize characteristic syndromes of signs and symptoms that point to *an underlying disorder* with a characteristic developmental history, biological and environmental risk factors, neuropsychological and physiological correlates, and typical clinical course" (p. 19, my emphasis); thus they have not altogether abandoned the idea of "underlying" conditions or structures, even if they tend to think of them as primarily biological in origin.

9. Exceptions to this may occur when an analyst believes that a particular patient is engaging in truly life-threatening activities without considering them to be in any way problematic, or doing things that jeopardize the continuation of the treatment.

10. Freud went on there to add: "The distinction between nervous health and neurosis is thus reduced to a practical question and is decided by whether the subject is left with a sufficient capacity for enjoyment and efficacy" (SE XVI, p. 457). Elsewhere he wrote, "It is not only that neurotics in themselves constitute a very numerous class, but it must also be considered that an unbroken chain bridges the gap between the neuroses in all their manifestations and normality" (SE VII, p. 171).

11. Recall that, strictly speaking, urges are *sup*pressed, whereas the thoughts and wishes associated with them are *re*pressed.

12. In most English translations of Freud's work, Freud seems to say that it is reality itself that forces us to give up certain pleasures, insofar as it repeatedly "frustrates" us, but two things should be noted here: (a) As I mentioned in Chapter 1, the term Freud usually uses in this context is *Versagung*, which means several things, including privation, denial, refusal, and disallowance—Lacan interprets it as "renunciation," perhaps basing this on the various uses of the verb *versagen* (implying, in certain instances, to fail, bungle, break down, or botch), not frustration (the German term for frustration is *Frustration*). "Renunciation" implies that one wanted to do something and gave up on it, often as if one were giving in to someone else's wishes (as in self-denial). In other words, it suggests a situation in which one allows someone else's will to prevail over one's own (or allows what one *imagines* someone else's will to be to prevail over one's own) and regrets it forever thereafter. (b) It should be clear that infants and toddlers are rarely confronted with reality directly (for example, with everything involved in producing food and shelter in the world as we know it); reality is, in large part, mediated for them by their parents and social environment. Taken together, these two points imply that young children are not "frustrated

by reality" but rather that they more or less willingly renounce certain urges and pleasures in order to deal with their parents' demands and wishes.

In her translation of "Some Character Types Encountered in Psychoanalytic Work," Louise Adey Huish helpfully translates *Versagung* as "refusal" in the opening line of Part 2: "Psychoanalytic work has bestowed on us the following dictum: people succumb to neurotic illness as a consequence of *refusal* [*Versagung*]" (S. Freud, 2002, p. 329). Her use of the term "refusal" here nicely leaves open the question of who it is that is doing the refusing (not to mention who is refusing what to whom); Strachey's translation ("People fall ill of a neurosis as a result of *frustration*" in SE XIV, p. 316) closes down or papers over this question.

Note, however, that at a couple of points Freud talks about "internal frustration" and "external frustration" (SE XVI, pp. 350 and 355), which is perhaps not quite so easy to translate in terms of renunciation or self-denial. Similarly for his discussion of "real frustration" arising from "deprivation of love, poverty, family quarrels, ill-judged choice of a partner in marriage, unfavorable social circumstances, and the strictness of ethical standards to whose pressure the individual is subject" (p. 432); and for his mention of frustration as involving "some privation in real life" (SE XII, p. 57). Note, however, that Blanton (1971) reports that Freud once commented to him that "there is a German school [of psychology] that thinks of neurosis as being caused by frustration" (p. 93), a view with which Freud seemed obviously to disagree.

13. In *Pretty Woman*, Edward Lewis (played by Richard Gere) is, for example, depicted as attempting to take over and break apart the company his own father founded.

14. Hence the terms *psychodynamic* and *dynamic therapy*, which are often code words for a kind of watered-down psychoanalysis, or as a colleague once put it, "psychoanalysis light." In many instances, "psychodynamic psychotherapy" has retained the notion of an interplay of forces but jettisoned the unconscious (except in a rather weak and often misguided sense) as one of the forces involved in the interplay, along with sexuality.

15. For a more detailed account of my work with this woman, see Fink, 1997, Chapter 8.

16. This was generally accompanied by the idea (or seemingly counterintuitive wish) that his father was dominating and victimizing him by taking all women away from him.

17. Had anyone attempted to give Anna O water in some other way (whether by spoon, squirting it in her mouth, or having her suck it in through a tube or bottle), she might have had no problem, since no glass would have been involved; if, alternatively, she had a total aversion to water itself after having seen the dog drink the water from her friend's glass, she might have been able to drink milk, juice, and so on from a glass; and if it was both the water and the glass that had become problematic for her, she might still have been able to drink other liquids from metal goblets, ceramic bowls, or wooden spoons. In this way it could have been determined which exact feature of the sight of the dog drinking out of the glass had taken on the most significance for her.

18. A symptom can thus be thought of as saying something, which is what the analyst does too when he or she speaks. "This assumes that the symptom and the analyst's intervention are of much the same order" (Lacan, 1976, p. 46).

19. People often become fixated on such overpowering past experiences, and their erotic fantasies and tastes remain durably influenced by them. In the case of Freud's patient, there may have been a strong erotic attachment to her father (whom her husband then reminded her of; SE XVI, p. 273). Several patients I have worked with were long fixated on people (often teenage girls or boys) who were the age they themselves were when they had their first significant sexual experiences and the age of their first sexual partners. See, in this connection, SE XVIII, pp. 230–231.

20. We might also postulate that remaining alone kept her from having to confront the fact that no relationship (involving love, desire, and jouissance) is ever perfect—there being, in Lacan's view, "no such thing as a sexual relationship"—and that it allowed her to continue to ignore the unconscious cause of her desire.

21. On the hysteric's maintenance of an unsatisfied desire, see Fink, 1997, pp. 123–127.

22. Her ritual may also have helped her feel she was, in spite of it all, the object of her husband's sexual desire, she perhaps having felt that he did not find her exciting enough on their wedding night (hence his difficulty maintaining an erection).

23. Freud suggests that one reason vomiting is so often encountered in female hysterics is that it is connected with the idea of (or wish for) pregnancy, insofar as pregnancy is associated in many people's minds with morning sickness (SE XII, p. 262).

24. We might well imagine that had she been willing to get divorced, the symptom would have disappeared or never have formed in the first place. Consider, in this context, what Freud says in SE VII: "Illnesses of this kind are the result of intention. They are as a rule leveled at a particular person, and consequently vanish with that person's departure" (p. 45).

25. As Freud tells us, a phobia is "constructed in order to avoid an outbreak of anxiety; the phobia is erected like a frontier fortification [*avant-poste*] against the anxiety" (SE V, p. 581). Thus, when one phobia is cleared up, another may eventually appear if the anxiety that generated the first phobia is still present.

26. Similarly, we must be careful not to too quickly associate a certain type of clinical presentation with a specific diagnosis. Whereas hysterics often present themselves as living in a world populated with lots of other people and spend a great deal of time talking about them in therapy, obsessives often present themselves as living in a world of their own and talk almost exclusively about themselves. Hysterics are also usually very attuned to the analyst's facial expressions and speech, whereas obsessives often avoid looking at the analyst altogether and pay little attention to what he or she says, seeming to prefer not to hear it. Hysterics may be very open to the analysts' views, whereas obsessives appear to want to be influenced and helped by no one but themselves. Nevertheless, these are merely broad generalizations, and cannot provide us with definitive diagnoses.

Lacan distinguishes hysteria from obsession differently from Freud, suggesting—roughly speaking—that obsessives feel they are lacking (feel they themselves are missing something) and try to fill that lack (or plug it up) by getting or taking something (an object that brings them jouissance) from another person, whereas hysterics see lack in others (the Other, as Lacan calls it, the mother or father at the outset) and try to fill that lack with themselves (they themselves playing the part of the precious object they believe the Other is missing). Furthermore, obsessives cannot stand to perceive lack in the Other and seek to plug it up as quickly as possible; hysterics, on the other hand, look for and cultivate the lack in the Other, as it gives them a place in life, a *raison d'être*. For a more complete articulation of this approach to distinguishing hysteria from obsession, see Fink, 1997, Chapter 8.

Despite all of this commentary on hysteria and obsession, we need not conclude that they are universal structures valid for all cultures and historical eras. It is far from clear, it seems to me, that they are valid for a culture like that of the Na people in China (see Hua, 2008).

27. "A symptom signifies the representation—the realization—of a fantasy with a sexual content" (SE VII, p. 47).

28. "Sexuality . . . provides the motor force for every single symptom, and for every single manifestation of a symptom. The symptoms of a disease are nothing other than *the patient's sexual activity*. . . . Sexuality is the key to the problem of the neuroses in general" (SE VII, p. 115).

29. *Thanatos* is a term that was introduced for the death drive by Wilhelm Stekel, not Freud. Freud appears never to have used it in his published work.

30. Conversely, one and the same function can, in the course of one's lifetime, be expressed in different symptoms.

31. These can be roughly rendered as "it gets me in the throat," "my throat is in knots" or "all knotted up," "I couldn't swallow it (because it was stuck in my throat)," "I have a lump in my throat," and "I've got lumps in my throat" (meaning I'm very upset or scared out of my wits).

32. "We have found it necessary to hold aloof from biological considerations during our psychoanalytic work and to refrain from using them for heuristic purposes, so that we may not be misled in our impartial judgment of the psychoanalytic facts before us" (SE XIII, pp. 181–182).

33. Freud also occasionally referred to "mixed neuroses"—that is, neuroses whose causes were both physical and psychical (SE II, pp. 257–259).

34. "Anxiety neurosis is actually the somatic counterpart to hysteria," hysteria being psychical (SE III, p. 115).

35. The most complete discussion by Freud of the actual neuroses that I know of is found in SE XVI, pp. 385–391; see also SE II, p. 258 n, SE III, p. 279 and n. 1, and SE XIV, p. 83. In Freud's terminology, the actual neuroses include neurasthenia, anxiety neurosis, and certain trauma states (that are caused by actual events, not by psychological conflict). On anxiety neurosis, see SE III, pp. 90–115; it is like "neurasthenia" (which is characterized by an "impoverishment of excitation"; SE III, p. 114) and is based on real causes like "overwork or exhaustion" (p. 102), coitus interruptus, or abstinence. It is not a psychologically caused neurosis, even though it may include thoughts like imagining one's husband dying or one's child falling out the window (p. 92). It can be brought on in virginal girls "by their first encounter with the problem of sex" (p. 99).

36. Freud seems to have called them "narcissistic" because he hypothesized that they involved the withdrawal of libidinal cathexes from one's objects and the focusing of virtually all of one's libido on oneself (SE XVI, pp. 415–418).

37. Note that the presence of a somewhat short-lived childhood phobia in someone's clinical history is not sufficient to call for a diagnosis of phobic structure. Such phobias are regularly found in hysterics and obsessives, but they usually disappear rather quickly. There is some question as to whether phobia deserves to be considered a separate diagnostic structure, even for those suf-

fering from long-lasting phobias; as Freud says, "It seems certain that [phobias] should only be regarded as syndromes which may form part of various neuroses and that we need not rank them as an independent pathological process" (SE X, p. 115). Yet Lacan at one point suggests that phobia is "the most radical form of neurosis" (Seminar VIII, p. 366), and elsewhere that it is "the simplest form of neurosis" (Seminar VI, p. 503). On this point, see Fink, 1997, pp. 163–164.

38. Lacan's contributions to the study of symptoms are many and wide-ranging, spanning as they do the half-century of his psychoanalytic work. They include such notions as:

- That symptoms have a "formal envelope" (*Écrits*, p. 52).
- That a symptom can serve as *a* "Name-of-the-Father."
- That symptoms form because, strictly speaking, "there's no such thing as a sexual relationship" (Seminar XX, p. 12).
- That a symptom takes the place of the sexual relationship, which does not exist.
- That symptoms can be classed under a broader heading, "sinthomes," which are ways of tying together the imaginary, symbolic, and real.
- That "identification with one's symptom" (Seminar XXIV, class given on November 16, 1976) is one possible positive outcome of an analysis.
- That one may learn through one's analysis to *savoir y faire avec* one's symptom (learn how to do things with it, learn how to get by with it, handle it, make do with it, or make it work for oneself) (Seminar XXIV, November 16, 1976).

Each of these contributions would require extensive commentary and are thus beyond the scope of this book. I have discussed a number of these perspectives on symptoms elsewhere (see Fink, 2007, 2014a, and 2014b) and interested readers can find additional useful commentary on these contributions in other texts (e.g., Miller, 1985; Soler, 1993, 2015). It should be immediately clear just from reading this short list that Lacan's focus is less on resolving or eliminating symptoms altogether, and—since symptoms may serve a number of important functions—more on finding a new and more livable stance with respect to one's symptoms.

Chapter 7: Beyond Freud?

1. Roughly half of the authors who defined the *DSM-IV* psychiatric disorders had financial relationships with the pharmaceutical industry at one time or another, suggesting likely conflicts of interest (Cosgrove, Krimsky, Vijayaraghavan, & Schneider, 2006). When it came to diagnoses for which drugs were listed by the *DSM* as the first line of treatment, 100% of the panel members had financial ties with Big Pharma. Steven Sharfstein, who was vice president and then president of the American Psychiatric Association in the 2000s, conceded that psychiatrists had "allowed the biopsychosocial model to become the bio-bio-bio model" (2005).

2. See, for example, SE XVI, pp. 264–269. Freud seems to have managed to help certain patients despite this contraindicated approach (see, in particular, p. 266).

3. See Koellreuter, 2016.

4. At times he even purportedly told analysands that he thought this person or that person had had a satisfactory analysis or not (see, for example, Blanton, 1971, p. 90), and told his analysands whether or not he felt they were competent enough to be training analysts themselves (p. 109).

5. Wortis (1954) comes off, in his account, as something of a simpleminded idiot who was as touchy as Freud himself and happy to provoke Freud into sterile debates about abstract topics.

6. He perhaps hoped to teach analysts-in-training what Henry Fielding taught us: "It is often safer to abide by the consequences of the first blunder than to endeavor to rectify it, for by such endeavors we generally plunge deeper instead of extricating ourselves" (1749/1979, p. 682).

7. Freud also apparently told Blanton that, although it was more difficult to analyze friends (like the Brunswicks), it *was* possible, and that even "brother and sister, or husband and wife, might be analyzed at the same time" (1971, p. 79).

8. Indeed, we might go so far as to conclude that Freud did not even aspire to become a better clinician when we read something he said or wrote to Abram Kardiner (1977; Kardiner did not indicate whether he was transcribing a letter or reporting more or less verbatim what Freud said to him in person):

> Frankly, I have no great interest in therapeutic problems. I am much too impatient now. I have several handicaps that disqualify me as a great analyst. One of them is that I am too much the father. Second, I am much too occupied with theoretical problems all the time, so that whenever I get occasion, I am working on my own theoretical problems, rather than paying attention to the therapeutic problems. Third, I have no patience in keeping people for a long time. I tire of them, and I want to spread my influence. (pp. 68–69)

Such comments—assuming they are true—might well be viewed as quite unforgivable on the part of a practicing psychoanalyst, and a betrayal of the profession as a whole on the part of its founder. Blanton claims that Freud told him that "the chief aim of psychoanalysis is to contribute to the science of psychology and to the world of literature and life in general," not to therapeutic needs, even if the latter "aim is not to be disparaged" (1971, p. 116).

9. This can go too far, leading analysts to overlook aspects of dreams, for example, that have nothing to do with transference. In one of my analysand's dreams, for example, the word *seven* appeared. I was aware that this particular analysand's sessions with me were at 7 a.m., but rather than immediately saying that and thereby suggesting that the dream was primarily about us, I asked, "What about seven?" His first association to seven was the "seven deadly sins," which led to a long discussion of his mother's fervent religiosity, and the fact that, for most of his childhood and adolescence, she got him to confess his every "sin" to her, including masturbation. Transference was not unconnected to *seven* in the dream, because he sometimes thought of analysis as like confession, but seven had at least two meanings—in other words, it was overdetermined.

As I have indicated elsewhere (Fink, 2007, Chapter 7), transference does not arise solely in psychoanalysis; it also arises in the classroom between teachers and students, in the workplace between those higher up and those lower down in the hierarchy, in "civil society" between voters and politicians, and in human relationships of all kinds. One of the earliest historical instances of transference we know of is the relationship between Socrates and his followers (see Lacan, Seminar VIII; and Fink, 2016).

10. One of my analysands once told me the following, in comparing me to his previous therapists: "You exist as little as possible to achieve the highest degree of efficacy."

11. For an account of them, see Fink, 2007, Chapter 7.

12. He wrote that "sufferers from narcissistic neuroses have no capacity for transference or only insufficient residues of it" and that "our therapeutic efforts have no success with the narcissistic neuroses" (SE XVI, p. 447).

13. He proffered that "we analysts see too few psychiatric cases," a synonym for cases of psychoses here (SE XVI, p. 423). It seems more likely that he saw a number of such cases without recognizing them as such.

14. This is mistranslated in the English edition as "reject of the unconscious."

15. Warner's (1994) account of Freud's work with Frink also indicates just how far Freud was from following somewhat widely accepted contemporary technique: Freud says that analysts must not dispense advice (and that "there is nothing we would rather bring about than that the patient should make his decisions for himself"; SE XVI, p. 433), but he himself gave plenty of advice to Frink about his marriage, in particular; and he engaged in "dual relations" by intervening in Frink's career. Kardiner's (1977) account of his own analysis with Freud in 1921–1922—which must obviously be taken with quite a few grains of salt given that it was written 55 years after the fact (perhaps on the basis of notes taken at the time, but perhaps not, since he does not tell us)—provides still more examples of Freud's deviation from what is now fairly widely accepted technique: Freud would apparently meet analysands arriving from distant shores at the train station with his wife and daughter (p. 16); told analysands that he needed to consult with his wife and daughter Anna about how to deal with a shortage of hours to devote to the excessive number of patients he had (p. 18); told certain analysts what he thought about others who were doing training analyses with him (he wrote to Frink that "Kardiner's analysis is complete and perfect. He ought to have a great career"; p. 68); and, to top it all off, engaged in small talk and gossip about other analysts and analytic candidates during sessions (p. 70). Kardiner is nevertheless full of praise regarding Freud's brilliance and the benefits he received from his analysis (pp. 93 and 97).

16. I have discussed the contentious topic of session length in detail in Fink, 2007, Chapter 4.

Appendix I

1. See SE IV, p. *xx*; and Jones (1953, p. 253, 1955, pp. 286, 335, 347). The Rat Man did, however, come to Freud for treatment after having briefly thumbed through the pages of *The Psychopathology of Everyday Life* (see SE X, pp. 158–159).

2. It seems that fellow physicians referred numerous potential patients to Freud, and that former patients told their friends and families about him as well—as is true today for a great many practitioners who are well respected in their communities. It should nevertheless be kept in mind that in the early decades of his practice, Freud was, like many Lacanians in America today still

are, a mental health provider of last resort, people often being sent to him only after they had tried virtually every other form of treatment known at the time. This meant that he was working with those who were considered to be among the most difficult patients (see SE VII, p. 21 n).

3. Freud is quite modest about the degree of success he achieved in his work with Emmy von N. and others in *Studies on Hysteria* (see, for example, SE II, p. 85).

4. I am leaving aside here, for the time being, the potentially dangerous side effects of the medications that may be used in the treatment of the acne.

5. As Shedler (2010, p. 103) points out, clinicians purportedly providing evidence-based or empirically validated therapies (e.g., manualized versions of CBT) do not all practice in the same way, and many incorporate psychodynamic elements into their work without acknowledging it:

> Even in controlled studies designed to compare manualized treatments, therapists interact with patients in different ways, implement interventions differently, and introduce processes not specified by the treatment manuals (Elkin et al., 1989). In some cases, investigators have had difficulty determining from verbatim session transcripts which manualized treatment was being provided (Ablon & Jones, 2002).
>
> For these reasons, studies of therapy "brand names" can be highly misleading. Studies that look beyond brand names by examining session videotapes or transcripts may reveal more about what is helpful to patients (Goldfried & Wolfe, 1996; Kazdin, 2007, 2008). Such studies indicate that the active ingredients of other therapies include unacknowledged psychodynamic elements.

Shedler goes on to say that

> In three sets of archival treatment records (one from a study of cognitive therapy and two from studies of brief psychodynamic therapy), the researchers measured therapists' adherence to each therapy prototype without regard to the treatment model the therapists believed they were applying (Ablon & Jones, 1998). Therapist adherence to the psychodynamic prototype predicted successful outcome in both psychodynamic and cognitive therapy. Therapist adherence to the CBT prototype showed little or no relation to outcome in either form of therapy. The findings replicated those of an earlier study that employed a different methodology and also found that psychodynamic interventions, not CBT interventions, predicted successful outcome in both cognitive and psychodynamic treatments (Jones & Pulos, 1993).

On the basis of his own research, Shedler (2010, p. 106) suggests that "Psychodynamic therapy may not only alleviate symptoms but also develop inner capacities and resources that allow a richer and more fulfilling life," going on to opine that, "Perhaps this is why psychotherapists, irrespective of their own theoretical orientations, tend to choose psychodynamic psychotherapy for themselves (Norcross, 2005)." This is quite telling indeed, and is a little-known fact (some might call it the "dirty little secret") about clinicians' own preferences:

when they themselves have problems or difficulties in life, they tend to seek out psychoanalysis, not CBT or whatever other form of therapy they have spent years being trained in.

6. On the imaginary and the symbolic, see Fink, 1995, 1997, 2004, 2007, 2014a, and 2016.

7. We see that he perhaps found a way to present, alongside the conclusions, at least some facets of the technique he employed in his write-up of the case of Ernst Langer (aka the Rat Man), insofar as he begins his account of his work with Ernst with something of a blow-by-blow description of the first six sessions. In the Dora case, Freud opines that he "would not have known how to deal with the material involved in the history of a treatment which had lasted, perhaps, for a whole year" (SE VII, p. 11); imagine, then, the difficulties facing an analyst presenting a decade-long analysis, who would like to include a feel for the moment-to-moment and day-to-day technique being employed!

Regarding the 2013 retranslation of the case, note that someone (either Anthea Bell herself or someone at Oxford University Press) chose for it the exact same cover image—a detail of *Portrait of a Young Girl* by Alexej von Jawlensky—as that found on the cover of Marie Cardinal's (1975/1983) *Les mots pour le dire* (*The Words to Say It*), which is the somewhat fictionalized account of the analysis of an hysteric that is about as diametrically opposed to Freud's as can be imagined. It was written by the analysand herself (not by her male analyst), and she did most of the analyzing in the course of it, the analyst seeming quite discreet and even self-effacing—staying out of her way, one might say. A funny choice of covers, to say the least! Marie Cardinal's book is, by the way, a highly recommended counterweight to Freud's.

Those critics who do take account of the fragmentary nature of the Dora case often express the view that they think Freud doth protest too much! See, for example, Marcus (1975/1990, pp. 265–270) and Mahony (1996).

8. Freud writes there: "Certain details of the way in which she expressed herself (which I pass over here, like most other purely technical parts of the analysis) led me to see . . ." (SE VII, p. 47).

9. Marcus' analysis of the Dora case from a literary standpoint is well worth reading, and he provides useful reflections on its fragmentary status (Marcus, 1975/1990, pp. 265–270).

10. If only he had been tongue-tied instead of feeling his hands were tied!

11. Mahony (1996, p. 18) argues—based on a widely circulated November 1, 1882, birthdate for Ida, whose origin he never reveals and that I have been unable to confirm in any source—that Ida was 13 when Herr K tried to kiss her, 15 when he propositioned her, and 17 when she started working with Freud, turning 18 after the first two weeks of therapy. (Her brother, Otto, said by Freud to have been a year and a half older than her, was reportedly born on September 5, 1881.) Mahony (1996), Decker (1991), and Rogow (1978; 1979) all claim to have gotten information from Peter Loewenberg, who claims to have had access to a letter written by Kurt Eissler to Hannah Fenichel on July 8, 1952, that is now in the Freud Archives in Washington; Loewenberg also claims to have had independent verification of Ida's identity and other facts about her from unpublished interviews with Marie Jahoda, Hilde Hannak, Paul Lazarsfeld, and Ida's son.

12. We might, however, note that, after the kissing incident, she continued to see Herr K as before, just not alone (SE VII, p. 28). Freud thinks it is obvious

that Herr K had an erection when he caught Ida in his arms, and thus that her memory of feeling his body against her torso was actually a displacement from the genital region upward; he mentions that after the kiss, she was unwilling "to walk past any man whom she saw engaged in eager or affectionate conversation with a lady" (pp. 29–30). Is it really true that there is no other plausible explanation of her unwillingness to do so than the possibility that Herr K had an erection? Couldn't it simply be that his eagerness or brusqueness in his shop that day had surprised and unsettled her? Or that she wanted a man to love and cherish her, not ravish her, preferring, at that age (13 or 14), romantic love to physical passion?

13. Freud indicates that she must have known that to fall asleep her father needed either sex or cognac (or brandy; SE VII, p. 98).

14. See, on this topic, Fink, 2007, Chapter 9. By the end of their analyses, analyzed people are probably some the most "abnormal" people around! They tend to follow their own bents, caring little about fitting into molds, and are slaves to neither social conventions nor the flouting of such conventions.

15. Note that instead of simply asking Ida if she ever recalled wetting her bed as a child (or recalled her brother wetting his), Freud presents it to her as something he is sure she did, as if to bully her into admitting to having done something shameful.

16. Bernheimer reads the Dora case "as a symptomatic continuation of [Freud's] ongoing self-analysis, as a fragment of the analysis of *his* case of hysteria" (1990, p. 17). Note that many of the contributors to the volume to which his paper serves as an introduction misinterpret Lacan's contribution to the debate owing to their total reliance on the unreliable English translation of his paper on the Dora case (*"Intervention sur le transfert"*) by Jacqueline Rose in *Feminine Sexuality* (1982), as well as the commentaries by Jacqueline Rose and Juliet Mitchell on Lacan's work in that same volume. Suzanne Gearhart's paper (1990), for example, manifests misunderstanding after misunderstanding of what Lacan means by the imaginary, the symbolic, transference, and countertransference (1990, pp. 108–118).

17. Suggestive of a certain lack of intellectual integrity, none of Sprengnether's (1990) comments on what Freud says about the kind of language to be used in speaking of sexual matters with patients (p. 261) or about the possibility of Ida reading his case write-up (pp. 262–263) takes into account the social and historical context of Victorian values and the medical prejudices of the time. Much that strikes me as dubious forcing and prodding in Freud's work with Ida is repeated by Sprengnether in identical (mirrored or mimetic) gestures, as in a kind of imaginary tit for tat.

18. Mahony even goes so far as to say that Herr K was a "statutory rapist" (1996, pp. 63–64). Mahony seems to have it in for all the men involved in Ida's story. This is not to say that Herr K was innocent: He clearly asserted that Ida had made up the whole story about the lakeside proposal, which is fairly typical of child abusers, rapists, and so on, and perhaps tried to intimidate her with his greater physical power as well.

19. Onfray, an *enfant terrible* on the contemporary French scene, makes numerous factual mistakes right from the very beginning of his book devoted to bashing Freud (Onfray, 2010), inadvertently making it clear that he has read precious little of Freud's work (or at least understood precious little of it). Pseudo-

intellectual critics like Onfray seem to be trying to obtain notoriety by riding the tide of Freud bashing that has become popular in recent years.

20. The incredible (almost delusional) flights of fancy engaged in by analysts and literary critics as they analyze Freud, bringing together everyone by the name of Dora in his past (including Joseph Breuer's daughter, the characters named Dora in Victorien Sardou's play entitled *Théodora* which Freud once saw, etc.; see Mahony, 1996, p. 43 n. 2), as if they knew which one of them was the most germane to Freud's choice of a pseudonym for Ida Bauer, as if they knew Freud far better than he knew himself—which perhaps his wife or daughter did, but few others, I would suspect—seem pretty patently absurd on the part of people who never even met the man. We can obviously postulate certain things about Freud based on his letters, writings, and so on, provided that we recall that letters written even to the best of friends rarely contain the truth, the whole truth, and nothing but the truth; but to assert that we have really figured out Freud as a person is even more far-fetched than to assert that we know everything about our patients, even those with whom we have worked for years (see Fink, 2014a, pp. xi–xii). This does not stop certain critics from believing they have also discovered Ida's "true motives" for what *she* did, said, and wanted.

21. In Seminar XX (p. 1), Lacan makes it quite clear that teaching puts him in the position of an analysand in front of his audience.

22. Mahony writes, "In the annals of Western culture, Dora has emerged as a paradigmatic example of how patriarchal forces in the nineteenth century— political, social, and medical—oppressed a Jewish girl who had to write out her pain in her body" (1996, p. 2). And Leader comments, "Deprived of any other means to communicate their malaise or their pain, [hysterical subjects] would use the symptoms available in a culture as 'idioms of distress'" (2016, p. 27).

23. We might note that she was subsequently "handed over" by her father to Freud for treatment (SE VII, p. 19).

24. We see here a conflation, on the part of certain feminists, of hysteria and femininity, as if they were coextensive. Consider Toril Moi's (1990) comment,

> Hysteria is not . . . the incarnation of the revolt of women forced to silence but rather a declaration of defeat, the realization that there is no other way out. Hysteria is, as Catherine Clément perceives, a cry for help when defeat becomes real, when the woman sees that she is efficiently gagged and chained to her feminine role. (p. 192)

25. Lacan's comment (*Écrits*) is, I think, worth considering at length:

> It is due to this indubitable origin, blatant in all of Freud's work, and to the lesson he left us as head of a school, that Marxism is unable—and I do not believe any Marxist has seriously contested this point—to attack his ideas on the basis of their historical extraction.
>
> I have in mind here his affiliation with the society of the dual monarchy, Freud remaining confined within Judaizing limits in his spiritual aversions; and [his affiliation] with the capitalist order that conditioned his political agnosticism . . . ; and, I would add, [his affiliation] with bourgeois ethics, for which the dignity of his life inspires in us a respect that has prevented his work from attaining a stature—otherwise than in our

misunderstanding of it and confusions about it—comparable to that of the only men of truth we still have: revolutionary agitators, writers whose style leaves its mark on language . . . , and the precursor of the thought that renews being. (pp. 728–729)

26. Wortis says that Freud told him at the beginning of his analysis with Freud that "psychoanalysis demands a degree of honesty which is unusual, and even impossible in bourgeois society" (1954, p. 22).

Appendix II

1. Freud, who studied with Charcot in Paris, once commented to Charcot that some clinical finding they had encountered at the hospital where Charcot worked (la Salpêtrière) contradicted a medical theory of the time (regarding hemianopsia), and Charcot famously responded, *"La théorie c'est bon, mais ça n'empêche pas d'exister"* (which, roughly translated, means, "Theory is all well and good, but it doesn't stop such clinical facts from existing"; see Freud, SE I, p. 139, and SE III, p. 13).

Appendix III

1. The attribution of this kind of omniscience to parents is probably not that unusual in young children, but it seems a bit mysterious in his case as it lasted quite a long time. What purpose might it have served for him? It might simply have represented a *wish* on his part for his parents to know all his thoughts so that he could hide nothing from them even if he tried. That way, he would receive immediate punishment for his evil thoughts and not have to shoulder the burden of meting out punishment to himself for them; his parents would do it for him. Later on he came to believe that if he had an evil thought about someone, that person would be harmed; this seems to be a clear case of *wishful thinking* (he wished his thoughts could be that powerful, whereas he generally felt rather impotent and unmanly) or *magical thinking*.

2. Note that Lacan says we are all a bit paranoid, inasmuch as the ego or self is an us-against-them, me-against-the-world type of construction (see Fink, 1997, p. 250 n. 44, and 2016, Chapter 5).

3. We might also recall here that one of his primary sexual drives involved looking (scopophilia); losing his glasses would obviously make *that* activity more difficult as well.

4. Yet at the same time, wouldn't he be making a fool of the cruel captain who was so obviously wrong?

5. The situation might be understood as still more complicated, since Ernst described what happened when the cruel captain told him to pay Lieutenant A as follows: "A 'sanction' took shape in his mind, namely, that he was not to pay back the money or *it* would happen" (SE X, p. 168): His lady and father would be tortured. If he did pay, they would be tortured; if not, they would be spared. The term *sanction* is a bit odd, but it seems to designate here a kind of rule, principle, or threat: "Don't pay or else." "Don't pay or your father will be attacked by rats." His objection to that might have been: "But my father is a rat, so let him be tortured!" Then he commanded himself to pay the money back

(but by paying his father's debt, wouldn't he make it such that his father was not such a rat anymore?).

Appendix IV

1. Freud adds to this list the following: depression, unsociability, and *taedium vitae* (boredom, being tired of life), oddly commenting that the latter "was probably not entirely genuine" (SE VII, p. 24). Unlike Anna O, Ida was not "subject to conditions of 'absence,' confusion, delirium, and alteration of her whole personality" (SE XI, p. 10).

2. See Fink, 2014a, pp. 20 and 143.

3. As Freud puts it, "Dora was overcome by the unpleasurable feeling that is characteristic of the tract of mucous membrane which lies at the entrance to the alimentary canal—that is, by disgust" (SE VII, p. 29).

4. Had she been an English speaker, we might have imagined the connection occurring via expressions like "having a tickle in one's throat" and having a little "slap and tickle." Had she been a French speaker, we might have imagined the connection occurring via an expression like *avoir un chat dans la gorge*, to have a cat (in English we would say a frog) in one's throat, and the vernacular *chatte* (pussy) for vagina. Mahony (1996, p. 28) points to the possible verbal bridge between the German *Kitzel* (itch or tickle, and figuratively thrill) and *Kitzler* (clitoris), which are cognates. But the connection would not have had to be purely verbal: Having at some point kissed a bearded man, she might have noticed that it itched and thought the same would happen with a woman's pubic hair.

5. Freud attempts to bolster his explanation with the fact that Ida believed she could write more fluently than usual when she lost her voice, as one might write to a distant loved one (at least at the time); yet, although we know Herr K wrote to her from afar, we do not know whether she wrote to him (SE VII, p. 40).

6. This would not necessarily explain, however, why she lost her voice for six weeks after seeing Herr K run over by a carriage in the street some time after her analysis ended.

7. Lacan argues that Ida desired Frau K insofar as she identified (at the level of her ego) with Herr K (and, perhaps by extension, with her father, insofar as she imagined taking his place in performing cunnilingus on Frau K), hence desiring her as though she were a man; see Seminar III, pp. 174–175.

8. Freud suggests that the labored breathing "and palpitations that occur in hysteria and anxiety neurosis are only detached fragments of the act of copulation" (SE VII, p. 80), and we certainly see this in what are currently referred to as panic attacks (for a case example, see Fink, 2014a, pp. 22–24).

9. He also writes, "the symptoms of the disease are nothing else than *the patient's sexual activity*" (SE VII, p. 115, emphasis in the original).

10. This obviously implies that Freud does not see masturbation itself as a symptom; it may speak of or be "symptomatic of" something going on in the child's household, but it is not a symptom in the psychoanalytic sense of being a compromise formation, a compromise between an id impulse and a superego counterinjunction.

11. Were there no crutches at the time?

Appendix V

1. I have not discussed how autism is conceptualized in psychoanalysis in this book (see Bettelheim, 1967; Fink, 1995, pp. 78–79, 1997, pp. 91 and 247 n. 30, 2007, pp. 18–19).

References

Adams, H. E., Wright, L. W., & Lohr, B. A. (1996). Is homophobia associated with homosexual arousal? *Journal of Abnormal Psychology, 105*(3), 440–445.

American Psychiatric Association (APA). (2013). *Diagnostic and statistical manual of mental disorders* (5th ed.). Washington, DC: Author.

Angus, L., Watson, J. C., Elliott, R., Schneider, K., & Timulak, L. (2015). Humanistic psychotherapy research 1990–2015: From methodological innovation to evidence-supported treatment outcomes and beyond. *Psychotherapy Research, 25*(3), 330–347.

Appignanesi, L., & Forrester, J. (1992). *Freud's women*. New York, NY: Basic Books.

Association mondiale de psychanalyse. (1994). *Comment finissent les analyses*. [How analyses end.] Paris, France: Seuil.

Austin, J. L. (1962). *How to do things with words*. Oxford, UK: Clarendon Press.

Baldwin, Y. (2015). *Let's keep talking: Lacanian tales of love, sex, and other catastrophes*. London, UK: Karnac.

Bateman, A., & Fonagy, P. (2008). 8-year follow-up of patients treated for borderline personality disorder: Mentalization-based treatment versus treatment as usual. *American Journal of Psychiatry, 165*, 631–38.

Baumeister, R. F., Bratslavsky, E., Muraven, M., & Tice, D. M. (1998). Ego depletion: Is the active self a limited resource? *Journal of Personality and Social Psychology, 74*(5), 1252–1265.

Bernheimer, C. (1990). Introduction, Part 1. In C. Bernheimer & C. Kahane (Eds.), *In Dora's case* (pp. 1–18). New York, NY: Columbia University Press.

Bettelheim, B. (1950). *Love is not enough: The treatment of emotionally disturbed children*. Glencoe, IL: The Free Press.

———. (1961). *Paul and Mary*. New York, NY: Doubleday.

———. (1967). *The empty fortress*. New York, NY: The Free Press.

———. (1982). *Freud and man's soul*. New York, NY: Knopf.

———. (1990). *Freud's Vienna & other essays*. New York, NY: Knopf.

Blanton, M. G. (1971). *Diary of my analysis with Sigmund Freud*. New York, NY: Hawthorn Books.

Bloom, H. (1973). *The anxiety of influence: A theory of poetry*. Oxford, UK: Oxford University Press.

Blos, P. (1972). The epigenesis of the adult neurosis. *The Psychoanalytic Study of the Child* (Vol. 27; p. 130). New York, NY: Quadrangle Books.

Bollas, C. (1983). Expressive uses of the countertransference. *Contemporary Psychoanalysis, 19*, 1–34.

Borch-Jacobsen, M. (1996). *Remembering Anna O.: A century of mystification.* London, UK: Routledge.

Borch-Jacobsen, M., & Shamdasani, S. (2012). *The Freud files: An inquiry into the history of psychoanalysis.* Cambridge, UK: Cambridge University Press.

Canedo, A. (2006). L'expérience dans un cartel de la passe. [The experience of the pass in a cartel.] *WUNSCH Nouvelle Série, 5,* 6–7.

Cardinal, M. (1983). *The words to say it* (P. Goodheart, Trans.). Cambridge, MA: Van Vactor & Goodheart. (Original work published 1975)

Carpenter, S. (1999). Freud's dream theory gets boost from imaging work. *APA Monitor, 30.*

Cicero. (1923). *On old age, on friendship, on divination.* Cambridge, MA: Harvard University Press.

Cixous, H. and Clément, C. (1990). The untenable. In C. Bernheimer & C. Kahane (Eds.), *In Dora's case* (pp. 276–325). New York, NY: Columbia University Press.

Consumer Reports Staff (1995, November). Does therapy help? *Consumer Reports,* 734–739.

Cosgrove, L., Krimsky, S., Vijayaraghavan, M., & Schneider, L. (2006). Financial ties between DSM-IV panel members and the pharmaceutical industry. *Psychotherapy and Psychosomatics, 75,* 154–160.

Crews, F. (1993, November 18). The unknown Freud. *The New York Review of Books,* 55.

David, C. (1974). A discussion of the paper by René Major on "The revolution of hysteria." *International Journal of Psychoanalysis, 55,* 393–395.

Decker, H. S. (1991). *Freud, Dora, and Vienna 1900.* New York, NY: The Free Press.

Deutsch, F. (1957). A footnote to Freud's "Fragment of an analysis of a case of hysteria." *Psychoanalytic Quarterly, 28*(2), 159–167.

Dominus, S. (2012, March 7). What happened to the girls in Le Roy? *The New York Times Magazine.* Retrieved from http://www.nytimes.com

Erikson, E. H. (1962), Reality and actuality. *Journal of the American Psychoanalytic Association, 10,* 451–474.

Fielding, H. (1979). *The history of Tom Jones, a foundling.* Norwalk, CT: The Easton Press. (Original work published 1749)

Fink, B. (1995). *The Lacanian subject: Between language and jouissance.* Princeton, NJ: Princeton University Press.

———. (1997). *A clinical introduction to Lacanian psychoanalysis: Theory and technique.* Cambridge, MA: Harvard University Press.

———. (2004). *Lacan to the letter: Reading* Écrits *closely.* Minneapolis, MN: University of Minnesota Press.

———. (2007). *Fundamentals of psychoanalytic technique: A Lacanian approach for practitioners.* New York, NY: Norton.

———. (2010). *The psychoanalytic adventures of Inspector Canal.* London, UK: Karnac.

———. (2013). *Death by analysis: Another adventure from Inspector Canal's New York agency.* London, UK: Karnac.

———. (2014a). *Against understanding: Vol. 1. Commentary and critique in a Lacanian key.* London, UK: Routledge.

———. (2014b). *Against understanding: Vol. 2. Cases and commentary in a Lacanian key.* London, UK: Routledge.

————. (2014c). *The purloined love*. London, UK: Karnac.

————. (2016). *Lacan on love: An exploration of Lacan's Seminar VIII, Transference*. Cambridge, UK: Polity.

Freud, A. (1966). *The writings of Anna Freud: Vol. 2. The ego and the mechanisms of defense* (Rev. ed.). New York, NY: International Universities Press. (Original work published 1936)

Freud, A., & Sandler, J. (Eds.). (1985). *The analysis of defense: The ego and the mechanisms of defense revisited*. New York, NY: International Universities Press.

Freud, E. L. (Ed.). (1960). *The letters of Sigmund Freud 1873–1939*. New York: Basic Books.

Freud, S. (1953–1974). *The standard edition of the complete psychological works of Sigmund Freud* (J. Strachey, Trans., Vols. I–XXIV). London, UK: Hogarth Press.

————. (1954). *The origins of psychoanalysis: Letters to Wilhelm Fliess, drafts and notes, 1887–1902* (M. Bonaparte, A. Freud, & E. Kris, Eds.; E. Mosbacher & J. Strachey, Trans.). New York, NY: Basic Books.

————. (1985). *The complete letters of Sigmund Freud to Wilhelm Fliess 1887–1904*. Cambridge, MA: Harvard University Press.

————. (2000). *L'homme aux rats : journal d'une analyse* [The Rat Man: Journal of an analysis] (6th ed.). Paris, France: PUF.

————. (2002). *The "Wolfman" and other cases* (L. A. Huish, Trans.). New York, NY: Penguin.

————. (2013). *A case of hysteria (Dora)* (A. Bell, Trans.). Oxford, UK: Oxford University Press.

Freud, S., & Breuer, J. (2004). *Studies in hysteria* (N. Luckhurst, Trans.). New York, NY: Penguin.

Freud, S., & Jung, C. G. (1974). In W. McGuire (Ed.), *The Freud/Jung letters: The correspondence between Sigmund Freud and C. G. Jung*. Princeton, NJ: Princeton University Press.

Friedman, R. A. (2015, July 18–19). Psychiatry's identity crisis. *The International New York Times*, p. 9.

Gallop, J. (1990). Keys to Dora. In C. Bernheimer & C. Kahane (Eds.), *In Dora's case* (pp. 200–220). New York, NY: Columbia University Press.

Gardiner, M. (Ed.). (1971). *The Wolf-Man by the Wolf-Man*. New York, NY: Basic Books.

Gearhart, S. (1990). The scene of psychoanalysis. In C. Bernheimer & C. Kahane (Eds.), *In Dora's case* (pp. 105–127). New York, NY: Columbia University Press.

Gherovici, P. (2003). *The Puerto Rican syndrome*. New York, NY: The Other Press.

Gill, M. M. (1982). *Analysis of transference: Vol. 1. Theory and technique*. New York, NY: International Universities Press.

Gill, M. M., & Hoffman, I. Z. (1982). *Analysis of transference: Vol. 2. Studies of nine audio-recorded psychoanalytic sessions*. New York, NY: International Universities Press.

Groos, K. (2007). *The play of man* (E. L. Baldwin, Trans.). Whitefish, MT: Kessinger. (Original work published 1898)

Grose, A. (2016). Introduction: Reclaiming hysteria. In *Hysteria today* (Grose, A., Ed.). London, UK: Karnac.

Gunn, D. (2002). *Wool-gathering*. London, UK: Routledge.

Herbart, J. F. (1824). *Psychologie als Wissenschaft* [Psychology as science]. Königsberg, East Prussia: Unzer.

Hirschmüller, A. (1989). *The life and work of Josef Breuer: Physiology and psychoanalysis* (2nd ed.). New York, NY: New York University Press. (Original work published 1978)

Hobson, A. (2015). *Psychodynamic neurology: Dreams, consciousness, and virtual reality*. New York, NY: CRC Press.

Horney, K. (1942). *Self-analysis*. New York, NY: Norton.

Hua, C. (2008). *A society without fathers or husbands: The Na of China*. New York, NY: Zone Books.

IRMA. (2005a). *La psychose ordinaire* [Ordinary psychosis]. Paris, France: Agalma-Seuil.

IRMA. (2005b). *La conversation d'Arcachon* [The conversation in Arcachon]. Paris, France: Agalma-Seuil.

IRMA. (2005c). *Le conciliabule d'Angers* [The discussion in Angers]. Paris, France: Agalma-Seuil.

Jacoby, R. (1975). *Social amnesia: A critique of contemporary psychology from Adler to Laing*. Boston, MA: Beacon Press.

Jones, E. (1953). *The life and work of Sigmund Freud*, Vol. 1. New York, NY: Basic Books.

———. (1955). *The life and work of Sigmund Freud*, Vol. 2. New York, NY: Basic Books.

Jouvet, M. (1999). *The paradox of sleep: The story of dreaming* (L. Garey, Trans.). Cambridge, MA: MIT Press. (Original work published 1993)

Jouvet, M., Dechaume, J., & Michel, F. (1960). Etude des mécanismes du sommeil physiologique [Study of the mechanisms of physiological sleep]. *Lyon Médical, 38*(18).

Kahane, C. (1990). Introduction, Part 2. In C. Bernheimer & C. Kahane (Eds.), *In Dora's case* (pp. 19–32). New York, NY: Columbia University Press.

Kanzer, M. (1966). The motor sphere of the transference. *Psychoanalytic Quarterly, 35*, 522–539.

Kanzer, M., & Glenn, J. (Eds.). (1980). *Freud and his patients*. New York, NY: Jason Aronson.

Kardiner, A. (1977). *My analysis with Freud: Reminiscences*. New York, NY: Norton.

Koellreuter, A. (Ed.). 2016. *What is this Professor Freud like? A diary of an analysis with historical comments*. London, UK: Karnac.

Koestler, A. (1964). *The act of creation: A study of the conscious and unconscious in science and art*. New York, NY: Dell.

La passe de B. [B's pass.] (2005). *Psychanalyse, 3*(4), 113–118.

Lacan, J. (1967–1968). *Le séminaire de Jacques Lacan, livre XV: L'acte psychanalytique*. Unpublished.

———. (1974–1975). *Le séminaire de Jacques Lacan, livre XXI: R.S.I.* Unpublished.

———. (1976). Conférences et entretiens dans des universités nord-américaines. *Scilicet, 6–7*, 5–63.

———. (1976–1977). *Le séminaire de Jacques Lacan, livre XXIV : L'insu que sait de l'une-bévue s'aile à mourre*. Unpublished.

———. (1984). Préface à l'ouvrage de Robert Georgin. In R. Georgin, *Lacan* (2nd ed., pp. 9–17). Paris, France: L'Age d'homme. (Original work published 1977)

————. (1988a). *The seminar of Jacques Lacan, book I: Freud's papers on technique (1953–1954)* (J.-A. Miller, Ed., & J. Forrester, Trans.). New York, NY: Norton. (Original work published 1975)

————. (1988b). *The seminar of Jacques Lacan, book II: The ego in Freud's theory and in the technique of psychoanalysis (1954–1955)* (J.-A. Miller, Ed., & S. Tomaselli, Trans.). New York, NY: Norton. (Original work published 1978)

————. (1990). *Television: A challenge to the psychoanalytic establishment* (D. Hollier, R. Krauss, & A. Michelson, Trans.). New York, NY: Norton. (Original work published 1974)

————. (1992). *The seminar of Jacques Lacan, book VII: The ethics of psychoanalysis (1959–1960)* (J.-A. Miller, ed., & D. Porter, Trans.). New York, NY: Norton. (Original work published 1986)

————. (1993). *The seminar of Jacques Lacan, book III: The psychoses (1955–1956)* (J.-A. Miller, ed., & R. Grigg, Trans.). New York, NY: Norton. (Original work published 1981)

————. (1998a). *The seminar of Jacques Lacan, book XX, Encore: On feminine sexuality, the limits of love and knowledge (1972–1973)* (J.-A. Miller, Ed., & B. Fink, Trans.). New York, NY: Norton. (Original work published 1975)

————. (1998b). *Le séminaire de Jacques Lacan, livre V: Les formations de l'inconscient (1957–1958)* [The seminar of Jacques Lacan, book V: Unconscious formations] (J.-A. Miller, Ed.). Paris, France: Seuil.

————. (2001). *Autres écrits.* Paris, France: Seuil.

————. (2006a). *Écrits: The first complete edition in English* (B. Fink, Trans.). New York, NY: Norton. (Original work published 1966)

————. (2006b). *Le séminaire de Jacques Lacan, livre XVI: D'un Autre à l'autre (1968–1969)* [The seminar of Jacques Lacan, book XVI: From one Other to another] (J.-A. Miller, Ed.). Paris, France: Seuil.

————. (2007). *The seminar of Jacques Lacan, book XVII: The other side of psychoanalysis (1969–1970).* (J.-A. Miller, Ed., & R. Grigg, Trans.). New York, NY: Norton.

————. (2013). *Le séminaire de Jacques Lacan, livre VI: Le* désir *et son interprétation (1958–1959)* [The seminar of Jacques Lacan, book VI: Desire and its interpretation] (J.-A. Miller, Ed.). Paris, France: La Martinière.

————. (2015). *The seminar of Jacques Lacan, book VIII: Transference (1960–1961)* (J.-A. Miller, Ed., & B. Fink, Trans.). Cambridge, UK: Polity. (Original work published 1991)

Leader, D. (2016). Hysteria today. In *Hysteria today* (Grose, A., Ed.). London, UK: Karnac.

Lear, J. (2005). Give Dora a break! A tale of eros and emotional disruption. In S. Bartsch & T. Bartscherer (Eds.), *Erotikon: Essays on eros, ancient and modern.* Chicago, IL: University of Chicago Press.

————. (2015). *Freud* (2nd ed.). London, UK: Routledge.

Leichsenring, F., & Rabung, S. (2008). Effectiveness of long-term psychodynamic psychotherapy: A meta-analysis. *Journal of the American Medical Association, 300*(13), 1551–1565.

————. (2011). Long-term psychodynamic psychotherapy in complex mental disorders: Update of a meta-analysis. *The British Journal of Psychiatry, 199,* 15–22.

Leray, P. (2008). L'expérience de la passe : De la décision aux conséquences. *L'en-je lacanien, 2*(11), 7–21.

Lewin, K. K. (1973). Dora revisited. *Psychoanalytic Review, 60,* 519–532.

Lindon, J. A. (1969). A psychoanalytic view of the family: A study of family member interactions. In *Psychoanalytic Forum, 3* (pp. 13–65). New York, NY: International Universities Press.

Loewenberg, P. (1983). *Decoding the past: The psychohistorical approach.* New York, NY: Knopf.

Lohser, B., & Newton, P. M. (1996). *Unorthodox Freud: The view from the couch.* New York, NY: Guilford.

Low, B. (1935). The psychological compensations of the analyst. *International Journal of Psychoanalysis, 16,* 1–8.

Mahony, P. J. (1986). *Freud and the Rat Man.* New Haven, CT: Yale University Press.

———. (1996). *Freud's Dora: A psychoanalytic, historical, and textual study.* New Haven, CT: Yale University Press.

Major, R. (1974). The revolution of hysteria. *International Journal of Psychoanalysis, 55,* 385–392.

Marcus, S. (1990). *Representations: Essays on literature and society.* New York, NY: Columbia University Press. (Original work published 1975)

Markowitz, J. C., Petkova, E., Neria, Y., Van Meter, P. E., Zhao, Y., Hembree, E., . . . Marshall, R. D. (2015). Is exposure necessary? A randomized clinical trial of interpersonal psychotherapy for PTSD. *American Journal of Psychiatry, 172*(5), 430–440.

Masson, J. (1984). *The assault on truth: Freud's suppression of the seduction theory.* London, UK: Faber & Faber.

Menand, L. (2010, March 1). Head case: Can psychiatry be a science? *The New Yorker.*

Miller, J.-A. (1985). Réflexions sur l'enveloppe formelle du symptôme. In *Actes de l'E.C.F., 9,* 67–71. [In English, see Reflections on the formal envelope of the symptom (J. Jauregui, Trans.). *Lacanian Ink, 4*(1991), 13–21.]

Miller, M. (2011). *Lacanian psychotherapy: Theory and practical applications.* London, UK: Routledge.

Mitchell, J. (2000). *Mad men and medusas: Reclaiming hysteria.* New York, NY: Basic Books.

Moi, T. (1990). Representation of patriarchy: Sexuality and epistemology in Freud's Dora. In C. Bernheimer & C. Kahane (Eds.), *In Dora's case* (pp. 181–199). New York, NY: Columbia University Press.

Muraven, M. & Baumeister, R. F. (2000). Self-regulation and depletion of limited resources: Does self-control resemble a muscle? *Psychological Bulletin, 126*(2), 247–259.

Muslin, H. & Gill, M. (1978). Transference in the Dora case. *Journal of the American Psychoanalytic Association, 26,* 311–328.

Newman, L. S., Duff, K. J., & Baumeister, R. F. (1997). A new look at defensive projection: Thought suppression, accessibility, and biased person perception. *Journal of Personality and Social Psychology, 72*(5), 980–1001.

Onfray, M. (2010). *Le Crépuscule d'une idole* [The dusk of an idol]. Paris, France: Bernard Grasset.

Paul, R. (2006). Purloining Freud: Dora's letter to posterity. *American Imago, 63*(2), 159–182.

Popper, K. R. (1959). *The logic of scientific discovery.* London, UK: Hutchinson.

Quinodoz, J.-M. (2005). *Reading Freud: A chronological exploration of Freud's writings.* London, UK: Routledge.

Rieff, P. (1971). Introduction. *Freud: Dora—An analysis of a case of hysteria.* New York, NY: Collier Books.

Roazen, P. (2001). *The historiography of psychoanalysis.* New Brunswick, NJ: Transaction Books.

Rogers, A. G. (2006). *The unsayable: The hidden language of trauma.* New York, NY: Random House.

Rogow, A. A. (1978). A further footnote to Freud's "Fragment of an analysis of a case of hysteria." *Journal of the American Psychoanalytic Association, 26,* 330–356.

———— (1979). Dora's brother. *International Review of Psychoanalysis, 6,* 239–259.

Rose, J., & Mitchell, J. (1982). *Feminine sexuality: Jacques Lacan and the Ecole freudienne.* New York, NY: Norton.

Rosner, S. (2000). On the place of involuntary restructuring in change. *Psychotherapy: Theory, Research, Practice, Training, 37*(2), 124–133.

Ross, D. A., Travis, M. J., & Arbuckle, M. R. (2015). The future of psychiatry as clinical neuroscience: Why not now? *JAMA Psychiatry, 72*(5), 413–414.

Satow, R. (1979). Where has all the hysteria gone? *Psychoanalytic Review, 66,* 463–477.

Saussure, F. de (1959). *Course in general linguistics* (W. Baskin, Trans.). New York, NY: McGraw-Hill. (Original work published 1916)

Schoenfeld, B. (2015, May 30–31). The wrath of grapes. *The International New York Times,* p. 2.

Searle, J. (1969). *Speech acts: An essay in the philosophy of language.* Cambridge, UK: Cambridge University Press.

Seidenberg, R., & Papathomopoulos, E. (1962). Daughters who tend their fathers. *The Psychoanalytic Study of Society, 2,* 135–160. New York, NY: International Universities Press.

Sharfstein, S. (2005). Big pharma and American psychiatry: The good, the bad, and the ugly. *Psychiatric News, 40*(16), 3–4.

Shedler, J. (2010). The efficacy of psychodynamic psychotherapy. *American Psychologist, 65*(2), 98–109.

Showalter, E. (1997). *Hystories: Hysterical epidemics and modern media.* New York, NY: Columbia University Press.

Soler, C. (1993). L'expérience énigmatique du psychotique, de Schreber à Joyce [The enigmatic experience of the psychotic, from Schreber to Joyce]. *La Cause Freudienne, 23,* 50–59.

————. (2006). *What Lacan said about women.* New York, NY: Other Press. (Original work published 2003)

————. (2015). *Lacanian affects: The function of affect in Lacan's work* (B. Fink, Trans.). London, UK: Routledge. (Original work published 2011)

Solms, M. (2015). *The feeling brain: Selected papers on neuropsychoanalysis.* London, UK: Karnac.

Solms, M. and Panksepp, J. (2012). The "id" knows more than the "ego" admits: Neuropsychoanalytic and primal consciousness perspectives on the interface between affective and cognitive neuroscience. *Brain Sciences, 2*(2), 147–175.

Solms, M. and Turnbull, O. (2002). *The brain and the inner world: An introduction to the neuroscience of subjective experience.* New York, NY: Other Press.

Spoto, D. (1993). *Marilyn Monroe: The biography.* New York, NY: HarperCollins.

Sprengnether, M. (1990). Enforcing Oedipus: Freud and Dora. In C. Bernheimer

& C. Kahane (Eds.), *In Dora's case* (pp. 254–275). New York, NY: Columbia University Press.

Sterba, R. (1934). The fate of the ego in analytic therapy. *International Journal of Psychoanalysis, 15*, 2–3.

Sulloway, F. (1979). *Freud, biologist of the mind: Beyond the psychoanalytic legend.* Cambridge, MA: Harvard University Press.

Swales, S. S. (2012). *Perversion: A Lacanian psychoanalytic approach to the subject.* London, UK: Routledge.

Vanheule, S. (2014). *Diagnosis and the DSM: A critical review.* London, UK: Palgrave.

Veith, I. (1965). *Hysteria: The history of a disease.* Chicago, IL: University of Chicago Press.

Verhaeghe, P. (2004). *On being normal and other disorders: A manual for clinical psychodiagnostics.* New York, NY: Other Press.

Warner, S. L. (1994). Freud's analysis of Horace Frink, M.D.: A previously unexplained therapeutic disaster. *Journal of the American Academy of Psychoanalysis, 22*(1), 137–152.

Weber, S. (1982). *The legend of Freud.* Minneapolis, MN: University of Minnesota Press.

Webster, R. (1995). *Why Freud was wrong: Sin, science, and psychoanalysis.* New York, NY: Basic Books.

Whitaker, R. (2002). *Mad in America: Bad science, bad medicine, and the enduring mistreatment of the mentally ill.* New York, NY: Basic Books.

———. (2010). *Anatomy of an epidemic: Magic bullets, psychiatric drugs, and the astonishing rise of mental illness in America.* New York, NY: Random House.

Whitaker, R. and Cosgrove, L. (2015). *Psychiatry under the influence: Institutional corruption, social injury, and prescriptions for reform* (Rev. ed.). London, UK: Palgrave Macmillan.

Winnicott, D. W. (1960). The theory of the parent-infant relationship. In *The maturational processes and the facilitating environment* (pp. 37–55). London, UK: Hogarth.

———. (1978). *The Piggle: An account of the psychoanalytic treatment of a little girl.* London, UK: Hogarth.

Wittels, F. (1971). *Sigmund Freud: His personality, his teaching, and his school.* Freeport, NY: Books for Libraries Press. (Original work published 1924)

Wortis, J. (1954). *Fragments of an analysis with Freud.* New York, NY: Simon and Schuster.

Index

Note: Italicized page locators refer to figures.